*Crosscurrents* / MODERN CRITIQUES

Harry T. Moore, *General Editor*

# A Dangerous Crossing

*French Literary Existentialism*
*and the Modern American Novel*

### Richard Lehan

WITH A PREFACE BY

Harry T. Moore

SOUTHERN ILLINOIS UNIVERSITY PRESS
Carbondale and Edwardsville

FEFFER & SIMONS, INC.
London and Amsterdam

*To Three Teachers I Have Remembered*
*Frederick J. Hoffman*
*P. Albert Duhamel*
*Brassil Fitzgerald*

Library of Congress Cataloging in Publication Data
Lehan, Richard Daniel, 1930–
    A dangerous crossing.

    (Crosscurrents: modern critiques)
    Based on the author's thesis, University of Wisconsin, 1958.
    Bibliography: p.
    1. American fiction—20th century—History and criticism. 2. Sartre,
Jean Paul, 1905–     3. Camus, Albert, 1913–1960. 4. Existentialism
in literature.
I. Title.
PS228.E9L4     813'.03     72–10233
ISBN 0–8093–0607–7

PS
228
E9L4

# Contents

340334

# Contents

## Preface

Richard Lehan's third book demonstrates how capable he is of continuing growth as a literary critic. In *F. Scott Fitzgerald and his Craft of Fiction*, published in this Crosscurrents/Modern Critiques series in 1966, Professor Lehan presented an in-depth study of one of America's most brilliant writers of fiction, a book which doesn't neglect to discuss Fitzgerald's weaker writing; altogether, the volume offers new perspectives on Fitzgerald and skillfully shows why his better work is so important. In *Theodore Dreiser: His World and His Novels*, published by Southern Illinois University Press, Dr. Lehan again dealt with an author who was made up of many contradictions; and once again Professor Lehan gave us a fine, full picture of a man and his career.

To say that those two books are highly significant contributions to the understanding of American literature is understatement; and now their author gives us a third book that reaches even beyond those predecessors. Its title suggests its range: *A Dangerous Crossing: French Literary Existentialism and the Modern American Novel*. Richard Lehan does more than develop the thesis to the effect that the postwar French novelists such as Sartre and Camus felt the influence of the American writers of the time, notably Dos Passos and Hemingway; for, after establishing this point, he goes on to show that there was, in the case of Mailer, Bellow, and others whom he examines, a reciprocal relationship and, further, he shows *that the writers in both countries had roots in somewhat similar situations and sources. Dr. Lehan works through such complexities in an admirably persuasive and clarifying way, consistently and convincingly developing his argument.*

*The genesis and growth of this book are interestingly described in his Acknowledgments section; this indicates how long this study was in the making and how thoroughly he has investigated his material in these rapidly changing times. He speaks of his experiences at the University of Texas, and of how he worked over what is the first draft of the present book—at a time when he was reading seventy-five freshman themes a week and teaching four classes. Yet he looks back on that time "with pleasure." He is one of the many living proofs that professors who publish are not dim in the classroom, for he has won distinguished-teaching awards both at Texas (1961) and at UCLA (1970), where he is now the department chairman.*

*In the madness of an era whose technical inheritance has been used so often and so hideously for destructive purposes, man has had to rediscover himself. A good part of this process of human self-realization takes place in the writings of the authors dealt with in this book, which is not only excellent literary criticism, but also a searching examination of our values.*

HARRY T. MOORE

Southern Illinois University
September 21, 1972

## Acknowledgments

Since this book has evolved with a number of starts and stops over a period of years, the debts I have incurred are many and varied. I first began this study in 1956 as a doctoral dissertation at the University of Wisconsin under the direction of the late Frederick J. Hoffman who has long been for me a model of professional dedication.

During the 1956 academic year I read the French and German existentialists as well as the novels on both sides of the Atlantic which seemed to have an affinity to their ideas. In 1957 I read at the Widener Library at Harvard University most of the French critics who had written about modern American literature, and there I completed a first draft of the dissertation. In 1958 I revised that draft while I was teaching four courses and grading seventy-five freshman themes a week at the University of Texas. While I have no desire to reread those themes, I do remember those days with pleasure, particularly the informed discussions I had with Ambrose Gordon.

When the dissertation was formally accepted in 1958, many of the novels I treat in this present study were not even written. I was convinced then that the pattern of literary history I was describing was still incomplete— that like a character in a Borges short story I had gone ahead of the documentation and had to wait for it to catch up. Catch up it did, and I have rewritten my earlier work, placing it in a much larger context, in an attempt to update the record.

Between 1958 and 1968 I published some of my ideas on literary existentialism in the form of articles, and I should like to acknowledge some of that material used in part and in different form in the present study:

Parts of Chapters 2 and 3 appeared as "Levels of Reality in the Novels of Albert Camus," in *Modern Fiction Studies* 10, Autumn 1964.

Parts of Chapter 3 appeared in the following: "Camus's *L'Étranger* and American Neo-Realism," *Books Abroad* 38, Summer 1964; "The Trilogies of Jean-Paul Sartre and John Dos Passos," *Iowa English Yearbook*, No. 9, Fall 1964; "Faulkner's Poetic Prose: Style and Meaning in 'The Bear,'" *College English* 27, December 1965.

Part of Chapter 5 appeared in "The Way Back: Redemption in the Novels of Walker Percy," *The Southern Review* 4, April 1968.

Part of Chapter 6 appeared as "Joseph Heller's *Catch-22*: The Making of a Novel," *The Minnesota Review* 7, No. 3, 1967.

In an attempt to keep footnotes at a minimum, I have added a Bibliographical Essay at the end. This essay acknowledges the translations that I have used as well as the editions I have quoted from, gives the reader a resumé of the major works treated in this study, lists some of the more important secondary works or bibliographical guides, and refers the reader to other writing relevant to literary existentialism and to the contemporary novel in general.

Once again I owe an immense debt to Professor Harry T. Moore who encouraged me to bring my ideas on literary existentialism together in a coherent study and who read this manuscript in its second draft.

Without holding them responsible for any of my shortcomings, I should also like to thank my colleagues at UCLA who read this study in manuscript, especially John Espey, Calvin Bedient, Kenneth Lincoln, and Richard Lanham.

In the spring of 1972 I had the enviable opportunity

of making a copy of this study available to a seminar of UCLA graduate students with whom I was reading some postwar American novels. Our discussions and their comments have been an invaluable aid in certifying, for me at least, the question if not the answer.

I am also grateful to Mrs. Marian Burson who did most of the typing and the retyping.

But my greatest sense of debt is to my wife, Ann, who first encouraged me to begin this study when we were both students at the University of Wisconsin and when I was already into another dissertation on Renaissance poetry. She has shared with me the conviction that the subject of this study touches us all. Perhaps the late Theodore Roethke, however, has said it better than anyone:

> *This shaking keeps me steady. I should know.*
> *What falls away is always. And is near.*
> *I wake to sleep, and take my waking slow.*
> *I learn by going where I have to go.*

# Introduction

"Man is something that is to be surpassed," said Nietzsche, by which he meant that man had the ability to remake himself, to become the product of his own mind. Nietzsche was not the first to formulate such an idea, and he documents his own intellectual debt to Dostoyevsky and even Byron. Jean-Paul Sartre shared Nietzsche's belief that man creates himself, and Albert Camus gave consent to Nietzsche's belief that man affirmed himself by saying yes to life in the face of death.

Sartre and Camus have been unjustly linked by the blurred term *existentialism*. While their ideas and their fiction are vastly different, Sartre and Camus, like Nietzsche, do believe that modern man has been restrained by the belief in God, Church, deterministic views of history, totalitarian forms of government, rational philosophy, and even by literature itself when it gives sanction to forms of bondage, either directly by advocating them or indirectly by assuming the point of view of a God-like narrator. Camus especially was interested in the means of rebelling against metaphysical and historical forms of bondage, and he sympathetically turned to the novels of Dostoyevsky, Melville, and Conrad to find in Ivan, Ahab, and Lord Jim characters who confront and struggle against their sense of absurd existence.

While Sartre and Camus were aware of a European tradition, they were also aware of an American tradition. At the end of the Second World War the American novel attracted French readers as it never had before. Camus was interested in the way Hemingway portrayed the innocent mind confronted with a violence it had to endure but could not understand. Sartre was interested in the technique of John Dos Passos which depicted a society gone rotten at the core. And Sartre and Camus were both interested in Faulkner's characters who struggled with a fate that they could not understand as they attempted to redeem themselves from the absurd.

The absurd occurs when man admits that his reason is limited, that it cannot supply answers to questions that are both metaphysical and personal. Accident, suffering, death—all invoke the absurd by challenging what we know with what we do not know, what we can understand with what is bewildering. A literature of the absurd begins by discarding fixed points of reference—God, history, rational philosophy, even the absolute of art—and drives the individual to an unsheltered sense of self. Nietzsche, Byron, Dostoyevsky, Melville, and Conrad all addressed themselves to this problem. Nietzsche's Zarathustra urged man to struggle beyond his sense of incompleteness—an incompleteness which Dostoyevsky's Ivan, Byron's Manfred, and Melville's Ahab hurled back in the face of God. The absurd results when meaning is overwhelmed by the unexpected and the unknown. Melville's Ahab experienced it when he was maimed by Moby Dick, Conrad's Lord Jim when he jumped from the *Patna*, Camus's Meursault on an Algerian beach when the sun triggered the bullet that drops the Arab, Camus's Dr. Rieux during the plague, Sartre's Brunet in a German concentration camp, Hemingway's Lieutenant Henry and Jake Barnes on the battlefield, and Faulkner's Quentin Compson as he tried to recapitulate the story of Thomas Sutpen and his children.

Man attempts to create himself in the face of his absurd limits, an idea which brings all of these writers together and gives a collective meaning to the term *existentialism*. To discuss existentialism in philosophical terms would involve us in a study of Kierkegaard, Heidegger, Jaspers, Gabriel Marcel, among others, and we would have needed to distinguish between a "Christian" and "atheistic" existentialism. I have chosen instead to discuss existentialism in literary terms, primarily as such terms can be derived from the works of Sartre and Camus, writers who were interested in American novelists and who attracted an interest in return. Despite their ideological differences, both Sartre and Camus describe man caught in a secular, godless world of flux that leads often to violence and displacement.

Such displacement cuts modern man off from his past and threatens his future. Existential man is often a stranger in a strange land. In extreme, he is the prisoner in the concentration camp, an idea thoroughly documented by Victor E. Frankl in *From Death-camp to Existentialism*. In a less extreme way, he is modern man aware that he has been swallowed up within the city, the corporation, the army—aware that he is subject to a bureaucracy so complete that reason stands helpless in the face of the unpredictable limits of the historical moment. As Sartre has pointed out, John Dos Passos depicted in *U.S.A.* a whole society in motion, a moment of historical flux. From 1919 to the beginning of the Second World War, America was experiencing tremendous political and social change which gave rise to conglomorates and new industries (like the airplane and movie industries) with the resulting rise of men and women like J. Ward Moorehouse, Dick Savage, Charley Anderson, and Margo Dowling. Dos Passos depicted a centripetal world, with money drawing men toward a common center, until the individual meaning could not be divorced from the meaning of the epoch. To be free in Dos Passos's world one has to assert himself against the very forces of history, remake himself in the face of institutional forms of death, an idea that compelled Sartre to make use of Dos Passos's technique in his own trilogy, *Les Chemins de la liberté*.

Existential man is the sum of what he does: his meaning follows from his actions and not some preconceived notion about human nature. He is man in motion. His values cannot be divorced from experience, an idea that attracted Camus to Hemingway's fiction even as Camus dismissed the mindlessness of Hemingway's characters.

Existential man embodies his fate. While he may struggle to bridge the absurd gap between his actions and the consequence of those actions, he believes that he has brought the ruin upon himself and that he remains the source of his own redemption, an idea that attracted both Sartre and Camus to Faulkner.

And if Sartre and Camus profited from reading American fiction, recent American novelists profited in turn from reading Sartre and Camus or from thinking about existentialism. Norman Mailer has declared that he was the first American existentialist. Mailer has equated the existentialist, the hipster, and the psychopath and depicted each in "a dangerous crossing" that leads toward Mailer's own version of Nietzsche's superman. General Cummings and especially Sergeant Croft of *The Naked and the Dead* anticipate the more consciously existential character of Stephen Rojack in *An American Dream*. Mailer drives all of these characters to the outer limits of experience and, in his later novels, engages them in a search for new forms of consciousness that involves them in a strange combat between God and the Devil.

The transition from Mailer to Richard Wright is not abrupt. Wright left America and became Sartre's disciple while he was working on *The Outsider*, an expressly existential novel. When Wright first read Sartre and Camus, he responded that "they are writing of things that I have been thinking, writing, and feeling all of my life!" Wright's characters, displaced by race, experience the dread that comes with the need to define themselves through violence and extreme situations. They are like civilians condemned to perpetual war. Bigger Thomas understands the meaning of such dread when he accidentally murders a white woman, an act that brings the consciousness of an outsider and which forces him to live in the face of the death that chases him. Such desire for life in the face of death becomes even more self-conscious in the character of Cross Damon, who reads Nietzsche and who feels that he has the right to become his own god, to remake himself beyond the laws of ordinary men.

Saul Bellow's *Dangling Man* has obvious similarities to novels like *La Nausée* and *L'Étranger* and establishes a pattern residual in other Bellow novels. While Bellow's characters do not seek new forms of psychic energy as do Mailer's and Wright's, their displacement separates them from the comforts of fixed points of absolute meaning. Family, friends, even history itself seems to betray them, and they often give way to self-indulgence and self-pity. They overcome this state of mind by affirming themselves through others, by accepting the human bond which demands from them understanding, compassion, sympathy, kindness, and which leads to a simple love of life and a joy of being among the living. They do not believe that man is limitless or that he is doomed, do not desire to be more nor less than human, and see in their simple possibilities the answers to both the absurdity of life and death. In their search for that essence which binds them to all men, they go beyond their own sense of defeat.

Walker Percy's characters have also been dehumanized by the brutal conditions of modern life. Even though they suffer from the boredom of "everydayness," they feel displaced in a world that has lost all fixed value. Percy has written about existentialism in philosophical and literary journals, and he brings the same vocabulary to his fiction. His characters break out of their destructive state of mind by putting themselves in motion, moving until they have the means to see themselves in double vision—as seer and seen. This state of mind demands to be shared—to be "certified." Redemption for Percy is always for two. Like Bellow's, Percy's characters go beyond their own sense of defeat when they can share their acceptance of life with others.

The estrangement of the modern hero cannot be separated from his loss of belief in God, history, society, and the rational self. Meaning lost to madness, fixity giving way to displacement, man striving to define himself in a world growing more inimical to the individual—all of these elements are part of the existential view of man. Many recent novelists feel that modern man has come to the dead end of history and must remake himself in the face of exhausted possibility. This view can be found in Ralph Ellison's *Invisible Man* and Thomas Pynchon's *V.*—also in Joseph Heller's *Catch-22* where the bureaucratic world of the Army Air Corps has gone mad and threatens life and limb as it makes a parody out of the very idea of man. When we last see Heller's Yossarian he is moving on, trying to get to Rome from where he believes he can get to Sweden. From Sartre's *Les Chemins de la liberté* to Percy's *The Last Gentleman* and Ellison's *Invisible Man* the reader is struck by the journey that brings with it the belief that one can find himself through experience on the road. But the journey itself is not enough. Experience has to be endowed with meaning, to be sanctioned by the mind. At a time when modern man seems to have exhausted the possibilities of history, a fiction is necessary. Such a fiction keeps Camus's Sisyphus moving the rock up the mountain, keeps Heller's Yossarian moving in the face of Colonels Cathcart and Korn, and keeps John Barth's Jacob Horner out of the insane asylum. The fiction may be self-consciously given (Sisyphus knows that his rock will roll back down) or it may be more literally given (Nietzsche's Zarathustra really believes that man can surmount himself). Nietzsche's sense of man's infinite possibility is diminished as man becomes more self-conscious of his absurd limitations, until the desire to create a new man gives way to Heller's simple lust for life. But even as Nietzsche's superman gives way to Thomas Pynchon's derelicts, we still find a residual man who strives to realize himself free of the restraints of God and system, especially a system that turns joy into despair and life into death. Man's fiction gives meaning to his motion, allows him to climb outside the system, and indeed may threaten the system itself as Ellison, Heller, and Barth all seem to be saying.

As a caveat to the reader, I should like to make clear that the account of Sartre and Camus in this study is in terms of their published work as it appeared up to roughly a decade after the Second World War—that is, roughly the time within which Sartre and Camus had expressed interest in American fiction and American writers were in turn looking at their writing. While I do discuss Camus's *La Chute* (1956), I do not consider the recent publication of his *La Mort heureuse*, the notebook draft of his early novel with a very different portrait of Mersault (as the name is there spelled). I also do not attempt to chart the modifications Sartre has made in his earlier philosophical views as he tried to accommodate his existential ideas to a more Marxist view of history. In the Bibliographical Note at the end, I do refer the reader to the studies which update this part of the record.

I should also like to make clear that this is not a source study. I am concerned with an affinity of mind, a sense of shared consciousness, that can be found in the literature of the nineteenth century as well as today. While Sartre and Camus did draw consciously on the American novel, and while Mailer, Wright, Bellow, Percy, Ellison, and Barth may admit or reveal an awareness of French literary existentialism, the ideological connection between and among these writers was never systematic or doctrinaire. The Second World War was the catalyst, but what is involved goes in part back to such an earlier spokesman as Henry Adams who saw the steady progression away from mythic centers, saw history as decline, saw modern man becoming displaced in a world where the center would not hold. A sense of the absurd becomes a condition of mind, a way of life, in an era of the dynamo, of moral relativism and religious doubt, of chaotic change, of distrust in institutions that were once the source of imaginative order.

This book reveals how on both sides of the Atlantic modern man has attempted to define himself against his sense of the absurd and then striven to go beyond his self-definition. Even as threats to the self from centralized sources of power become more real, modern man seems compelled to re-create himself in the face of these limits —to affirm his sense of life against the continuing forms of institutional death which surrounds him.

RICHARD   LEHAN

University of California at Los Angeles
July 4, 1972

# A Dangerous Crossing

# 1

# Man the Redeemer

"Man is a rope stretched between the animal and the Superman—a rope over an abyss." Such rope-stretching "is a dangerous crossing." So says Nietzsche in *Thus Spake Zarathustra*, where he insists that man is his own creator, can make himself what he will be so long as he has the courage and persistence to strive. "Man is something that is to be surpassed," Zarathustra continues. "What is the ape to man? A laughing-stock, a thing of shame. And just the same shall man be to the Superman: a laughing-stock, a thing of shame." Nietzsche's superman was the new Prometheus, the man who challenged the gods, who rejected Apollonian order, and who obtained by crime what most ennobled man. Like Dionysus, the superman embodies the spirit of joy, strength, exuberant health, overfullness, radical freedom; he acts in the name of Titanic impulses, stretching against his limits. "Have you understood me?" Nietzsche asks. "*Dionysus* versus *Christ*."

Such words make it easier to understand why Nietzsche has been called the father of modern existentialism. Like the existentialists, he does not believe that man's nature is pre-given or fixed. Man is his own creation; he is what he makes of himself. As he struggles to be the product of his own mind, he is in pursuit of himself. He is man in motion. Nietzsche believed that man had been diminished by the nay-sayers who turned him against his own instincts and created a sense of doubt and shame.

This is why the battle is between Dionysus and Christ: Nietzsche rejects original sin and a God-sent redeemer in favor of Dionysus, the god of fertility as well as chaos and destruction. Dionysus symbolizes sublime achievement and embodies primitive instincts. Nietzsche's faith in the instinctual made him suspicious of rational philosophy, whether it was the belief that reason precedes existence (Descartes's "I think; therefore I am") or the belief that categories are independent of the mind (Kant's space, time, condition, relationship, and modality). Nietzsche insisted upon subjective reality, life as a fiction of the mind, created by our needs, in a world of our own making. He affirmed life against death by postulating a pattern of eternal recurrence within which life renewed itself as energy, was formed and released in a tragic rhythm of rise and fall, day and night, joy and pain, happiness and sadness. Within this pattern the individual exercised the eternal will to strive, to grow and create, to live in the face of suffering, to say yes to life as it renewed itself around him. Camus knew of what Nietzsche spoke and repeated the idea when he told us that in spite of the eternal repetition of "every pain and every joy, every thought and every sigh . . . all is well." And Bellow's Herzog enlisted the name of Nietzsche and the idea of eternal recurrence as he affirmed life against death.

At the same time that Nietzsche could reconcile man to his human fate, he was unrelentingly hardhearted and came to believe that the superman had the moral responsibility to fulfill himself regardless of the cost to others. "All that proceeds from power is good," he said; "all that springs from weakness is bad." He exalted the "hardier virtues" of egotism, cruelty, arrogance, retaliation, and appropriation and ridiculed the "softer virtues" of sympathy, charity, forgiveness, loyalty, and humility. He believed in a master-morality, maintained that the race would develop only when the strong men had control, and called for "a class of immoralists," pointing to Napoleon as one of the few enlightened leaders who put his ideas into action. He demanded for the strong man those rights which the state had reserved for itself, arguing that an official of the state has the authority to hang (kill), imprison (enslave), tax (rob), and, as undercover agent, to deceive and trap (lie).

Nietzsche yanked God from the heavens, questioned the rational philosophers, and challenged the state in the name of extreme individualism. He wanted a hardheaded visionary who had the courage to act against Church and State in the name of his own version of man. His call was to the supreme individualist whose radical action would serve as an answer to nihilism and as a model for the new race he would in effect be recreating:

> This man of the future, who in this wise will redeem us from the old ideal, as he will from the ideal's necessary corollary of great nausea, will to nothingness, and nihilism; this tocsin of noon and of the great verdict, which renders the will again free, who gives back to the world its goal and to man his hope, this Antichrist and Antinihilist, this conqueror of God and of Nothingness—*he must one day come.*

Nietzsche's ideas cannot be totally divorced from the romantic movement. The romantic psyche revealed itself in two different ways. Certain romantics had the desire to lose themselves in some version of the absolute with the resulting desire to merge with a living, organic universe. Others, like Nietzsche, tried to assert themselves as supreme individualists with the resulting urge to reject established dogmas and to find self-awareness through heightened experience. Wordsworth gave consent to an organic and mystic nature, Shelley to an equally mystic conception of a kingdom of love. Goethe's *Werther* or Byron's *Childe Harold*, on the other hand, retain an individualized, albeit skeptical, sense of life which saved them from romantic mysticism by encouraging truths based on first-hand experience and sensation. Byron, for example, wrote "that the great object of life

is sensation—to feel that we exist, even though in pain."
*Childe Harold* closes on this note, which we find again
in both *Manfred* and *Cain.* Carlyle's Teufelsdröckh
could also accept this view before German idealism made
his position top-heavy, and so could Arnold's vocal
skeptic Empedocles and Clough's self-contained Dipsy-
chus. Interestingly enough, Nietzsche read Byron and
tells us that "I must be profoundly related to Byron's
Manfred: I discovered all his abysses in my soul."

Manfred does embody many of Nietzsche's ideas. He
links himself with Prometheus, quests after "hidden
knowledge," and has a sense of destiny which sets him
apart from other men. As he tells us, "From my youth
upwards/ My spirit walk'd not with the souls of men.
. . . / My joys, my griefs, my passions, and my powers,/
Made me a stranger." He refuses to kneel before the
Spirits and is intolerant of Christian arguments, telling
the Abbot that "there is no power in holy men,/ Nor
charm in prayer." He sees in the hunter a man of simple
life and simple mind who has been spared the agonies
that accompany Manfred's more intense vision. Yet
Manfred will not exchange his lot and insists that he can
bear what life demands of him. He masters himself and
makes "his torture tributary to his will." He is the self-
contained product of his own mind which is responsible
"for its good or evil thoughts—/ Is its own origin of ill
and end—/ And its own place and time."

The mind is "its own place"—free to create its own
scheme of order and value. With these words Byron
frees man from God. For all his melancholy Manfred
insists that he has made himself: that he is his "own destroyer" and not the victim of religious or cosmic spirits.
In his final speech Manfred rejects the gods and the hope
for supernatural deliverance, and he accepts man and
the struggle to understand an amoral universe, even
though its final meaning is ultimately unknown and un-
knowable. Man can accept his dreadful freedom and
choose to die as he has lived—alone. Byron takes back
some of this radical freedom with Cain, who is left dis-

satisfied with his human condition once Lucifer gives him the means of evaluating it in cosmic perspective. Cain regrets his killing of Abel and accepts the mark of his crime, the brand still hot on his brow. He also accepts his own mortality and finds satisfaction in the limited, human love Adah and his children give him. Thus, in Cain, Byron brings the cosmic journeyer back into the family of man at the same time that he sends him into the wilderness to work out his own redemption.

As Nietzsche read Byron, he also read Dostoyevsky, especially *Notes from Underground*, to which he responded enthusiastically in 1887. In *Notes from Underground*, the speaker attacks modern rationalism which he felt imprisoned man in formal systems of thought that frustrated action. He advocated acting against reason in order to "break down all our classification" and to "shatter systems." His conclusion was that man is a creative animal who "incessantly and eternally desires to make new roads, *wherever they may lead.*" Where the road takes us "is less important than the process of making it." Along with Nietzsche and Byron who helped release man from the supernatural so that he could be the product of his own mind, Dostoyevsky's underground man helped release man from the bondage of rational thought which justified the individual only in terms of absolutes outside himself. All of these spokesmen were trying to create a residual man, unencumbered, unrestrained, free.

Dostoyevsky, to be sure, saw dangers in such a creature, and in *The Possessed* he tried to document his foreboding. After completing *The Idiot*, the story of a modern Christ, Dostoyevsky turned to "The Life of a Great Sinner," a novel he never completed but from which emerges the character Stavrogin, his strong man. Dostoyevsky modeled both Stavrogin and Pytor Verhovensky on a steel-willed radical named Nechayev.[1] In Stavrogin we have the saint turned criminal; in Pytor we have the criminal turned clown. Pytor himself recognizes this distinction, and when he feels that Stavrogin might fail in his demonic mission, he tells him, "All right, I am a clown, but I do not want you, my more important half, to be a clown." Stavrogin in turn has two disciples—Shatov and Kirillov—who seem to be a composite of his saintly-demonic nature. His very name—*stavros* (the Greek word for cross) and Nikolay (conqueror of nations) and Vsevold (master of all)—reveals Stavrogin's double nature. He is both saint and sinner—Myshkin and Raskolnikov—and his attempt to rise above ordinary men seems doomed. Through his suicide at the end of the novel, Stavrogin renounces his demonic self in the name of human limits. Dostoyevsky refused to give Stavrogin what Nietzsche granted his superman—the right to crush others in the pursuit of his own fulfillment. Stavrogin is one of the first failed supermen, a character whose fate calls a momentary halt to ruthless freedom.

Kirillov is another character who embodies such freedom. His concerns, however, are primarily metaphysical. Kirillov wants to prove once and for all that God does not exist. If God does not exist, then all human action becomes arbitrary, a point the underground man made in a different way. If all human action is arbitrary, then it matters little if one lives or dies, because no absolutes can justify either. Kirillov believes that man has invented God to give life purpose, and he chooses to take his own life so as to mock that sense of purpose:

> I have no higher idea than disbelief in God. I have all the history of mankind on my side. Man has done nothing but invent God so as to go on living, and not kill himself; that's the whole universal history of mankind up till now. I am the first one in the whole history of mankind who would not invent God. Let them all know it once for all.

In killing himself, Kirillov believes that he has become his own god and hence has freed man from God. If Stavrogin turns his superman's hate toward others, Kirillov turns his hate of God toward himself.

While Nietzsche pursued the effects of a world without God, Dostoyevsky presented the psychological and ethical implications of godlessness in literary terms. Perhaps the novel that speaks best to this point is *The Brothers Karamazov*. The three brothers are seeking the new man: Dmitri's struggle is emotional, Ivan's intellectual, and Alyosha's religious as he tries to realize the God he carries within him. Most important is Ivan's story of the Grand Inquisitor. The Grand Inquisitor imprisoned the returned Christ for telling men that happiness is achieved through freedom of choice. The Inquisitor insists on controlling man's will and conscience through the forces of mystery and authority, and he boasts to Christ that he and his church "have vanquished freedom." He condemns Christ for thinking "too highly of men," for man in general is nothing but "slave . . . though rebellious in nature." Ivan's story is a condemnation of the Roman Catholic Church and other forces that attempt to regulate the individual; it is also a "praise of Jesus," although a kind of secular and humanistic Jesus, as Alyosha tells him.

Like Camus and Sartre, Ivan insists that the individual must bear the responsibility of his choices and that guilt must be accepted individually and not communally. The individual is solely responsible and must bear guilt alone. All the brothers come to this realization. Dmitri Karamazov lacks the means personally to expiate his guilt. In the court scene, when Katerina's evidence has practically cleared him of his father's murder, cleared him at the expense of her own honor, Dmitri cries, "Katya, why have you ruined me? . . . Now I am condemned." Dmitri was not thinking of his father's murder, but of his own right to spiritual suffering and expiation. And Ivan, who believes he is guilty of his father's murder because he wished it and hinted his wish to Smerdyakov, confesses his guilt at the trial. Unable to make people aware of his guilt, unable to atone for his sense of wrong, he remains imprisoned within his own consciousness and goes mad. Even Alyosha, the most spiritually pure of the brothers, feels the need to expiate the sensual Karamazov blood in his veins and takes Father Zossima's suggestion, refuses to lead a cloistered life, and dedicates himself to being a spiritual buffer between his brothers and his father. In his long philosophical conversation with Alyosha, Ivan explicitly defends the need for personal suffering, here and now, and not in some kind of hell after life. "I must have justice, or I will destroy myself," he says. "And not justice in some remote infinite time and space, but here on earth, and that I could see myself."

As Ivan says, a mother who has her son unjustly slain by a torturer can forgive the torturer for her own personal suffering, but she has no right to forgive him for the suffering of her son. Consistent with this feeling, Ivan rejects the traditional notion that Christ's suffering expiated the sins of all mankind: "I don't want harmony," he says, "from love for humanity I don't want it. I would rather be left with unavenged suffering. I would rather remain with unavenged suffering and unsatisfied indignation." Unavenged suffering, unsatisfied indignation—this can be the starting point of the existential journey: the starting point for Meursault in the face of the misunderstanding jury, for Roquentin alone in Bouville, for Dr. Rieux with the plague dead, for Mathieu in prewar France, and for Brunet in the German concentration camp. Camus and Sartre move toward different existential positions, but they each begin where Ivan ends.

One cannot, of course, determine exactly what Dostoyevsky himself believes in *The Brothers Karamazov*. The debate is an important device in the novel, but exactly how far Dostoyevsky aligns himself with a specific point of view becomes impossible to say. One can say, however, that both Father Zossima and Ivan, who represent extreme points of view, believe in the dignity of the individual and that man personally must be responsible for his actions (cf. Zossima and the Lady of Little Faith). However, while Zossima sees sense and meaning

in God's creation, Ivan, the first of the modern existentialists, sees no cosmic order or logic—sees the world as
absurd. Ivan, in fact, is the first of the metaphysical
rebels when he insists that if evil is essential to divine
creation, then creation is unacceptable. While Dostoyevsky may have rejected Ivan's view personally, he made
dramatic use of it in the novel, and he brought this
problem—along with the problem of individual commitment, free choice, the nature of guilt and expiation—
into focus, a focus that prefigures and anticipates modern
existentialism.

Like Dostoyevsky's Ivan, Melville's Ahab also refuses
to accept God's universe so long as it means accepting
evil, an evil embodied in the whale which has ripped off
his leg. In perhaps the novel's key passage, Melville tells
us that "all evil, to crazy Ahab, [was] visibly personified,
and made practically assailable in Moby Dick. He piled
upon the whale's white hump the sum of all the general
rage and hate felt by his whole race from Adam down;
and then, as if his chest had been a mortar, he burst his
hot heart's shell upon it." Unlike the captain of the
*Samuel Enderby* who accepts in a Job-like way the arm
that he lost to Moby Dick, and unlike Father Mapple
whose sermon praises the patience of Jonah, Ahab stands
in opposition to Job and Jonah. He has been afflicted
and demands an answer. He refuses his fate and shouts
his revenge in the face of God: "I misdoubt me that I
disobey my God in obeying him!" Starbuck tells us
near the end of the three-day chase, repeating the words
that Father Mapple used in his sermon: "But all the
things that God would have us do are hard for us to do
—remember that—and hence, he oftener commands us
than endeavors to persuade. And if we obey God, we
must disobey ourselves; and it is in this disobeying ourselves, wherein the hardness of obeying God consists."
Ahab refuses to disobey himself, exalts the self over God,
and becomes the first American existentialist, albeit a
misguided one from Melville's own point of view. Ahab
is misguided because he has become so fascinated with

evil that he is unable to see the beauty and even the good in nature; he becomes monomaniacal, indeed demonic, as Melville suggests by naming him after the biblical Ahab who gives false homage to the God of Tyre and by connecting him with Fedallah the Parsee, a Zoroastrian, who along with Ahab baptizes the harpoon in the name of the devil. Ahab is even more a metaphysical rebel than Camus's plague-stricken. Dr. Rieux rejects human suffering but not creation itself. He goes to the aid of the afflicted with the hope of easing their pain but not with the desire to change the nature of reality. He believes that the suffering of one man obligates another, an important theme in *Moby Dick*, but not one that Ahab accepts when he refuses to help the captain of the *Rachel* look for his son who has fallen overboard. And after the demonic Ahab has torn the bird from heaven and sunk the *Pequod* and its crew, it is the *Rachel* which picks Ishmael from the sea and thus brings the rejected son of Abraham back into the family of man.

Like Dostoyevsky's Ivan, Ahab feels betrayed by God. When he refuses to serve a God he cannot understand, he becomes a metaphysical rebel. His sense of evil throws him solipsistically back upon himself, and he becomes his own god, a pattern of action that he will share with many more consciously developed existential characters. While Ahab confronts the evil that he sees, he does not become his own redeemer in the way Joseph Conrad's characters do. Most of Conrad's characters better understand themselves by seeing that others are evil or frail— as Almayer sees evil in Lakamba, as Willems (in *An Outcast of the Islands*) sees it in Aissa, as Lord Jim sees it in Brown after he has seen it first in himself, as Marlow (in "Heart of Darkness") sees it in Kurtz, and as Heyst (in *Victory*) sees it in Ricardo. Conrad's characters are tormented and lonely men, plagued by grief and wracked with guilt. They are often in flight from themselves, modern-day Cains whose crimes have alienated them from society. Some are destroyed by their encounter with the "destructive element" (Almayer, Wil-

lems, Kurtz, Decoud and Nostromo, Mr. Verloc and
Winnie), while others are morally strengthened by their
ordeal, even though it at times costs their lives (Lord
Jim, Rasumov, Flora de Barral, and Heyst). Sometimes
those who are saved are helped back by the love of someone else as Aissa helps Willems before her love turns to
destructive jealousy, as Nathalie helps Razumov in *Under
Western Eyes*, as Anthony helps Flora in *Chance*, and as
Lena helps Heyst in *Victory*. In all cases, those who are
saved have undergone a change; they have peeled away
their early illusions, abandoned their hopeless dreams,
and accepted themselves for what they are and can do.
The man of illusion immerses himself in the destructive
element and he is sustained by his dreams at the same
time as the dream is tempered by experience. "Woe to
the man whose heart has not learned while young to
hope, to love—and to put its trust in life," says Heyst.
Conrad's characters must first lose themselves in order
to find themselves, and Conrad was giving his own answer to the romantic concept of self.

We can clearly see the way Conrad dismissed the romantic self in *The Shadow-Line*, the story of a young
officer who deserts his ship because he is restless at sea.
As he waits in an officer's club for passage home, he accepts the command of a ship whose captain has recently
died. Once at sea, fever levels his crew, except for himself and a Mr. Ransome, the cook, who has a bad heart
and could not sign aboard for more strenuous work. The
first mate, Mr. Burns, is burdened by the death of the
old captain whom they buried at sea. He fears the captain is haunting the ship and will destroy them all. Like
the fever, Burns's fears become contagious, a problem
the captain finds compounded by an approaching storm.
During the storm even the binnacle lights go out: "The
last gleam of light in the universe." As Burns raves in his
fever about the evils of the old captain, the new one—
assisted by Ransome—tries to steer a "wildly rushing
ship full of dying men." The ship metaphorically is the
Conradian universe, where men labor against the ele-

ments as well as sickness, madness, and death. In their struggle, the young captain sees in Ransome the source of man's tragic weakness and strength. He becomes aware of "the shadow-line" between life and death and realizes that all men, like Ransome, have weak hearts—hearts which allow us the dignity of struggle, that bind us together, and that can betray us at any moment. Our strength—like Ransome's tragic strength—is really in our weakness. When Conrad's characters become aware of this truth they become their own redeemers. Like Lord Jim, Nostromo, Razumov, Flora de Barral, they recognize their mistakes in judgment, accept their limits, and find enough strength, even when confronted with death, to redeem their pasts.

Both Melville and Conrad depict metaphysical rebellion; but unlike Ahab, Conrad's characters become aware of their limits. While Ahab tries to overvault himself, Lord Jim and Nostromo do not. It is between these two extremes—the superman as opposed to the man of self-imposed limits—that we find character motives in existential fiction. Nietzsche, Sartre, Norman Mailer, and Richard Wright all give consent to radical freedom—a freedom which ironically often brings self-destruction to their characters. Camus, Conrad, Faulkner, Saul Bellow, and Walker Percy in different ways come to realize that one cannot be free of God at the expense of other men —that while man may be his own redeemer he is still not beyond good and evil.

## 2

# French Literary Existentialism: Sartre and Camus

In the essay "Philosophy and Fiction," Albert Camus described the philosopher as a creator: "He has his characters, he has his symbols and his secret action. He has plot-endings." Camus believed that the novel was perhaps the best medium for the philosopher to express his ideas because in the novel "abstract thought at last returns to its prop of flesh. And likewise, the fictional activities of the body are regulated a little more according to the requirements of the world." And in *Qu'est-ce que la littérature?* Sartre said that "a fictional technique always relates back to the novelist's metaphysic." Sartre believes that the philosopher does not have to be abstract once he knows how his ideas relate to life, once he tries to "embrace from within the human condition in its totality." Sartre wants a novelist who not only has a sense of philosophy but also a sense of history, and he describes a great tradition of French writers who were "engaged," who spoke to the problems of the historical moment. Literature has a moral dimension for Sartre. The writer must not only create a fictional world, he must also bring the reader *through* it. If the writer is successful, the reader will experience "esthetic joy" or the delight of re-creating the fictional universe. The writer thus introduces "order where there was none, by imposing the unity of mind on the diversity of things." Sartre and Camus turned to the novel with very explicit philosophical and historical views in mind. They wrote an extremely self-conscious fiction, one that spoke in moral terms to their age. They believed that fiction not only could describe man's plight but that it could change it by making man aware and willing to act. Their fiction is both a statement about their times and a call to action.

## Jean-Paul Sartre

The first of Sartre's tenets is that the world is irrational and without plan. Sartre denied God and put man in his place. The belief that one's fate is God's will, says Sartre, is a rationalization and can encourage the complacent attitude of accepting human evil as inevitable and foreordained. Sartre maintained that all reality is contingent upon human consciousness, and he turned to Edmund Husserl, the nineteenth-century phenomenologist, for support of his belief in this dual reality. One aspect of reality Sartre termed *en-soi* (in-itself); the other, *pour-soi* (for-itself). *En-soi*, being in its most encompassing sense, constitutes the world of real objects, the objective, universal, abstract, timeless, all-embracing, determined, passive element. *Pour-soi*, or consciousness, is the subjective, personal, individual, concrete, limited, free, undetermined element. A table has being without one's knowing it, but it does not truly exist until consciousness brings it to life.

Sartre's famous nausea stems from this disjunction between consciousness and being. In the novel *La Nausée*, Roquentin is unable to differentiate between things by inventing categories which conceal the true nature of reality. The world to him appears amorphous, pulpy, gelatinous. He feels like a drop of honey in a honey jar, feels lost within his viscous surrounding, and he is overcome by the physical sensation of nausea:

No necessary being can explain existence. . . . It is complete gratuity [*de trop*]. All is gratuitous, this garden, this town and myself. When one happens to realize it, then it turns one's heart, all begins to float . . . : that is the *Nausea.*

Husserl's epistemology has important ethical implications. If all reality is dependent on human consciousness, then goodness and evil do not exist outside of the mind. Man himself, "in situation," creates good and evil, creates his own values in a world void of any absolute and ethical meaning. In *L'Être et le néant, essai d'ontologie phénoménologique,* Sartre maintained that

> I neither have nor can have any value in which to take refuge from the fact that it is I who maintain values in being. Nothing can guarantee me against myself. . . . I have to realize the meaning of the world and of my essence. I decide it alone, unjustified, and without excuse.

An ethical vacuum often exists at the core of an existential novel. The heroes live in an unknown or strange world to which they must adjust. A good many of Sartre's ideas came out of his Resistance experience, and his philosophy lends itself to the conditions of a prison world. In *Huis Clos,* hell becomes a prison. In *La Nausée,* Bouville (Mudville) confines Roquentin. In *L'Âge de raison,* Marcelle, Mathieu's mistress, is confined to her bedroom. In *Le Sursis,* the invalids who are being evacuated in the face of the German advance find themselves imprisoned in a boxcar. And in *La Mort dans l'âme,* the concluding action takes place in a concentration camp. In all these works, prison life separates the characters from their past environment, encloses them in a strange and hostile world, and forces them to find a meaning, often in the face of a choice that reveals that good and evil are inextricably related. Some characters, for example, have to decide whether they will save themselves at the expense of another (cf. Sartre's "Le Mur"). Others have to decide if their integrity is more important than their life (cf. Sartre's *Les Mains sales*).

Since we choose ourselves "in situation," Sartre believed that we cannot go beyond the finite modes of thought. Sartre repudiated transcendent being, denied absolute reality, and rejected the infinite and all-encompassing mind. God died, and man must rule. The worlds of Sartre and Camus—different in many respects—are without center and beyond conventional morality.

Man acts and his nature follows from his actions. That is what Sartre means when he says in *L'Existentialisme est un humanisme* that existence precedes essence:

> We mean that man first of all exists, encounters himself, surges up in the world—and then defines himself afterwards. If man as the existentialist sees him is not definable, it is because to begin with he is nothing. He will not be anything until later, and then he will be what he makes himself. Thus there is no human nature, because there is no God to have a conception of it. Man simply is. Not that he is simply what he conceives himself to be, but he is what he wills, and as he conceives himself after already existing—as he wills to be after that leap toward existence. That is the first principle of existentialism.

As long as one can act, one can change his nature, and only death solidifies essence and transfixes destiny. In Sartre's plays and novels, we see his characters embodying this belief in the permeable quality of human nature, a belief that necessitates he endow his fictional world with a future, with time as a process of becoming.

Because Sartre's characters project themselves into the future, their destiny becomes a matter of what one commentator called "dreadful freedom." As Sartre put it in *L'Existentialisme est un humanisme*: "If existence really does precede essence, man is responsible for what he is. Thus existentialism's first move is to make every man aware of what he is and to make the full responsibility of his existence rest on him. . . . Man's destiny is within himself. . . ." Responsibility must be accepted individually and not communally. One acts alone and not in the name of a political party or a religion. Communal motivation is considered not only an unauthentic evasion of self but also a means of sanctioning the worst kind of moral atrocities, an idea that Sartre would eventually have difficulty reconciling with his support of the Communist party in France. In *Les Mains sales*, written in his pre-Communist days, Sartre revealed the folly of living in terms of an abstract party dialectic.

As he projects himself toward what he wants himself to be, as he sees his consciousness "divided from its essence by nothingness, or separated from the future by its liberty," the existentialist re-creates man. To deny freedom is to admit "bad faith," and one is conscious of his bad faith. Sartre maintains that Freud's theory of the unconscious—his insistence upon the id and repressions—merely sanctions unauthentic living and replaces free will with unconscious motives over which an individual has no control. Sartre's concept of bad faith is as central to his whole philosophy as the concepts of the unconscious, censorship, and repression are to the psychology of Freud. Sartre's "projection theory" replaces Freud's theory of libido. The objects that we "project ourselves into," the objects we choose and desire, tell us more about our psychological makeup than consideration of unconscious sexual motives. Sartre's psychology would hence search for a hidden choice, Freud's for a hidden complex. Sartre believed that one is what one prefers.

Sartre's characters are committed, self-dependent, and free. They are an ethic unto themselves and choose destiny in anguish, the only alternative to bad faith, a conscious process that reveals itself in choice. While Sartre's individual is free, he does not, however, live free of other people's expectations or demands. Sartre speaks of a constant tension between conflicting egos. One exists for someone else as well as himself. Of the three great categories of human existence—having, making, being—Sartre lists "otherness" under having. In social relationships, one attempts to appropriate another's freedom, to reduce the other to an object of consciousness, a mere being. But the other is also a conscious being, and a struggle of wills can develop. Since existence is contingent upon awareness of possibilities, one does not really exist at all if consciousness and will are subordinated to a superior personality. Sartre's characters are not too far removed from power maniacs. They have Nietzsche's will to power and Adler's superiority complex, walk in the footsteps of Stendahl's Julien Sorel, and hate anyone who has ever degraded or humiliated them, as Dostoyevsky's narrator hates Zverkov, the young Russian officer in *Notes from Underground.*

Being-for-others is thus basically conflict, a struggle of consciousnesses. It is no wonder that in *Huis Clos* Sartre maintained that "Hell is other people." The play itself is a classic demonstration of the conflict of otherness. Like the action in *Les Jeux sont faits,* the play takes place in a world after death. There are three principal characters. Garcin, executed by a firing squad, has tormented his wife and deserted his political party in the war. Estelle, an egocentric adulterer, has murdered her illegitimate child and driven her lover to suicide. Inez, a lesbian, has driven her cousin to death and morally destroyed Florence, his mistress. Florence, then Inez's lesbian consort, despondently turned on the gas one evening and killed both Inez and herself. When each character realizes that the other knows his sin, he is filled with shame, the emotion which stems from and is proof of another's existence. The shame that each feels leads him to try to overcome the other's consciousness and to reinstate himself in the other's mind. Garcin can easily overcome Estelle's consciousness because she needs his attention to bolster her vanity. But Garcin cannot subdue Inez, who remains an eternal reminder of his past failings. Estelle can lord it over Inez, who is physically attracted to her. But before Garcin, whose love she needs as proof that she still has power over men, Estelle is powerless, Inez, having no physical need of men, is easily able to dominate Garcin because she knows that he is a coward and will not surrender this ignoble attitude toward him. But Inez cannot win the favor of Estelle, whom she needs as a consort to justify her lesbianism. Each character tries to escape his past and to reestablish his integrity. He is successful only to the degree that he can dominate the other's point of view. Coward Garcin cannot transcend his cowardice so long as Inez transfixes him with her glare; baby-killer Estelle finds her sin eternally written in the look of Garcin; and lesbian Inez is aware of her abnormalities so long as Estelle's opinion of her is unfavorable. Garcin summarizes the situation: "We're chasing each other, round and round in a vicious circle, like the horses on a roundabout. That's part of the plan, of course. . . ." Although the three characters think that they are locked in the room, they find the door is really open. Yet none can leave. Each realizes that if he leaves the room he will be damned forever in another's consciousness. They thus willingly submit themselves to an eternal imprisonment and attempt to rectify themselves in the others' eyes. This is Sartre's modern hell.

Sartre fears the other as a threat to freedom and mental equilibrium. One man sees another as an object, solidifies him, labels him, reduces him to *en-soi*, the lowest form of being. In Sartre's world, love seems next to impossible, because with it comes the threat that one will surrender his freedom to another.

### Albert Camus

Albert Camus has never expressed the misanthropic views of Sartre. Meursault is more indifferent than hostile to other persons, and he never considers someone else a threat to his sanity. He dislikes the judge and the priest because they cannot understand the absurd nature of the Arab's death, and because they so arrogantly believe that they have all the right answers. The universe or a cold bureaucracy are often the antagonists in Camus's novels, not other men, although men like the priest and the judge can be the human connections between the absurdity of nature and the absurdity of society. Meursault becomes a victim of society; the plague-stricken become victims of nature. The only power-maniac in Camus's fiction is Jean-Baptiste, a satirical embodiment of Jean-Paul Sartre. Unlike Sartre's, when Camus's characters become aware of their absurd condition, they become benevolently reconciled to each other. Where Sartre's characters are often bound by hate, Camus's characters are more often bound by love. While Sartre's characters are more cerebral, Camus's characters are more compassionate.

Camus, of course, was not a systematic philosopher. While Sartre built an elaborate theory of consciousness, of freedom, and of social struggle, Camus held a more simple view of man. Camus's was a more lyrical and direct belief in life based upon man's ability to feel and think, to respond to the joy of living without abandoning oneself to a nature that can bring the plague as well as the pleasures of the sea and sun. While Sartre did not believe that man was morally boundless, it was Camus who continually insisted that man must know his limits. To fully understand Camus's fiction, one has to see how he moved his characters from indifference to commitment, from mere physical response to a lyrical consciousness which brought with it a sense of life's joys and responsibilities.

In Camus's fiction action takes place on two levels of reality—the realm of sensation and the realm of the mind. When we initially see Meursault, he lacks the dimension of mind. He responds mechanically to immediate sensation, lives on the level of feeling, has no subjective reality, and lacks moral awareness. When his mother dies, when Marie asks him to marry her, when his boss asks him to take on new responsibilities, when Raymond asks him to write a letter—Meursault is indifferent to all these people. The point is that Meursault is a personification of nature, an incarnation of the absurd. He is a kind of inverted Christ, an avatar of unrelenting cosmic indifference. Meursault's consciousness comes at the moment he becomes aware of the absurd. And this moment awaits on the beach when the gun "happens" to go off, and the Arab falls at his feet. The shooting is as accidental and gratuitous as the world Meursault personifies. The four other shots he fires are, of course, not accidental. They are a symbolic commitment to and acceptance of an absurd world. It is at this moment that Meursault begins to acquire consciousness. Like Sisyphus, he accepts his fate—and he eventually knows why he accepts it.

Whereas Meursault is a mere automaton in the earlier part of the novel, he eventually grows more complex as he moves from the man of simple responses to one capable of higher thought. Most of the humor in the earlier sections of *L'Étranger* stems from Meursault's inability to get beyond the literal and to think abstractly. This creates a "verbal innocence" because for Meursault everything is unique, and he tries to clarify the obvious. At the trial, for example, he says: "Then Céleste was called. He was announced as a witness for the defense. The defense meant me." Meursault is a stranger because his experience has been almost entirely sentient and, quite comically, the processes of society are new to him: "For the nth time I was asked to give particulars of my identity and, though heartily sick of this formality, I realized it was natural enough; after all, it would be a shocking thing for the court to be trying the wrong man."

Both language and silence in *L'Étranger* reveal a quality of mind and a philosophical view of reality. When the examining magistrate asks Meursault why he fired four additional shots, Meursault answers with silence. The shooting was gratuitous and absurd; the absurd is unreasonable and inexplicable; thus the language of absurdity is silence. It is most significant that when the Arab appears on the beach "all was sunlight and silence except for the tinkle of the streams." And Meursault's world narrows to a "little strip of sand between sunlight and sea, the twofold silence of the reed and stream."

As Meursault thinks back on how he adjusted to the

routine of prison, it becomes obvious that he can now think abstractly. He begins, for example, to discuss ideas of liberty and boredom, the idea of sleep, and the concept of time. Meursault has passed through the realm of silence to understanding. It is easy to miss in *L'Étranger* that Meursault possessed such understanding from the outset. One must remember that Meursault is a retrospective narrator, and the events are taking place in his memory. The reflective Meursault, in the jail cell, describes the elemental Meursault who was most happy on the Algerian beaches. One must also remember Camus's remark about the American novel and Proust. The Meursault who shot the Arab was a fictional brother of the American tough guy; the Meursault who begins telling his story in the prison cell "unites . . . memory of the past and immediate sensation" because "rebellion . . . can find satisfaction only in . . . affirming this interior reality and not denying it."

Thus Meursault becomes the rebel. He is aware that the sun can kill, but he loves life under the sun; and his own impending death intensifies this love. In this way, Meursault comes to understand why his mother, at death's door, takes on a fiancé. "Mother," he says, "must have felt like someone on the brink of freedom, ready to start life over again. . . . And I, too, felt ready to start life all over again." Through love of his own life, Meursault can understand the lives of others, and justify life in general. For Camus, rebellion begins here. Meursault becomes one of Camus's ideal spokesmen because his thought is tested by feeling. The absurd stems from an irreconcilable disharmony between the world as man would like it and the world as it is. Meursault's final gesture is an act of absurdity: he lays his heart open to nature and accepts the world of indifference—so much like himself—with lyrical excitement and lucid belief: "gazing up at the dark sky spangled with its signs and stars, for the first time, the first, I laid my heart open to the benign indifference of the universe. To feel it so like myself, indeed, so brotherly, made me realize that I'd been happy, and that I was happy still." Meursault

moves beyond the machinelike puppets who make up
society (cf. Salamano who regularly walks a dog he supposedly hates, and the "robot-woman" who ticks off
radio programs in a newspaper as she wolfs down her
restaurant food). They will never come to terms with
the absurd because they are separated from it by a comfortable barrier called society with its mummifying routine.

The Meursault who embraces creation—absurd and
unreasonable as it may be—has moved from an elemental behaviorist (like the American tough guy), to a man
of memory, to a man of understanding—understanding
which came through experience and which can never be
divorced from feeling, from his joy of life itself. Meursault moves through sensation to memory and desire,
finally to memory and understanding. And it is understanding which is the dimension absent in the characters
of American neorealism.

We again find two realms of reality in Camus's second
novel. *La Peste* is a story of both public and private catastrophe, a documentary as well as a personal history.
There are also two realms of time in this novel—a historical and an existential realm; and there are two narrative
voices—one objective and factual, the other subjective
and interpretive. Reading *L'Étranger* involves climbing from the literal to the symbolic level and following
the progress of a narrator who reveals first a sentient and
then an abstract mind. Reading *La Peste* involves de-
scending from the level of abstraction (the meaning of
the idea of plague) to the realm of human feeling (the
effect of the plague on the individual). Dr. Rieux is
Camus's public voice: he discusses how the town works,
loves, and dies—and how the plague interrupts and
changes their lives. Jean Tarrou is Camus's idiosyncratic
voice: he observes "events and people through the wrong
end of the telescope," lists conversations overheard on
streetcars, watches a man spit on cats from his balcony,
and observes an asthmatic decant peas from one can to
another. Camus uses Tarrou's commentary to suggest
that these unusual pastimes are no more or less idiotic

than the functionary tasks of the people who make up society in general. Like the "robot-woman" in *L'Étranger*, people think that their lives are necessary and consequential. In *La Peste*, however, the plague destroys the daily routine as well as the difference between rich and poor, magistrate and criminal. All life becomes one when time is emptied of meaning. And the moment remains empty until the people begin fighting the plague.

Camus's method in *La Peste* is to make a number of abstractions—the plague, the meaning of suffering and death, the meaning of exile—so concrete that they become "felt realities." We begin, for example, with a discussion of plague in terms of statistics. Rieux "recalled that some thirty or so great plagues known to history had accounted for nearly a hundred million deaths." He then discusses how unreal statistics can be: "But what are a hundred million deaths? When one has served in the war, one hardly knows what a dead man is, after a while. And since a dead man has no substance unless one has actually seen him dead, a hundred million corpses broadcast through history are no more than a puff of smoke in the imagination." Camus tries to make these figures real by discussing the plague in personal terms and by creating an emotional context for them. Rieux, for example, must get the health committee to think of the plague in emotional terms in order to initiate prophylactic measures. The three medical attitudes toward the plague parallel the three philosophical attitudes toward reality that Camus discusses in *The Rebel*. Castel assumes a Nietzschean position: he is willing to recognize evil, but he accepts it instead of fighting it. Dr. Richard thinks in Marxist terms: he insists that only time (history) can justify the legitimacy of action, and then a program of action can be dictated by a manifesto. Dr. Rieux's position is primarily existential: he wants immediate action and is willing to accept the consequences of any mistakes made in the pursuit of overcoming the plague with its suffering and deaths.

Dr. Richard will not take action allowed by the Code because to do so would be to admit the plague and thus cause public hysteria. Camus dramatizes the folly of such reason-without-feeling. Soon after Rieux leaves the meeting, "as he was driving down a back street redolent of fish and urine, a woman screaming in agony, her groin dripping blood, stretched out her arms toward him."

Each character in *La Peste* represents a typical response to the plague. Some respond on both the level of thought and feeling. Rieux, Tarrou, and Grand become —in different ways and for different reasons—the rebels who pit their wills against affliction and struggle to alleviate suffering. While Rieux's first contact with the plague is impersonal, and his chronicle is very much a documentary, he has the basis for understanding the plague in emotional and in human terms. His wife, whom he loves dearly, has been committed to a tuberculosis sanitorium outside the city; her health is a constant concern to him, her absence a continued source of pain. The experience allows him to empathize with those in Oran who are suffering or exiled by the plague. I would hesitate to call Rieux "dehumanized," as does one commentator. Dr. Rieux's reaction to the horrible suffering of M. Othon's child is genuine and sincere and reveals, as does his nightswim with Tarrou, the capacity of feeling as well as thought. Rieux, as Camus tells us, followed "the dictates of his heart," took "the victim's side and tried to share with his fellow citizens the only certitude they had in common—love, exile, and suffering."

Rieux's alter ego, Tarrou, also understands the plague in both abstract and emotional terms because he equates it with the institution of capital punishment. When he was seventeen, Tarrou saw his father, a prosecuting attorney, have a prisoner sentenced to the guillotine. Up until that time, says Tarrou, "my notions on the subject were purely abstract." After that Tarrou realized that the whole idea of capital punishment rested on an abstraction; it was justified by a system that unfeeling people took for granted. He listens to his father speak in formulas, "telling the jury that they owed it to society to find him [the prisoner] guilty." Tarrou goes on to point out the horrible discrepancy between the idea people have of an execution and "the real thing." For Tarrou, both capital punishment and plague are gratuitous, and he fights each with feeling and conviction.

Joseph Grand, we are told, is the real hero of *La Peste*. When we first meet him, he is a disillusioned minor clerk, abandoned by his wife, rewriting the first sentence of what he hopes to be a "perfect" novel. He will, of course, never complete his task because he lacks the ability to realize his Platonic concept of the novel. When the plague comes, he uses his energy more realistically, and for two hours every night he works on Rieux's records and files. Grand is a functionary—not a man capable of great thought or immense feeling—but on a lower frequency "this insignificant and obscure hero who had to his credit only a little goodness of heart and a seemingly absurd ideal" is as dedicated as Rieux and Tarrou.

Other characters in *La Peste* respond to the plague only on the level of abstraction. Fr. Paneloux, for example, thinks of the plague in terms of divine punishment for sin. Tarrou, pointing out the difference between speculative and existential knowledge, maintains that Paneloux "hasn't come in contact with death; that's why he can speak with such assurance of the truth—with a capital T. But every country priest who visits his parishioners and has heard a man gasping for breath on his death-bed thinks as I do. He'd try to relieve human suffering before trying to point out its excellence." Even after Paneloux sees M. Othon's child die a horrible death, he still continues to think of suffering in terms of abstractions. In his second sermon, Fr. Paneloux says that "the sufferings of children were our bread of affliction, but without this bread our souls would die of spiritual hunger."

Others, in counterpoint to Fr. Paneloux, respond to the plague only on the level of personal feeling. For Cottard, who has committed some kind of crime—possibly (like Meursault) that of murdering a man on an Algerian beach—the plague brings a kind of release. The police are so busy enforcing the quarantine that Cottard no longer fears arrest. More to the point, the plague brings Cottard emotional release; when everyone has to suffer, Cottard can find consolation for his own suffering.

Rambert, at first, responds to the plague on the level of feeling. He is a journalist, assigned to study living conditions in the Arab section of town. When the city is quarantined, he is cut off from his mistress, who is still in Paris. Rambert insists that he should be allowed to go home. "He explained that his presence in Oran was purely accidental." The word *accidental* is a key one in Camus's thought, and the reader of *La Peste* realizes that Camus's Oran is a microcosm when Rieux tells Rambert, "I know that it's an absurd situation, but we're all involved in it, and we've got to accept it as it is." Rambert's problem is that he lives only in terms of feeling, and he has to learn to reconcile his feelings with what the plague means as an abstraction. As Rieux puts it:

> To fight abstraction you must have something of it in your own make-up. But how could Rambert be expected to grasp that? Abstraction for him was all that stood in the way of his happiness. Indeed, Rieux had to admit the journalist was right, in one sense. But he knew, too, that abstraction sometimes proves itself stronger than happiness; and then, if only then, it has to be taken into account. And this was what was going to happen to Rambert, as the doctor was to learn when, much later, Rambert told him more about himself. Thus he was enabled to follow, and on a different plane, the dreary struggle in process between each man's happiness and the abstractions of the plague—which constituted the whole of our town over a long period of time.

Rambert, who longs for his "wife," knows what love means. Before he can become the rebel, however, he has to abstract from his experience a concept of love and widen his definition. Rambert finally does something like this when he tells Rieux that it is "shameful to be happy by oneself." In Camus's world, one has to feel in order to understand. Consciousness can never be directed inward; it must have an object; and experience always precedes empathy. Before going to bed at night, Dr. Rieux often heard on the radio well-meaning speakers outside the city trying to voice their sympathy for the plague-stricken. " 'Oran, we're with you!' they called emotionally. But not, the doctor told himself, to love or to die together—and that's the only way. They're too remote." *La Peste* is a journey through agony; and out of the agony comes the meaning of death, suffering, exile, and love.

*La Chute* is Camus's most explicit attack on those who live in terms of self-enclosed, abstract systems. As a number of commentators have pointed out,[1] Camus's third novel is his answer to Jean-Paul Sartre's and Francis Jeanson's attack on him. In *Les Temps Modernes*, Sartre and Camus debated their ideas on history. Sartre was trying to reconcile existentialism with Marxism, and he insisted that man could endow history with ends that would justify suspect political means. Defending his arguments in *L'Homme révolté*, Camus said that the end never justified the means when the means themselves were inhuman. Camus was speaking specifically about the Russian forced-labor camps, and he insisted that the USSR had violated the very freedom that an existentialist was supposed to defend. Sartre agreed that the forced-labor camps could not be justified in and of themselves. He maintained, however, that in the postwar power struggle between East and West, the forced-labor camps were no worse than the disguised slavery of capitalism, and that Camus was an intellectual idealist who refused to commit himself to history. Sartre went on to say that communism could be the means to existential ends, and he insisted that anti-Stalin Russia offered the most expedient means to secure a masterless state. What Sartre was saying in effect was that communism was the lesser of two evils. Camus rejected such expediency, said one must live for today and not tomorrow, and insisted that no government had the right to sacrifice men in the name of the future.[2]

The debate between Camus and Sartre was so heated that the two men broke as friends, and Camus brought his wrath to the writing of *La Chute*. As Adele King explains, Clamence is at first "a caricature of Camus, seen through Sartre's eyes" who finally becomes "a spokesman for, and practitioner of, Sartre's own method." This illuminating insight becomes the key that unlocks the meaning of Camus's most difficult novel. Everything Clamence says must be placed in double context. Thus, when Clamence speaks of the Zuider Zee, Camus is likening Sartre's philosophy to a boat at float on a dead sea, devoid of landmarks: "So we are steaming along without any landmarks; we can't gauge our speed. We are making progress and yet nothing is changing. It's not navigation but dreaming." Other references to Sartre are unmistakable. Sartre's ideal of radical freedom is well known: "Once upon a time," says Clamence, "I was always talking of freedom. At breakfast I used to spread it on my toast." Sartre believed that the novel should be a mirror and reflect for the reader various states of ethical existence. Camus seems to have this in mind when Clamence says, "the portrait I hold out to my contemporaries becomes a mirror." Sartre also believed that as a matter of expediency one had to align himself with the Communists. Camus pointed out to Sartre that the end never justified the means, that suffering in the forced-labor camps could not be justified in the name of future ideals, and that Sartre was choosing a master in choosing communism. In this context, Clamence's remarks are most significant: "Ah, mon cher, for anyone who is alone, without God and without a master, the weight of days is dreadful. Hence one must choose a master, God being out of style. . . . In short, you see, the essential [*sic*] is to cease being free and to obey, in repentance, a greater rogue than oneself. . . . I'm well aware that slavery is not immediately realizable. It will be one of the blessings of the future, that's all."

Camus makes Clamence into such a convincing caricature because Clamence is exactly the kind of person Camus had criticized in his previous fiction. Clamence thinks only on the level of abstractions, and he can move almost fluidly from the idea of universal innocence to the idea of universal guilt. Clamence lives without feeling. Compassion is an idea to him, and he is motivated by head and not heart. He sees himself as he wants others to see him, and his sense of duty stems from a Platonic conception—an idea that he has of himself. For this reason his altruism is empty and turns back upon itself—as, for example, when he helps a blind man across the street and then tips his hat.

Clamence's system allows him to stand outside humanity. As he tells us, "I lived with impunity. I was concerned in no judgment; I was not on the floor of the courtroom, but somewhere in the flies like those gods that are brought down by the machinery from time to time to transfigure the action and give it its meaning." Clamence becomes fond of the dead because he has no obligation to them and they cannot puncture his system: "They leave us free and we can take our time, fit the testimonial in between a cocktail party and a nice little mistress, in our spare time." Even his life of debauchery is related to a fixed system; such a life, he says, was "liberating" and created "no obligations." "In it you possess only yourself."

Clamence's sense of guilt is no more real than his sense of innocence; both are fictions of his mind. His feeling of guilt stems from his failure to help a drowning woman who jumped into the Seine. Clamence has abstracted a concept of universal guilt from this event which is as unjustified as the drowning is almost unreal. The woman is not personalized, she is left vague, and the object of Clamence's concern is made intangible to suggest how much it is really a product of his abstract thinking. The whole affair is further abstracted when Clamence sees, from the top-deck of an ocean liner, a black spot moving on the sea. The speck turns out to be refuse, but he generalizes and insists that "that cry which had sounded over the Seine" had been "carried by river to the waters of the Channel, to travel throughout the world, across the limitless expense of the ocean." Clamence needs to sustain his concept of guilt; that is why he keeps van Eyck's "The Just Judges." As long as he has this panel, he destroys the sequence of the altarpiece, "The Adoration of the Lamb"; and the judges will be kept forever from the Saviour, and Clamence will be able to sustain his belief in universal guilt.

Clamence's capacity for abstract thought stems from his gigantic ego. His mind reaches out, and the world has to fit his conception of it. "I lived," he says, in terms of "I, I, I," and "thus I progressed on the surface of life, in the realm of words as it were, never in reality." Clamence's ideas change in *La Chute*, but that is all that changes. At the beginning of the novel he expresses a preference for "summits." At the end of the novel, after his ideological shift, he repeats that preference: "Once more I have found a height to which I am the only one to climb and from which I can judge everybody." Clamence's "exposed heights" parallel Sartre's philosophical dogmatism and trust in an abstract concept of history. Clamence refused to join the Resistance because underground activity did not suit his temperament or his idea of right action.

Clamence in many ways is like Mathieu, the central character in Sartre's *Les Chemins de la liberté*. He is so concerned in trying to abstract the idea of right action that he never acts. It is very important to follow the quality of the language in *La Chute*. Clamence talks in continued paradox, and the very logic of his language reveals the contradictory nature of his thought. Paradox could be the language of absurdity because it sustains continued contradiction. Clamence at times uses paradox in this way: "It seems to me," he says, "that I was half unlearning what I had never learned and yet knew so well—how to live." However, in *La Chute* paradox usually reveals a mind working on the level of abstraction, contradicting itself as it moves from idea to idea. Speaking of Christ and the Slaughter of the Innocents, for example, Clamence says, "It was better to have done with it, not to defend himself, *to die*, in order not to be the only one to live, and *to go elsewhere* where perhaps he would be upheld" (italics mine). While many other examples could be cited, a few will serve to document further this point:

1. What does it matter, after all, if by humiliating one's mind one succeeds in dominating everyone?

2. Tubercular lungs are cured by drying up and gradually asphyxiate their happy owner.

3. Don't lies eventually lead to the truth? And don't all my stories, true or false, tend toward the same conclusions?

4. You see in me, *très cher*, an enlightened advocate of slavery.

5. At the end of freedom is a court sentence.

6. Satanism is virtuous.

7. The more I accuse myself, the more I have a right to judge you.

Camus has told us that the germ of *La Chute* was Conrad's *Lord Jim*, a study of moral inadequacy brought about by an unjustified idea of self.[3] Jean-Baptiste Clamence also has an abstracted idea of self that frustrates moral action—as the very last paragraph of *La Chute* suggests. Sartre's Mathieu tried to come to terms with an ambiguous world, and was so busy thinking about life that he never lived. In this context, it is most significant that Clamence speaks in the language of paradox and vacillates when action is most needed. "History may perhaps have an end," Camus says in *L'Homme révolté*, "but our task is not to terminate it but to create it, in the image of what we henceforth know to be true." But the image is not enough. "One can reject all history," Camus continues, "and yet accept the world of sea and stars."

Camus and Sartre were of different temperaments, never spoke in the same idiom, and their philosophies rested on different assumptions. Camus loved the natural life, especially the oceans and deserts of North Africa, while Sartre loved the city, especially Paris. Camus was a man of deep emotion, Sartre of deep thought; Camus's response to life was lyrical, Sartre's cerebral. Camus was concerned with the meaning of justice, Sartre with the meaning of reality. The difference, in fact, between Sartre and Camus was the difference between what Sartre meant by *nausea* and what Camus meant by the *absurd*. Nausea had its source in human consciousness, absurdity in cosmic creation. Camus was concerned with the nature of creation, man's fate, and the justification of existence. Sartre is concerned with the nature of the mind's operation and perception, its relationship with others, and the character of one's existence. The difference between *absurdity* and *nausea* is the difference between Sartre's emphasis upon freedom and Camus's emphasis upon rebellion. For Sartre, the free man overcomes the contingency of his immediate situation, projects future goals, and consciously strives to redefine himself in time. For Camus, the rebel recognizes that nature and society are antagonistic and hostile, continually redefines himself in terms of threats from each, and sets moral limits beyond which the human becomes inhuman.

While Camus and Sartre are thus at philosophical odds, there are points of common agreement: both are concerned with threats to the self from without, with the battle between an interior and an exterior reality. For Sartre, one is at odds with his surroundings, at odds with a viscous, gelatinous world that seems ready to envelop him. For Camus, one is threatened by the disharmony between man and his unresponsive environment. Sartre's Roquentin tries to reconcile himself to Bouville (that is, to "mudville"). Camus's Meursault tries to reconcile himself to that beautiful expanse of Algerian beach upon which the sun can kill, just as Dr. Rieux tries to reconcile himself to plague-infested Oran.

Within this context, the supreme figure for both Sartre and Camus is the artist. In *L'Homme révolté* Camus maintained that the artist was the man best able to live the absurd life, and in *La Nausée* Roquentin desired to be absorbed by a song he heard on a phonograph. Roquentin, however, wanted to become a part of the song because music is the most harmonious and complete form that consciousness can take and thus a means of self-perfection. Camus retreated into art because it offered a sense of self-proportion, a means of living the absurd, of affirming existence and of rejecting such extremes as the Nietzschean will to power and Marxian dogmatism. Camus believed in a given creation where the scheme of things could not be changed but where one could change his attitude toward what is given. Sartre, on the other hand, believed that reality could be phenomenologically bracketed, believed in a world in which one could transcend reality, could project the self beyond the glutinous contingency of nausea, because ultimate reality was contingent upon the consciousness of it. Art for Camus was thus a way of life, a means of giving proportion to one's actions. Art for Sartre was a mode of reality, a desired end of being that consciousness should strive to attain.

Despite their ideological differences, postwar Europe found a common denominator in the writing of Sartre and Camus. Both men were trying to reconcile modern man with his uprooted surroundings, to formulate a philosophy of self, and to construct a purely secular ethic. Both were trying to put man in motion.

# 3

# French and American Literary Existentialism
Dos Passos, Hemingway, Faulkner

Perhaps the most systematic and complete account of the American novel in postwar France has been made by Thelma Smith and Ward Miner in a book entitled *Transatlantic Migration: The Contemporary American Novel in France*. The book makes no pretense to being critical; it is expressly historical and bibliographical, and the authors concentrate upon the French critical studies of American fiction and the French reactions to the American novel. Smith and Miner list almost two dozen books that were either fully or partially devoted to the American novel, as well as articles too numerous to count, all written between 1946 and 1950. The more important full-length studies of the American novel include Maurice Coindreau's *Aperçus de littérature américaine* (1946), Pierre Bodin's *Les Écrivains américains de l'entredeaux-guerres* (1946), Jean Pouillon's *Temps et roman* (1946), Claude-Edmond Magny's *L'Âge du roman américain* (1948), and Jean Simon's *Le Roman américain au XX° siècle*.

Perhaps the greatest encouragement to Amercan fiction came from the popular magazines. During the war, for example, a number of Algerian magazines published anthologies of American fiction. In 1943, one such magazine, *Fontaine*, published an issue entitled "Écrivains et Poètes des États-Unis," containing selections from the works of Hemingway, Steinbeck, Faulkner, and Caldwell. *Confluences*, another magazine of similar nature, got out an issue entitled "Problèmes du Roman" and discussed the American influence on the French novel. After the liberation of Paris, these special issues were printed in book form. Also at this time, special series containing selections from the American novel were issued by such popular French journals as *L'Arbalète*, *Cahiers des Langues Modernes, Esprit, Renaissances*, and *Les Temps Modernes*. The American library in Paris undoubtedly also influenced the popularity of American fiction. The library contains over eighty thousand American books and its subsidiary libraries are also well stocked. These libraries were established primarily for the American serviceman in France, but counts have shown that 60 percent of their subscribers were French. The final encouragement to American fiction came from the National Ministry of Education. Before the war only the Sorbonne gave a course in American literature and civilization. Now such courses are being given at universities in Aix-Marseilles, Alger, Bordeaux, Caen, Clermont, Dijon, Rennes, and Strasbourg. Modern American literature is often featured prominently in French graduate literary studies, and symposiums on American literature have also been frequently given and popularly attended in France.

French enthusiasm over the American novel has been perhaps no better expressed than by Jean-Paul Sartre himself. Sartre maintained in "American Novelists in French Eyes" (*The Atlantic Monthly*, August 1946) that

> The greatest literary development in France between 1929 and 1939 was the discovery of Faulkner, Dos Passos, Hemingway, Caldwell, and Steinbeck. . . . These authors have not had in France a popular success comparable to that of Sinclair Lewis. Their influence was far more restricted, but infinitely more profound. . . . To writers of my generation, the publication of the *42nd Parallel, Light in August, A Farewell to Arms*, evoked a revolution similar to the one

produced fifteen years earlier by the *Ulysses* of James Joyce. . . . At once, for thousands of young intellectuals the American novel took its place together with jazz and the movies, among the best of the importations from the United States. The large frescoes of Vidor joined with the passion and violence of *The Sound and the Fury* and *Sanctuary* to compose for us the face of the United States—a face tragic, cruel, sublime.

American fiction was new and different to the French. It was distinct from any narrative genre France had yet known. On the one hand, it was removed from the deterministic, highly documented, socially determined naturalism of Zola. On the other hand, it was faster-paced and more down-to-earth than the bloodless, over-refined Proustian novel of psychological analysis, and more concrete and objectively rooted than the abstract or heavily symbolic writing of Gide, Valéry, and Giraudoux. In his *Atlantic Monthly* essay, Sartre maintained that the French did not want a heavily documented, ponderous, intellectual, or psychological novel in an age of Buchenwald and Hiroshima. The novel of intellectual analysis, he says, "was no longer anything but an old mechanism badly adapted to the needs of the time. . . . Could it take into account the brutal death of a Jew in Auschwitz, the bombardment of Madrid by the planes of France?" The French wanted a novel of action, and they found it in the repertoire of Hemingway, Dos Passos, and Faulkner. "Here," said Sartre, "a new literature presented its characters to us synthetically. It made them perform before our eyes acts which were complete in themselves, impossible to analyze, acts which it was necessary to grasp completely with all the obscure power of our souls." The success of Faulkner, Hemingway, Dos Passos, Sartre said in *Qu'est-ce que la littérature*, "was the defensive reflex of a literature which, feeling itself menaced because its techniques and its myths no longer permitted it to face the actual situation, grafted on itself foreign methods in order to fulfill its function in dealing with the problems placed before it." The objectivity of presentation, the inversion of time, the collectivist view and wide social range, the extended intensity of emotion —all these literary qualities were new in France and account in part for the popularity of the American novel.

The existentialists also admired the American novel because it organically dramatized a world view. They stressed, in particular, what they called its sense of *dépaysement*, which can be translated as "uprootedness" or as "deracination." As one French critic, Claude-Edmond Magny in *L'Âge du roman américain*, put it:

> Le roman américain est venu circuler un souffle plus large dans la République des Lettres. Aussi son charme est-il en particulier celui de l'exotisme non tant au sens banal de l'éloignement dans l'espace, que grace au prestige plus profond du dépaysement social. Il nous montre des vagabonds, des chomeurs, des ivrognes invétéres; de mauvais garçons dénués de tout romantisme.

America, still in the process of growth, was a relatively young country to the French. While America offered the individual much more freedom than the more fixed Continent with its age-old traditions, for some it was a hostile and brutal prison. The novels of Faulkner, Dos Passos, Steinbeck, Hemingway, and Caldwell are populated with floundering expatriates or itinerant workers who live on the periphery of society and are forever looking for new adventure or for a new start. The Hemingway, Dos Passos, Faulkner hero is seldom cerebral or (with the obvious exception of characters like Quentin Compson) self-involved and often wanders alone and aimlessly through a land devoid of tradition, defining himself through immediate action. In his *Atlantic Monthly* essay, Sartre in particular called attention to the solitary heroes of American fiction who seem to have lost contact with past tradition:

What fascinated us all really—petty bourgeois that
we were, sons of peasants securely attached to the
earth of our farms, intellectuals entrenched in Paris
for life—was the constant flow of men across a whole
continent, the exodus of an entire village to the or-
chards of California, the hopeless wanderings of the
hero in *Light in August*, and the uprooted people who
drifted along at the mercy of the storm in *The 42nd
Parallel*, the dark murderous fury which sometimes
swept through an entire city, the blind and criminal
love in the novels of James Cain.

## John Dos Passos

Sartre has admitted his debt in matters of technique to John Dos Passos's panoramic trilogy *U.S.A.* "It
was after reading a book by Dos Passos," he said in the
*Atlantic Monthly*, "that I thought for the first time of
weaving a novel out of various lives with characters who
pass each other and who all contribute to the atmosphere
of a historical period." Sartre went on to say in "John
Dos Passos and 1919" (in *Situations I*) that "I regard
Dos Passos as the greatest writer of our time." One questions Sartre's literary values after such a statement. The
praise becomes more understandable, however, when one
realizes that Sartre is carried away with Dos Passos's
ability to immerse a reader in a historical situation and
to create a kind of existential reality. Sartre is also interested in Dos Passos's experimental technique which allows a sense of history at the same time as it does away
with the omniscient point of view.

Sartre is certainly correct when he points out that
Dos Passos's heroes are very much a part of history and
keep pace with the turbulent and chaotic growth of
America. One of the controlling motives in *U.S.A.* is the
desire for quick money. The lives of many of the main
characters even parallel the Horatio Alger formula.
J. Ward Moorehouse rides the waves of ambition until

he becomes the head of a leading advertising firm. Dick Savage outdistances his humble beginning and eventually becomes an executive in the Moorehouse firm. Eleanor Stoddard goes beyond her sordid childhood environment, becomes a successful interior decorator, and finally marries into Russian nobility. Charley Anderson leaves North Dakota to become eventually a wealthy airplane manufacturer. Margo Dowling runs away from Long Island poverty to become a wealthy movie star.

These are some of the people involved in the frenetic activity that accompanied postwar prosperity. Along with this mad scramble for wealth, rioting and fighting run through U.S.A. and engage Charley Anderson, Mac, and Joe Williams. The chaos of the times is reflected by the chaotic lives. A kind of abandon characterizes Dos Passos's unheroic men and women. Almost all the characters are promiscuous: Eleanor Stoddard and Eveline Hutchins sleep with Moorehouse, Margo Dowling with Charley Anderson, Anne Elizabeth Trent (daughter) with Dick Savage. All the characters move away from their families and childhood surroundings and wander aimlessly through life, never seeming to mind their deracinated conditions. These lives never have any sense of completion. Even Dos Passos's "good people" lead rootless lives. Mac, Joe Williams, Benny Compton, and Mary French flounder about as badly as the others. The various characters in U.S.A. come and go and disappear. Their problems are rarely resolved in the manner of the traditional novel because they are the unresolved problems of an age.

In Les Chemins de la liberté there is also a direct relationship between the historical and the individual situation. The historical situation contains all of the characters, and yet they remain autonomous and free to define themselves. The novels take place a year before World War II, at the time of the Munich conference, and during the French capitulation to Germany. Sartre saves his characters from becoming types by personalizing what would otherwise be a general state of mind. France is restless, fearful, anxious, yet unable to grasp the meaning of the situation or to act meaningfully in terms of it. Like the country as a whole, the freedom of the individual is often wasted because it is undirected and unengaged. Mathieu, for example, restlessly looks for the single act that will define him. Boris lives aimlessly because he greatly admires Mathieu and does not know what he wants to be. Lola demands the love of young Boris to prove that she is not growing old. Daniel desires to be punished because he is a homosexual, tries to kill his prize cats, then to castrate himself, and finally marries Marcelle as a form of self-punishment. He likes to see others suffer because he is a sufferer, and he longs for war. Gros-Louis, a shepherd, is too stupid to understand the meaning of war. Jacque, Mathieu's brother, never has to think because he accepts without question the values of the bourgeoisie. These wasted and pitiful lives are Sartre's objective correlative, his dramatic metaphor, of the political and social situation of France at this time.

The characters in the fiction of Sartre and Dos Passos are either a part of the historical moment or in some way embody that moment, and they do this without losing their autonomy. This is not to say that there is no difference between the novels of Sartre and Dos Passos. Their fiction does differ in one essential way—and that is in the manner in which they handle time. Dos Passos's characters exist in a well of time. At first everything is seen in a historical perspective, then follows a sudden shift from a very general to a specific time. A typical passage in *U.S.A.* reveals Dos Passos's method:

Winters the brick sidewalks were icy. . . . One winter they got in the habit of walking up the hill. . . . One afternoon she asked Pearl to come in and they played dolls together. . . . Summer evenings when the twilight was long after supper they played lions and tigers with other kids from the neighborhood. . . . About once a week Joe would get spanked. . . .

Once a drizzly Saturday night she stood against the fence in the dark looking up at the lighted window. She could hear Popper's voice and Joe's in argument.

Dos Passos here sets time in motion with such general words as *winters, summer evenings*, and then jumps into a more particular realization of time with words like *one afternoon* and *once* serving as transitional links. The following fragment reveals the method again:

> July was hot that summer, in the office they worked in a continual whir of electric fans, the men's collars wilted and the girls kept themselves overplastered with powder; only Mr. Drefus still looked cool and crisply tailored as if he'd just stepped out of a band-box. The last day of the month Janey was sitting a minute at her desk when Jerry Burnham came in.

Sartres novels never lose a sense of duration as do those of Dos Passos. Sartre adds the dimension of freedom to his fiction by constructing a narrative future, the realm of time in which the reader's will functions. The character may remain consistent with the first image he creates of himself, but he always has the opportunity to transcend his initial nature. In *Les Chemins de la liberté* the moment continually weighs upon the reader. Sartre often prefaces chapters with the hour of the day in which the following action is to take place; he continually makes the reader aware of the passing of time by working the hour of day into the dialogue. *L'Age de raison* takes place in 48 hours and 35 minutes, and every minute can be accounted for. *Le Sursis* starts at 4:30 P.M. Berlin time (3:30 P.M. London time), Friday, September 23, and ends a few minutes past 1:30 A.M. on Friday, September 30. Every ten pages of the novel equals approximately one hour of time. It is 4:30 on page one, 5:30 on page eleven, 8:10 on page 31, 4:00 A.M. on page 64, 6:00 A.M. on page 74, 7:00 A.M. on page 81, and so on.

Despite the difference in the handling of time, the final effect of *U.S.A.* is strangely enough the same as

*Les Chemins de la liberté.* As Sartre himself pointed out, Dos Passos's novels seem to take place in the present. The reason for this is that they sustain a horizontal structure, a quantitative time in which one action or event is made to seem as important as the next. There are no real crises in *U.S.A.* One action also never seems to be the result of another. As Sartre puts it, "not for an instant does the order of causality betray itself in chronological order. There is no narrative, but rather the jerky unreeling of a rough and uneven memory. . . . As a result of this, past things retain a flavour of the present; they still remain, in their exile, what they once were, inexplicable tumults of colour, sound and passion. Each event is irreducible, a gleaming solitary *thing* that does not flow from anything else."

In the collective novel the reader is the real source of this temporal unity. He also holds the various scenes together. Not only does the camera tend to move toward a common center and catch lives crossing and recrossing, but the various candid shots—the individual pictures— follow each other in such rapid succession that the novels of Sartre and Dos Passos are a prose form of the film technique. Claude-Edmond Magny had pointed out in *L'Âge du roman américain* that the technique of the camera eye and the newsreel are not limited merely to Dos Passos's interlinking sections, and Sartre himself seems to be aware of this. In *Le Sursis* Sartre sets the film in motion and employs quick narrative transitions to smash the life of one character into that of another. Such montage often produces a certain mood or emotional effect and the transition from one mood to another produces a third. In *U.S.A.* and *Les Chemins de la liberté* characters are in such bad faith, so similar, that the transition from one to the other is fluid, and the reader becomes aware of a world gone rotten at the core. Thus instead of diffusing the effect, montage in these novels intensifies and reinforces the controlling mood. The tone of the novel solidifies, so at the end of the novel the reader sees each character in terms of all the others, the bad faith of one magnifying the unauthenticity of the other. In *Le Sursis*, for example, Daladier is troubled about the French commitment to protect Czechoslovakia against Hitler. Sartre comments obliquely on his vacillation by juxtaposing Daladier's reflections against a picture of Philippe, the deserter, in the arms of a Negro prostitute: the pronoun "he," which opens the second paragraph, refers by implication to Daladier as well as Philippe:

> He [Daladier] stared at the dark flowers in the carpet and felt a little dizzy. Peace—war. I have done all I could to preserve peace. But he now wondered whether he didn't actually want to be swept away like a straw in this vast torrent, whether he didn't long for that tremendous holiday—war.
>
> He [Philippe] looked about him in bewilderment and exclaimed: "I haven't gone." She had opened the shutters and was now back beside the bed, leaning over him. He felt her warm body and inhaled her fishy odor.

The plight and moral failure of one character is transferred to another until the reader is submerged in the evidence of a helpless and hopeless society.

Another narrative device Sartre seems to have borrowed from Dos Passos is that of shifting from outside to inside a character in order to secure transition from the world of things to the world of consciousness and from the individual to the collective consciousness. Sartre, himself, refers to the passage in 1919 in which Joe Williams is killed in a barroom brawl:

> Joe laid out a couple of frogs and was backing off towards the door, when he saw in the mirror that a big guy in a blouse was bringing down a bottle on his head with both hands. He tried to swing around but he didn't have time. The bottle crashed his skull and he was out.

"We are inside him," says Sartre, "until the shock of the bottle on his skull. Then immediately, we find ourselves outside with the chorus, part of the collective memory." The passage in *Le Sursis* which describes the beating of Gros-Louis seems consciously to employ what Sartre describes as Dos Passos's method.

"They are going to kill me," thought Gros-Louis, and fear froze him to the marrow, he seized Mario by the throat with his free hand and lifted him off the ground; but at the same moment his head was cloven to the chin, he let go of Mario and fell to his knees, blood pouring over his eyebrows. He tried to steady himself by grabbing Mario's coat, but Mario jumped backwards, and Gros-Louis saw him no more.

To say that there is an interior reality here overstates the quality of narration. There is an overwhelming sense of fact in the writing of both Sartre and Dos Passos. Each incident has the quality of a *thing*. And yet the facts are related to personal consciousness ("he saw in the mirror that . . . ," " 'They are going to kill me,' thought Gros-Louis. . . ."). And suddenly that consciousness disappears. The very identities of Joe and Gros-Louis become just another fact, another descriptive detail with the words "and he was out," "and Gros-Louis saw him no more." Characters disappear into the gelatinous realm of "things as they are," a realm Sartre described at length in his first novel, *La Nausée*. And as such, they can be judged. I think this is what Sartre means when he says, "we find ourselves outside with the chorus, part of the collective memory."

Sartre, of course, reads into Dos Passos's novels much more than can be justified textually. Sartre has a tendency not only to read literature but to judge it in terms of his existential ideas. That is why Sartre makes a great deal out of Dos Passos's ability to describe a character from without and then to personalize the facts. Such transition is important for Sartre because it takes into account his philosophical duality—*en soi* and *pour soi*—and admits both an objective and a subjective existence. In *U.S.A.* and *Les Chemins de la liberté* the reader is allowed to participate in the two realms. The reader identifies himself with the various protagonists, becomes a part of the social consciousness, and engages himself in the freedom of the characters. Such a point of view forces the reader to participate in the novel as part of a chorus, a social conscience. He pieces together the fragmented images, views them in relation to the main social problem, and finally passes judgment on himself at the same time that he passes judgment on the characters. "If you name the behavior of an individual," Sartre has said, "you reveal it to him; he sees himself. And since you are at the same time naming it to all others he knows that he is *seen.*" Thus the final image in the mirror—and it is often an ugly one—is really that of the reader himself, and the final problem is one of identity. Sartre uses the technique of John Dos Passos to show man, sick of soul, in motion at the crossroads of modern history.

## Ernest Hemingway and James M. Cain

Sartre's debt to Dos Passos parallels Camus's debt to Hemingway and James M. Cain. Hemingway has always been a popular novelist in modern France. Almost all of his novels have been translated, and all the translations have sold exceptionally well. Maurice Coindreau translated *The Sun Also Rises* in 1933 (*Le Soleil se lève aussi*, Paris: Gallimard), and the year before he had translated *A Farewell to Arms* (*L'Adieu aux armes*, Paris: Gallimard). Marcel Duhamel translated *To Have and Have Not* in 1945 (*En avoir ou pas*, Paris: Gallimard). *For Whom the Bell Tolls* (*Pour qui sonne la glas*), which had been translated in 1944 by Denise V. Ayme and published by the London firm of Heinemann and Zsolnay, was reissued in 1948 by the Paris branch of the same publishing house and by Le Club Français du Livre in 1950. *The Old Man and the Sea* (*Le Viel Homme et la mer*) was translated by Jean Dutourd in 1952 and published by Gallimard.

In "A Natural History of the Dead" (which appe
in both *Death in the Afternoon* and *Winner Take
Nothing*) Hemingway postulates an ordered and God-
governed universe and then undercuts the assumption
with a description of the agony, horror, and pain of
violent death. Death is at the very center of Hemingway's fictional world. In *The Sun Also Rises*, Jake Barnes
comes out of the war with his life but not with his
masculinity, and he realizes that the only way he can
make his absurd condition a way of life is to bring to it
a private discipline and a capacity to endure. Jake's
wound separates him from both family and community,
and he feels most at home with a group of profligates and
social outcasts. An outsider, Jake's is an existential situation: he must construct a way of life in an absurd world,
a world he no longer understands. "I did not care what
it was all about," he says. "All I wanted to know was
how to live in it."

The title of the novel, taken from Ecclesiastes, prefaces and reinforces the theme of circular and meaningless motion. The novel itself makes use of this circular
pattern. At the beginning, Jake and Brett ride in a taxi
through the streets of Paris. At the end, they ride in a
taxi through the streets of Madrid, still separated from
each other, still hopelessly alone in the crowded city.
When Brett gets into the Paris taxi, she says, "Oh, dar-
ling, I've been so miserable." Later in the novel, she repeats the same words, and Jake tells us that "I had
the feeling of going through something that has all happened before. . . . I had the feeling as in a nightmare
of it all being something repeated, something I had been
through and now I must go through again." Jake's situation does not change, but he changes himself in relation
to his situation. When Jake undercuts Brett's sentimen-
tality at the end of the novel, he is trying to keep himself in emotional order. He learns in the course of the
novel that if he is to cope with the absurd, he must
condition himself emotionally, become emotionally hard,
a kind of neostoic.

The only values that exist are those the individual tests against his own sense of experience and preserves for himself. The trouble with Robert Cohn is that he cannot bring himself emotionally into order. He lives secondhand, once-removed from immediate experience, his ideas tainted by preconceived impressions he has received from reading such romantic novels as *The Purple Island* or such satirists as H. L. Mencken. Cohn is unable to go beyond his romantic illusions. He cannot accept the fact that Brett Ashley is promiscuous; he feels superior to the rest of the expatriates, is egocentric and self-centered, fails to control his emotions, breaks down in public, and makes a ridiculous spectacle of himself before the moral control of Pedro Romero. Since he lives at one remove from reality, Cohn is guilty of the worst kind of bad faith. He never sees himself realistically and is forever trying to escape his condition, to evade the present moment by traveling to new countries in search of a phantom self.

Since all values for Hemingway are relative, since meaning is created by man himself, to live in terms of absolutes is to court disillusionment. *A Farewell to Arms* is a study in twofold disillusionment—disillusionment in love and war. At the beginning of the novel, Lt. Henry thinks of war as if it were some glorious football game and that he is playing a totally necessary part; he is slightly disillusioned when, behind the lines, eating a piece of cheese and drinking wine, he suffers his absurd and gratuitous wound; and he is totally disillusioned and makes his "separate peace" when he is almost shot by Italians during the retreat from Caporetto. If he idealizes war at the beginning of the novel, Lt. Henry has at this point no illusions about love. He encourages Catherine Barkley because she is a beautiful woman and he sexually wants her: "This was better than going every evening to the house for officers." His attitude becomes less cynical as Catherine nurses him in the hospital and accompanies him on his leave, and he is totally in love with her when they escape from Italy and spend a kind of Edenic winter in the Alps. At this point, Lt. Henry has raised love to the same absolute realm that he had placed war. When Catherine dies in childbirth, love is negated as an absolute just as war had previously been negated. Lt. Henry is washed of all illusions, and *A Farewell to Arms* ends where *The Sun Also Rises* begins—with the main character trying to find a kind of existential meaning, a more realistic kind of commitment in this indifferent universe.

Like Jake Barnes, Frederic Henry is embarrassed by untested ideals. He cannot, for example, share the patriot Gino's belief that the Italian defeat "this summer cannot have been done in vain." Henry "did not say anything. I was always embarrassed by the words sacred, glorious, and sacrifice and the expression in vain. . . . Abstract words such as glory, honor, courage, or hallow were obscene beside the concrete names of villages, the number of roads, the names of rivers, the numbers of regiments and the dates." Count Griffi, the old diplomat with whom Henry plays billiards at the Stresa Hotel, is a man of empirical wisdom who has experienced life fully and deeply and now has a right to talk about it. He represents an ideal compromise between the values of Rinaldi and the priest. Rinaldi is the nihilist, the priest, the absolutist. Rinaldi's world is like the black lake in Switzerland with no definable boundaries since nothing is real beyond the moment. In contrast is the priest's Abruzzi, the mountain world "where the roads were frozen and hard as iron, where it was clear cold and dry powdery and hare tracks in the snow and the peasants took off their hats and called you lord and there was good hunting." Henry plans to go to the Abruzzi, but goes instead to the city, with its cafes and "nights when the room whirled and you need to look at the wall to make it stop." Love is impossible in this world. Rinaldi knows that when he says, referring to Catherine, "thank God I did not become involved with the British." This is the world where Lt. Henry, in a scene not unlike that between Meursault and the Arab, kills a sergeant for not helping him disengage his demobilized ambulance.

If Jake Barnes has to choose a course of life that falls

between the idealism of Robert Cohn and the nihilism of Mike Campbell, Lt. Henry has to choose a course of life between the absolutist views of the priest and the moral abandonment of Rinaldi. In *The Sun Also Rises*, Pedro Romero offered a point of reconciliation between moral extremes. Neither Jake Barnes nor Frederic Henry can be a bullfighter, but they can use Romero's life as a model for their own and approximate it in their own way by ordering themselves against the chaos of life, especially the final chaos—death. If Rinaldi's cynicism is justified, it also leads in his case to moral abandonment and syphilis. If the priest's faith in God is gratuitous, it leads to a life with proportion and meaning. The ideal Hemingway character must redeem Rinaldi's cynicism with the pride that comes from doing a job well, with the joy of living close to the senses, and with the integrity that comes with courage—that all-important Hemingway virtue, which he once defined as grace under pressure. One redeems himself through the self-integrity of his actions—an idea that brings Hemingway to the very doorstep of French existentialism.

A *Farewell to Arms* shows the Hemingway hero becoming aware of the absurd. *The Sun Also Rises* shows him living the absurd. In 1937, Hemingway published *To Have and Have Not*, one of his poorest novels. Smith and Miner tell us that in France this novel has been given a continued existentialist reading, even more so than Hemingway's earlier works. This is surprising because it was written at a time when Hemingway was expressing a half-hearted interest in power politics, and the conclusion of the novel reveals Hemingway beginning to doubt, as Jean-Paul Sartre would also doubt, the ability of one man to change his world. "A man alone ain't got no bloody . . . chance," Harry Morgan concludes.

Despite this conclusion, *To Have and Have Not* sustains many of Hemingway's existential ideas. Harry Morgan is the outsider who smuggles aliens and contraband into the United States because he cannot find the means to live the respectable life. In direct contrast to Morgan are the rich and influential vacationers. Mr. Johnson is a clumsy sportsman, a fraud and cheat as well. Richard Gordon, a popular novelist, is intellectually superficial, a writer without personal conviction who caters to bourgeois taste. A snob, he changes political horses at opportune moments. Too weak-willed to escape the clutches of Helène Bradley, a nymphomaniac, he is a failure as both husband and serious writer. Gordon's wife does not come out any better. She knows of his affair, accepts Gordon for what he is, and carries on an affair of her own with Professor John MacWalsey, a drunkard. Hemingway, of course, reveals his own prejudices here as well as when he makes Wallace Johnson and Henry Carpenter into effete intellectuals and homosexuals. Hemingway not only distrusted the rich, he had contempt for the kind of social world that Henry James used in his novels, and he had equal contempt for intellectuals. Camus saw Hemingway's limitations here, saw that Hemingway's characters were really one-dimensional. Hemingway repeatedly maintained that the man who lived bravely, close to violence, was the true man, with an integrity and sexual vitality that put men of social status or of intellectual ability to shame. As unjustified as Hemingway's portraits may be, they duplicate the views repeatedly found in American men's magazines, and they tap a national consciousness, which perhaps explains why Hemingway has always been such a popular writer. Harry Morgan is a character right out of *True Adventure* or *Argosy*. In contrast to the socialites and intellectuals, he and his wife are healthy, live more fully, do not need luminal to sleep, and are not sexually inadequate.

Despite Camus's reservations about such American tough guys, Harry Morgan is the apotheosis of existentialism. He is courageous, acts spontaneously, has the will to endure, and never (like Henry Carpenter) contemplates suicide, even though his life is far more difficult than the Wall Street barons. Unlike the Negro mate, he never whimpers or reveals his emotion when he is wounded. While he may be unscrupulous, he also has feelings of responsibility toward his friends and toward Marie. After her husband's death, Marie expresses the same sense of stoical endurance that sustained Morgan.

Lt. Henry made a separate peace and rejected social responsibility. Like Frederic Henry, Jake Barnes isolated himself from a society in which he had lost faith. Like Jake, Harry Morgan tried to remake his life after the demoralizing wound and would not commit himself to anything beyond immediate experience. Harry is most annoyed by the Cuban who robs the bank and murders in the name of Revolution. "What the hell do I care about his revolution," he thinks. "To help the working man he robs a bank and kills . . . a working man." In *For Whom the Bell Tolls* (1940), Hemingway once again had to ponder how a man can live consistent with his own sense of values and still commit himself to a political cause. Robert Jordan tries to reconcile his own sense of values to that of the Loyalist cause during the Spanish Civil War. While he recognizes that he ultimately is fighting for an abstract ideal, he concentrates more on what he as an individual brings to the war— his knowledge of Spanish, of the terrain, of guns and demolition work, and his skill as a hunter. Hemingway depicts Robert Jordan as the man of conscience, turning himself toward history. He maintains that his commitment is only for the duration of the war, and that he has no real trust in political movements which substitute a historical ideal for a Christian heaven. Concerned with exactly the same problems that led to the split between Camus and Sartre in 1952, Jordan becomes aware that men can justify their atrocities in the name of ideals. He learns, for example, how Pablo's Republican band brutally murdered the leaders of a small village because of their politics. He also sees the terrible discrepancy between Jordan's plight behind the enemy's lines and life on the high command where Jordan and his group are merely a part of an abstract plan. The officers at Gaylords believe that the Fascists have bombed their own troops when in reality they have bombed El Sordo's band. There is an absurd gulf between the simple life of an Anselmo, the peasant who tells Robert Jordan that "a man must be responsible to himself," and that of a General Golz, the Russian adviser who thinks of the war as so many marks on a tactical map as well as a dialectical point in history.

One of the serious weaknesses of existentialism was its inability to move the individual beyond himself and give him a way of reconciling his own sense of purpose with a projected theory of history. Camus was most skeptical of historical ideals which could justify moral expediency. Unlike Sartre, he stressed the need for moral limits that would prevent power maniacs from acting in the name of the future. André Malraux had wrestled with this problem in *La Voie royale* (1930), where death which is the source of the absurd ("La mort est là, comprenez-vous, comme . . . comme l'irrefutable presence de l'absurdité de la vie") can also be a monument to the individual's life. The theme of a dedicated death runs through such Malraux novels as *Les Conquérants, La Tentation de l'occident, La Condition humaine,* and *Les Noyers de l'Altenburg.* Man can fulfill an otherwise empty condition if his death has significance.

Hemingway echoes Malraux in *For Whom the Bell Tolls.* When Robert Jordan is wounded on the pine floor of the Spanish mountains, he justifies his death in the name of duty. In *Across the River and into the Trees,* Hemingway abandons the socially dedicated hero. In *The Old Man and the Sea,* Santiago is the self-fortified hero engaged in the gratuitous struggle against the powers of nature. This same theme pervades Hemingway's *Islands in the Stream,* written in the late forties and early fifties, but not published until October of 1970, almost ten years after Hemingway's suicide. If Hemingway began his career in *The Torrents of Spring* by parodying Sherwood Anderson, he seems to have ended his career by parodying himself. Perhaps because *Islands in the Stream* is so unconvincing, it best serves as the novel which shows in transparent fashion the internal structure of his fictional world. The novel divides into three parts. "Bimini" treats a fishing trip that Thomas Hudson goes on with his three sons, one by his first wife, the others by his second. "Cuba" takes place primarily in a bar, the Floridita, where Thomas Hudson drinks enough frozen double daiquiris to get even the reader drunk. The Second World War is in progress, and Hudson is using his powerful motor boat to patrol the coast off Cuba in search of German submarines. Hudson's two youngest sons have been killed in a traffic accident, and he has just received word of his oldest son's death in action. "At Sea," the third section of the novel, involves Hudson and his ragbag crew in searching the islands off Cuba for some sailors off a destroyed German submarine. Hudson takes pride in the job well done, which includes his ability to hunt well, his skill in handling his boat, his knowledge of the sea and its currents, and his ability to predict the weather from a gust of wind or the look of a cloud, or to anticipate his prey from the broken flight of a bird. Like the best of hunters, he identifies with what he is hunting, anticipates their moves, and closes in for the kill. Only the hunter becomes hunted in turn. The Germans ambush Hudson's boat, and before the German crew is wiped out, he is killed.

Despite the hard drinking and the final violence, *Islands in the Stream* is a child's world. The first section of the novel deals directly with children and depends upon their sense of wonder and adventure, their love of stories. This gives Hemingway the chance to satisfy his own sense of adventure and nostalgia by allowing Hudson to recount his memories of Paris where he knew James Joyce, Ezra Pound, Ford Madox Ford, and Picasso. Honest Lil, the barroom prostitute who has his ear for most of the second part of the novel, also has a child's mind and demands the same kind of storytelling. And the story of the destroyed submarine with its escaped crew is pure childhood fantasy, a modern Huck Finn or Tom Sawyer adventure.

Beneath the wonder and adventure, however, is the

reality of life's horror. The sea is beautiful, but it is also cruel. Sharks and barracuda remind us that death lurks below the surface. Interestingly enough, the German sailors are never individualized, and they fire upon Hudson from out of the jungle, as if the jungle itself, rather than human beings, had turned upon him. Like so many other Hemingway stories, *Islands in the Stream* is a story of man against nature—a nature that is both incredibly beautiful and cruelly destructive.

The ambiguity within nature parallels the ambiguity within Hudson the man. Like other Hemingway heroes, he is both arrogant and self-pitying, tough and sentimental, brave yet anxious, disciplined and self-indulgent, confident yet insecure, one moment joyful the next depressed, caught up in the moment and yet capable of terrible nostalgia, and confused about life's meaning and yet cruel to anyone who violates the law of his self-styled code.

*Islands in the Stream* duplicates many of the situations we find in other Hemingway novels and stories. The tourists come in for the same kind of abuse they receive in *To Have and Have Not*, and we have the same kind of love-hate battle with the marlin that we had in *The Old Man and the Sea*. As in most of Hemingway's fiction, death continues to prey on life, and man seems only once-removed from the world of the animals. We also have the same stock barroom conversations, the same fishing and hunting adventures, the same frantic desire for life in the face of death. Perhaps only the fact that Thomas Hudson seems more broken than other Hemingway heroes separates him from the rest, and here we can see Hemingway anticipating his own crack-up. While this novel, along with the others written at the time, had no influence on Albert Camus or French existentialism, it reveals in a transparent way why Hemingway's fictional world edges toward existentialism—a violent world where man is always testing himself against the complexities of nature and against that final reality —death itself. From the beginning to the end of his career, Ernest Hemingway was working unconsciously within terms more coherently expressed by modern existentialism.

Jean-Paul Sartre first saw the relationship between existentialism and Hemingway. "I was told," says Sartre, "that *L'Étranger* was Kafka written by Hemingway." Sartre then goes on to say "I confess that I have found no trace of Kafka in it. The comparison with Hemingway seems more fruitful." Like so much of Sartre's criticism, these statements reveal flashes of brilliant insight at the same time as they distort the main character of the work he is discussing. In an essay entitled "Art and Rebellion," Camus maintains that the modern novel is limited because it depicts feelings and passions in one dimension only—externally in terms of surface gesture. In another essay entitled "Hope and Absurd in the Work of Franz Kafka," Camus discusses the admirable way that Kafka is able to establish "perpetual oscillation between the natural and the extraordinary, the individual and the universal, the tragic and the everyday, the absurd and the logical . . . that coincidence of the general and the particular." Camus has thus been quite explicit in qualifying the virtue of American neorealistic technique as technique. He has been just as specific in analyzing the way the symbol functions in the fiction of Kafka. I should like to suggest that Camus's *L'Étranger* is a symbolic novel which uses the style of Hemingway and the neorealists for a very specific purpose. Sartre is right when he speaks of Hemingway's influence; he is wrong when he rejects the symbolic structure of the novel. Like so many other critics, Sartre has failed to see the inseparable relationship between symbol and style in Camus's first novel.

In order to understand the idea of this novel, one must understand the philosophy which underlies *Le Mythe de Sisyphe*. Like Meursault's, the development of Sisyphus's character involves first that he become aware that his task is meaningless and second that he commit himself to his absurd life as if it had meaning. Awareness and commitment—these are the most important aspects of Sisyphus's character. He becomes a symbol of absurd commitment. Because critics have often failed to see the symbolic function of Meursault, they have misinterpreted the novel. Perhaps the greatest critical confusion has centered on the murder scene, the scene on the beach where Meursault shoots the Arab and then fires four more shots into his prostrate body. Carl A. Viggiani, one of the most perceptive critics of the novel, discusses at length the significance of the death to the structure of the novel, but when it comes to interpreting the meaning of the murder scene the best he can say is that it "remains a mystery . . . just as for Camus, the universal and eternal murder of men, i.e., the reality of death, is a humiliating and incomprehensible phenomenon."

Viggiani is unable to see the significance of the murder scene because he is unable to see the significance of *L'Étranger* as a symbolic novel. Meursault commits a symbolic murder on the beach. As we have seen, the point is that the murder of the Arab is as accidental and gratuitous as Camus's world itself. Meursault does not mean to kill the Arab. He goes to the spot by accident. He meets the Arab by chance. The sun happens to be unpleasantly hot, and Meursault happens to feel terribly uncomfortable. When the Arab draws a knife, the blade by chance catches the sun and the reflection flashes into Meursault's eyes whereupon he responds mechanically —like a coiled spring—and the gun goes off.

The rest of the novel supports an interpretation of an accidental murder. The prosecutor asks Meursault if he went back to the stream with the intention of killing the Arab. Meursault tells him no, that "it was a matter of pure chance." Raymond also tells the judge that the murder was pure chance:

> Raymond told him that my presence on the beach that morning was pure coincidence.
> "How comes it then," the Prosecutor inquired, "that the letter which led up to the tragedy was the prisoner's work?"

Raymond replied that this, too, was due to mere chance.

To which the Prosecutor retorted that in this case "chance" or "mere coincidence" seemed to play a remarkably large part.

And so it does. As well as being an avatar, an incarnation, a personification of the absurd world, Meursault is also a human symbol of cosmic indifference. To love or not love his mother, to write or not write a letter for a pimp, to marry or not marry Marie, to shoot or not shoot the Arab—it all comes to the same thing. Unilateral values exist in the absurd world. This idea runs continually through the novel.

As a character, Meursault is more than just an abstract symbol of gratuity and indifference, primarily because the novel is also a kind of moral progress toward self-realization and cosmic understanding. As we have seen, Meursault's awareness comes at the moment he fires the first accidental shot that fells the Arab. The four following shots are, of course, not accidental. They are a commitment to belief in the reality of the absurd. In French the pun on Meursault's name—*meurt-sault*, which means "death-leap"—further suggests this kind of commitment. With awareness of the absurd and commitment to it, Meursault has become Sisyphus. From this point on Meursault sees that the meaning of life is in the struggle. He understands, for example, how his mother, even on the brink of death, could reaffirm her life by taking Perez as her fiancé. Just before he is executed Meursault says:

> Almost for the first time in many months I thought of my mother. And now, it seemed to me, I understood why at her life's end she had taken on a "fiancé"; why she'd played at making a fresh start. There, too, in that Home where lives were flickering out, the dusk came as mournful solace. With death so near, Mother must have felt like someone on the brink of freedom, ready to start life all over again.

Meursault, then, comes to terms with the absurd world he symbolically represents and of which he is an elemental part. In *L'Homme révolté*, Camus said that the American novel finds "its unity in reducing man either to elementals or to his external reactions and his behavior." He also has said that "the life of the body, reduced to its essentials, paradoxically produces an abstract and gratuitous universe." Since this kind of universe reduces man to a physical part of the world, "it is possible to explain," concludes Camus, "the extraordinary number of 'innocents' who appear in this universe."

Camus's observations are important because what he is suggesting is that the American neorealists created a character—the innocent—who functions in a one-to-one way with the world in which he lives and is thus a symbol of that world as well as a particular part of it. In other words, Camus saw in American neorealism a means of effecting a symbolic presentation of the absurd.

The essential difference, then, between the American innocent and Meursault is that while the innocent remains simple-minded and often is as bewildered at the end of the novel as he was at the beginning, Meursault develops consciousness and conscience. Speaking of the American neorealist novel, Camus has said that it reduces "man either to elementals or to his external reactions and to his behavior." This kind of novel, he continues, gives rise to the innocent, the "simpleton" who can "be defined—and completely defined—by his behavior." The unity of such a novel, Camus concludes, "is a degraded unity, a levelling off of human beings." The novel has to reveal an "interior reality." "To deny it totally is to refer oneself to an imaginary man." In contrast to American neorealism is the novel of Proust:

> If the American novel is the novel of men without memory, the world of Proust is nothing but memory. . . . Proust chooses the interior life and, of the interior life, that which is more interior than life itself in preference to what is forgotten in the world of

reality—in other words, the purely mechanical and blind aspects of the world. But by his rejection of reality he does not deny reality. He does not commit the error, which would counterbalance the error of American fiction, of suppressing the mechanical. He unites, on the contrary, into a superior form of unity, the memory of the past and the immediate sensation, the twisted foot and the happy days of the past.

These modes—the realm of memory and the elemental—represent the terms within which Meursault's character is defined, the difference between what Meursault is at the beginning and at the end of *L'Étranger*. In many ways this is a novel about being and becoming.

Hemingway's novels have no sustained symbolic structure or metaphysical frame of reference. Yet characters like Lt. Henry, Jake Barnes, and Harry Morgan are, as we have seen, the progenitors of Meursault. Camus undoubtedly had the Hemingway hero in mind when he referred to the American innocent. In the unreal and chaotic world of Caporetto, for example, Lt. Henry, in a scene not unlike that between Meursault and the Arab, mechanically triggers the revolver that brings down the wayward sergeant, who would not help him disengage his demobilized ambulance.

In the Burguete scenes, Hemingway reduces Jake's life to essentials, and, as Camus has said, "the life of the body reduced to essentials paradoxically produces an abstract and gratuitous universe." Certainly Meursault is an "elemental character," and it was Camus who pointed out that the American neorealist's novel finds "its unity in reducing man either to elementals or to his external reactions and his behavior." Both Meursault and Jake Barnes are innocents; they live on the surface of life in terms of physical reality; they have been reduced to their behavior, to "external reactions." The fragmented sentences, the lack of subordination, the separate quality and unrelated character of each object—all reveal a world in which physical objects exist in a gratuitous and acci-

dental relationship. As Hemingway has said, "the real
thing" is "the sequence of motion and fact which [makes]
the emotion." In Hemingway's style, the nouns are syn-
tactically structured with anticipatory subjects or with
predicate adjectives, so that a noun usually precedes an
adjective, emphasizing that the narrator first becomes
aware of things and then responds to their qualities. In
Hemingway's prose, we often have sentences like "the
fields were rolling and grassy," "the grass was short,"
"the log was surfaced off," "the trees were big, and the
foliage was thick." The object of each sentence usually
becomes the subject of the next clause. Mind and emotion are caught up in the natural sequence of things. The
noun-adjective order, the mind working in a moment of
time, the narrator trying to impose order on the jumble
of reality and sense impressions—all reveal a mind that
never gets beyond the realm of physical existence. These
two things—an accidental and gratuitous world and a
mind that responds to physical stimuli—are the motives
for the Arab's murder. In the first part of *L'Étranger,*
Meursault is a personification of the gratuity and indifference of nature itself because he is never able to get
beyond the physical realm. Meursault initially embodies
Camus's definition of nature as expressed in *Le Mythe de
Sisyphe.* After the murder scene, Meursault grows away
from his initial character—illustrating Camus's interest
at this time in the difference between man and his absurd condition, the difference between humanity and
nature.

If the French existentialists admired the newness and
the sense of *dépaysement* in American fiction in general,
they admired the American detective story in particular.
They linked under this category a number of writers that
American critics do not often connect with each other
—and they called this kind of fiction *la littérature noire.*
In 1946 Marcel Duhamel started a series of detective
stories entitled *Série Noire.* Gallimard published three
books in this series a month, selling for about half to
one-third the price of an ordinary novel. According to

Smith and Miner, about 90 percent of these books were translations from the American and included such writers as W. H. Burnett, Horace McCoy, James M. Cain, Dashiel Hammett, Raoul Whitfield, Don Tracy, and P. F. Wolfson.

These novels were popularly read and respected by even the most serious writers. In fact, until about mid-century, French criticism of American fiction tended to lack discretion and sensitivity, and it was not surprising to find a commentator seriously maintaining that a Hammett or a Cain was of the same literary magnitude as a Faulkner. In all fairness to the critics, the French saw the detective novel as a significant genre, and even Camus's *L'Étranger* owes a significant literary debt to a work like James M. Cain's *The Postman Always Rings Twice*. The climax of each novel is a murder, followed by litigation; the novels conclude in a murder cell with Meursault and Frank Chambers waiting to be executed, talking or writing to a priest; each novel ends ironically with the main character dying for a crime other than the one of which he is guilty; each novel is told from a first-person point of view, secures narrative compression, and becomes tendentious at the end.

But the most obvious as well as the most important parallel between *L'Étranger* and *The Postman Always Rings Twice* is that both Meursault and Frank Chambers are misfits, passive heroes who respond to immediate stimulus and are described in terms of their external behavior, who react rather than act. Compare, for example, the swimming scenes which appear in each novel. In the first passages, Frank Chambers describes two visits to the beach—one after visiting Nick in the hospital, the second after he and Cora are married:

> Then one day, stead of her going in alone, we both went in, and after she came out of the hospital, we cut for the beach. They gave her a yellow suit and a red cap, and when she came out I didn't know her at first. She looked like a little girl. It was the first time I ever really saw how young she was. We played

in the sand, and then we went way out and let the swells rock us. I like my head to the waves, she liked her feet. We lay there, face to face, and held hands under the water. I looked up at the sky. It was all you could see. I thought about God. . . .

We got married at the City Hall, and then we went to the beach. She looked so pretty I just wanted to play in the sand with her, but she had this little smile on her face, and after a while she got up and went down to the surf.

"I'm going out."

She went ahead, and I swam after her. She kept on going and went a lot further than she had before. Then she stopped, and I caught up with her. She swung up beside me, and took hold of my hand, and we looked down at each other. She knew, then, that the devil was gone, that I loved her.

In the following passage, Meursault describes a day at the beach with Marie:

L'eau était froide et j'étais content de nager. Avec Marie, nous nous sommes éloignés et nous nous sentions d'accord dans nos gestes et dans nôtre contentement.

Au large, nous avons fait la planche et sur mon visage tourné vers le ciel, le soleil écartait les derniers voiles d'eau qui me coulaient dans la bouche. Nous avons vu que Masson regagnait la plage pour s'étendre au soleil. De loin, il paraissait énorme. Marie a voulu que nous nagions ensemble. Je me suis mis derrière elle pour la prendre par la taillet et elle avançait à la force des bras pendant que je l'aidais en battant des pieds. Le petit bruit de l'eau battue nous a suivis dans le matin jusqu'à ce que je me sente fatigué. Alors j'ai laissé Marie et je suis rentré en nageant régulièrement et en respirant bien. Sur la plage, je me suis étendu à plat ventre près de Masson et j'ai mis ma figure dans le sable. Je lui ai dit que 'c'était bon' et il était de cet avis. Peu après, Marie est venue. Je me suis retourné pour la regarder avancer. Elle était toute visqueuse d'eau salée et elle tenait ses cheveux en arrière. Elle s'est allongée flanc à flanc avec moi et les deux chaleurs de son corps et du soleil m'ont un peu endormi.

Marie m'a secoué et m'a dit que Masson était remonté chez lui, il fallait déjeuner. Je me suis levé tout de suite parce que j'avais faim, mais Marie m'a dit que je ne l'avais pas embrassée depuis ce matin. C'était vrai et pourtant j'en avais envie. 'Viens dans l'eau,' ma'a-t-elle dit. Nous avons couru pour nous étaler dans les premières petites vagues. Nous avons fait quelques brasses et elle s'est collée contre moi. J'ai senti ses jambes autour des miennes et je l'ai désirée.

[The water was cold, and I felt all the better for it. We swam along way out, Marie and I, side by side, and it was pleasant feeling how our movements matched, hers and mine, and how we were both in the same mood, enjoying every moment.

Once we were out in the open, we lay on our backs and, as I gazed up at the sky, I could feel the sun drawing up the film of salt water on my lips and cheeks. . . .

That sound of little splashes had been in my ears so long that I began to feel I'd had enough of it. So I let go of Marie and swam back at an easy pace, taking long, deep breaths. . . . Presently Marie came back. I raised my head to watch her approach. She was glistening with brine, and holding her hair back. Then she lay down beside me, and what with the combined warmth of our bodies and the sun, I felt myself dropping off to sleep.

After a while Marie tugged my arm and said Masson had gone to his place; it must be nearly lunchtime. I rose at once, as I was feeling hungry, but Marie told me I hadn't kissed her once since the early morning. That was so—though I'd wanted to several times. "Let's go in the water again," she said, and we ran into the sea and lay amongst the ripples for a moment. Then we swam a few strokes, and when we were almost out of our depth she flung her arms around me and hugged me. I felt her legs twining around mine, and my senses tingled.]

The Cain and Camus passages are remarkably alike. We have the same detached, objective, narrative eye, describing surface reality, speaking in clipped sentences, each sentence recording a physical impression, and each impression a distinct and separate thing. Frank Chambers and Meursault live in a one-to-one way with physical reality; they could never abstract the idea of love because to them it is no more than a kind of physical euphoria. "My physical condition at any moment influenced my feelings," Meursault says to the investigating magistrate, but he could have been describing Frank Chambers as well as himself. In the Cain passage we have a series of objects (Cora in her yellow suit and red cap, the sand, the swelling waves, the sky) and then we get a physical response to these stimuli. "I thought about God," says Frank Chambers, an absurd remark, but most appropriate because for him there is little difference between God and pleasing sensation.

In Camus's passage, life is also reduced to the level of sensation. Although there is less the catalogue of objects, we do have an object and then a response to it. "The water was cold," says Meursault, "and I felt all the better for it." "Marie and I, side by side, and it was pleasant feeling how our movements matched." Meursault dutifully records many other sensations: "As I gazed up at the sky, I could feel the sun drawing up the film of salt water on my lips." "Then she lay down beside me, and what with the combined warmth of our bodies and the sun, I felt myself dropping off to sleep." "I rose at once, as I was feeling hungry." "I felt her legs twining around mine, and my senses tingled." Camus was willing to use American neorealism for his own symbolic purposes, but the "innocent" victim represented a point of departure and not an ideal conclusion for him. Camus believed that the responsible man employed both his senses and his reason, was both able to interpret as well as immediately react to stimuli. He disliked the American "tough guy" who lived on the surface of life, lacked the dimension of interior reality, and whose behavior embodied the very indifference of nature itself. Camus saw, however, that in *L'Étranger* he could use the fast narrative pace of the detective novel to secure the interest of the reader in a novel that would have philosophical implications. He further saw that the world in the detective novel was not dissimilar from the violent world of the twentieth century and that it compactly organized and dramatically revealed a hostile and indifferent universe—the world of the absurd. Camus also saw that the world of the detective novel was the world of the outsider. The heroes of Cain's and Hammett's novels, for example, are social malcontents who live dynamically on the fringes of society. Finally, the dramatic structure and the extreme situation in the detective novel offered a narrative vehicle for Camus's ideas about the structure of society, the nature of motivation, the nature of guilt, and the general psychological makeup of the social rebel. Dostoyevsky's *Crime and Punishment* is a form of the detective novel in its highest sense. In *L'Étranger*, Camus used a similar vehicle for dramatic speculation about the structure of existence and the need to live in the face of the absurd—questions discussed at expository length in *Le Mythe de Sisyphe*.

While Melville's "Billy Budd" is not a detective novel, there is also an affinity between it and *L'Étranger*. Billy Budd is also the innocent hero who is overwhelmed by a situation he cannot cope with or understand. So also is Melville's Bartleby who, once confronted with the wall of death, becomes indifferent to life.

While we would have to go outside of American literature to do it, we could also compare Meursault to Moravia's Michele in *Gli indifferenti*, who initially suffers from ennui, whose life lacks purpose and direction, and who almost murders the lover of both his mother and sister, not out of hate, but out of an absurd desire to assert his identity. Near the beginning of the novel, Michele, in a scene very similar to scenes in *L'Étranger,* is baffled by the rush of the busy crowd, going about its daily business:

> All these people, he thought, know where they're going and what they want, they have a purpose in life and that's why they hurry and torment themselves, and are sad or happy. They have something to live for, whereas I . . . I have nothing . . . I have no purpose. If I don't walk, I sit: it makes no difference.

Meursault also has points of similarity to Garine in Malraux's *Les Conquérants*, who feels that even society lacks a principle of order, who mechanically shoots a Chinese prisoner of war, and who behaves like Meursault in court when, early in his career, Garine is involved indirectly in an abortion case (as Meursault is indirectly involved with the Arab because of Raymond). When he appears in court:

> His first feeling was one of bewilderment. He knew that his proceedings were illegal; but the absurdity of bringing such matters into court amazed him. He had no idea of what the sentence was likely to be. I saw him constantly at that time; for he had been left free on bail. The evidence of witnesses did not interest him in the least. As for the cross-examination carried on by a bearded judge whose one object seemed to be to make it a kind of judicial allegory, it seemed to him a struggle against all automaton, who was but a second-rate dialectician.
>
> One day, in response to a question of the judge, he said: "What does it matter?"

Finally, Meursault's murdering the Arab is similar to Kirillov's "metaphysical" suicide. The act of Dostoyevsky's character was an assertion of will against an absurd world and, to him, proved that he was independent of God. Meursault, as pointed out earlier, commits himself to the world of the absurd when he fires the additional shots.

The difference, however, between Meursault and these

other characters is that he is far more elemental and be-
havioristic. While Michele and Garine may be aware of
the absurd, only Meursault, like Jake Barnes and Frank
Chambers, lives in a one-to-one relationship with this
kind of world. In *L'Étranger* a Hemingway-like style
dramatically realizes and sustains a gratuitous world.
Camus never used Hemingway and Cain after his first
novel because he was never concerned with depicting the
absurd in the same way. But to see the effect of Hemingway and Cain in *L'Étranger* is to see in part the deriva-
tive sources and resources of Camus's imagination at the
outset.

### William Faulkner

Another connection between American fiction
and French literary existentialism stems from what the
French called the tragic world of American fiction. In
his preface to *Sanctuary*, André Malraux maintained
that Faulkner's novel is "l'intrusion de la tragédie grecque
dans le roman policier." Unfortunately, Malraux did not
elaborate. One might question the similarity of Faulkner's characters and the more noble and more enlightened characters of Aeschylus, Sophocles, and Euripides.
But if Malraux is referring to the similarities between
the dramatic world of Faulkner and that of the Greeks,
his observations are suggestive and worthy of further in-
vestigation. Like the early Greeks, Faulkner constructs
a moral world. His characters may not always seem to
possess free will, but they are all obsessed with sin and
guilt. Faulkner's sense of sin and guilt is, in fact, so
strong that the French critics continually talk about his
underlying Puritanism. In *Aperçus de littérature américaine*, Maurice Coindreau, for example, maintains that

> L'oeuvre de Faulkner est l'oeuvre d'un puritan qu'-
> abide l'idée de la fatalité, la crainte et l'horreur du
> péché et de ses conséquences. C'est un réquisitoire

passionné centre le vice, et il serait aisé d' y démasquer
un grand idéalisme. Alors que William Faulkner
regrette que l'homme resoit pas un ange, Caldwell
voudrait qu'il fut le plus possible un bête.

While the tension and the complexity in much American literature stems, as Coindreau suggests, from an inability to reconcile a feeling about the natural baseness
of man with that of his ultimate dignity, Faulkner's fiction goes beyond Coindreau's "l'idée de la fatalité." As
Coindreau connects Faulkner directly with Puritanism,
other critics have connected him with naturalism. If
Faulkner's characters have "fallen," and if there is a sense
of naturalistic darkness in his fiction, man seems to have
caused his own fall, to have brought the naturalistic
disorder down upon himself. In a novel like *Absalom,
Absalom!* we see a pattern that can often be found in
Faulkner's fiction. First we have a time of order and
harmony, a kind of Eden before the Fall, when Thomas
Sutpen was living in the mountains of West Virginia in
a world where everyone was equal and one man was as
good as the next. When his father takes him down
from the mountains to the Tideland area of Virginia,
the descent is both a metaphorical and a literal fall. In
Virginia, Sutpen is totally robbed of his innocence when
he is turned away from the plantation door—an incident
that violates everything that he had taken for granted,
destroys his old way of looking at himself, and turns
him toward his monomaniacal design. The design, in
time, leads him to repudiate his son, Charles Bon, which
parallels in a very real way what happened to him at the
plantation door and which becomes an act of irreparable
evil that is always at the center of Faulkner's fiction (this
act varies in the novels but is usually connected with
miscegenation). Sutpen's repudiating his son leads in
turn to Henry Sutpen's murdering Bon (a fratricidal
act which has parallels to the Civil War, the novel moving from the personal to a historical level of meaning).
Throughout the novel, we have an inevitable sense of

doom, Sutpen planting his own tragic seed, the *fleur de mal*.

The same pattern can be observed in Faulkner's story "The Bear." The death of both the bear and of Sam Fathers represents the passing of an old order. Their deaths occur simultaneously with the loss of the wilderness as it is ruthlessly raped by the timber company. The novel, in fact, opens on this theme, as Faulkner describes "that doomed wilderness whose edges were being constantly and punily gnawed at by men with plows and axes who feared it because it was wilderness."

The death of the bear parallels, to be more exact, what happened to the South after the Civil War when the older agrarian order was disrupted, when an industrialized North tried to make it over in its own image. Boon and Lion destroy the bear, just as the timber company, the spirit of industry, destroys the wilderness—and again Faulkner makes this point through descriptive detail. In the passage describing the death of the bear, perhaps one of the most moving passages in contemporary fiction, he describes Boon and Lion, both astride the bear, Boon with his knife probing for the bear's heart, the knife rising and falling once:

> It fell just once. For an instant they almost resembled a piece of statuary [cf. Keats's Grecian urn]: the clinging dog, the bear, the man astride its back, working and probing the buried blade. Then they went down, pulled over backward, by Boon's weight, Boon underneath. It was the bear's back which reappeared first but at once Boon was astride it again. He had never released the knife and again the boy saw the almost infinitesimal movement of his arm and shoulder as he probed and sought; then the bear surged erect, raising with it the man and the dog too, and turned and still carrying the man and the dog it took two or three steps toward the woods on its hind feet as a man would have walked and *crashed down*. It didn't collapse, crumple. It fell all of a piece, *as a tree*

*falls*, so that all three of them, man, dog, and bear, seemed to bounce once. (Italics mine)

The death of the bear and the loss of the wilderness are thus thematically spliced through descriptive detail. The bear did not fall, it "crashed down," "as a tree falls," and the death of the bear and the loss of the forest become one.

If the death of the bear and the loss of the wilderness parallel each other, there is, at least in Faulkner's imagination, a cause for both—and that cause is the "sin" of Carothers McCaslin, Ike's grandfather, who felt his slaves were as much his property as the lumber company feels the wilderness is its property. Faulkner's world— and this is true in *Absalom, Absalom!* as well as "The Bear"—is initially one of harmony, a kind of Eden before the Fall. Man himself destroys this harmony, throws the world out of joint, and at the very center of a Faulkner novel is a moral error which causes the disorder— here Carother's sin of miscegenation and incest.

Carother's story is told in the ledger, itself a symbol of the moral payment that Ike feels he owes the past. In "The Bear," again as in *Absalom, Absalom!*, the sins of the fathers are passed down to the sons, and Ike takes it upon himself to expiate the misdeeds of Carothers. Time becomes obligation, a prison, and it is most appropriate that in the center of Yoknapatawpha County is the courthouse on top of which, in the center, is the clock and the bottom of which, again in the center, is the jail. Time becomes a prison; there is always the ghost of the past in Faulkner's fiction. The death of the bear and the rapaciousness of the lumber company find their counterpart in the past, find it in the "original sin" of Carothers McCaslin. McCaslin violated nature by accepting slavery and by entering into a miscegenous and then incestuous relationship with his slaves, acts which parallel the rape of the forest and the loss of the old order. Carothers's act, in other words, becomes a kind of "poetic" or emotional cause for the death of the bear, the rape of the forest, the loss of the Old South. It also explains why Ike McCaslin repudiates his inheritance, repudiates the land: his grandfather's land, which Carothers "had bought with white man's money from the wild men whose grandfathers without guns hunted it, and tamed and ordered or believed he had tamed and ordered it for the reason that the human beings he held in bondage and in the power of life and death had removed the forest from it and in their sweat scratched the surface of it to a depth of perhaps fourteen inches in order to grow something out of it which had not been there before and which could be translated back into the money he who believed he had bought it had had to pay to get it and hold it and a reasonable profit too. . . ."

And so, Ike repudiates his land, or rather he does not repudiate it, because, as he puts it, " 'I can't repudiate it. It was never mine to repudiate. It was never Father's and Uncle Buddy's to bequeath me to repudiate because it was never grandfather's to bequeath them to bequeath me to repudiate because it was never old Ikkemotubbe's to sell to Grandfather for bequeathment and repudiation. Because it was never Ikkemotubbe's . . . because on the instant when Ikkemotubbe discovered, realized, that he could sell it for money, on that instant it ceased ever to have been his forever. . . .' "

Ike allows his second cousin to inherit the land, leaves his wife, who thinks that she can use her nakedness—the power of sex—to force him into accepting the land, and Ike becomes a carpenter, a Christ in the modern world. As Christ takes it upon himself to redeem the sins of Adam and Eve, Ike takes it upon himself to redeem the sins of Carothers McCaslin—and the novel moves into another dimension of meaning. In section four, Ike is twenty-one. In section five, which is chronologically out of sequence, we move back to the time that Ike was eighteen. He has returned to the scene of the bear hunt, and he finds that the wilderness is greatly destroyed. As he looks out across the land, he sees a train disappearing into the remaining forest. Faulkner describes the train as a "snake vanishing into weeds, drawing him with it too until soon it ran once more at its maximum clattering speed between the twin walls of unaxed wilderness as of old," and again the descriptive detail is appropriate. The train becomes a modern parallel to the serpent, the Devil himself, in the Garden of Eden. In fact, soon after he sees the train, Ike comes upon a rattlesnake, and the descriptive detail is further reinforced and the story moves from historical allusion to myth.

"The Bear," then, has really three stories in one; it is first of all a story of a young boy coming of age and participating in the ritual of the hunt. If we stop here, as Faulkner did when he published the first three sections of the novel in *The Saturday Evening Post*, we have a moving and exciting hunting story. The plot, however, does not stop here, and we can move to a second story about the destruction of the wilderness, the loss of the old order, the death of the Old South itself. It is easier to stop at this point, but to do so would be to leave the novel still incomplete. Once more the story spirals out, like ripples in a pond, and the third story is about the loss of Eden, the story of Carothers McCaslin, whose "original sin" is connected with, even the cause of, the death of the bear and the end of the old order. "The Bear" thus functions on three levels of reality—the level of the individual (the hunter), the level of history (the loss of the Old South), and the level of myth (the loss of Eden).

In "A Rose for Emily," Emily lives out her days "married" to—and sleeping with—a dead man, a man who came to the South to do Reconstruction work. Here we have an image—to be sure, an unpleasant one—of what happened when the industrialized North was "married" to the agrarian South. In *Sanctuary*, the rape of Temple Drake by Popeye, whom Faulkner describes in terms of machine and mechanical imagery, is another metaphor for what happened to the South after the Civil War. And yet, as we see in "The Bear," the South cannot go

unblamed. The Carothers McCaslins destroyed the initial harmony, brought an end to the wilderness, and it
is their burden which has been imposed on the living;
they have put a curse on the land. As Christ accepted
the burden of Adam and Eve, Ike accepts the burden
of Carothers McCaslin. The death of the bear, the loss
of the old order, the end of Eden—all are metaphorically
and emotionally related in Faulkner's imagination to the
sin of Carothers McCaslin. The bear "crashed down"
the night Carothers McCaslin put his property rights
before human rights. Carothers destroyed the realm
outside of time where Ike first saw the bear. He brought
an end to Eden and, as in the Old Testament, the sins
of the father are passed down to the sons.

Although the chronology of the novel belies it, there
is a tremendous sense of causality in *Absalom, Absalom!*
and "The Bear": all *was is*, as we are told, sins are handed
down, the past is contained in the present, even though
Sutpen and Carothers McCaslin will not admit this.
Sutpen in particular is doomed, but he is doomed because of his own monomania—and this is what separates
Faulkner from the naturalists who think of tragedy in
purely environmental terms, and from Coindreau's Puri-
tans who think of it in terms of God's will. If God's will
is at work in the novel, it is working beyond man's ability
to understand it. Faulkner's novels are often told by a
young man (a Quentin Compson or an Isaac McCaslin)
with a tormented consciousness, a young man who struggles to impose meaning on events that seem to defy
meaning, events that go beyond explanation.

Thus Faulkner's world is absurd because it has the
capacity to erupt violently and because it transcends reason. We seem to have motion without meaning. In *The
Sound and the Fury*, Quentin does not want a world
without meaning, because if Caddy's sin is meaningless
then his love for Caddy is also meaningless. Quentin's
suffering lacks temporal purpose and significance, and
he tries to destroy time. Quentin is so obsessed with giving life meaning he chooses to be absolutely condemned

and to solidify his suffering in eternal damnation. As Quentin looks at the bottom of the Charles River, he says, "If it could just be a hell beyond that: the clean flame the two of us more than dead." Quentin refused to accept Christ's sacrificial death ("from what wound in what side that not for me died out") because he wants his own sacrificial death.

In *As I Lay Dying*, we also have motion without meaning. The journey to bury Addie reaps only misery. At journey's end, Addie's body is a mass of liquid corruption. Darl has been committed to an insane asylum, Cash has again broken his leg, Dewey Dell is seduced by a drugstore clerk, Anse loses his mules and has mortgaged his farm equipment, and Jewel has lost his horse and is badly burned. While Addie has communicated her presence in death in a way she never could in life, she too seems badly foiled when Anse returns with the duck-shaped woman as his new wife.

In *Sanctuary*, Horace Benbow is also fully aware that he lives in a world without ends and purpose, especially when he realizes that Goodwin's death is completely unjustified and that justice has certainly not been attained. As Horace and his sister drive home after Goodwin has been condemned, he is startled by the discrepancy between the new spring life and the utter meaninglessness of suffering and death. New life replaces the old, but birth and death seem to have no meaning outside of themselves.

In *Light in August*, we once again have motion without meaning as Joe Christmas completes the circle of his life and returns to his birthplace only to be brutally murdered by Percy Grimm. In contrast to the possibility of hope which comes when Byron Bunch (the simple decent man) becomes the protector of Lena Grove (the very spirit of the earth), Joe Christmas's life runs itself to destructive conclusions. Shaped by Doc Hines to hate the Negro in him, Joe becomes a product of self-hate. The reason that Joe antagonizes people is to make them hate him, perhaps to make them hurt him so that he can satisfy his need to suffer. Joe turns with rage upon the white prostitute who is not offended when he tells her that he is a Negro and she has just had sex with a black man. He is as angry with her as a white supremist would be, beating her viciously: "It took two policemen to subdue him. At first they thought the woman was dead. He was sick after that. He did not know until then that there were white women who would take a man with a black skin." Scenes like this help us see the principle behind Joe's motives. As in so many of Faulkner's novels, miscegenation is at the very center of *Light in August*, and if Joe is not part black in fact, he believes that he is black, and out of a terrible sense of guilt, inculcated by Doc Hines, he tries to destroy himself. This is why Joe repeats over and over that he will not be anything else than what he is. "No, if I give in now," he says, "I will deny all the thirty years that I have lived to make me what I chose to be." Joe spends all his life waiting for the moment of Percy Grimm to kill him, and this moment of agony is his moment of release, because it relieves his guilt, offers the final suffering that could not be anything less than death itself. At this moment, Joe can for the first time look up with "peaceful eyes." As his name suggests, Joe Christmas is a modern Christ—that is, an inverted Christ. Whereas the biblical Christ lived a life of compassion and love, Joe lives a life of hate and guilt. He embodies what modern religion, especially bible-belt religion, has done to Christianity. The dehumanized feelings of Doc Hines, Joanna Burden, and McEachern, all fanatic Christians, have been passed down to Joe. In *Light in August*, Faulkner examines the motives that make a man the neurotic product of self-destruction. Joe's is the existential quest which becomes demonic, an existential story that has been repeated in other American fiction, as we shall see in the next chapters.

Joe Christmas is existential man trying to realize a demonic image of himself. His mad journey is not too far removed from Thomas Sutpen's, who bends his whole will toward another kind of "design," only to be rewarded by frustration and tragedy, proof of the difficulty of imposing rigidity upon the chaotic motion of events once he has put his plan into motion. *Absalom, Absalom!* reveals the inability of one man to understand fully the total consequences of his choices, which is why such choice must always be made in dreadful freedom. Sutpen starts a chain of events which gets out of his control. Faulkner's universe is perverse at times; a malignant force seems out to frustrate man. Sometimes this force is a Player (*Light in August* and *Sartoris*), a Judge (in *Absalom, Absalom!*), a Cosmic Joker (*The Wild Palms*), a capricious God (*Go Down, Moses*), and an Arbiter, Architect, Umpire (*Intruder in the Dust*). The effort to understand and impose meaning on the universe seems quite futile. As a result, a constant irony pervades Faulkner's fiction. Caddy's sin works adversely twice against Jason. Addie is laid in reverse position into the coffin that Cash has measured so carefully to her body. Throughout the Bundrens' journey they pass a sign, "New Hope." Temple finds sanctuary not in a church but a Memphis brothel. Lee Goodwin kills a fellow soldier in the Philippines with impunity, only to become the innocent victim of a holocaust in Jefferson. Popeye gets away with the brutal murders of Tommy and Red only to be executed for a murder he never committed. Joe Christmas and Hightower only want peace. Roger and Laverne Schumann are completely indifferent to money, but Roger dies for the financial benefit of men like Feinman, and the money the reporter and Jiggs concealed in little Jack's toy plane is misconstrued as the coin of Laverne's adultery. Thomas Sutpen tries to escape responsibilities of time and is killed with a scythe. The Negro Jim Bond is the last descendant of the man whose tragedy was initiated by miscegenation. Sam Fathers participates in his own death ritual when he helps track the bear. The tall convict likes jail and gets (temporary) freedom. Wilbourne enjoys freedom and gets jail. The corporal dies for world peace and is buried in the tomb of the Unknown Soldier. Irony prevails in the absurd world where events defy comprehension.

As the result of the void between an act and its significance, we have a continued gap between the meaning of an act and the narrator's ability to verbalize that meaning. Quentin (especially in *Absalom, Absalom!* but also in *The Sound and the Fury*), Darl, Wilbourne, the tall convict, Isaac, Charles Mallison, Jr., even Gavin Stevens struggle with problems which far transcend them. The Faulkner hero is overwhelmed by the meaning of his identity (Joe Christmas, Charles Bon, Isaac, Darl), by the meaning of the past (Quentin, Addie, Hightower, Miss Burden, Thomas Sutpen, Henry Sutpen, Isaac), by the meaning of the community (Joe Christmas, Lucas Beauchamp, Lee Goodwin, the rootless aviators, Wilbourne, the tall convict). The tall convict in *The Old Man* felt "an outrageous affronting of a condition purely moral, the same raging impotence to find any answer to it."

For Camus, the world became absurd when man lost his power to give it meaning, when reason broke down in the face of the unknown. Like the existentialists, Faulkner continually demonstrates the void between an act and the narrator's ability to find its meaning. An outer conflict creates an even deeper inner conflict; an act in the past short-circuits meaning in the present. When the flow of events loses meaning, time can only be endured—and meaning can only be found in the struggle. One can perhaps now better understand why Camus translated and adapted *Requiem for a Nun* for the Paris stage. Nancy Mannigoe was bound to fascinate him, Nancy that mysterious, dark, brooding figure who solitarily stands under sentence of death and accepts the sentence with quiet heroism.

Faulkner, of course, was not an existentialist, and one can become carried away by Camus's and Sartre's interest in him. Even the existentialists did not give him total consent. Sartre disliked the way Faulkner made his characters victims of their memory, the way he created an inevitable sequence of events which man's will could not break, the way his characters became prisoners of time. While Faulkner saw the absurd struggle in terms of redeeming the past, the existentialists saw it in terms of living the present (Camus) or projecting oneself toward the future (Sartre). Faulkner's characters, cut off from an Edenic past, momentarily restore the initial order by finding the more simple and natural life, like Wilbourne and Charlotte in *The Wild Palms* when they escape to a timeless Eden deep in the Wisconsin woods. Perhaps this is why Faulkner put so much faith in such simple, often earthy, characters as Lena Grove, Byron Bunch, Horace Benbow, and Isaac McCaslin. Yet, if Faulkner postulated an ideal world in his fiction, his characters do not function in this ideal world but only in relation to it. If the ideal world is an Edenic past, the real world is a lost paradise, a world where a simple agrarian life is giving way to a more complex industrial one, a world without order, often violent and malevolent, moving with no seeming end or purpose. Within such a world, the individual can bring about his own destruction with the violence of a Meursault or a Joe Christmas, or he can fulfill himself with the love of a Dr. Rieux or a Lena Grove. And if Faulkner's characters seem helpless to change their fate, the events in the novel do not suggest a mechanistic and dehumanized universe because man—in one way or another—has planted his own seeds of ruin, is the source of his own fate, and remains the source of his own redemption. When the sins of the father are handed down to the son, time is humanized and becomes a personal burden. Like Dostoyevsky's Ivan, Faulkner's characters must become their own Christ. We can thus understand why, for this reason if no other, Sartre said, "Faulkner's humanism is probably the only acceptable kind."

# 4

## The Outer Limits: Norman Mailer and Richard Wright

Sartre's and Camus's debt to American fiction can be well documented and, in return, Sartre and Camus had a demonstrable influence on recent American fiction. Paul Bowles, for example, has translated Sartre's *Huis Clos* for the Broadway stage. I have elsewhere demonstrated the existential elements in such Bowles novels as *The Sheltering Sky, Let It Come Down*, and *The Spider's House*.[1] Moving to Paris in 1946, Richard Wright came under the influence of Sartre, who published parts of *Black Boy* in *Les Temps Modernes*. In Wright's *The Outsider*, Cross Damon speaks and acts out obvious existential motives. Saul Bellow's characters have also been in search of existential values and so have Walker Percy's and Norman Mailer's.

Yet the problem is not entirely one of influence. The influence of Continental fiction on Mailer and Bellow is at best remote. The problem is more one of an affinity of mind. A number of American writers—Mailer, Bellow, Wright, Percy, Barth, Heller, among others—approximated some of the key ideas of Sartre and Camus, adapting these ideas to a more purely American experience which also involved depicting a fragmented world without mythical or moral center. The new American hero is as displaced—as uprooted and puzzled—as his prototype in the French existential novel. He is sometimes on the verge of insanity or suicide as with the characters of Heller and Barth. But in all instances, he is his own redeemer, sometimes violently so as with Mailer and Wright, sometimes with compassion as with Bellow and Percy. In his efforts to go beyond his various limitations, in his effort to force a meaning on the dead end of history, he is man in motion.

## Norman Mailer

Norman Mailer's is the embattled vision. His characters are often threatened by power maniacs and become power maniacs in turn. In his earlier novels, the threat comes from the far right, men seeking military or political power. In his later novels, the threat seems to have cosmic sources, and his characters seem to participate in a strange battle between God and the Devil—indeed, participate as agents, never fully understanding how in trying to fulfill themselves they either complete or diminish God, as the cells in the human body complete or deplete the individual. With this leap, Mailer carries the existential idea of man as his own creator into the heavens. In creating himself, man creates God, and the forces of God seem to be losing to the counterforces of the Devil, or so Mailer suggests in his later novels.

But we must back up for a moment and look at Mailer's early novels. The first of these, *The Naked and the Dead*, is a brilliant study of the absurd in the context of war, a more serious and less farfetched interpretation than Heller's *Catch-22*. In this massive novel, Mailer interrelates microcosm and macrocosm, individual and group behavior, to show men driven by the lust for power in a world that has become totally absurd. While Mailer treats more than a dozen characters at some length, three main characters emerge. General Edward Cummings is an ambitious, authoritarian, power-hungry leader. He believes that history "has been working toward greater and greater consolidation of power," and that "the only morality of the future is a power morality." He believes that fascism will eventually control the world and is pleased to think that it will be an American rather than German fascism. Even though Germany's fascistic world domination "was sound enough," Germany could not win because of "limited physical means." Only America had the "intrinsic potential to power" to perpetuate and preserve "the concept of fascism" which Cummings finds "far sounder than communism . . . for it's grounded firmly in men's actual nature." As a result, he believes the purpose of the Second World War is "to translate America's potential into kinetic energy"—that is, to bring about the triumph of a right-wing totalitarian order.

General Cummings explains his idea in detail to Lieutenant Robert Hearn, a Harvard graduate from a wealthy and conservative Midwest family who has repudiated the ideas of his father and become a liberal. Hearn is more fumbling than General Cummings, more vague about the political future and less convinced that the Left has the answer, even as he fears the Right. He moves head-on into a personal collision with Cummings when, as his aide, he mashes a cigarette butt into the boards of the general's immaculate tent. When Cummings forces the moment to a crisis, Hearn is humbled and humiliated, aware of how ruthlessly power can be exercised when the general forces him to pick up another cigarette butt. This kind of scene, one man powerless before another, is duplicated over and over in the novels. The suggestion is that what is true between individuals is also true between political groups and between nations. Life seems to be one unresolved power struggle.

The character who is intuitively aware of this truth is Sergeant Croft from Texas, whose lust for power is both blind and sadistic. In many ways, Croft embodies the blind power of America. He has a cruel, ambitious will to succeed, and once directed toward an end, he will work with superhuman strength and unquestioning obedience. He willfully allows Lieutenant Hearn to be killed so that he can take over command of the platoon and complete Cummings's instructions. He is in effect the unenlightened extension of a Cummings: blind energy waiting to be directed, waiting unquestioningly without morals or conscience. In *The Naked and the Dead*, Mailer is saying that the liberals like Hearn, men of simple good will, are really helpless in the face of Cummings and Croft who embody one aspect of the mentality and force at work in America. This is an idea that Mailer will develop more explicitly in such political-journalistic books as *Cannibals and Christians*, *The Presidential Papers*, *The Armies of the Night*, and in the novel *Why Are We in Vietnam?*

But in *The Naked and the Dead*, Mailer places the theme of power in an existential context, for despite Cummings's masterminding, the battle is ultimately won by accident when Cummings is not even on the scene. When Major Dalleson gets word that Japanese troops have deserted a section of the Toyaku line, he blindly sends his own troops into the gap and they fortuitously overrun General Toyaku's headquarters, killing him and half his staff. As a result, the whole purpose of Lieutenant Hearn's reconnaisance patrol is negated and Hearn, Wilson, and Roth die in vain. The mission that takes their lives comes to nothing, as do Goldstein and Ridge's efforts to return Wilson's body. Croft's Herculean attempt to have his troops scale Mount Anaka is also no more meaningful than Sisyphus's absurd efforts up the hill. This is the truth that painfully emerges from the novel, and Mailer adds a Melvillian touch when the official campaign history gives credit for the campaign to Cummings's invasion of Botoi Bay. Mailer brilliantly reveals an absurd discrepancy between the campaign itself and the record of the campaign, between Cummings's plan and the actual events, between the simple reality of the men's lives and the meaningless events which lead to their death. At the end of the novel, life goes on. The illusion is indeed restored when Major Dalleson builds a new training field and imposes strict military discipline in preparation for the move on the

Philippines. The circuit is again connected, the circuit of power that produced a Cummings and a Croft with their symbiotic need for each other. By his ending, Mailer contends that such power will always exist and always be a threat when it is in the hands of Cummings and Croft, men whose conscious aims are capable of tremendous destruction before they are countered by the blind and gratuitous power of the absurd. Even in his first novel, Mailer brought power motives into focus with an existential idea of absurdity, recognized that human and technological power functioned within the limits of forces unknown.

*Barbary Shore*, Mailer's second novel, is so uninspired that he probably would not have been able to publish it if he had not established his reputation with *The Naked and the Dead*. As political types, the characters discuss at interminable length the Marxist view of modern history, and the novel seems like a cross between Hawthorne's *The Marble Faun* and Jack London's *The Iron Heel*. The main character is Edward McLeod, a one-time member of and secret agent for the Communist party. Although he has left the party and even worked for a federal investigating agency, he has remained faithful to Marxist ideas. McLeod is being pursued by Leroy Hollingsworth, an American agent, who knows that he has stolen a secret object, perhaps key documents. The novel takes place in a Brooklyn rooming house where McLeod and Hollingsworth are living in separate attic rooms, and where they are joined by the novel's narrator, Michael Lovett, who has been wounded in the war and is suffering from amnesia. Lovett, one of the many nowhere heroes of modern fiction, is in a kind of no-man's-land since he has neither a past nor a future. His displacement stems thematically from the fate of McLeod at the hands of Hollingsworth—that is, the defeat of world socialism at the hands of capitalism. State capitalism, we are told, will eventually become a military state in perpetual war, will exploit the backward countries, will eliminate all forms of nonproduction, and finally will dominate the globe until the world resources are depleted. At this point "the deterioration [will] continue until we are faced with mankind in barbary" as "the boat drifts ever closer to the shore."

As in *The Naked and the Dead*, Mailer sees postwar America and all its financial-technological power on the road to right-wing totalitarianism. All of the characters in the novel are developed in terms of this idea. For example, Guinevere, McLeod's wife, symbolizes a "struggle for a vulgar gentility." She embodies the past at the same time that she embodies the ideal American consumer: her appetite for consumer goods is insatiable, and she dreams of marrying into money or of having her daughter succeed as a Hollywood star. Mailer is far from subtle when, at the novel's end, McLeod commits suicide and Guinevere runs off with Hollingsworth.

A more puzzling character is Lannie Madison, a member of the party until she turned informer. She has become infatuated with Hollingsworth and later Guinevere, with whom she has a lesbian affair. When Hollingsworth runs off with Guinevere, she is doubly cheated and, at the end of the novel, she has painted her room windows black and is sitting on a couch facing the wall. When Lovett comes to her after McLeod's suicide, Lannie notices that he is bleeding from a head wound he received at the hands of the government agents, and she calls him her "blood brother." The metaphor is justified because she, like Lovett, is waiting for the end. They have exhausted the possibilities of history and are staring at a blank wall in a room with windows painted black. At best, she is simply "waiting for the signs which tell me I must move on again," as Lovett says at the end. As "man grew smaller . . . the machine grew larger," Mailer tells us in *Barbary Shore*. Like Henry Adams and Oswald Spengler combined, Mailer is depicting history on the decline, a world running down to a "barbary shore" as capitalism gives way to a new kind of barbarism. Lannie and Lovett are left at the edge of history, one step away from despair, their life devoid of meaning. They are left, that is, at the point where every existential journey begins.

After the publication of *Barbary Shore*, Mailer's literary reputation was at its lowest ebb. These were bad days for him, as he tells us at length in *Advertisements for Myself*: "Maybe it was right that this first of the existentialist novels in America (unless one labels Faulkner correctly as an existentialist) should have had an existential fate, have been torn from its expected reception and given a shrunken life which was to react on the life of the author and reduce him as well." His faith in himself shaken, Mailer turned first to writing some short stories in the hope of regaining his confidence. When that failed, he came up with an extremely ambitious narrative which involved a prologue followed by an eight-part novel. The prologue turned out to be "The Man Who Studied Yoga," which treats a day in the life of Sam Slovada, "a small frustrated man, a minor artist manqué," who has neither the energy nor the ability to write his long-conceived novel and who spends a drab Sunday afternoon and evening watching a pornographic movie with his tired wife and jaded friends. Sam lives a kind of death-in-life, a point Mailer explicitly makes at the story's conclusion: "So Sam enters the universe of sleep, a man who seeks to live in such a way as to avoid pain, and succeeds merely in avoiding pleasure. What a dreary compromise is life." When Sam goes to sleep he was to become a Joycean dreamer, and the eight novels to follow the prologue "were to be eight stages of his dream later that night, and the book would revolve around the adventures of a mythical hero, Sergius O'Shaugnessy, who would travel through many worlds, through pleasure, business, communism, church, working class, crime, homosexuality and mysticism."

In "The Man Who Studied Yoga," Mailer introduced a number of themes he planned to develop in the eight-part sequence and which he did develop in *The Deer Park*, the first and last novel of this aborted series. As Sam watches and rewatches the pornographic film, he thinks of the way that Louis XV amassed immense personal power which he then used to perpetuate his own pleasure. Modern man still lusts after power but has lost the capacity for pleasure. In the century of Louis XV,

> men sought wealth so they might use its fruits; this epoch men lusted for power in order to amass more power, a compounding of power into pyramids of abstraction whose yield are cannon and wire enclosure, pillars of statistics to the men who are the kings of this century and do no more in power's leisure time than go to church, claim to love their wives, and eat vegetables.

The key to *The Deer Park* is in this passage. Sergius O'Shaugnessy tells us from the beginning that he has come to Desert D'Or (Palm Springs) "to look for a good time." There everything was "in the present tense," the hedonistic moment controlling all action until time became nonexistent. As Sam Slovada was about to fall asleep, Sergius tells him: "Destroy time and chaos may be ordered." Drinking around the clock in dimly-lit, luxurious bars, Sergius destroys time: "I never knew whether it was night or day, and I think that kind of uncertainty got into everybody's conversation." Although he has a short-lived affair with Lulu Meyers, a beautiful Hollywood actress, Sergius refuses to make pleasure into a way of life when he turns down an offer to become an actor and have his life story (orphan boy becomes hero) turned into a Hollywood movie.

Sergius's story is counterpointed against that of Charles Francis Eitel and Elena Esposito. Eitel was a successful director until he appeared as a hostile witness before a Congressional "Subversive Committee," at which time he was blacklisted in Hollywood. He meets Elena when Collie Munshin, an influential producer, is tiring of her as his mistress. Half out of pity, half out of boredom, Eitel takes Elena as his own mistress, and their affair is emotionally exhausting as each feels that his own life is purposeless and blames the other for this sense of frustration and of defeat. When Eitel cooperates with the Subversive Committee and is reinstated in

Hollywood, he leaves Elena, only to marry her later when she is in a serious automobile accident. The novel ends with Eitel caught in this loveless marriage and for diversion carrying on an affair with Lulu Meyers. Pleasure, we are told, cannot be an end in itself but must "end as love or cruelty . . . or obligation."

Never does the novel make this central idea convincing, and Mailer was unable to move in *The Deer Park* from idea to character. We can see this when we turn in *Advertisements for Myself* to Mailer's discussion of the difficulties he had in writing this novel. The novel originally was to be like *The Great Gatsby* with Sergius O'Shaugnessy a Nick Carraway-like character describing, with cynical awe, the life of Charles Francis Eitel. When Mailer realized that O'Shaugnessy's impoverished background and war experience made him substantially different from Nick Carraway, he roughened the style and made Sergius more tough and confident. As his point of view changed, so did Mailer's concept of character, or so he tells us: "I was no longer telling of two nice people who fail at love because the world is too large and too cruel for them; the new O'Shaugnessy had moved me by degrees to the more painful story of two people who are strong as well as weak, corrupt as much as pure, and fail to grow despite their bravery in a poor world, because they are not brave enough and so do more damage to one another than to the unjust world outside them." While Mailer's key characters do have paradoxical natures, we never see in what way they are better than "the unjust world outside them," and we also never see what alternatives can save them from their sad fate. They are ego-maniacal, lust-ridden, money-minded people who have the delusions that they are better than others when in reality they embody the very world they reject.

Mailer tells us that as a character Sergius was becoming too much like himself, and so also—perhaps even more so—was Eitel. Eitel thinks of himself as a man of principle even as he goes against conscience and cooperates with the Subversive Committee and writes and directs a pot-boiler movie. Mailer also thought of himself as a true artist when he condemned the Rinehart Company which was reluctant to publish *The Deer Park* even as Mailer worried about reviews and the place his novel would find on the best-seller list. Just as a novelist cannot go beyond history, he cannot go beyond himself, and while Norman Mailer toyed with existential ideas in *The Deer Park* (for example, that history cannot be divorced from man's actions, which are at best ambiguous, just as God and the Devil may be locked in cosmic battle) these ideas never go beyond cliché. Sam Slovada, Charles Eitel, and Sergius O'Shaugnessy are all artists manqués—and so, in *The Deer Park*, was Norman Mailer.

*An American Dream* is Mailer's attempt to characterize the hipster, or the American existentialist, as he called him in *Advertisements for Myself*:

> Hip is an American existentialism, profoundly different from French existentialism because Hip is based on a mysticism of the flesh, and its origins can be traced back into all the undercurrents and underworlds of American life, back into the instinctive apprehension and appreciation of existence which one finds in the Negro and the soldier, in the criminal psychopath and the dope addict and jazz musician, in the prostitute, in the actor, in the—if one can visualize such a possibility—in the marriage of the call-girl and the psychoanalyst. Unlike the rationality of French existentialism, which has its point of inauguration in the work of Sartre, Hip is an American phenomenon, and it has come into being without an intellectual mentor.

More than any other American writer, with the possible exceptions of Richard Wright and Walker Percy, Mailer has clearly indicated that he is working within American forms of French existentialism. In trying to give body to these forms, Mailer equated the existentialist, the hipster, and the psychopath, the last of whom his friend Robert Linder, a psychoanalyst, had treated at length in *Rebel Without a Cause—The Hypnoanalysis of a Criminal Psychopath*. The psychopath is aimlessly rebellious, concerned totally with his own gratification, impatient with conventions or social graces. He will murder when frustrated and will rape because he does not have the patience to court. He lives under sentence of death (embodying the collective condition of modern man), is divorced from society, and is obsessed with the meaning of his own self and with ways of immediately tapping the resources of his unconscious as well as fulfilling his capacity for orgasm. As a result, the hip has its sources in such sexually obsessed writers as D. H. Lawrence, Henry Miller, and Wilhelm Reich, and even more immediately in the Negro and in jazz since both find their meaning outside social convention in acts of improvisation.

As the hipster stands halfway between forms of life and forms of death, he "conceives of man's fate being tied up with God's fate." Mailer believes that man exists in relation to God as the cells in the human body exist in relation to the individual so that God's growth cannot be divorced from human action just as the individual cannot divorce himself from the condition of his cells. As Mailer puts it: "God Himself is engaged in a destiny so extraordinary, so demanding, that He too can suffer from moral corruption, that He can make demands upon us which are unfair, that He can abuse our beings in order to achieve His means, even as we abuse the very cells of our body." And as healthy and diseased cells may battle in the human body, Mailer believes that God and the Devil may battle within space—that God is perhaps "trying to impose upon the universe His conception of being against other conceptions of being very much opposed to His." Man may indeed be the agent of both God and the Devil—pawns in a cosmic battle, an "embodiment of that embattled vision . . . engaged in a heroic activity, and not a mean one."

Not only did Mailer bring these strange ideas to *An*

*American Dream* but the novel is an allegorical embodiment of them. The main character in the novel is Stephen Rojack, a professor of existential psychology and host of a television talk show. The novel begins with his killing his wife, Deborah Kelly, after a violent argument and then throwing her body out the window. He talks the police into believing that his wife committed suicide because she had cancer (which indeed the autopsy coincidentally proved). He then takes up with a girl named Cherry, a jazz singer who is having an affair with Shago Martin, a Negro jazz musician. Rojack beats up Martin when the musician comes to renew his affair with Cherry, and then Rojack goes to the Waldorf Towers where he has been summoned by Oswald Kelly, Deborah's father. There Kelly asks Rojack if he still believes the words he once spoke, perhaps on television, "that God's engaged in a war with the Devil, and God may lose." This becomes a question that only the novel itself will eventually answer. For Rojack does indeed believe that life is a struggle between God and Devil, and he further believes that both Kelly and Deborah are the agents of the Devil, a point documented by Rojack referring to Deborah as the Devil's daughter and by Kelly's description of Deborah's conception in terms of a journey to hell.

After he had murdered his wife, Rojack was not sure whether this act would take him to heaven or hell, an idea that is also reinforced in the next scene when he has both vaginal and anal intercourse with Ruta, the maid, entering her by both the Lord's and the Devil's (that is, forbidden) door and leaving his seed with the Devil. Rojack's confidence is restored by Cherry who had previously been Kelly's mistress, another unlikely coincidence. Cherry is on the side of the angels, and Rojack is able to lead her for the first time to that penultimate experience, successful orgasm. Now convinced that his powers are magical and hence divinely sent, Rojack is the square becoming hip, proved in the next scene when he beats up and takes upon himself the power of Shago Martin, the hippiest of the hip, even going to the extent of carefully wiping up Martin's vomit (as he wipes up Deborah's excrement) because food once eaten becomes a part of the person and hence a source of magic power in its own right. Armed with Shago's umbrella—a kind of magic wand, a stick of power, and symbolic phallus—Rojack does not take his trial by ordeal in the dark streets of Harlem but on the parapet of Kelly's apartment, thirty floors above Lexington Avenue. This walk in the sky proves to him that his actions have been blessed by God. As he is about to complete his walk on the third and final side of the parapet, Kelly, the Devil's agent, tries to push him over, but Rojack strikes him with Shago's umbrella and then spares his life, throwing the umbrella away as proof that his courage is a part of and not external to himself. If Rojack now believes that his own psychic power is greater than Kelly's financial and political power, he also finds that he has gone beyond Shago (who perhaps dies so that Rojack may live since Shago is found murdered in the streets of Harlem) and of Cherry (who is murdered in her apartment). Rojack leaves New York, goes to Las Vegas where he recoups his finances, and then walks into the desert—into a kind of crater of the moon (moon imagery has dominated the novel)—where he places a phone call to Cherry in heaven, once again proving the extraordinary psychic reach of his power. From there he is off to Guatemala and Yucatan—that is, off once again into the unknown—to test himself against the limits of his past knowledge and experience, presumably still engaged in God's war with the Devil.

To read *An American Dream* as realistic fiction is to make it an idiot's delight. *An American Dream* is an existential allegory—an examination of the self overcoming dread in its open-ended journey into an understanding of primitive and psychic energy. The trouble comes with Rojack's belief that he is fighting God's war and that this allows him to act with impunity—a kind of meglomania that would have satisfied Nietzsche but shocked Camus. The problem, however, is even more complicated than this because Mailer's surface terms have subsurface meanings. Although Mailer tells us that the war is cosmic (with a correspondence existing between God-Devil and man, and between man and his bodily cells), the war is in reality sexual, since the orgasm is the only link between man and Mailer's God. In *An American Dream*, Kelly, who has financial power, is set against Rojack who has libidinal power—the Devil faces God, and technological man is outwitted by the psychopath. In this world, the Deborahs must give way to the Cherrys because the pilgrimage is to orgasm, that moment for Mailer beyond good and evil when man and God touch. In Mailer's embattled vision, the Oswald Kellys are a source of a new barbarianism. An important weakness of that vision is that Mailer fails to see that the Rojacks also have no moral limits, have indeed the license to murder in order to create, and may be an even greater source of barbarianism.

Mailer once again pursued the theme of modern barbarianism in *Why Are We in Vietnam?* (1967), a novel narrated by a foul-mouthed young man named D. J. Jethroe, the son of Rusty Jethroe, a plastics-corporation executive from Texas. Along with his friend Tex, D. J. accompanies his father and two junior executives into the wilds of Alaska, where with the help of guides from the Moe Henry and Obungekat Safari Group they hunt bear and other wild life. From birth, D. J. has been taught by Rusty that to win is all: "You got to be a nut about competition. That's the way. You got to be so dominated by desire to win that if you was to squat down on the line and there facing you was Jesus Christ, you would just tip your head once and say, 'J. C., I have to give you fair warning that I'm here to do my best to go right through your hole.'" The meaning of Rusty as a character is not too far removed from that of Cummings and Croft in *The Naked and the Dead* or Oswald Kelly in *An American Dream*. He "sees himself as one of the pillars of the firmament . . . the fulcrum of the universe." He has a centripetal will, drawing all things into his ego, absorbing, consuming, triumphing. He embodies the evil triumph of technological power. He brings an arsenal of weapons into Alaska and, along with his friends, he cuts down the animals with his gun, the most destructive of machines. Annoyed that he has not yet been able to claim a bear, Rusty takes his son away from the others in order to go in separate pursuit. It is at this moment that D. J. feels the urge to kill his father, "to turn his gun and blast a shot into Rusty's fat fuck face, thump in his skull, whang!" D. J. is motivated here by his childhood memory of the serious beating his father gave him when he was five. He is also motivated by an Oedipal desire to destroy his mother's lover, a theme which Allan J. Wagenheim believes dominates *An American Dream.*[2] Finally, he is motivated here by an intuitive sense that his father's egomania is evil, a feeling that is reinforced when D. J. actually shoots a bear and his father takes the credit: "Wheh. Final end of love of one son for one father." Disgusted with his father after Rusty took claim of the bear, D. J. awakens Tex and together they go deep into the Endicott Range.

Their experience is in direct contrast to the earlier, wanton shooting of deer, wolf, and bear. Reminiscent of Faulkner's Ike McCaslin and Sam Fathers, they divest themselves of guns and compass and happily spy on the wild life around them. When they see an eagle and wolf in combat and later when they see a giant grizzly bear rip open and devour a caribou faun, they realize that nature itself is hostile—that God does not exist apart from combat. Yet the death that his father and father's friends brought seemed a wanton justification of ego, while the death of the faun seemed a part of a larger, more mysterious plan. Later that night D. J. for the first time feels a homosexual desire for Tex, but as he reaches for him "the Northern light shifted on that moment and a coil of sound went off in the night like a blowout in some circuit fuse." The experience is cosmic as if some "radiance of the North went into them," their self-control passing over to a "prince of darkness, lord of light, they did not know [which]." Once again we see Devil and God war in Mailer's universe. In this instance, the Devil seems to win, for when they return to Texas, D. J. once again becomes his father's son. The last section of the novel describes a going-away party for D. J. "because tomorrow Tex and me, we're off to see the wizard in Vietnam." The square wins, unless, of course, D. J. as narrator is really a black hipster in disguise, Harlem putting down Dallas. "You never know. You never know what vision has been humping through the night." While it ends on a note of ambiguity, *Why Are We in Vietnam?*, like *An American Dream*, postulates a world at war—God against Devil, man against animal, animal against animal, black against white, hipster against square. Like Oswald Kelly, Rusty Jethroe embodies this principle of war in its worst form. It is his mentality of winning at any cost, of destroying the wilderness in the name of progress and technology, of killing for the sake of ego, which sent America into Vietnam. The result is as devastating to the nation as cancer cells are to the flesh. The battle, however, still goes on, and Mailer's characters participate in the furious struggle that pulls them toward God or Devil, that keeps them in motion, which adds up to Mailer's own, very distinct vision of the existential self.

## Richard Wright

Richard Wright was born in Natchez on September 4, 1908 to a sharecropper family. In 1914 his father moved the family to Memphis, where he later deserted them. When Wright's mother fell seriously ill, he and his brother were placed in an orphanage. Wright later lived with his aunt and then his grandmother before he was reunited with his mother in Jackson, Mississippi. In 1925 Wright himself left home to live in Memphis where he held several menial jobs. In 1927 he moved to

Chicago, and like his Cross Damon, worked in the post office, then for a Negro burial society, and finally as publicity agent for the Federal Negro Theater. In 1932 he joined the John Reed Club, closely connected with the American Communist party, and in 1937 moved to New York as Harlem editor of the *Daily Worker*. When he received a Guggenheim Fellowship in 1939, he was able to complete *Native Son*, the novel which brought him immediate recognition. This was followed by *Black Boy*, Wright's biography, published in 1945. Both *Native Son* and *Black Boy* are deeply American books and portray how completely the American Negro was controlled by the psychology of fear. When Wright met Gertrude Stein in Paris, he told her, "I feel that fear is the greatest thing that Negroes feel in America; it influences them all, from the black Ph.D. to the janitors." In 1946 Wright met Jean-Paul Sartre when the French existentialist was visiting America. When he read Sartre and Camus, Wright responded, "they are writing of things that I have been thinking, writing, and feeling all of my life!" Perhaps because of the strong influence that Sartre had upon him, Wright went to Paris in 1946 and established permanent residence there the next year. He became a close friend (perhaps disciple is a better word) of Sartre who obviously influenced the expressly existential *The Outsider*, published in 1953. In 1954 Wright published the poorly received *Savage Holiday* which was followed in 1958 by *The Long Dream*, his last novel. Wright died in Paris of a heart attack on November 28, 1960.

*Native Son* deals with the growing consciousness of Bigger Thomas after he commits two murders—one accidental, the other intentional. Combining the naturalistic elements of Dreiser with the psychological gothicism of Hawthorne, Wright introduces us to Bigger as he awakens in his rat-infested Chicago ghetto, follows him into the luxurious residence of Mr. Dalton for whom Bigger works as chauffeur, records Bigger's first impressions of Mary Dalton and Jan (her Communist friend), and analyzes the hidden motives that lead Bigger—out of both fear and hate—to murder Mary, decapitate her, and burn her body in the house furnace. When Bigger is exposed, he takes flight, and we follow him as he murders his girl friend and unsuccessfully tries to avoid the pursuing police. His trial allows Wright to discuss social and political concerns. When Bigger is found guilty, Wright can question the whole matter of innocence and guilt.

Bigger as we first see him is very different from Bigger as we last see him. The early Bigger has no real self-understanding. He is maddened by the fact that the welfare department has found him a job at the Daltons and that his choice is a limited one—work or starve. Although he has robbed before, all of his victims have been black. When he thinks of robbing Blum's Delicatessen with two of his friends, he is unwilling to recognize that he is gripped by fear because Blum is white, and the robbery "would be a violation of ultimate taboo." The fear that grips him turns to violence toward his friends—an act that anticipates his murdering Mary Dalton.

Mary Dalton is a wealthy radical whose motives are both sincere and quixotic. When she drinks too much rum with Jan, Bigger ends up driving her home and putting her into bed. Although Mary has passed out, their lips touch when Bigger tries to stand her up. As he puts her on the bed, his hands fondle her breasts. When "he tightened his fingers on her breasts, kissing her again, feeling her move toward him," the bedroom door opens and Mrs. Dalton—blind, always dressed in bright white —enters, and Bigger's lust turns to fear. In panic, he buries Mary's face into the pillow to keep her from speaking, until she stiffens, dead, as the unknowing Mrs. Dalton prays by the bed. This is the act—in many ways the gratuitous act that we often find in novels more expressly existential than *Native Son*—that brings with it the dimension of consciousness. Bigger suddenly feels "outside his family now, over and beyond them." He sees them as blind and looks at them differently—in fact, so differently that his sister wilts before his gaze and pleads, "Stop looking at me, Bigger!"

While Dreiser's characters are trapped within their bodies and environment, Bigger Thomas is also trapped within his mind—a mind which begins to expand under the shock of violence. Fear and submerged hate lead to the killing of Mary Dalton, and fear and submerged hate remain with Bigger. When he returns to the Dalton house, he finds food left out, but he hesitates to eat because he is not sure that the white man's food is for him. Suddenly he realizes how absurd are his fears: "He had killed a rich white girl and had burned her body after cutting her head off and had lied to throw the blame on someone else and had written a kidnap note demanding ten thousand dollars and yet he stood here afraid to touch food on the table, food which undoubtedly was his own." What Bigger must do is find a way out of his fear and hate. After Mr. Dalton finds Bigger's kidnap note, Bigger has a kind of existential moment: "He could run away; he could remain; he could even go down and confess what he had done. The mere thought that these avenues of action were open to him made him feel free, that his life was his, that he held his future in his hands." When he finally does run away, he murders again—this time Bessie, his girl friend, whom he fears will give him away. This killing parallels the murder of Mary Dalton, only the same motives have now risen to the surface, and Bigger acts consciously, first forcing himself sexually upon Bessie and then brutally—fear and rage driving him on—beating in her skull with a brick. When the morning comes, Bigger looks out at a Chicago covered with snow and is conscious that in more ways than one he is a black man in a white world—a cold, white world. He feels totally outside that world and ponders, "Why should not this cold white world rise up as a beautiful dream in which he could walk and be at home?" The question has no answer; he has murdered twice and created a new world from which he can never escape.

When Bigger is finally brought to trial, he is represented by a Communist lawyer whose ideas become the
frame of reference against which Bigger's story unfolds.
Bigger's sense of despair is tempered by Max's political
hope. While some critics have felt that a Bigger Thomas
is not intellectual enough to put such faith in ideas, Bigger's own desire to find a way out of fear and despair is
convincing, especially as he anticipated death in the
electric chair: "He had to make a decision: in order to
walk to the chair he had to weave his feelings into a
hard shield of either hope or hate. To fall between them
would mean living and dying in a fog of fear. He was
balanced on a hair-line now." In *Native Son*, Bigger
moves through fear, hate, murder, flight, and despair
to hope, even though the source of hope—the Communist party—will not convince Wright himself for long.
While the specifics of the situation may give pause, the
psychology of the situation is convincing. The two murders, each in their different ways motivated by hate and
fear, become an extension of Bigger's life, as Max tells
us at the trial: "The hate and fear which we have inspired in him, woven by our civilization into the very
structure of his consciousness, into his blood and bones,
into the hourly functioning of his personality, have become the justification of his existence." Only when Bigger begins to see differently, only when his blindness
gives way, is he free—ironically freed by his crime: "free
for the first time in his life." In Bigger's world, men are
blind and invisible until a violent crime separates them
from their past and gives them both sight and the insight of the outsider: "I didn't know I was really alive in
this world until I felt things hard enough to kill for
'em," Bigger says at the very end of the novel.

The political insight which comes so unconvincingly
as the source of new hope to Bigger gives way to an existential insight in *The Outsider*. Although Wright
wrote *The Outsider* in Paris after he had come under
the obvious influence of Jean-Paul Sartre, Wright has
told us that his own sense of experience had made him
an existentialist long before he had ever met Sartre. This

remark seems justified by the many existential elements that can be found in *Native Son*—especially the gratuitous murder, the absurd motives that condition it, Bigger's developing sense of a privileged self, Bigger's ability to see himself reflexively, and his belief that he must create himself anew in the face of his despair.

*Native Son* was completed in 1939 and published the next year. Between 1942 and 1944, Wright broke with the American Communist party. In 1942 he published a long story, "The Man Who Lived Underground," in the spring issue of *Accent* and then expanded the story two years later for Edwin Seaver's *Crosssection*. The two versions of "The Man Who Lived Underground" explicitly reveal how Wright was moving away from a political explanation of life in America toward a philosophical existentialism. Since this story was finally published two years before he fell under Sartre's influence, Wright's existentialism at this point stemmed very much from his own thinking.

"The Man Who Lived Underground" is a story that reveals the influence of Dostoyevsky and influenced in turn the last section of Ralph Ellison's *Invisible Man*. It is the story of Fred Daniels, a Negro falsely accused of murder, who escapes from the police, takes refuge in the sewer from which he crawls to dig a network of tunnels through buildings that take him into a church, an undertaker's embalming room, a movie, a butcher shop, a radio repair shop, and a jewelry store. Once underground, his whole perspective is changed. The people in the church and the movie theater seem grotesque, men and women from another planet who have no awareness of what life is all about. They "were children, sleeping in their living, awake in their dying."

Daniels's experience robs his life of goals. When he robs the jewelry store of diamonds and money, these valuables have no meaning to him, are no more important than the meat cleaver, the radio, and the typewriter which he has also stolen. All acts and all things take on unilateral significance once Daniels believes that the aboveground life is purposeless and has no meaning ("the world above ground now seemed to him a wild forest filled with death"). He papers his dirt cave with hundred-dollar bills and sprinkles his floor with diamonds. Although he has stolen a number of watches, their hands all tell a different time, because now time has no meaning at all. What he comes to realize is that life is a fiction, a plot invented by other people who have made his life superfluous. He is aware that in the world above life preys on life—the meat cleaver is proof of this truth—and he feels that "if the world as men had made it was right, then anything else was right, any act a man took to satisfy himself, murder, theft, torture." While this thought takes the form of a hypothetical syllogism, Daniels is incapable of such thought, and he feels rather than reasons to this truth. He comes to feel that even he, an underground man, will never be able to escape fully the events above that have conditioned him, the fears that control a black man in a white man's world. When he says that "it seemed that when one felt this guilt one was retracing in one's feelings a faint pattern designed long before . . . forgotten by the conscious mind, creating in one's life a state of eternal anxiety," some critics feel that Wright is talking about the birth trauma. But one is equally justified in believing that he is talking about social conditioning, a theme that emerges so distinctly in *Native Son*.

When Daniels climbs from the underground, he cannot communicate these fragile ideas because the outside world "demands logical answers and he could no longer think with his mind; he thought with his feelings and no words came." He is thrown out of the black church and is shot down by the police who better understand that he is dangerous ("You've got to shoot his kind. They'd wreck things"). When he first enters the sewer, Wright's underground man sees a baby floating past him. At the end of the story he is shot dead in the sewer and the water also carries him away. Both the underground man and the baby are innocent, victims of a cruelty and a system which they can neither understand nor control. Their deaths are pathetic proof that civilized life expresses itself in absurd ways. Fred Daniels in many ways anticipates Wright's most existential character, Cross Damon.

When Cross Damon is listed by mistake among the dead of a horrible train wreck, he rejects his dismal life (his aging mother with a mind addled by religion, his vindictive wife from whom he is estranged, his mistress who holds over him the fact that she is under the age of consent) and tries to start life anew, to remake himself in existential fashion. Even before the subway accident, Damon feels that he is the outsider, has a "pending threat of annihilation," and debates over who he is and what he should be. Where Bigger Thomas is controlled by emotions of fear and hate, Cross Damon cannot escape emotions of fear and desire. Although he is convinced that "good or evil" must come "through his own actions," he is not free of his past fears and growing desire, and he wishes "to be a God who could master feeling! If not that, then a towering rock that could feel nothing at all." His desire makes him restless, dissatisfied with his lot, and convinced that it is his future which must be decided as vague as that future may be: "He was a man tossed back upon himself when that self meant only a hope of a hope." Like Bigger Thomas, Cross Damon finds himself responding to a gratuitous situation. Once more like Bigger Thomas, he moves from an accident to deliberate murder, motivated in great part by fear. With this deliberate act, Cross Damon brings existential motives into play: "the outside world had fallen away from him now and he was alone at the center of the world of the laws of his own feelings."

When he takes flight from Chicago to New York, he comes in contact with the Communist party through Gilbert and Eva Blount. Outraged by Gilbert's desire to mastermind the lives of others, and incensed by the racism of a landlord named Herndon, Damon kills both of them as they fight between themselves. His action is a travesty because he has become what he was trying to defeat, a tin god. "Was all action doomed to this kind of degradation?" he asks, in a novel that seems to give positive answer to that question. Beyond religion, beyond family, beyond everyday society, Damon lives beyond the realm of the human. While he loves Eva Blount, his actions drive her to suicide. He has merely substituted aimless desire for Bigger Thomas's political hope, and his own death at the hands of a party member seems inevitable, for there is no place for either Damon or Wright's plot to go.

Damon's dilemma is the dilemma of all existential characters who believe in radical freedom, which includes Mailer's megalomaniacal overreachers, "the dilemma of the ethical criminal, the millions of men who lived in the tiny crevices of industrial society completely cut off from humanity, the multitudes of little gods who ruled their own private worlds and acknowledged no outside authority." Cross Damon embodies the absurd in its most destructive form. Even though he has murdered four men, he is supposedly innocent, because he can see to the core of a corrupt society and can find no values in which to believe or act, a theme Wright had developed in another context in *Native Son*. Once Damon strays beyond, he finds that there is no return to the ordinary, no redemption from his extreme existence. He is exposed by Ely Houston, the district attorney, a hunchback who has the psychological make-up to understand his demonic motives. One demonic consciousness upends another, and when Damon recants at the end of the novel, he is in essence expressing the tragic consequences of radical freedom, the danger of the self-enclosed existence. Damon's end was in his beginning. Nietzsche's man of power assumes a satanic mask, and the flight toward self leads up a road that never turns back to man.

Because of their dubious literary merits, both *Savage Holiday* and *The Long Dream* could be omitted from our consideration. Yet, because it was Wright's last novel, *The Long Dream* should be briefly considered, especially because it treats life in Mississippi, revealing in many ways the source of motives that Wright's characters bring with them to the industrial North.

The central character, Fishbelly, is the son of a wealthy black man who owns the black funeral home and who has money invested in black houses of prostitution and in a dance hall which turns out to be a firetrap. Fishbelly learns at an early age that a black man can have at best tenuous relationships with the white world. He experiences the agony of this truth when a friend is tortured and lynched for having sex with a white woman. When Fishbelly sees Chris's mutilated body on his father's table, he becomes haunted by the fear of what the white man can do with impunity to the black man. When his father's dance hall catches fire and forty-two Negroes are burned to death, the local chief of police protects himself by throwing the blame on Fishbelly's father. When his father is shot to death in a police trap, Fishbelly comes fully to realize the truth of what his father told him: "A black man's a dream, son, a dream that can't come true. Dream, Fish. But be careful what you dream. Dream only what can happen. . . . there's too many dreams of a black man that can't come true." In some ways, these words are prologue to all of Wright's fiction. Controlled by fear, acting in dread, Wright's characters dream dreams that are destined never to happen. Neither Bigger Thomas's inchoate Marxism nor Cross Damon's radical existentialism is enough to save them from this web of events. It is indeed significant that at the end of *The Long Dream* Fishbelly is leaving America for France—any kind of solution still beyond him, flight once again his only option. Tormented, driven by hate and fear, refusing to accept racist limitations, Wright's characters become the victims of the violence that befalls them and which they inflict on others. They cannot escape their final state of mind which completes their initial alienation.

Since Sartre's philosophy also leads to destructive conclusions, one can perhaps see why Wright might have been intuitively drawn toward Sartre's version of existentialism. While Wright's characters define themselves in social and political terms, Sartre's characters usually define themselves in epistemological terms. They often see life as a struggle between mutually exclusive states of being—matter and consciousness. They believe that the most perfect form of human attainment is that state which simultaneously contains pure matter and pure consciousness. Sartre recognizes that such a state is a form of self-destruction: to be pure fixity and pure consciousness at one and the same time is to be both God and dead, mutually inclusive terms. Since it is in the very nature of Sartrean freedom to overreach oneself, to strive for total completion, the Sartrean hero continually destroys himself at the very moment he achieves a kind of self-completion. It is no accident that characters such as Mathieu and Hugo die at the moment they most fully realize their freedom. Sartre often compounds his hero's trouble, often frustrates the will of his hero, by insisting that he recognize the need for social commitment as well as the need to be a *causa sui*, obviously exclusive pursuits. The irresolute Mathieu, torn between a desire to engage himself in the Spanish Civil War and a desire to pursue his own individual preoccupations, lacks the capacity for unimpeded action and almost destroys himself by an inability to direct his restless energy toward a definite end. Sartre was unable to finish *Les Chemins de la liberté* tetralogy because he was unable to decide whether Brunet should pursue his ideals within or outside the Communist party, within or outside society.

Unlike Sartre, Wright after 1944 did not believe that the Communist party would bring salvation; but like Sartre, he never found the means to make his characters both autonomous and socially responsible, self-contained and socially committed. Like other radical existential characters, once Wright's Fred Daniels and Cross Damon go underground or climb to Nietzschean heights, they never find the means to return to man. Saul Bellow's characters often feel cut off from a world that they can neither understand nor accept, a world of the dead which seems about to possess them; but Bellow never takes his characters so far beyond man that they are unable to find their way back.

# 5

## Into the Ruins: Saul Bellow and Walker Percy

Mailer's and Wright's characters try to overcome the system with their ego—an ego that gives them the right to destroy others in the vague name of their own salvation. Mailer tells us as much when he insists that God and the Devil are locked in a war within which we participate but do not understand. Richard Wright's Cross Damon embodies the idea that salvation will come through the surmounting of self. For Mailer and Wright the journey is indeed a dangerous crossing.

Saul Bellow's characters never take us so far: they insist on limits and live between extremes. They may be cut off from family, mate, society, God—may feel more dead than alive—but they eventually try to isolate and perpetuate those qualities which make them human and to force these virtues into the face of death. Kindness, sympathy, compassion, a simple love of life and a joy of being among the living—these are the virtues that redeem life from death, that turn Bellow's characters from nay to yea sayers. Unlike the characters of Mailer and Wright, they find no satisfaction in destroying others to justify themselves. If they emerge like Lazarus from a kind of death, they have no desire to become demonic supermen. While they believe that man must be his own redeemer, they do not believe that he is a satanic redeemer. They do not glorify the past or make deliverance a matter of the future. Like Herzog, they can accept neither extreme in the dialectic between the romantic self and modern apocalypse, between the romantic idea that man is limitless and the modern idea that he is doomed. While they are often self-indulgent and give way to self-pity, they desire to be neither more nor less than human, await no moment of the burning bush, and see in their own simple possibilities the answer to both the absurdities of life and death.

Walker Percy's characters redeem life by "certifying" reality. A movie can help certify reality if it depicts a setting we know well but have taken for granted. Suddenly seeing it on the screen gives it new life, moves us from our sense of "everydayness," gives us the means of sharing our reality with others. Percy's characters have been dehumanized by the brutal condition of modern life: they live in a world that has lost all fixed value, often become victims of a meaningless workaday routine, try to find love but are often taken for granted. They struggle to move beyond everydayness by putting themselves in motion, breaking the circuit of their existence through what Percy calls *rotation*. The "return" brings new focus, a double consciousness, a sense of one's being that is accompanied by a consciousness of that sense of being, so that one begins to see himself as an actor in a play or movie, playing a part that one certifies by consciously choosing to play it. At the end of *The Moviegoer*, Binx Bolling is both actor and director, describing the scene as it should be played, playing the scene he describes. Percy's existential man moves with double vision: he sees and then reflexively is seen in his mind's eye. His final sense of being comes when he can share his own vision of himself, can certify it by having it accepted by another. Even the ruins are tolerable when one can justify his being through love.

### Saul Bellow

Saul Bellow's characters seem to delight in being agonized. The source of their agony stems from a sense of displacement, cut off as they often are from wife, family, friends, or a sense of life's purpose. They seem to be surrounded by countless forms of death, even as they go in search of life. Indeed, like modern-day Lazaruses, they are sometimes the risen dead, climbing out of death's ditch and back into life as did Mr. Sammler. They know, if only intuitively, that they are their own redeemers. They know also that they will find their humanity somewhere between romantic affirmation and apocalyptic despair. Life as opposed to death, the need for life to move in the face of its limits—these ideas compel Bellow's characters who usually see in their own simple possibilities an answer to the absurdity of both life and death. They are men in motion—in flight from death, the inhuman, the barbaric, and the joyless.

These themes can be found in all of Bellow's novels, including his first, a work that has many similarities to Sartre's *La Nausée* and Camus' *L'Étranger*. *Dangling Man* is set in the early days of the Second World War. The main character, named Joseph, comes in contact with the absurd when the draft board holds up his induction papers because he is a Canadian citizen. The routine that he could once take for granted is suddenly interrupted, and he is left dangling. Joseph begins to live at a distance from himself, outside the realm of ordinary men, aware of the full weight of his undirected life. He comments, "I am forced to pass judgment on myself to ask questions I would far rather not ask: 'What is this for?' and 'What am I for?' and 'Am I for this?' My beliefs are inadequate, they do not guard me."

Joseph sees his friends and relatives as snobbish and pretentious. At Mitta's party, he suddenly realizes that his friends band together for mutual protection, behave the way the group expects them to behave, assert the group values, scorn all that is outside the clique, and ridicule all that threatens the general definition. He is both annoyed and jealous of them—annoyed at their sense of self-righteousness, jealous that they can participate in the general experience from which he is excluded.

Like Augie March, Joseph is equally annoyed by his older brother, who has married into wealth and repudiated his class and family background. When Joseph's anger explodes during a holiday dinner, he proves that his indifference is merely a posture and that he resents his in-laws' attitude toward him more than he is willing to admit. He even begins to resent Iva, his wife, who is sympathetic but not really understanding of his problem.

Joseph's disillusionment with people prefaces his disillusionment with the whole nature of creation. "The world suddenly comes after you," he says, and there is a "feeling of strangeness, of not quite belonging to the world at large." An indifferent world precludes a beneficent and personal God, and Joseph asserts that "there are no values outside of life. There is nothing outside of life." Joseph rejects God because God is born out of "a miserable surrender . . . out of fear, bodily and imperious . . . I could not [he says] accept the existence of something greater than myself." Cut off, left out, metaphysically superfluous, Joseph becomes bitter and argumentative. He finds himself growing anxious and short-tempered, often making a public spectacle of himself. Caught in a prolapsed world, caught in a state of moral suspension, he can act in terms of no emblem, can live in terms of no future—except death. Joseph seems surrounded by death. The Chicago of 1942 anticipates the decline of the modern city. The streets are black with dirt, the houses are run down, everything is "ugly and blind," and the horror seems "related to interior life." Joseph's boozy neighbor, Mr. Vanaker, embodies Joseph's own spiritual state of deterioration; his story is told against the fact that his landlady's mother, Mrs. Kefer, is dying beneath him.

Like so many of Bellow's characters, Joseph feels that his life has been short-circuited and that death has thrown the switch. Like so many existential characters, he questions how he can give life meaning, how a life force can come from him when he is surrounded by so many forms of death at a time when his own life is so empty. He rejects a romantic solution—a belief in an idealized humanity—because man "must have limits and cannot give in to the wild desire to be everything and everyone and everything to everyone." On the other hand, freedom imposes a burden so great that he finally finds it too overwhelming and longs for the army: "I am in the hands of others, relieved of self-determination, freedom cancelled. . . . Long live regimentation!" The ending is heavily ironic, and for Bellow the solution is to be found between romantic idealism and mass conformity. Joseph comes closest to a solution when he listens to a Haydn *divertimento*. Without transcending the human condition or abandoning his own sense of the moment, he finds the music unifies a previously shapeless sense of experience, orders discordant time, and justifies human suffering. Moreover, the music tells him how to respond to such suffering—"with grace, without meanness. And though I could not as yet apply that answer to myself, I recognized its rightness and was vehemently moved by it. Not until I was a whole man could it be my answer, too. And was I to become this whole man alone, without aid?"

In many ways *Dangling Man* ends with this question, a question that many of Bellow's characters strive to answer. Joseph is a prisoner of his own fear, cannot brave alone the unknown and unordinary, and for him the struggle is too much. While his world folds in and weighs him down, some of Bellow's other characters will get beyond fear and put themselves in motion—will assert their humanity, their brotherhood, their desire for life in the face of death. In *Dangling Man* Bellow introduces us to his own version of existential man—cut off from family, wife, friends, city, society, and God; trying to affirm his humanity in the face of the unknown, in the face of his own unfixed condition. No American writer has better portrayed the psychology of this experience.

In *The Victim*, Bellow once again treats a dislocated

character, Asa Leventhal, who feels lonely and empty when his wife leaves him for a short visit with her mother. Two events happen that sorely test him at this time. He receives a call from the wife of his brother, informing him that her husband is still working in Galveston and that their youngest boy is critically ill. He is also set upon by Kirby Allbee, an old acquaintance, who informs Leventhal that he was fired from *Dell's Weekly* when Leventhal insulted Mr. Rudiger, the owner, during a heated argument after Allbee had arranged the meeting between the two. Allbee holds Leventhal to blame for his bad luck which involves also the death of Allbee's wife in an automobile accident.

These two events are both coincidental and thematically related. Both lead Leventhal to a wracked sense of blame, especially when his nephew dies after Leventhal insists he be brought to the hospital, and when Mr. Williston (a mutual friend of Leventhal and Allbee) tells him that he is at fault for Allbee's bad luck. Both events involve the theme of brotherhood. Leventhal barely knows his brother's family—indeed, he barely knows his brother—so far apart have the two families drifted. Max, a laborer, has become an itinerate worker and his wife, Elena, is from an Italian Catholic family which is wary of Max's Jewish background. Leventhal feels put upon by the demands of Elena and is annoyed that he should have to accept the responsibility for his brother's troubles, especially when his brother is not even in the city. Leventhal also feels Allbee's demands are unjust, that Allbee was and is a drunk, that *Dell's Weekly* would have eventually fired him anyway, and that Allbee may even have arranged the interview with an idea of what would happen between Rudiger and Leventhal. Just as Sartre maintained that the anti-Semite will blame the Jews for his own failures, Allbee holds Leventhal responsible for his recent failures and refuses to accept any of the blame.

Given this situation, Bellow is able to study the questions of bad faith and brotherhood. Questions of where individual responsibility begins and ends are not easy and the answers are slow in coming. Allbee's weakness of character jeopardized his career, but Leventhal inadvertently injured Allbee's chances. When Allbee refuses to recognize his own culpability, Leventhal begins to feel totally responsible. At this point the relationship between Allbee and Leventhal is as symbiotic as it is destructive. Leventhal begins to act like Allbee, begins taking upon himself many of Allbee's own prejudices. Allbee, for example, believes that Jews succeed because they "stick together" and believe in "connections." Even as Leventhal refuses to admit this, he remembers that he went to Rudiger in the first place because of his connections with Williston and because of Rudiger's connections with the publishing world. He later thinks of getting Allbee an interview with Shifcart because of the agent's connections, even though he knows that Shifcart is an actor's agent and cannot really help Allbee. This moral change in Leventhal is paralleled by a physical change. When Allbee spends a drunken evening asleep on Leventhal's couch, Leventhal is disgusted, but the next evening Leventhal himself drinks too much wine at Harkavy's party and spends a drunken evening on Harkavy's couch.

Leventhal and Allbee become each other's victims. Allbee is Leventhal's victim because so long as he insists that Leventhal has ruined his life, Allbee will find no need to change his life. And Leventhal is Allbee's victim because so long as he admits that he is responsible for Allbee, he is simply weighed down by what is base in human nature. Each character becomes locked in the bad faith of the other, becomes fixed by a relationship which prevents the possibility of change. Man is no longer in motion as each becomes the absurd victim of the other's distorted view, until each begins grotesquely to resemble the other.

This theme is brought to the surface in an exchange between Leventhal and Harkavy's friends, Schlossberg and Shifcart, when Leventhal meets them in a Fourteenth Street cafeteria. Leventhal finds himself arguing against the motives of Disraeli, a man who becomes a national leader because "he was a Jew, not because he cared about empires. People laughed at his nose, so he took up boxing; they laughed at his poetic silk clothes, so he put on black; and they laughed at his books, so he showed them. He got into politics and became the prime minister. He did it all on nerve." Disraeli tries to become "more than human" to prove that Jews can be heroes, and in so distinguishing himself he proves that Jews are different—that their motives are controlled by what others think of them. When Leventhal applies this lesson to himself, when he refuses to accept what Allbee thinks of him, he can then be free of all the Allbees. In the discussion which follows between Shifcart and Schlossberg, this theme is put in relief. As an actor's agent, Shifcart sees people as so much meat to be packaged, wrapped, and sold. Whereas Disraeli tried to be more than human, Shifcart is less than human, an idea that Schlossberg completes when he says, "More than human, can you have any use for life? Less than human, you don't either." In accepting Allbee's and Elena's blame, Leventhal realized that he was being more than human while they were being less because to be human is simply to be accountable—"accountable in spite of many weaknesses—at the last moment, tough enough to hold."

The idea of responsibility to neither an exaggerated nor diminished sense of the human is the key idea in *The Victim*, an idea reinforced at the end when Leventhal finally dismisses Allbee once he is finally convinced that Allbee is beyond redemption, that Allbee will never admit his own profligacy or his hypocrisy about his dead wife whose death he uses to gain pity. Leventhal calls Allbee a "dirty phoney! . . . a liar, with your phoney tears and your wife's name in your mouth, every second word. . . . You're not even human." When Allbee breaks his way into Leventhal's apartment later that evening and tries to commit suicide by turning on the gas, the plot comes full circle, for Allbee almost inad-

vertently kills Leventhal as well as himself, just as Leventhal had inadvertently hurt Allbee with Rudiger. Such
is the nature of brotherhood since one life is bound to
touch upon another. The meaning of brotherhood can
follow when one becomes human and accepts (as Allbee
refuses to accept) the consequences of his actions.

Set in a world that is fast losing all sense of tradition,
*The Victim* presents ordinary characters trying to give
their lives a sense of meaning at a time of radical change.
Allbee, who actually is descended from Governor Win-
throp, is the drunken, cowardly embodiment of the dead
past, a scavenger in a society in which he no longer really
belongs. Leventhal, whose father was a devout Jew, a
small Hartford clothing-store owner, feels only grotesque
connection to that grim past and to his mother who
died in an insane asylum. He feels even less connection
to his brother, dressed as he is in the kind of work
clothes that his father once sold, mourning his baptized
child buried in consecrated ground. Devoid of a meaningful past, cut off from family, living at best tenuously
with everyone except his absent wife, Asa Leventhal
refuses to become a victim and thereby learns the meaning of his own life and the meaning of brotherhood in
this novel at once so European (Dostoyevsky's and
Camus's handling of these themes come to mind) and
so American.

*The Adventures of Augie March* is very different from
Bellow's earlier fiction. Indeed, the novel cannot be rele-
gated to any one specific narrative mode but is a composite of three or four. The beginning has some parallels
to the *Studs Lonigan* novels of James T. Farrell. Like
Farrell, Bellow describes what it is like to grow up in a
poor family in the slums of Chicago. The theme of the
family gives way to the theme of success, and Bellow's
novel becomes as American as Horatio Alger, anticipating Philip Roth's *Goodbye, Columbus*. Simon, Augie's
brother, learns to hustle early, and he succeeds in marrying Charlotte Magnus for her money while Augie, with
less success, courts her sister, Lucy Magnus, just as he had

earlier failed to win Esther Fenechel or her sister Thea. Unlike his brother, Augie is willing to put human values ahead of money. He helps Mimi through her abortion even at the expense of losing Lucy and her money. In this section of the novel, the theme of success gives way to the theme of compassion, and in his hell-with-society attitude, Augie anticipates some of the characters in such recent novels as James Purdy's *Eustace Chisholm and the Works* and Robert Stone's *A Hall of Mirrors*. Bellow sustains this narrative element in the mad car trip to Mexico with Thea Fenechel and a bald eagle they train to hunt primitive lizards. When this absurd journey runs its inevitable dead-end course, Augie returns to Chicago in the hope of starting a family of his own. The novel, however, does not come full circle because Augie and Stella are far different from their parents. The novel ends with Augie going into the merchant marine in a world so totally changed that no continuity exists between the present and the past. Augie's ship, the *Sam MacMangus*, is sunk by a German submarine off the Canaries, and before he is saved Augie spends his last ordeal with a mad scientist in a lifeboat.

*The Adventures of Augie March* is the story of a young man in search of meaning—in search of his own human essence. Over and over, Bellow talks about Augie in search of his "fate"—a fate that always seems ahead of him swirling away with the flux of Heraclitus's stream, as indeed the very first paragraph of the novel suggests. Augie is looking for something durable in a world of change. He fails to find it in the family, or from his friends, or outside the law, or within the university, or on the road. Augie is in search of Man with a capital letter. Clem Tambow isolates Augie's problem:

> "You want there should be Man, with capital M, with great stature. As we've been pals since boyhood, I know you and what you think. Remember how you used to come to the house every day? But I know what you want. O *paidea*! O Kind David! O Plutarch and

Seneca! O chivalry, O Abbot Suger! O Strozzi Palace,
O Weimar! O Don Giovanni! O lineaments of grati-
fied desire! O godlike man! Tell me, pal, am I getting
warm or not?"

"You are, yes you are," said I.

Augie discovers that man longs to be more than he is.
There are dangers in such desire, as Augie realizes when
he is stranded with Basteshaw in the lifeboat, a detail
too narratively perfect to be a narrative accident. Basteshaw is a biochemist who believes that he can create and
control life. Even more than Augie he is in search of an
idealized form of life. He wants Augie to give up any
desire to be saved and returned to America and to go to
the Canaries with him, where he plans to set up a laboratory and continue his research and experiments. "Boredom starts with useless efforts," he tells Augie, in some
ways summarizing Augie's life up to this point. According to Basteshaw, "the simple cells wish for immortality
whereas the complex organisms get bored? The cells have
the will to persist in their essence." Basteshaw believes
that he can control the cells in such a way as to create
a new breed of man who will be so perfect, so self-contained, that he will be "liberated from boredom." At
this moment, "every man will be a poet and every woman
a saint. Love will fill the world. Injustice will go, and
slavery, bloodshed, cruelty. . . . I am going to create a
serum—a serum like a new River Jordan. With respect
to which I will be Moses. And you Joshua. To lead an
Israel consisting of the entire human race across it. And
this is why I don't want to go back to the States." Augie
settles for less. He tells Basteshaw:

> "I'm dead against doing things to the entire human
> race. I don't want any more done to me, and I don't
> want to tamper with anyone else. No one will be a
> poet or a saint because you fool with him. When you
> come right down to it, I've had trouble enough becom-
> ing what I already am, by nature. I don't want to go
> to the Canaries with you. I need my wife."

Man must be his own redeemer—not destroyer. When Augie comes to realize what it means to be a man with a small and not capital letter, he arrives at an existential conclusion. He learns that to be human is to be in flux, to be in motion, and that it is better to live out one's own sense of the absurd than to die for the utopian vision. This is why Augie compares himself in the last paragraph of the novel to Columbus, the eternal voyager who remained faithful to his own vision even as he was led away in chains. This is also why the novel ends in Paris, "the capital of hope that Man could be free without help of gods.' There is a conscious play upon Man with a capital M, for Augie concludes that "if it was for Man why shouldn't it be for me too?"

Augie puts the individual self in the center of history, sees man as his own creator and redeemer, as both tragic and comic in his attempt to define the limits of his own possibilities. Augie is existential man in motion, a "sort of Columbus"—the "flop" who discovers America in this novel about America. Augie March must choose his own roads to freedom, totally blind to where they can or may lead. To decide otherwise is to choose to be less than human. In his own unique way, Bellow used the central idea of existentialism in this very American study of the picaresque, of man in search of himself.

In *Seize the Day*, Bellow combines the themes of *The Victim* and *The Adventures of Augie March*. Tommy Wilhelm is the loser who is wracked with a terrible sense of guilt by his defeats. As a result, he suffers with the intensity of Asa Leventhal and is so burdened by his past that he cannot change his life, cannot be his own creator but gives way to agonized thoughts about Man with a capital M, a state of mind that Augie March had overcome. Once again Bellow sets up two poles of being and defines characters in terms of whether they *construct* or *destruct* their lives. Those who construct have a sense of the possibilities of life, are moved by the joy of being. Those who destruct have a sense of life as death, choke for air, beseech others for help, complain about their troubles, and make their defeats into a way of life. Such people are married to suffering. "If they go with joy they think it's adultery. . . . suffering is the only kind of life they are sure they can have, and if they quit suffering they're afraid they'll have nothing."

Tommy Wilhelm's problem stems in great part from his father, Dr. Adler, whose values are totally shaped by money. In his own desire for quick money, Wilhelm went to Hollywood in the hope of becoming an actor. There he married, and it was soon clear that both his marriage and his career were mistakes. Bringing his family East, Wilhelm sold baby furniture for the Rojax corporation. This brief success turned to defeat when the president gave his son-in-law half of Wilhelm's territory. Separated from his wife, in love with another woman that he probably can never marry, jobless with a thinning bank account, Wilhelm falls into the hands of Dr. Tamkin, a con man who persuades him into investing his last seven hundred dollars in the stock market where Wilhelm is wiped out. The novel ends with Wilhelm stumbling into a funeral parlor in search of Dr. Tamkin. As he stands in front of the corpse, Wilhelm breaks into tears and sobs for the plight of man in general and of himself in particular in a pathetic display of total defeat.

Like so many of Bellow's other characters, Wilhelm is cut off from any meaningful kind of life. He is fatherless, having given up his father's name in Hollywood where he also lost the old man's respect. He is childless, having lost his two sons to his estranged wife. And he is loveless, having become cut off from his only sister, his wife, the girl he loves. Only Dr. Tamkin offers the possibility of hope, a hope that cannot be separated from the suspicion that Tamkin is a crook. Although Wilhelm (and the reader as well) is suspicious of him, Dr. Tamkin is the closest thing we have to a spokesman in a Bellow novel, and Tamkin's advice comes very close to the logotherapy of such existential analysts as Victor Frankl. Tamkin tells him that, like much of humanity, he is making his emotional sickness into a way of life. He insists that Wilhelm (there is probably a pun on the idea of "will") has the capacity to be more than he is, that he must become his own redeemer because "your own betrayer is inside of you and sells you out." Tamkin wants to bring people into "the here-and-now." He tells Wilhelm that what is important is "the real universe. That's the present moment. The past is no good to us. The future is full of anxiety. Only the present is real— the here-and-now. Seize the day." Tamkin tries to make Wilhelm see that he should not "spend the entire second half of your life recovering from the mistakes of the first half" and that a great number of men are more in love with death (as the end of the novel demonstrates) than with life. "There's [only] a small percentage . . . who want to live," Tamkin tells Wilhelm. "That's the only significant thing in the whole world today. Those are the only two classes of people there are. Some want to live but the great majority don't." Although these words fill Wilhelm with new hope, with desire for a new beginning, he is suddenly wiped out on the stock market, and his will is once again broken by defeat. While Tamkin may be a con man, he speaks truths that run through almost all of Bellow's fiction. Too much his father's son to think in any other terms but money, Wilhelm knows that the doctor has cheated him but fails to see that in another sense he received his money's worth. Life is too much for Tommy Wilhelm, who leads a choked, constricted, timid, mechanical, guilty, and meaningless existence, who constantly thinks of death because it is more real to him than life. As Wilhelm passes a hoary old fiddler in the street, the fiddler twice points his bow at him, a symbol that he is marked for death, indeed is part of the living dead. Wilhelm is incapable of going beyond the most restricted limits of his humanity. He is manipulated by others and overcome by a sense of the leaden city which weighs down upon him. What most distinguishes Bellow's fiction is his ability to depict the absurdity of everyday life, the casual horror of typical men whose lives are breaking apart, leaking the last drops of life. Because he is able to suggest that human possibilities await to be fulfilled, that human nature is something potential waiting to be realized, Bellow's novels are not pessimistic. Even as both Tommy Wilhelm and Augie March long for a new beginning, a new life with meaning, Wilhelm gives way to despair while Augie March is capable of hope. As in most existential fiction, the source of hope seems to be somewhere up ahead, luring us on. Like Augie, one must go in search of it before one can "seize the day." The urban claustrophobia of Wilhelm gives way to the hope of Augie on the road.

*Henderson the Rain King* goes beyond *Seize the Day* and shows Henderson in search of his destiny, in search of human possibilities, of a new beginning. Henderson, the first of Bellow's explicitly non-Jewish characters, is a WASP: his father was a friend of Henry Adams and William James, his great-grandfather was secretary of state, and his great-uncles were ambassadors to England and France. When his father died, Henderson inherited three million dollars, a large estate at Danbury, Connecticut, and a terrible sense of emptiness into which he pours quarts of bourbon. While Wilhelm was forty-four, Henderson at fifty-five is the oldest of Bellow's characters, except for Mr. Sammler. Twice married, he is the father of five children, of whom three are grown and separated from him. He plays the violin hoping to find the means of reaching something beyond himself, perhaps the spirit of his dead father. Like Wilhelm, Henderson often gasps for breath, as life suffocates him. A voice in his ear repeats "I want, I want," but he does not know what he wants, and he suffers from an aimless sense of dissatisfaction and restlessness. Seemingly he has everything; in reality he has nothing.

Where *Seize the Day* ends with the theme of death, *Henderson the Rain King* begins with this theme. Henderson's wife, Lily, asks him, "are you going to waste the rest of your life?" and Henderson does not know what to reply. His life is so empty that he often thinks of suicide, particularly in places like Chartres Cathedral "in the very face of this holy beauty"—that is, when, like Henry Adams, he confronts a source of meaning that is now dead for him and his era. In a marine station at Banyules, an octopus glares at him through the glass tank, and Henderson feels that "Death is giving [him] notice."

Henderson is physically as well as spiritually gross. Six feet four, a hulk of a man, his gut hanging over his belt, he feels most at home with—indeed, feels a part of —the pig herd that he has brought onto his estate. When his wife rents one of the smaller houses on the estate to a young couple, Henderson rebuilds it so cheaply that his tenants almost freeze in the winter. When they complain, Henderson rants so violently that he literally frightens to death the fragile Miss Lenox, who cooks his breakfast. With Miss Lenox's death, Henderson realizes that he was a destroyer, a wrecker—that if he does not change, "Death will annihilate [him] and nothing will remain, and there will be nothing left but junk."

In his desire to overcome his sense of life as death, Henderson goes on a quest which takes him to Africa. There he is told by Queen Willatale of the Arnewi that he has *grun-tu-molani*, which means "desire to live." When he sees a herd of cattle dying of thirst because they are forbidden to drink from a cistern of water filled with frogs, he is shocked by the absurdity of this taboo, until he realizes that back in the States he was "dying of misery and boredom" at a time when he had material goods "abundant as the water in that cistern which cattle were forbidden to drink." If the mind can be a destroyer, it can also be a creator. But before he learns this truth, he learns that to know a problem is very different from solving it, and Henderson blows open the cistern when he meant only to blow out the frogs. If Henderson is here the schlemiel, his misguided act also marks an advance in his attempt to move from becoming to being. When Henderson comes to the aid of the Arnewi, he is acting for the first time for someone besides himself.

Despite his failure, Henderson goes beyond his pigness and asserts his humanity, a humanity as frail as his motives were misguided, but a humanity nevertheless. Henderson is learning what it means to be human.

In self-disgrace, Henderson leaves the Arnewi, moves deeper into the interior, where he is captured by the Wariri. When he is questioned about why he is traveling in this aimless way, Henderson comes to a conclusion that is the key to the novel, even though he knows that his inquisitor will never be able to understand this truth:

> What was I going to tell this character? That existence had been odious to me. It was just not the kind of reply to offer under these circumstances. Could I say that the world, the world as a whole, the entire world, had set itself against life and was opposed to it—just down on life, that's all—but that I was alive nevertheless and somehow found it impossible to go along with it? That something in me, my grun-tu-molani, balked and made it impossible to agree?

Henderson is here expressing an idea that Camus treated at length in *Le Mythe de Sisyphe*—that while death sets the limits for man, man must always oppose his death, instinctively assert his desire to live in the face of his limits. Man defines himself against the absurdity of death, keeps in motion, defies the emptiness of life circumscribed by death, and finds meaning in the moment. To do less was to be less than human and led to death-in-life, the kind of mentality from which Henderson is in flight. Life as opposed to death, the need for life to move in the face of its limits—these are the main ideas in not only *Henderson the Rain King* but also *Seize the Day* and *The Adventures of Augie March*.

As Henderson moves from pig to man, he learns not to go beyond what is human—to be more than human is as bad as to be less. Henderson tells Dahfu, the King of the Wariri, that "I had a great desire to do a disinterested and pure thing—to express my belief in something higher. Instead I landed in a lot of trouble." The king responds, "Do you not rush through the world too hard, Mr. Henderson?" Indeed he does, and in order for Henderson to learn to seize the day, arrest the moment with its simple meaning, he must not only give up the crudeness of the pig but learn the truth of the lion. Dahfu brings the terrified Henderson face to face with the lion Atti, telling him that Atti "will force the present moment upon you . . . lions are experiencers. But not in haste." Dahfu forces Henderson to contemplate the lion, to watch the way she strides, saunters, gazes, breathes, particularly the way she breathes, a point not lost upon Henderson who begins the novel with a terrible sense of suffocation:

> "I stress the respirator part," [Dahfu] said. "She do not breathe shallow. This freedom of the intercoastal muscles and her abdominal flexibility" (her lower belly, which was disclosed to view, was sheer white) "gives the vital continuity between her parts. It brings those brown jewel eyes their hotness. Then there are more subtle things, as how she leaves hints, or elicits caresses. But I cannot expect you to see this at first. She has much to teach you."
>
> "Teach? You really mean that she might change me."
>
> "Excellent. Precisely. Change. You fled what you were. . . . You have rudiments of high character. You could be noble. Some parts may be so long-buried as to be classed dead. Is there any resurrectibility in them? This is where change comes in."

The Lazarus theme runs through *Henderson the Rain King* and reaches a climax here. Henderson may indeed rise from the dead and join the living if he can simply realize the possibilities of his humanity which lies buried within him. Henderson has felt overwhelmed and intimidated, has made defeat into a way of life. If he can change his state of mind, he can change himself as well. While Bellow arrives at this conclusion from different sources than the existentialists, he also believes that human nature is not fixed, that existence precedes essence, that man can re-create himself, make himself into something different. That instead of repeating the "procession of human monsters the human imagination has created. . . . Think of what could be instead by different imaginations," Dahfu tells Henderson in words that bring the novel to its thematic peak. This involves risks, proved by the king himself when he falls victim to the half-trapped lion. We can betray and be betrayed; we can also create and re-create. Henderson comes out of "the prehuman past" and brings this truth back to civilization, hoping to overcome his "dead days" with a new beginning that involves Lily and a possible career as a doctor.

Henderson no longer feels as he did in the beginning that his going to medical school is a joke. After Miss Lenox died Henderson walked over to her house and looked at a cat in her tree; near the end of the novel this scene is reversed when the lion comes under the tree house and Henderson stares into his wild eyes. Henderson's brother Dick drowned, a fact that filled Henderson with guilt; in Africa Henderson found another brother in Dahfu, whose death is a source of inspiration. Henderson refused to let his fifteen-year-old daughter adopt a Negro child she found abandoned in the street; on the plane back to the States Henderson takes to his bosom a young boy whose parents have died in India. All of the elements at the beginning of the novel are reversed with Henderson's reversal of mind. His sense of death gives way to a sense of life, defeat to possibility, and despair to joy—joy in being alive and ready to tap the new-found (it is not an accident the plane lands in Newfoundland) possibilities that each man carries in his human heart. In *Henderson the Rain King*, Bellow takes us beyond existential despair, and the absurd gives way to new life.

The pattern which controls *Henderson the Rain King* is very much evident in *Herzog*. At the beginning of the novel, Moses E. Herzog feels much put upon. His second wife, Madeleine, has divorced him and is living in Chicago with Valentine Gersbach, once his best friend. With Madeleine, Herzog was attempting "a fresh start," and his disappointment is almost as complete as his sense of betrayal. Exhausted by anger, sickened by the loss of his little daughter, confused by the gratuity of his situation, Herzog is unable to concentrate on his university extension classes or upon his scholarly book—a study of the need to renew "universal connections in order to overturn the Romantic belief in the uniqueness of the Self." Herzog's scholarly subject mocks him because, ironically, he feels his own situation is unique but finds no universal connections to relieve his sense of misery. In search of order and meaning, he finds only chaos and misery.

More than any other of Bellow's death-obsessed characters, Herzog thinks of death and is closer to the dead than the living. "Do I want to exist, or want to die?" he asks himself at one point. He often recalls his dead father who came to Canada from Russia and failed as a farmer, baker, jobber, failed also in the dry-goods business, and as a sack manufacturer in the war "when no one else failed," failed as a junk dealer, marriage broker, and finally as a bootlegger when he was double-crossed by his own friend (the irony of repeated history is not lost on Herzog) when their loaded truck is hijacked and his father is severely beaten and thrown in a ditch. While his love for the family thrived, Herzog never forgot the way his father was berated in family discussion. Years later, he thinks back on these painful days when he "listened to the dead at their dead quarrels."

Death surrounds Herzog. Sandor Himmelstein arranges for an insurance policy as part of the divorce settlement, an act which enrages Herzog who screams, "Just now I don't feel like making arrangements for my death." Herzog journeys to Martha's Vineyard to visit an old friend, only to look into her face and think, "Death, the artist, very slow, [was] putting in his first touches." He visits his stepmother in Chicago and is touched by her frailty, her realization that she is part of "the living dead." Life in the city intensifies his sense of death. Herzog sees the buildings weighing upon the suppressed citizenry who are dulled, controlled, mechanized—turned into instruments of a workaday world. He is amazed by the demographers' estimate that half of the human beings born are alive in the twentieth century and thinks the very best and the very worst must be at work in human nature. The very best escapes his leaden eyes; the very worst seems omnipresent. When he goes into the New York subway, for example, he sees in the scribbling on the wall an intelligence less than human, and thinks of it as "minor works of death" and the crowd as mere "trans-descendence," intelligence turned downward.

All that he sees reinforces his "infantile terror of death" which has "bent and buckled his life into these curious shapes." Given this kind of mentality, we are not surprised to find Herzog writing letters to newspapers, public figures, friends and family, and to the dead, "his own obscure dead, and finally the famous dead." He asks himself, "But why shouldn't he write the dead? he lived with them as much as with the living—perhaps more." Behind Herzog's obsession with death is the fear that he "would die when thinking stopped." As a result, Herzog never stops thinking, tortures himself with abstractions, and tries to turn reality into language by writing the endless letters that he never mails. All in the name of Death.

Because Herzog is more obsessed with death than any of Bellow's other characters, the road back to life is more difficult for him to find. He perhaps begins this journey when he remembers his mother telling him that man cannot be separated from the earth from which he came. Just before she died, he is shocked by her nails "turning already into the blue loam of graves. She had begun to change into earth." Herzog begins to think of man as matter struggling into life—that is, into consciousness—with a desire to be more than his origins. More than mere earth, less than pure spirit, man is earth in-fused with spirit, flesh capable of consciousness, matter subject to desire and suffering. Herzog comes to believe that man must not deny his possibilities or forget his limits, that "I must . . . keep tight the tensions [be-yond] which human beings can no longer be called humans"—a residual truth in a Bellow novel.

All of Herzog's thinking touches this idea. As a scholar of intellectual history, he keeps in his mind the dialectic between the Romantic Self and Modern Apocalypse—between the romantic idea that man is limitless and the modern idea that man is doomed. Whereas Nietzsche's ideas led to an unwarranted optimism, Heidegger's ideas led to an unjustified pessimism. Nietzsche believed that nature, infused with a Dionysian spirit, had the capacity to absorb evil and forever renew itself. Opposed to Nietz-sche are the "German existentialists who tell you how good dread is for you, how it saves you from distraction and gives you your freedom and makes you authentic. God is no more. But death is." If he erred, Nietzsche at least erred on the side of life, and Herzog rejects the modern nay-sayers. Once he rejects the idea that "Death is God," he can fight his own way out of the living grave. At the root of modern man's pessimism is the mind, "our murdering imagination . . . which starts by ac-cusing God of murder" in order to satisfy "a sense of grievance."

Herzog's own sense of death and grievance sends him to Chicago bent on revenge. As he waited for his own lawyer in the New York courtroom, he listens to a num-ber of cases which depressed him—first that of a Negro who beat up a friend, then that of a transvestite, later a homosexual medical student who was entrapped in a subway toilet, and finally the horrible case of a mother who beat her child to death while her lover watched from the bed. Twice Herzog flees these courtroom scenes, choking for breath, thinking of death, insisting that "he must live"—that is, must find the justification to live—in the face of such inhumanity. The fear that Madeleine and Gersbach might, like the couple in the courtroom, be beating June sends Herzog to Chicago, where he retrieves his father's old pistol before he goes to Madeleine's house. The sight of Valentine giving June her bedtime bath is so tender that murder is forced from his heart. Like his father, Herzog will never use the gun. Before he can take satisfaction in the meaning of their common defeat, Herzog is once again victimized, or so he thinks—first by the truck driver who rams him from behind, then by the Chicago police who arrest him for carrying a loaded pistol, and finally by Madeleine herself who confronts him at the police station. It is thematically significant that Herzog is saved by his brother. "I really believe," he tells us at one point, "that brotherhood is what makes a man human. . . . 'Man lives not by self alone but in his brother's face.'"

Leaving his brother, Herzog goes to his run-down, forty-acre farm in Ludeyville, Massachusetts, where he finally puts aside "the question of death," finally rejects the modern prophets of apocalypse who tell us *that this is a doomed time, that we are waiting for the end, and the rest of it, mere junk from the fashionable magazines.*" While he does not give way to Nietzsche's excessiveness, Herzog comes close to it, especially when he feels in himself the vitality of the earth renewing itself as summer takes over. "He was surprised," he tells us, "to feel such contentment . . . contentment? Whom was he kidding, this was joy." Here, finally, his sense of death gives way to life—his dread to joy. No longer is Herzog forced to think in order to escape death. Instead he walks quietly into the woods "where the silence sustained him." It is at this moment—and again significantly —that his brother appears, so solicitous of his well-being that Herzog is brought to tears by his love. Although he rejects his brother's sincere help, Herzog does not reject his brother. He also does not reject Ramona, who followed him into the Berkshires from New York where, much like Arnold's lovers in "Dover Beach," their love affair seemed all that was good in a cruel, irrational world.

At one with his pastoral setting, confident of his brother's love, warmed by the love of Ramona, Herzog realizes that life is worth living. The simplicity of the novel's ending reinforces Herzog's final trust in simple things. He no longer needs abstractions to save him from his fear of death. He no longer needs to reject reality by turning it into the language of his letters, and he stops writing the letters altogether. Even words, for the moment, are too much for him, and he hesitates to tell Mrs. Tuttle to dampen the floor before sweeping for fear that it will break his new-found trust in simple reality, his simple faith that life will go on in the face of death—and carry Herzog with it. Once again, one of Bellow's quiet heroes has worked his way beyond the absurd, turning as he went from nay- to yea-sayer.

Bellow's Mr. Sammler is almost literally a Lazarus figure. Stripped naked, blinded in one eye by the butt of a German's rifle at the outset of the Second World War, he is forced to help dig a mass grave, fired on, and tumbled into the pit along with his dead wife. Sammler lives, crawls out from under the dead bodies, out from under the dirt that has been shoveled into the grave, and takes flight. In the Zamosht Forest he surprises a German soldier who pleads for his life just before Sammler shoots him. Later, Sammler will have second thoughts about this shooting, will answer the radical freedom of novelists like Mailer and Wright who allow murder in the name of self-fulfillment. Although he is brought to it by a desire for self-preservation rather than for reasons of ego, Sammler repudiates his act and goes on to reject "the idea that one could recover, or establish, one's identity by killing." In retrospect, Sammler feels that he was not really himself when he shot the German, that he was "less than human." He might have acted differently if he had "been eating, drinking, smoking," if his blood had been "brimming with fat, nicotine, alcohol, sexual secretions." In his flight from the barbaric and inhuman, Sammler finds a man who has kept a good deal of his humanity in the person of a Polish under-

ground fighter named Cieslakiewicz, who helps him escape the Germans by hiding him in a cemetery tomb,
once again inflicting upon Sammler the feeling that he
is one of the risen dead.

Years later, in New York with his eccentric daughter
Shula, Sammler feels obsolete. "Born in the old century
in the Austro-Hungarian Empire," Sammler stands in
incongruous contrast to the modern world with its constant change. He is misunderstood by his daughter, who
thinks that his book on Wells will make him famous;
by his niece, who provides for him out of a sense of pity;
by the children of his nephew—by Angela, too much the
victim of her own female chemistry; and by Wallace,
too much the victim of his madly pathetic get-rich
schemes. When Sammler attempts to speak on the
causes of the Second World War at Columbia, he is
shouted down by a new barbarian who charges that his
"Balls are dry. He's dead."

Indeed, Sammler seems to have escaped one grave
only to be entombed in another. New York embodies
for him "the collapse of civilization" as Western man
has known it. "You could smell the decay," he insists.
Mr. Sammler avoids the subway which reminds him of
a grave, of death, of entombment. He suffers from a
"tightness of the heart" and has trouble breathing, a
symptom he shares with many of Bellow's living dead.
The people he meets—the hustler Feffer, for example,
so much like Wallace Gruner—are mad, lead "a high-
energy American life to the point of anarchy and breakdown." Telephones give only busy signals, telegrams are
not delivered, and the mail is late. He cannot turn away
from a shabby building marked for demolition because
it symbolizes for him "future nonbeing." Mr. Sammler's
New York simply and clearly reflects "the suicidal impulses of civilization pushing strongly." He concludes
that everything was being done "to make it intolerable
to abide here, an unconscious collaboration of all souls
spreading madness and poison."

But if Sammler has risen from the dead once, he seems

capable of doing it again. Although New York entombs him, he is still aware of the seasonal change from winter to spring, and he takes heart in the new life renewing itself before his eyes. Although he has a sense of apocalypse, he works on his book on H. G. Wells which will reflect a "faith in an emancipated future, in active benevolence, in reason, in civilization." Convinced that Western civilization is doomed, Sammler thinks of men beginning a new form of life on the moon; obsessed by a sense of an ending, he ponders a new beginning.

On the 72nd Street bus, he sees a big, handsome, immaculately dressed black man—easily a brother of the king Henderson meets in Africa. Sammler watches in fascination as the Negro picks pockets and purses. When the pickpocket realizes that Sammler is on to him, he follows Sammler to his apartment, corners him in the empty lobby, and forces Sammler to look at his penis. Later Sammler thinks of this man "unbuttoning his puma-colored coat in puma silence to show himself. Was this the sort of fellow called by Goethe *eine Natur?* A primary force?" That is exactly what he seems to be—a life force in a city of death, a fact that becomes more obvious when Sammler's sadistic son-in-law opens up the Negro's face by hitting him with a bag of metal medallions.

The thematic meaning of the pickpocket is expressed again in the person of Dr. Gruner, Sammler's nephew by marriage, who has generously supported Sammler and Shula from the time they came to America. Gruner lies in a hospital bed, one of the many Bellow characters who waits to die as the story unfolds. The inevitability of Gruner's death stands in contrast to Sammler's desire for life. When Gruner dies at the end, Sammler looks into the dead face and ponders a man at once noble and limited (Gruner more than likely performed illegal operations for the Mafia), courageous and weak, unselfish and yet demanding, generous to his children and yet unforgiving. Gruner embodies human nature—man as both large and small, tragic and pathetic. As Sammler looks into his nephew's face, he realizes that we all live in the face of death, and he thinks of death as life's contract. Dr. Gruner met "the terms of his contract"— his life justified his death. Bellow cannot ask more of a character, and what is true of Dr. Gruner is also true of Mr. Sammler. Sammler tries to keep his humanity in a world that is falling apart; he embodies the Bellow hero at his best. Although he was born in a past era, Sammler is modern man caught in a world that seems both cruel and senseless. He lives in the face of death in all its forms, tries not to be less or more than human, and recognizes his limits as he bravely goes on in the face of them. Caught between the dead past and the dubious future, Mr. Sammler embodies life over death, good over evil, the human over the barbaric. In his own simple way, he is modern man in motion.

## Walker Percy

As in existential fiction, Walker Percy's novels take place in a prolapsed world, often cut off from the ordinary workaday world, where characters are haunted by the past and bound by the absurdity of their situation. Percy adds to this two states of narrative consciousness, one of perception and the other of reflection, and also a sense of the grotesque. We can document Percy's interest in existentialism from his many philosophical articles as well as from the novels themselves. His philosophical essays, usually written in a very technical and abstract language, have appeared in such journals as *Partisan Review, Philosophical and Phenomenological Research, The Modern Schoolman, The Journal of Philosophy, The Commonweal*, and others. The most important of these essays, "The Man on the Train: Three Existential Modes," is a study of alienation, its causes and possibly its cure. Percy is fascinated by the psychological condition of displacement, the kind of existential estrangement from self and surrounding that Camus described so brilliantly in *L'Étranger*. The alienated man no longer knows or cares who he is, where he is going, or why he is going there. He is Percy's man on a train, the commuter, staring blankly out the window at a landscape that both terrifies and bores him—bores him because it is all too familiar, terrifies him because he does not know what awaits him when he steps off the platform—alone.

Percy's alienated man is lonely and unloved, an isolated consciousness. He can find peace, however, through social communion, through sharing his concerns with someone equally or even more greatly plagued. The Bomb, for example, is not a real source of anxiety for him because "when everything else fails, [he can] always turn to [his] good friend back from Washington or Geneva who obliges [him] with his sober second thoughts—'I can tell you this much, I am profoundly disturbed.' "

There is a comfort in sharing such dread, a warmth like spending a sheltered evening by a cabin fire while the wind and sea roar outside. A far more disturbing question, according to Percy, is "What if the Bomb should not fall? What then?" This question implies no hope of deliverance, no way of escaping what Percy calls *everydayness*, no way out of the rat trap that the Bomb would bring so comfortably and so quickly. Percy believes that a sense of well-being often accompanies a public catastrophe, that the individual exorcises his personal fears when he knows that his suffering will be shared—something Camus described in *La Peste* when Cottard, a murderer hunted by the police, finds a sudden sense of well-being when the citizens of Oran fear the plague, just as he feared the police. One experiences dread only when the catastrophe is his alone, when the cancer is eating his loins or when the burden to succeed becomes his personal task, especially when those who have climbed the ladder did it alone and then abstracted the key to their success. "It is just when the alienated commuter reads books on mental hygiene which abstract immanent goals that he comes closest to despair." Abstract dictums on how to attain mental health are the surest cause for suicide. When the alienated commuter is told that Socrates, Jesus, Buddha, St. Francis were "emotionally inclusive," he "shook like a leaf."

What Percy repeatedly describes in his learned articles is a kind of "existential communion"—an overlapping of consciousness which breaks down the barriers between individuals, moves them from an I-It to an I-Thou relationship. He rejects Sartre's idea that hell is another person. "*L'enfer c'est autres*," Percy says. "But so is heaven." [1] Percy, in fact, rejects all phenomenological theories of consciousness—all attempts to "bracket" sense data and to regard it, as do most of the existentialists, as distinct in itself, beyond interpretation, explanation, and evaluation. Borrowing much from George H. Mead,[2] Percy maintains that the phenomenologists start with consciousness and never get back to reality. For Percy, consciousness is a public, not a private matter, "arising from the social matrix through language." [3] All consciousness is shared, the beauty or strangeness of an object linking people together, binding them like an accident to a common moment—to even a common fate. Thus, where Descartes would say, "I am conscious of this chair," and where Sartre would say, "There is consciousness of this chair," Percy says, "This is a chair for you and me."

Life thus becomes a search for shared consciousness, for a communion of mind, for the affirmation of self which can only be found in the reflection of another. Failure to find this—and what we are talking about, of course, is love—leads to nothingness, an emptiness of mind and soul, the blank stare of the commuter from the window of the eight-fifteen.

The way one moves from an I-It to an I-Thou relationship is by what Percy somewhat pretentiously calls *rotation*. The commuter breaks the circuit and destroys "everydayness." "The road is better than the inn," said Cervantes, a remark Percy takes literally to mean that salvation is in the journey, especially the aimless journey, which allows "pure possibility." Here the commuter is in motion, on the road, open to all experience that may come his way, under no personal or social pressure whatever. Here also the commuter is a kind of voyeur, seeing but not being seen, walking silently through dark streets and blackened fields, fondling the world with his eyes, or parking his camper at night noiselessly beside a house as does the central character in *The Last Gentleman*. The road becomes an escape from the responsibility others have to accept. This is the journey of Huck Finn, and like Huck's journey it is not an isolated one. Huck, Percy points out, has Jim, "a prepuberty vision of *la solitude à deux*."

What Percy is describing here is the romantic journey, the journey that dominates such twentieth-century novels as Sartre's *Les Chemins de la liberté*, Salinger's *The Catcher in the Rye*, Ellison's *Invisible Man*, Kerouac's *On the Road* and *Lonesome Traveler*, Bowles's *Let It Come Down*, Bellow's *The Adventures of Augie March*, and Styron's *Set This House on Fire*. One of the first romantic journeys was that of Childe Harold, an aimless pilgrimage, a search for oneself on the road. Percy's hero is in search of love—a communion of consciousness—and returns to the prolapsed world from which he escaped with the new-found hope that he can begin to put the pieces together.

The "return" (or the "repetition," as Percy also calls it) is a return to the past in search of self—a coming to terms with a haunted and guilt-laden world, a theme that abounds in Southern fiction. The traveler, delivered from everydayness, has a new perspective; this is a true "existential reversal," to use Percy's term, the mind now its own place, seeing what is unique in the scene, seeing the grotesque nature of reality, consciousness dominating the landscape, mind now ruling matter, the I and It at one.

These existential modes—alienation, rotation, and return—give the critic a cutting edge to examine Percy's novels—for *The Moviegoer* is a brilliant analysis of alienation, and *The Last Gentleman* is an ambitious attempt to describe the process of rotation and return.

*The Moviegoer* is the story of John Bickerson Bolling, sometimes called Jack, sometimes Binx. He runs a small branch of his uncle's brokerage firm, selling mainly a diversified stock and suffering horribly from everydayness: I lived, he says, "the most ordinary life imaginable."

In "The Man on the Train," Percy spoke of the strange gulf between the reality of the movies and the reality of life. Destry when challenged shoots all the knobs off the saloon sign and frightens away those who confront him. But "what if he missed?" asks Percy, "what if he missed?" There is no anxiety for the movie hero because the script is already written. The moviegoer, however, emerges from this staged world with a headache, and he is at best a poseur, modeling himself on William Holden or Gary Cooper, but aware that any moment he might "bump his nose." When the hero in the movie crosses a gulf, the rope is a foot above the ground. When the moviegoer does the same thing, he "is over the abyss."

John Bickerson Bolling is aware of the abyss, but his cousin Kate is really over it. Suffering from extreme anxiety, she is suicidal. Bolling treats her at first like a friend, then a lover, finally marrying her. When he takes her to a movie, she emerges at first as a "role player," until their "old friendship . . . falls victim to the grisly transmogrification . . . [the] horror."

Bolling himself is a kind of professional nice-guy, easily amused, jovial, understanding, and tolerant. Part of his easy-goingness stems from his indifference—or at least seeming indifference—and he appears at times like Camus's Meursault. When Meursault's boss asks him if he wants a better position in Paris, Meursault tells him that "I was quite prepared to go; but really I didn't care much one way or the other." When Bolling's Aunt Emily (Kate's stepmother) asks him if he wants to take up a more serious discipline—become a research scientist or a doctor, "make a contribution"—he answers, " 'No 'm.' "

He is neither happy nor unhappy in his everydayness. While he is indifferent to everything but simple and immediate pleasures—getting an immense satisfaction in patting the bovine behind of his luscious secretary (he has gone through a string of secretaries) and in movie-going—he is also sensitive to suffering, especially the physical suffering of his half-brother Lonnie, a hopeless cripple, and the mental suffering of Kate. There is also something sadomasochistic about him, cuffing around both Sharon (his secretary) and Lonnie, enjoying (more than as just a means to get Sharon's sympathy) a shoulder hurt in an automobile accident, and taking the suffering Kate upon himself with puzzling willingness. These qualities of character seem to be accidentally bestowed upon him, qualities of which Percy does not seem totally aware.

The novel is more consciously related to the ideas Percy worked out in "The Man on the Train." Bolling is aware of the "search"; he wants to get deeper and deeper into things, to "unify" them. He tells Kate: "[The search helps] you understand more and more specimens by fewer and fewer formulae. There is the big excitement. Of course you are always after the big one, the new key, the secret leverage point, and that is the best of it."

I am not exactly sure what this means, but Percy appears close to a definition of the romantic journey—the quest for a kind of essential self through an existential experience—an experience, that is, which brings a moment of sudden illumination and complete fulfillment. Such a moment is, of course, impossible—at least this side of death—and Percy seems well aware of this fact. Bolling, speaking of his romantic past, says: "A regular young Rupert Brooke was I, 'full of expectancy.' Oh the crap that lies lurking in the English soul." Later he is very hard on a young romantic he meets on the bus, feeling that "he will defeat himself, jump ten miles ahead of himself, scare the wits out of some girl with his choking silences, want her so desperately that by his own peculiar logic he can't have her; or having her, jump another ten miles beyond both of them and end by flee-ing to the island where, propped at the rail of his ship in some rancid port, he will ponder his own loneliness." This is a brilliant psychological insight into the romantic imagination, and one could not find a better description of Binx Bolling, even if he is aware of the romantic gulf between the ideal (the movies) and the real (life).

If there is "rotation" and "return" in *The Moviegoer* it is of a prosaic sort. Before they are married, Bolling and Kate venture to Chicago, a trip that is part business, part escape, and even part search. When Aunt Emily summons them home, she tells him of her disappoint-ment, that he has no sense of honor, no " 'sense of duty, a nobility worn lightly, a sweetness, a gentleness with women—the only good thing the South ever had and the only things that really matter in this life.' " She tells him that he is not really a gentleman, not really the last of this Southern breed, a discovery which, if it does anything, frees him from what seems to be a holy (or an unholy) burden.

The aura of the past—heroes and heroism—clutch at Bolling throughout the novel. His father, perhaps the crux of the problem, met a hero's death, and when Bolling and Kate in Chicago visit Harold Graebner who heroically saved Bolling's life in the war, Bolling gets a sadistic pleasure in tormenting him, in showing him how ten years have cut him off from his heroism, how in reality he is buried in the everydayness that anchors places like Wilmette, Illinois.

Thus Bolling returns also to a kind of everydayness, only now with Kate who, with his help, may also be able to make "the return." The novel ends with his sending her on a trivial errand, an errand that nevertheless fright-ens her. She is afraid to go—"alone"—but finally con-sents when Bolling tells her that while she is on the streetcar he will be thinking of her. He picks a cape jasmine, sticking through an iron fence, and gives it to her. As Kate leaves, she turns to him and says:

"I'm going to sit next to the window on the Lake side and put the cape jasmine in my lap?"

"That's right."

"And you'll be thinking of me just that way?"

"That's right."

"Good by."

"Good by."

This is a moment of communion, more religious than the host, and the only way back for Kate; it is a communion through consciousness, the comfort that comes with the understanding of love, that overlapping of consciousness which Percy has described in much different terms in his learned philosophical essays.

*The Last Gentleman* is in many ways similar to *The Moviegoer*. Two young boys, minor characters in each novel, await death. The main character in both novels devotes himself to helping either the physically or mentally ill. The dead father looms large—a model of conduct frighteningly hard to keep up with. The two central characters come from good Southern families; both have inherited a plot of land, a small cash settlement, and a larger moral and cultural endowment. Like Binx Bolling, Williston Bibb Barrett has a sense of the haunted past; he visits Civil War battlefields and ponders what Richmond, Virginia would be like today if the South had won the war. Most of all, Barrett is burdened by the memory of his father and tries to live an honorable, courteous, dutiful life, to be a protector of women, a real gentleman. Despite his good intentions, he has his problems, primarily because he suffers from displacement and because he has a sense of unlimited possibility —so unlimited that he is unable to commit himself to anything. He also suffers from occasional attacks of amnesia which Percy has termed "the perfect device of rotation," because it wipes out in an instant everydayness. Perfect rotation can only be attained by progressive amnesia in which the forgetting keeps pace with time, so that every face is that of a stranger, every woman loved is a new affair.

In *The Moviegoer*, objects exist in a well of consciousness, as objects in themselves and as objects for contemplation. In *The Last Gentleman*, objects exist in a well of time also, the past always superimposed on the present because Barrett, an engineer in charge of Macy's air-conditioning, has a continued sense of *jamais vu*: "he forgot things he had seen before, but things he had heard of and not seen looked familiar." As a result, he is continually dislocated, never at ease wherever he is, with the landscape a continual assailant. He can be at home only where people were homeless, and for this reason has come to New York because there everyone seems happy because everyone is unhappy, as if the Bomb were about to fall: "his own happiness had come from being onto the unhappiness beneath their happiness. It was possible for him to be at home in the North because the North was homeless." He is a voyeur's voyeur, attempting to discover the essences of things—not on the road, at least at first—but with a $1,900-canister-jam-packed-with-the-finest-optical-glasses-and-quartzes-ground-annealed-rubbed-and-roughed-tinted-and-corrected-to-a-ten-thousandth-millimeter-telescope.

Here we are again back with the moviegoer in search of essences, a crystallizing experience, a moment caught and held, perhaps in the finely ground lens of an expensive telescope; when this happened "he would know the secret of his life." Barrett finds no such moment, although focusing the telescope from point zero (as described in the *New York Times*) of a possible atomic attack, he spies a woman who eventually leads him out of Central Park and up to a hospital in Washington Heights where he meets an old Southern family, acquaintances of his father (such a sinister and mysterious network of paths his father left behind). A strange family it is with its Big Daddy, a D.A.R. mother, a beautiful twenty-one-year-old daughter (Kitty, who becomes "the love of his life"), and her brother (Jamie, who is slowly dying of leukemia).

At this point the novel falls to pieces—Barrett agrees to return (the word is significant) South with them where, in various unlikely ways, he encounters a photographer (modeled most likely on the novelist, John Howard Griffin, author of *Black Like Me*) who has dyed his skin black and is passing as a Negro, becomes involved in what appears to be the James Meredith riot at the University of Mississippi, becomes entangled in the violence of the civil rights movement, meeting during this experience a movie star (who appears to be Marlon Brando) and a Negro playwright (modeled on James Baldwin), and eventually ends up in New Mexico attending to Jamie on his deathbed.

Two other characters also "oversee" Jamie's death: Jamie's derelict brother, Dr. Sutter Vaught, an agnostic, who attends to Jamie's physical state; and his sister Val, a Roman Catholic nun, who is preoccupied with his soul and insists that Jamie be baptized before he dies. Barrett is caught in the crossfire between this strange couple. While he is willing to entertain Val's religious beliefs, he is particularly drawn to Sutter for his own release, feeling that Sutter can give him the truths for which he is in search. What he wants more specifically is for Sutter to limit his sense of possibility, reduce the area of choice, tell him what to do. As Sutter angrily remarks to him:

> "You either want me to tell you to fornicate or not to fornicate, but for the life of me I can't tell which it is."
> "Then tell me," said the engineer smiling.
> "I will not tell you."
> "Tell me to be chaste and I will do it . . . [or] tell me not to be chaste."
> "I will not."

In his notebook, Sutter has shrewdly perceived that "Barrett . . . thinks . . . if only he can locate the right expert with the right psychology, the disorder can be set right and he can go about his business." Sutter must release him from the words of his father who told him that the white trash, with whom the father has battled, have won out: "Once they [the white trash] were the fornicators and the takers of bribes and we were not and that was why they hated us. Now we are like them. . . . They know they don't have to kill me." When the father thought the new South was hopeless, beyond salvation, he committed suicide. It was for this reason that Barrett is reluctant to let Sutter go after Jamie's death, fearing that Sutter, like his father, might commit suicide (Sutter has so threatened), and fearing also that he will lose his last chance of salvation—for as much as he loves Kitty and wants to "return" to the "everydayness" of the South, he cannot do it unless Sutter approves. He needs Sutter to "certify" his own existence. " 'Do you have to know what I think before you know what you think?' " Sutter asks him at the end. The answer, of course, is yes; it is Sutter, not the priest, who must shrive him, and the novel concludes open-ended, Barrett racing after Sutter, stopped in his beat-up Edsel, hoping for the answer he wants to hear.

The "return" in Percy's novels is always for two, never one, and Sutter in his own way needs Barrett as much as Barrett needs him. Kitty is not really a major character in this novel; she offers Barrett a *way* of life; Sutter offers him the *means* to that life. The novel thus stops far short of any kind of final consent—to religion, to the domestic life, to the routine of everydayness.

*Love In the Ruins* (1971), Percy's most recent novel, in some ways picks up where *The Last Gentleman* leaves off. Dr. Thomas More is cut off from his religion (the novel is subtitled "The Adventures of a Bad Catholic at a Time Near the End of the World"); from anything like domestic life (his wife has deserted him, his daughter has died of neuroblastoma, and he has taken to the bottle); and finally More is cut off from the everyday world (he cannot bridge the chasm between body and mind, between what he thinks and what he sees). While More shares many qualities with Percy's other characters, *Love In the Ruins* is a very different kind of novel for Percy. It is both fantasy and satire. Set in the future, it describes a divided America that finally comes to ruin: "Americans have turned against each other; race against race, right against left, believer against heathen." The Catholic Church has split into three groups and feuds among itself at the same time that it battles nonbelievers. The most powerful branch is the American Catholic Church which emphasizes property rights and the integrity of neighborhoods, and which plays *The Star-Spangled Banner* at the elevation of the host.

Like so many others in this mad world, Dr. More is a walking contradiction. He suffers from simultaneous depression and exaltation, hate and love, trust and mistrust. Unable to reconcile the contradictions that sunder himself from himself, Dr. More suffers a mental breakdown. He thus joins the many characters in modern fiction for whom madness is the final end, or the final end but one —suicide. When Dr. More cuts his wrists, he asks himself that question that connects him with characters as diverse as Meursault and Jacob Horner: Is life worth the effort? Like his predecessors, he decides to believe that life can be joyous. He recovers enough to work on his invention, a lapsometer, which allows him to measure the electrical activity of the brain and correlate his reading with personality traits. Dr. More is thus able to determine the anxiety or rage level of his patients. While this work does not cure him, he finds that his own "insanity" gives him a means of understanding. Once again, being crazy in modern America seems preferable to being sane. "Not being crazy, being sane in a sane world, is the craziest business of all," Dr. More concludes.

Dr. More's story would end here if Dr. Immelmann did not come upon the scene. Immelmann has discovered the means of using the lapsometer to both generate and relieve emotional conditions. Ideally, this will lead man back to paradise, will allow him to reconcile body and spirit, control love and hate, anxiety and ennui, depression and exaltation. However, for political reasons, Immelmann uses the lapsometer to increase the contradictions within the individual. This leads to a state of emotional war between Christian and atheist, the Right and the Left, poor and rich, black and white, and scientist and humanist. When disaster seems inevitable, More retreats with three of his girl friends to an abandoned Howard Johnson motel to wait out the holocaust. The novel ends with More marrying Ellen, his nurse. Like a new-day Adam, he starts all over again in a new world. But the world is not really that new. The old arguments are revived to justify the old injustices, although now the oppressed is sometimes the oppressor, and the old feelings of anxiety and distraction-of-self seem all too visible. Ellen is a consolation, perhaps Dr. More's only consolation, proving that love can make even the ruins tolerable.

Like so many recent novels, *Love In the Ruins* describes a world gone mad, a world that challenges understanding. Like Bellow's Mr. Sammler, Dr. More is a secular saint who refuses to become the victim of the absurd or to accept the madness that others impose upon him.

# 6

# Man and his Fictions: Ellison, Pynchon, Heller, and Barth

When the metaphysical rebel rejects God, he assumes that man is responsible for history. When man can no longer define himself in relation to God, he can at least define himself in relation to the past and to his own immediate times. Unlike Hegel and Marx, the existentialist rejects the teleological belief that history is being directed toward some predetermined end. He can accept Carlyle's belief that history is the record of the human mind as it manifests itself in action without, of course, the Carlylean belief that these motives are being directed from beyond. Faulkner's Quentin Compson despairs when he can find no meaning in the past; and while Sartre disliked Faulkner's obsession with the past, Sartre's own Mathieu suffers the same kind of bewilderment when he tries to come to terms with events in Europe before the Second World War. In fact, in *Les Chemins de la liberté*, as we have seen, Sartre used the techniques of John Dos Passos to describe the way modern man miscommitted himself to the historical moment, a question Camus pursued in *L'Homme révolté*. When history loses its meaning life becomes absurd.

The theme of the betrayed past as the source of the absurd has been more vividly portrayed by American than by French writers. Perhaps the classic treatment of this theme is *The Education of Henry Adams*, a book which I see as central to an understanding of modern American literature. Writing about events—some of which occurred over a hundred years ago—Adams depicts a vanishing genteel world that is completely different from the postwar worlds of Sartre and Camus. Adams, however, shared Sartre's and Camus's sense of displacement, their struggle to arrest and give meaning to the absurd moment. *The Education* is an unsuccessful attempt to find meaning and belief in the face of history. It is the story of a patrician, the great-grandson of one American president and grandson of another, who tries unsuccessfully to find his place in a world that will no longer accommodate his class. *The Education* begins with Adams telling us that "for him, alone, the universe was thrown into the ashheap and a new one created." Adams discovers that his eighteenth-century education with its faith in reason cannot resolve the problems of a new financial-industrial world.

As he struggles to find something that he can believe in, Adams's education becomes a journey into self, really a paring away of the self until it is devoid of illusion. *The Education* develops the history of personal miscommitment, a sense of the betrayed past, as Adams becomes disillusioned in turn with the Quincy of his childhood, with Boston being invaded by a new financial class and by Irish immigrants, with Washington and the Free Soil Party, with Harvard and its genteel education, with Berlin University and its dreary lecture system, with England and her pro-Confederate sympathies during the Civil War, with the ideas of Darwin which maintained a line of progress that Adams could not find, with his teaching at Harvard when he could not answer his own questions, and with the corruption of the Grant administration which embodied for him what America was becoming. The Virgin could give the illusion of meaning to the Middle Ages, could supply the imaginative means of a mythical unity and centripetally pull an age together. The Dynamo offered no such syncretistic resolution for modern man but became instead a symbol of centrifugal force, of the fragmented self caught in a process of motion which the mind could neither arrest nor give meaning.

Mark Twain also felt that man was caught in a spiral

descent which we ironically call civilization. As man moved from bows and arrows to gunpowder and dynamite, he increased the means of destruction without increasing the moral means of controlling himself as history became nightmare. This apocalyptic idea can be found at the end of *A Connecticut Yankee in King Arthur's Court* as well as "The Chronicle of Young Satan" version of "The Mysterious Stranger." Twain offers us an escape hatch of sorts when Philip Traum (dream) tells Theodore, "But I, your poor servant, have revealed you to yourself and set you free. Dream other dreams, and better!" Traum explicitly connects man's fate with his dream—his conception of himself. If man is approaching what appears to be the dead end of history, it is because he has failed to see other possibilities, has become the victim of his own vision. "Dream other dreams, and better."

Hart Crane picks up the theme of the downward drift of history in *The Bridge* as he moves us from the unified vision of Columbus, to the equally vital vision of Pocahontas, to the passing of the Indians, to the passing of the frontier and the great cutter ships, to the drunken sailor in the saloon, to the mythic woman now belly dancer, to the airplane that falls from the sky over Cape Hatteras, to the city as modern hell. Like Twain, Crane also tells us that we have failed our vision, that modern man is doomed unless he can create and perpetuate a new vision—"a better dream."

Crane, of course, was influenced by Walt Whitman. He was also influenced by Nietzsche; and when we scrape away the residue of Emersonian Transcendentalism, we come close to the existential idea that man can become the product of his own mind, which leads to a form of radical individualism. Such belief in the individual frees man from God and Church and a deterministic view of history. It frees him from the demands of class, the fixed manners agreed upon and shared by the characters in a Henry James or Edith Wharton novel. Those manners had already begun to crumble by the time we get to F. Scott Fitzgerald, whose Gatsby and Dick Diver are separated from the establishment by birth, and whose Nick Carraway realizes that the Buchanans are really the new destroyers. The Buchanans parody "the old courtesies," the code of honor, indeed chivalry, that Dick Diver can admire in his father but not find in himself or his contemporaries. The radical freedom of existentialism also freed man from the idealized past—the past of a William Dean Howells who in a *Traveler from Altruria* and *Through the Eye of the Needle* tried to return us to a kind of rural utopia at a time when the big city and technology had already sealed us off from another era, and the idealized past of Ezra Pound who tried to return us to the Quincy of John Quincy Adams and later the city-state of fifteenth-century Italy. Finally, existentialism freed man from the genteel despair of T. S. Eliot who depicted the fragmented self entrapped in an industrial, power-driven wasteland made up of displaced aristocrats, idle rich, bad-teethed women, and pathetic clerks, all of whom are bored and loveless in an ugly city where machines throb in the twilight hour.

All of these writers capitulated to a world that was too much for them and found solutions that allowed the individual to escape responsibility: Howells into Christian socialism, Pound into fascism, James and Eliot into the fixed comforts of their class and then into the insulated comforts of artistic consciousness before Eliot took the final step and gave consent not only to Adams's Virgin but to her Church as well. Caught between a world that was dying and another powerless to be born, they gave us characters who embody their own sense of helplessness, portrayed men of paralyzed will like John Marcher, Prufrock, Mauberley, and Nick Carraway. These men cannot move on; at best they take flight into the world of the past, like Mauberley and Carraway; they are just the opposite of men in motion.

These characters seem to have lost the sustaining myth, an idea that most concerned Henry Adams, who felt that the myth of the Virgin gave medieval man a sense of purpose which modern man had lost. The dynamo could not supply a countermyth; moreover it fed on natural resources and thus depleted nature physically while it depleted man spiritually. Adams decried undirected motion, but he saw no way of directing human motion without a redeeming fiction which could subsume the dynamo and restore human priorities. With the second law of thermodynamics in mind, Adams saw modern man caught in the forces of entropy, dependent upon the machine which accelerated waste until the whole process burned itself out and we were left with— and one can choose the image—a wasteland (T. S. Eliot), a Valley of Ashes (F. Scott Fitzgerald), Pisa after the war (Ezra Pound), Mr. Sammler's New York (Saul Bellow), an underground coal pile near riot-torn Harlem (Ralph Ellison), a bombed-out Rome (Joseph Heller), or the frozen land of Vheissu (Thomas Pynchon).

Adams's own despair was genuine enough, and perhaps all that saved him from it was his ability to create his own personal redeeming fiction—an ironic mode which allowed him self-consciously to depict himself as the last embodiment of the landed gentry, an honorable man born a century too late and thus displaced by the materialism of the new Caesers who control the dynamo. In disparaging his education, Adams ironically affirmed it, substituting his own fiction for that of his age, which perhaps gave him at the end of *The Education* the capacity to take charge of his fate, as the title of the last chapter indicates: "Nunc Age" means "act now."

## Ralph Ellison

While it works with a different notion of experience than Adams's *Education*, Ralph Ellison's *Invisible Man* is also a kind of education and reveals even more clearly how such a work approaches existential meaning. *Invisible Man* has its most obvious origins in Negro experience, especially in a boy's memories of being black in the South, in his hope of succeeding in the industrial North after he has left the agrarian South, in his Harlem experiences, in his stereotyped experiences with characters like Rinehart and Ras the Exhorter, in his understanding of the rhythms of jazz and the blues, and in his experiences with black colloquialism as it is found in the sermon and the street. Yet *Invisible Man* is more than a novel about race. As the narrator asks in the very last sentence of the novel, "Who knows but that, on the lower frequencies, I speak for you?" Elsewhere he says, "Our task is making ourselves individuals. We create the race by creating ourselves." Even more to our point, he says, "I knew it was better to live out one's own absurdity than to die for that of others." While the influence may be remote, Ellison himself has documented his interest in existentialism. In his essay "Society, Morality, and the Novel," he says that Sartre, Camus, Kierkegaard, and Unamuno are the chief heroes of the modern world.

*Invisible Man* is a novel about commitment and mis-commitment, about order dissolving into disorder, sanity giving way to madness, visibility to invisibility, and (ironically) illusion to reality, and darkness to light. From the beginning to the end of the novel, the un-named narrator intuits forces at work—various forms of power—which seem ready to absorb him, until at the end, illuminated of mind, he has tapped into Monopo-lated Light & Power and made the power work for him. Even at the college, a kind of Eden, he is aware of "the black powerhouse with its engines droning earth-shaking rhythms." As he listens to Homer Barbee's impassioned speech about the founder, he hears "the power engines far across the campus throbbing in the night like an ex-cited pulse." Bledsoe later tells him that he controls this power: "I's big and black and I say 'Yes, suh' as loudly as any burrhead when it's convenient, but I'm still the king down here. . . . When you buck against me, you're bucking against power, rich white folk's power."

Bledsoe is the white man's flunky; he is the custodian

of the white man's power. He signs his letters to the white trustees "your humble servant." As president of the black college, he enslaves the black man to the white man's God, educates him to accept the white man's stereotypes, and sells the black man the white man's dream. He keeps the black man running, as he sends the narrator running, toward those promises that are always just beyond the horizon. Without Mr. Norton, however, there would be no Bledsoe. As benefactor to the college, Norton thinks of himself as a god, and he insists that the black man's fate is a part of his destiny. Each spring he returns to the campus to renew that sense of destiny, ironically unaware of the pitiful black life that surrounds the campus. While the campus is amazingly green, it is really a wasteland: a broken fountain, corroded and dry, belies even the hope of water; and the road by the powerhouse crosses a dry riverbed before it moves on to the insane asylum.

The narrator takes Mr. Norton down this road where he meets Mr. Trueblood and then the vets at the Golden Day. Trueblood embodies the black man in his most elemental state, once removed from slavery, the victim of his ignorance and passions, uninhibited even to the extent that he seduces his own daughter, a fact that shocks Norton who had subliminal desires about his own daughter. The vets at the Golden Day represent the other extreme. They embody the black man in his most inhibited state, broken by the system. Most were formerly doctors, lawyers, teachers, civil service workers —that is, products of the college. The road from Trueblood's shack, past the college, runs indeed for some to the insane asylum—or the coal pile. Whereas Trueblood is pure libido, the vets are pure superego, restrained as they are by an attendant with the thematically obvious name of Supercargo. When the vets overcome Supercargo, they are free of inhibitions and go wild, whirling "about like maniacs." Their frenetic rioting anticipates the apocalyptic moment when the black race will throw off its psychological shackles and engage in a dance of death, as indeed seems to happen at the novel's end with the riot in Harlem.

Between the uninhibited madness of Trueblood and the inhibited insanity of the vets stands the college wherein the narrator expects to find himself. When he is expelled, he loses not only a sense of place but a sense of self. The last words spoken to him as he leaves the South are those of Crenshaw, the craziest (sanest?) of the vets, who is being removed to St. Elizabeth's hospital in Washington because he is too dangerous. "Remember," says Crenshaw, "the world is possibility if only you will discover it," words that will be picked up at the end of the novel.

As the unnamed narrator found himself caught between extremes in the agrarian South, so also he finds himself caught between extremes in the industrialized North, where the possibilities that await him are at best illusions. (On Wall Street he sees black runners, slaves to the system, "with leather pouches strapped on their wrists" instead of manacles. The misplaced hope of freedom seems best symbolized by the Statue of Liberty, "her torch almost lost in the fog.") Once he moves beyond the workaday world of Liberty Paints (which surrealistically helps keep black and white distinct), he finds himself involved at one extreme with the Brotherhood, a euphemism for the Communist party, which seems to offer solidarity of purpose. Brother Jack convinces him that history is on their side. Bledsoe spoke in the name of the blacks but had his own selfish motives in mind. When Tod Clifton is gunned down, the narrator realizes that Brother Jack also has his own selfish interests in mind, that he wants to organize the blacks for the good of the party and not for the good of the blacks. Tod had "fallen outside of history," abandoned the party and parodied his race by selling Sambo dolls. The narrator refuses, however, to judge Tod because he no longer believes that men can be judged absolutely against a Marxist view of history, against a mechanical process that turned men into machines. As for Tod, he felt that he "knew neither the extent of his guilt nor the nature of his crime." The narrator refuses to substitute one form of tyranny for that of another, Brother Jack and the Brotherhood for Bledsoe and Norton, history for God, one illusion for another. "What if history was a gambler, instead of a force in a laboratory experiment," he asks, "or a madman full of paranoid guile?"

Opposed to Jack and the Brotherhood is Ras the Exhorter, a black nationalist, an inverted racist, who encourages the blacks to overthrow the whites. The narrator learns to his horror that Ras and the Brotherhood, deadly enemies with opposed motives, are unwittingly working together to bring about a race riot in Harlem. Ras wants the blacks to revolt because he hates the whites; the Brotherhood wants blacks to revolt because they need martyrs for their cause. As the race riot is about to begin, the narrator shouts to the crowd that he has been betrayed by the Brotherhood. He then points to Ras and tells them that the Brotherhood wants the riot and "needed this *destroyer* to do their work. They deserted you so that in your own despair you'd follow this man to your destruction. Can't you see it? They wanted you guilty of your own murder, your own sacrifice!"

Between the extremes of the Brotherhood and Ras the Exhorter stands Proteus Rinehart, the man of many masks, the creature of his own imagination. His world is total possibility so long as he is willing to play the part: "The world in which he lived was without boundaries. A vast seething, hot world of fluidity." If the college offered the narrator a fixed sense of self, Rinehart offered no sense of self at all, or every sense of self, which amounted to the same thing. Rinehart embodied the purest form of invisibility with the important difference that he kept himself from being seen rather than merely being taken for granted by Bledsoe, Norton, Emerson, and Brother Jack. Rinehartism fails the narrator because its consequences are too dangerous. The role he plays with Brother Maceo almost turns into a deadly fight, and he finds it too difficult to act the part with Sibyl who wants to be "raped" by a black man: "Such games were for Rinehart, not me."

Like Adams's *Education, Invisible Man* is a journey into self. Before he can find out who he is, the unnamed narrator has to find out who he is not. As in *The Education*, we move through history, in this case the history of the black man in America in an unsuccessful search for commitment. Each experience is a kind of death as he leaves his past irretrievably behind him. He says good-bye to home, long remembering the words of his grandfather who was once in slave's chains. He leaves his home town after he talks at the men's smoker, the blood from the free-for-all choking his words. He leaves the college, bewildered by Bledsoe and Mr. Norton and his experience with Trueblood and the vets at the Golden Day. In all of these scenes, he is restrained by his "superego," the restricting voice of society. Like the vets, the narrator must divest himself of all forms of false restraints before he can free his unconsciousness and "create his race by creating himself." He is helped along by Mr. Emerson, who shows him Dr. Bledsoe's letter in a scene that derives its meaning from Ralph Waldo Emerson's work as an abolitionist. (Ralph Ellison's middle names are Waldo Emerson.) Now cut off from the agrarian South, the narrator must move through the historical experience of the industrial North, a fact rather obviously suggested by the electric nodes attached to his head and navel in his operation, after which he says "I could no more escape than I could think of my identity. Perhaps, I thought, the two things are involved with each other. When I discover who I am, I'll be free." Before he can be free, he must reject the Lucas Brockways (Blockways?) who want to see other blacks kept in their place so they will be no threat to him, even though he has a most menial job himself. He must also reject Mary, the prototypical mother, who wants him to be careful, to conform, to succeed in the white man's world. As we have seen, before his journey into history is over, he must reject Jack and the Brotherhood because to Jack he is simply an economic pawn in the dialectical play of history. He must also reject Ras the Exhorter, the black nationalist whose belief in Negro racial supremacy leads to violence and death.

At this point, the narrator has exhausted modern history. He has no other forms of commitment. The end of *Invisible Man* is even more of a beginning than Adams's *Education*. The hero is now aware of who he is not, aware also that he was destined to exhaust the historical moment so that his end was absurdly contained in his beginning. This realization comes in the glare of his highly illuminated underground room, a Dostoyevskian detail which suggests that he has gone beyond his own early blindness (he is blindfolded when he fights at the stag party) and the blindness of those he meets (Homer Barbee is blind and Brother Jack has only one eye):

> And now I realized [concluded the narrator] that I couldn't return to Mary's, or to any part of my old life. I could approach it only from the outside, and I had been as invisible to Mary as I had been to the Brotherhood. No, I couldn't return to Mary's or to the campus, or to the Brotherhood, or home. I could only move ahead or stay here, underground. So I would stay here until I was chased out. Here, at least, I could try to think things out in peace, or, if not in peace, in quiet. I would take up residence underground. The end was in the beginning.

Despite the retreat to the coal pile, Ellison's hero tells us in an epilogue that between the fixity of Jack and Ras and the freedom of Rinehart are "infinite possibilities," by which he means that the imagination can re-create and thus redeem history, an idea that Ellison leaves at best vague and perhaps even contradictory. "I whipped it all except the *mind*. And the mind that has conceived a plan must never lose sight of the chaos against which that pattern was conceived," says the narrator at the end. Rinehart embodies the mind at its most inventive work, but the mind that steps outside of historical reality steps into chaos. As a black man, Ellison's protagonist is invisible on the coal pile, which embodies the absurd moment, history exhausted of meaning. He cannot go back to Mary, Bledsoe, Norton, Emerson, or Jack, personifications of the dead past, of the historical possibilities that he has rejected. He is also discontent with thinking on the coal pile, with pure thought disembodied from action, and will eventually come out. But in the meantime the mind seems unable to commit itself to action, fiction seems unable to redeem history by creating a new sense of possibility. Historical possibility is fuel for the imagination, but Ellison's protagonist has exhausted his sense of historical possibility. Jack cannot save Rinehart or Rinehart save Jack. *Invisible Man* ends on an ambiguous note. Ellison's protagonist believes that the final source of order is within himself, but he also believes that he has jumped ahead of history and must wait for it to catch up. Then he will be able to move from thought to action. Even though it ends with the protagonist giving us the existential message that "life is to be lived, not controlled; and humanity is won by continuing to play in the face of certain defeat," Ellison's novel stops short of an existential conclusion. The strict existentialist believes that thought is action, that thought leads to motion. Unlike Ellison's narrator, he believes that man makes rather than waits for history.

### Thomas Pynchon

Like Ellison's *Invisible Man*, Thomas Pynchon's *V.* shows us that when we exhaust the possibilities of history we are left with the absurd. *V.* is a long, madcap novel with two plots that eventually converge. In one plot, Herbert Stencil is in frenetic pursuit of the mysterious woman V. whom we suspect and later learn is his mother. She appears in many guises—first as a nineteen-year-old Yorkshire girl named Victoria Wren, then as a young temptress in Florence seducing Stencil's father, later as a lesbian in Paris where she is having an affair with a young ballerina who dresses as a boy, then as Veronica Manganese in Malta, and later as Vera Meroving in southwest Africa, and finally as a "bad" priest in Malta where she dies in an air raid during the Second World War. As V. moves through the novel she loses various parts, until at the end she is disassembled by a bunch of children who find her imprisoned under a roof beam in a demolished building. In as grotesque a scene as we have in modern literature, the children pull off her wig, take out her glass eye with a clock for a pupil, detach her artificial legs, and finally kill her when they dig a star sapphire from her navel.

V. embodies the historical decline of Woman from sex goddess to lesbian and transvestite—from mother to manufactured object, from the human to the grotesque. As Don Hausdorff has admirably pointed out, she embodies what has happened to Henry Adams's Virgin: "Adams's Virgin-Venus, the fertility goddess of medieval illusion, never grasped by an American mind that was dominated by business and technology, has its counterpart in a V. that is progressively devitalized—and despoiled." [1] Indeed, the very key to this novel is Henry Adams's belief that history is running down, that life is a matter of *entropy*, to use the word that Pynchon entitled one of his short stories. Stencil is told this secret by a drug-wise, old sea captain:

> "You're old," the skipper mused over his nightly hashish. "I am old, the world is old; but the world changes always; we, only so far. It's no secret, what sort of change this is. Both the world and we, M. Stencil, begin to die from the moment of birth."

Herbert Stencil is contemporary man in search of his identity. What he learns from his extended and mad search is that history is a long, dead-end street:

> "Which way does it go? As a youth I believed in social progress of my own. Today, at age sixty, having

gone as far as I am about to go, I see nothing but a dead end for myself, and, if you're right, for my society as well."

"The only change is toward death," Pynchon tells us, and this truth has both personal and cultural meaning. Like Adams, Pynchon believes that Western man—with his expanding technological know-how, his dynamo— is moving further and further away from his own humanity, further and further away from the meaning of Adams's Virgin—the warm belief that humanity as symbolized by the life-giving woman is central to all belief, a centripetal idea that pulls everything into focus and gives man a sense of direction when in reality life is simply a matter of purposeless force working to exhaust itself. Western civilization has lost this saving illusion, has substituted the machine for humanity and decadence for belief. The key to the novel's whole meaning comes when we are told: "A decadence . . . is a falling—away from what is human, and the further we fall the less human we become. Because we are less human, we foist off the humanity we have lost on inanimate objects and abstract theories."

The second plot—the story of Benny Profane and the Whole Sick Crew—takes its meaning from the fate of V. Their whole absurd existence is the final outcome of V.'s story. Benny is the schlemiel as modern hero. Familyless, rootless, indifferent to all but creature comforts, he gets his greatest kicks from "yo-yoing," simply riding the subway up and down Manhattan—going nowhere. As Hausdorff points out, Pynchon's yo-yo is the *reductio ad absurdum* of Adams's dynamo. The yo-yo translates into human terms the idea of motion without direction, energy without thought, life without meaning. To yo-yo is to abandon the will and to let the machine move us— to become a mechanical man. As a result, when Benny goes to work as a guard at Anthroresearch Associates, he feels a kinship with two plastic "men" named Shroud and Shock, who are used to test the amount of radiation and physical force that man can withstand. Profane feels especially close to Shock who "was the first inanimate schlemiel he'd ever encountered." The only trouble with Shock is that the air in his lungs was controlled by a motor, the cooling vent of which was located in his crotch. Thus when a sexual injury was simulated, it blocked the cooling vent so Shock "could not therefore have a sucking chest wound and mutilated sexual organs simultaneously." The technicians, however, were hoping to resolve this deficiency.

Such humor reveals Pynchon at his best and reveals also his deep concern with the way that man is simply becoming an adjunct to the machine. As Shroud surrealistically tells Profane, "Me and Shock are what you and everybody will be someday." Indeed, after Dr. Schoenmaker "saws the hump" off Ester Horowitz's nose, he remakes her face as if it were a manufactured object. Moreover, he does not want to stop with her face, and later wants to work on her spine. The whole operation is like a sex act—he works "gently, like a lover"—and suggests in what way this kind of mechanical remodeling has replaced love. Just before Benny makes love to Rachel, he ponders if someday "there would be an all-electric woman. . . . Any problem with her, you could look it up in the maintenance manual."

In both plots, we see man becoming dehumanized, mere mechanical object, and the Benny Profane plot is directly related to the story of V. The death of Adams's Virgin is contained in both Schoenmaker's nose operation and in the equally gruesome scene in which the young ballerina dies impaled upon a spear in a dance appropriately titled the "Sacrifice of the Virgin." Pynchon believes that the machine age pushed the Puritan fear of women—that is, of sex—to its final destructive conclusion, led modern man "deeper into fetish-country" until the woman "became entirely and in reality . . . an inanimate object of desire." To this extent, the story of V. and the story of Rachel and Esther and all the other women in the novel is really one story. The V. story ends on Malta, "a matriarchal island," a detail that reinforces Pynchon's suggestion that perhaps "history is a woman."

In tracing the fate of Woman, Pynchon takes us metaphorically to the end of history, and where history stops the absurd begins, an idea that he shares with both Henry Adams and Ralph Ellison. We see this clearly in V. when Benny Profane goes underground to hunt crocodiles through Father Fairing's parish. History is put in absurd perspective when Father Fairing, convinced that except for its rats New York was doomed, moves into the sewer system and tries to convert to Catholicism all the rats between Lexington and the East River and between 79th and 86th streets. Although he runs into some difficulty with rats who have Marxist inclinations, he has more success with the rat Veronica, his mistress and/or nun-to-be, who reveals that the spirit of V. is all-pervasive. Since time is running out for all of us, it is no surprise when time runs out for Benny, who loses his job in the sewer. In words that echo the end of *Invisible Man*, he comes back to the surface and "what peace there had been was over." Benny's quest for meaning and Stencil's quest for V. and the lost city of Vheissu are two forms of modern "education." As with Henry Adams, history is a foe—an undirected, self-defeating force that cancels human certitude as surely as death cancels life.

The embodiment of this progression seems to be Vheissu. The second law of thermodynamics would guarantee that Henry Adams's universe would lose heat as entropy did its work. Pynchon's Vheissu, located roughly at the South Pole, reached by ascending large mountains and then through an elaborate network of caves, is motionless, lifeless, barren, and frozen. When Hugh Godolphin reaches it, he digs down several feet beneath the snow to find the corpse of a spider monkey buried in the ice. The monkey represents not only the last sign of life, but a mockery of human existence. As Godolphin says, "If Eden was the creation of God, God only knows what evil created Vheissu." The source of the evil seems to be within man himself, "falling away from what is human," giving himself to monster machines and monster systems that guarantee the lifelessness of a Vheissu.

While Vheissu embodies the main theme of V.— the belief that man is caught in a universe that is running down to an ultimate state of inert uniformity—its very existence may only be a figment of Hugh Godolphin's imagination: "Does it make any difference?" Godolphin asked. "If it were only an hallucination, it was not what I saw or believed I saw that in the end is important. It is what I thought. What truth I came to." Here Pynchon seems to be insisting that all reality, whether it be good or evil, is first a state of mind. Pynchon had told us earlier that Stencil "had decided long ago that no Situation had any objective reality; it only existed in the minds of those who happened to be in on it at any specific moment." Thus if Vheissu is a final nightmare state of human existence, man seems to have cooperated in his own destruction, seems to have created the state of mind that made a Vheissu an ultimate reality. Near the end of the novel, Benny is asked if he has learned anything. "Profane didn't have to think long. 'No,' he said, 'offhand I'd say I haven't learned a goddamn thing.'" Benny Profane, as his name implies, holds nothing sacred; unfortunately his dearth of imagination prevents him from supplying new myths to replace the old ones that he tears down. In Thomas Pynchon's V., modern man seems to be the victim of his dying imagination, of his inability to create the fictions that give meaning to motion.

## Joseph Heller

One source of the absurd in modern literature is the prolapsed world of Camus and Sartre, Oran in *La Peste* or the concentration camp in *Les Chemins de la liberté*, where the plague or military surrender has led to a world without a center, and where one has been cut off from an old way of life. In this fragmented world, one must construct himself once again, find new meaning, a new routine, a new system of moral and social values, a new way of measuring everything, including social status. Until there is once again a way of life which one can take for granted, every situation is unique and the individual lives estranged from everyone else, in an absurd and grotesque world.

The other source of the absurd is exactly the opposite kind of world—not the prolapsed world of Camus and Sartre but the overstructured and bureaucratic world of Kafka, where one does not exist if he does not have an I.D. card. This is the world of Heller's *Catch-22* (1961), where one is dead if his 201-file says he is dead, even if he is there to protest that the file is wrong.

Both worlds are sources of the absurd because they destroy meaning—the first destroys all preestablished social and moral dictums so that the individual becomes a kind of hopeless wanderer in a foreign land; the second destroys the validity of sensory data and of human communication by reducing all meaning to tons of official forms and to a chain of command that passes all responsibility up and then back down, until someone like ex-P.F.C. Wintergreen decides what should happen by forwarding some letters and destroying others. The two sources of absurdity—the chaos of the war and the mad system of bureaucracy—exist side by side in *Catch-22*, but the system for Heller is even more absurd than the war—a fact Captain Yossarian, Heller's main character, discovers one night in Rome when Lieutenant Nately rapes an Italian girl and then with impunity throws her out a window while Yossarian is arrested for being on leave without a pass.

While it reveals the dark underside of life, while it is at times amusing, *Catch-22*—inchoate and incohesive, cracking in places under its own weight—is not entirely successful. Heller is best at depicting an upside-down world where one wins by losing and loses by winning.

As an exercise in the absurd—the negation of a rational and meaningful world—not many novels can compete with *Catch-22*. Heller creates a sense of the grotesque and the incongruous—of *déjà vu*, that condition of mind which accepts the strange as familiar; and of *jamais vu*, that condition which accepts the familiar as strange. *Catch-22* presents a hallucinatory world which exists in reality: one in which the mind refuses to believe that a naked man *is in fact* sitting in a tree; in which one can get into serious trouble by disobeying an order given by an officer who has disobeyed orders in giving that order; in which one has to be insane to be discharged from the Air Corps, but in which the insane are willing to fight and thus have no desire to be discharged. The far-fetched and ludicrous events in this novel sometimes contain truths that freeze the smile in horror. Captain Black's Loyalty Oath Crusade is ridiculous only because it is a slight exaggeration of the truth: the captain, demanding that the men sign the oath before every meal, insists that Major Major, his hated rival, is a Communist because he has not signed the oath which the Captain refuses to let him sign. " 'You never heard him denying it until we began accusing him, did you?' " Corporal Whitcomb's classic letter, signed by Colonel Cathcart, only slightly distorts the sincerity of official letters of condolence:

> Dear Mrs., Mr., Miss, or Mr. and Mrs. ———: Words cannot express the deep personal grief I experienced when your husband, son, father or brother was killed, wounded or reported missing in action.

Such passages in *Catch-22* go beyond comedy. As Heller puts it, "I wanted people to laugh and then look back in horror at what they were laughing at." Heller is less successful in *Catch-22* when, trying to use irony and paradox for purposes of caricature, he flies off into the realm of ludicrous fantasy; or when Milo Minderbinder, the mess officer and a capitalist's capitalist, bombs his own troops because the Germans, who pay their bills promptly, have so contracted; or when Captain Flume, the public relations officer, lives for months off berries and wildlife deep in the forest, afraid of returning to headquarters because of Chief Halfoat who has once threatened to kill him; when Major Major Major Major runs through a ditch at top speed and sneaks into his office through a back window and is available for conference only when he is not available; or when Captain Yossarian parachutes an Italian prostitute behind German lines because she is ubiquitous, continually appearing from nowhere and trying to kill him. Heller has overextended himself in these scenes and heavy-handedly destroyed the underlying truth by allowing them to become mere farce.

*Catch-22* should have been scrupulously edited, whole sections removed, until we had one consciousness, Captain Yossarian's, breaking under the weight of the absurd; until we had, that is, a credible point of view, a consciousness that absorbed experience which was less than slapstick and adolescent fantasy. When Heller succeeds in *Catch-22*, and his success is sometimes considerable, he depicts Yossarian fighting the machine, Yossarian desiring to stay alive in an organization that finds him expendable, an organization that has lost the sense of humanity which Yossarian refuses to surrender.

It was Heller's closest friend, George Mandel, who had the greatest influence on *Catch-22*. The character of Yossarian is modeled on both Heller and Mandel. The physical description of Yossarian matches Mandel, and Yossarian's attempt to make a "separate peace," as well as his strange appearance at Snowden's funeral, is reminiscent of Mandel's behavior as a soldier. Mandel, a thoroughgoing nihilist, served as an infantryman in the European theater of the Second World War (the setting of his novel, *The Wax Boom*) and was severely wounded in the head. Today, Mandel lives only two blocks from Heller in Manhattan, and they often collaborate on screenplays. Mandel is an associate editor for Random House and the author of three novels, *Flee the Angry*

*Strangers* and *The Breakwater,* in addition to *The Wax Boom.*

An important influence on both the early careers of Mandel and Heller was Louis-Ferdinand Céline (Destouches). Heller discovered Céline's novel *Death on the Installment Plan* (1938) while he was in Europe during the war. He later read *Journey to the End of the Night* (1934), and was reading *Guignol's Band* (1944) while working on *Catch-22. Guignol's Band* is an absurdist novel, a wildly irrational and nonsensical series of interior monologues woven into an equally irrational and almost nonexistent plot. Cascade, the main character, trapped by the insanity of his wartime world, attempts to reenlist in the army but is rejected because he receives a pension of 2,000 francs a year and is therefore considered disabled. The reason for his failure—he is rejected not because he is unable to perform his army duties but because some bureaucrat has decreed that all pensioners are unfit—exemplifies the kind of illogic which permeates *Catch-22.* The source of the absurd in both Céline and Heller is the bureaucracy which negates common sense and frustrates individual action.

Céline's *Guignol's Band* and Heller's *Catch-22,* however, differ greatly in tone and method. There is at best an affinity of mind between these two novelists. A much more direct influence on Heller at this time was that of George Mandel himself, especially Mandel's *The Wax Boom* (1962), a novel written before but published after *Catch-22.* Heller, who read the manuscript of *The Wax Boom* as Mandel wrote it, was obviously impressed, particularly with the forceful way in which his closest friend had attacked the army as an institution.

Like *Catch-22, The Wax Boom* reveals the evil that can come from the chain of command. It shows how the army can be a senseless and inhuman institution where lives are jeopardized by incompetent or ambitious officers and where men are helpless to protect themselves in the face of the all-powerful system. The incompetency of Captain Stollman and Lieutenant Simmons threatens the lives of everyone in the Second Platoon. As in *Catch*-22, most of the men are either so crazy that they do not care what happens to them (like Sergeant Riglioni, who is the "brother" of Captain Yossarian just as Mandel is the "brother" of Heller) or so impotent that they are unable to change their circumstances.

Dobbs in *Catch*-22 thinks seriously of murdering Colonel Cathcart; Sergeant Riglioni, in *The Wax Boom*, of murdering Lieutenant Simmons. Like Yossarian, Riglioni has an awareness of *déjà vu*: "Riglioni went through demolished rooms searching for Gingold. And the room he found him in seemed a room he had been in before; the moment itself seemed a repetition of one recently gone by." As Captain Yossarian ministers to the badly injured airman, Snowden, who repeatedly murmurs, " 'I'm cold,' " so Riglioni ministers to the badly wounded Gene Proctor, who repeatedly whispers, " 'Pretty please.' "

Perhaps because there is a tremendous sense of necessity—an inexorable sense of fate—in *The Wax Boom*, it is a far grimmer novel than *Catch*-22. There can be no escape for Sergeant Riglioni, no way out, nowhere to go—not even Sweden. He can never escape the stupidity and the ambition of a Captain Stollman, and Mandel never effects a humorous relief of the tension as Heller does. Such humor as there is in *The Wax Boom* is, however, like that in *Catch*-22, stemming from the profane (posted inside a gun turret is a picture of Christ, inscribed "To Ken Atman, with admiration, Jesus") and the ridiculous:

> "Give your call sign."
> "Huh? Reliable."
> "No . . . you're Mayflower!" It was First Sergeant Muldoon at Troop. "This is Reliable."

At the end of *The Wax Boom* Riglioni throws down his rifle, turns in his sergeant's stripes, and refuses to lead his men into battle. In like manner Captain Yossarian in *Catch*-22 refuses to fly futher combat missions. Captain Stollman tries to bribe Riglioni by offering him the job of First Sergeant the same way Colonel Korn tries to bribe Yossarian by offering him a hero's trip back to the States. Riglioni refuses the bribe—and also refuses to fight—sitting mesmerized by the flicker of candlelight in a cellar, as the Germans attack the town, killing him and his men, except Gingold, who lives through the same kind of wound that Mandel suffered in combat.

*Catch*-22 ends on a more optimistic note: Captain Yossarian has, like Sergeant Riglioni, made his separate peace, is now committed only to noncommitment, and is planning to run away to Sweden and the promise of better things. We are hardly expected to accept this resolution literally. All we are expected to accept is a certain attitude or quality of mind. Yossarian escapes from the system, triumphs in his escape, and has a sense of new-found promise. Riglioni is trapped by the system, defeated by it, and dies because (for Mandel) there is no way back.

We must go back to *Catch*-22, however, to understand how Yossarian comes to the decision to escape and what that escape means. What he wants most, from the beginning to the end of the story, is to stay alive in a world where his death seems imminent. Even in the hospital, where his faked liver condition gives him respite from the threat of death, he is confronted by the soldier in white, covered from head to foot with bandages, fed out of one bottle which empties into another, alive so long as his temperature indicates life, dead when it does not. The soldier in white is merely the semblance of human life, more machine than man; and Dunbar and Yossarian are filled with horror when one soldier in white is replaced by another, as if the machines were interchangeable. In flight, Yossarian is confronted with Snowden, whose wounded thigh shocks him, until that horror turns into a greater horror when he opens Snowden's flack suit and sees his guts spill out. "Man was matter, that was Snowden's secret. . . . Bury him and he'll rot like other kinds of garbage. The spirit gone, man is garbage. That was Snowden's secret."

Yossarian wants to preserve his "spirit," the ineffable quality that separated man from garbage, that kept him human and among the living. He learns early that his life is in as much danger from the Colonel Cathcarts and Korns, from the men of unscrupulous ambition who both embody and preserve the system, as it is from the Germans. Yossarian tells an unbelieving Clevinger that "the enemy is anybody who's going to get you killed, no matter *which* side he's on, and that includes Colonel Cathcart. And don't you forget that, because the longer you remember it, the longer you might live." The words mean nothing to Clevinger who soon dies when Colonel Cathcart raises once again the number of missions. Indeed, everyone in the original fighting group dies—even Captain Halfoat who is smothered in his sleep by a cat —with the exception of Yossarian, who like Ishmael lives to tell his sad tale.

Most of the others—the Applebys and Havermeyers who believe in flag, mother, apple pie, and duty; the Milo Minderbinders, the supreme capitalists, who personally exploit the misery of war in the name of a collective good; the McWatts who think of combat flying as high adventure; the Dobbses whose hatred of the system does not go beyond the desire to save their own skin; the Daneekas whose hatred of the system does not go beyond self-pity; the Danbys whose inept idealism leave them helpless in the face of Korn and Cathcart; the Tappmans whose Christian passivity make them equally easy victims—think that Yossarian is insane. Yossarian knows differently, knows that the terms have been reversed, that he is on the side of life while the others are on the side of death, that he is sane and they insane. Yossarian makes his point in a discussion with Major Sanderson, the company psychologist:

> "You have a morbid aversion to dying. You probably resent the fact that you're at war and might get your head blown off any second."
> "I more than resent it, sir. I'm absolutely incensed."

"You have deep-seated survival anxieties. And you don't like bigots, bullies, snobs or hypocrites. Subconsciously there are many people you hate."

"Consciously, sir, consciously," Yossarian corrected in an effort to help. "I hate them consciously."

"You're antagonistic to the idea of being robbed, exploited, degraded, humiliated or deceived. Misery depresses you. Ignorance . . . Persecution . . . Violence . . . Slums . . . Greed . . . Crime . . . Corruption [depress] you. You know, it wouldn't surprise me if you're a manic depressive.

"Yes, sir. Perhaps I am.". . .

"Then you admit you're crazy, do you?"

"Crazy," Yossarian was shocked. "What are you talking about? Why am I crazy? You're the one who's crazy!"

Only Orr can understand what Yossarian is saying. Like Yossarian, Orr finds temporary relief in the hospital by paying a whore to give him a concussion by beating him over the head with the high-pointed heel of her shoe. Once back on flying duty, he makes longer-range plans, ditching his plane on every mission, practicing for the long row that will take him outside the system to Sweden. Only when the missions are hiked from seventy to eighty and Nately is killed on Yossarian's seventy-first mission does Yossarian begin to think like Orr. When he tells Nately's whore that Nately is dead, she tries to kill him. He tries desperately to persuade her that he was not responsible, until he suddenly realizes with horror that he was responsible—that so long as he cooperated with the system he could not maintain impunity. At this point Yossarian comes to his moment of moral truth. Someone had to short-circuit the crazy flow of power: "Someone had to do something sometime. Every victim was a culprit, every culprit a victim of inherited habit that was imperiling them all." He realizes also at this point that Catch-22 did not exist, or that it existed as a figment of the mind, a fiction, which made it "much worse, for there was no object or text to ridicule or refute." Yossarian suddenly understands that he has given consent to a fiction that kills. He can no longer justify this in the name of country. With seventy-one missions to his credit, he has done his share of the fighting. But more to the point, while the war is almost over, this will not stop the Cathcarts, Korns, and Minder-binders whose frame of mind will rule the postwar world. Nor will it stop the Scheisskopfs who love a parade. He knows that he cannot march to their drum. His attempt to save himself from Nately's whore, who embodies his own sense of shame, is an attempt to save his conscience. Just when he sells out to Cathcart and Korn, she stabs him in the side: "Getting stabbed by that bitch was the best thing that ever happened to me," Yossarian cries in delight. Indeed it is, because as he recuperates in the hospital, he learns that Orr is safe in Sweden, and he suddenly realizes that Orr had planned his own deliver-ance and that the opportunity is waiting for him. Yos-sarian even convinces Chaplain Tappman, for whom there might also be hope: "It's still a miracle, a miracle of human intelligence and human endurance. Look how much he accomplished!" shouts Tappman. At this point Yossarian makes up his mind. He will not cooperate with Cathcart and Korn and thus condone their madness by returning to the States as a hero: this would be to sell out to the system. He will not fly any more missions either: this would only perpetuate the system and per-haps lose him life. He will not defy them and bring upon himself a court-martial: this would only be another kind of self-destruction. Like Ellison's Invisible Man, what he wants is time: "ripeness is all," he tells us at the end. He has exhausted his possibilities within the sys-tem; outside it he can try to create himself anew.

When we last see Yossarian, he is man in motion, struggling to reach Rome from where he believes he can get to Sweden. Orr has given him hope that he can save his life in more ways than one—can save the "spirit" that separates the human from the inhuman. Even

Chaplain Tappman has a new sense of hope: "A Real miracle. If Orr could row to Sweden, then perhaps I can triumph over Colonel Cathcart and Colonel Korn, if I only persevere." While it is unlikely that Orr ever rowed from Italy to Sweden, that is not important. The fiction alone is enough.

## John Barth

John Barth's later novels like *The Sot-Weed Factor* and *Giles Goat-Boy* are very different in technique from his early novels which deal with existential despair, a sense of man at road's end, with nowhere to go. Morally paralyzed, on the verge of suicide, Barth's earlier characters struggle to go on, to either put themselves in motion or to force death to give way to life.

The first novel, *The Floating Opera*, is a free-wheeling narrative that gets much of its interest and comic force from the central plot which involves a strange *menage à trois*. Todd Andrews renews his friendship with Harrison Mack, an old college friend open-minded enough to reconcile his patrician background with an interest in the Communist party. His radical days behind him, Harrison has married a twenty-six-year-old Ruxton-and-Gibson-Island type, by which is "meant a combination of beauty and athleticism." Confident in their love of each other, proud that they are beyond jealousy, the Macks decide that they can best show their friendship for Todd by allowing Jane to sleep with him, and between 1932 and 1937 Todd makes love to her six hundred and seventy-three times. When Todd does not seem grateful enough, the Macks break off the relationship but eventually renew it, even though everyone feels a bit uncomfortable when Jeannine is born, possibly fathered by Todd. At the end of the novel, the Macks have arbitrarily decided to live for a time in Italy and to break off the relationship between Jane and Todd.

While the love plot is of surface concern in *The Float-

*ing Opera,* the philosophical question of whether Todd should live or commit suicide is of deeper concern, and *The Floating Opera* is really an American version of Camus's *Le Mythe de Sisyphe,* even though Barth disclaims any direct influence. Todd moves from yea to nay saying until he is confronted with the final "why"—why live? The victim of a weak heart, Todd (as his name suggests) is under sentence of death which may come at any moment. He has been able to function by role-playing, inventing a series of masks which give him at least the illusion of meaning. As a student at Johns Hopkins, he was a college-man-about-town; after trouble with his prostate gland, he became an ascetic of sorts and played at being a modern saint; and after his father's suicide he took on the role of cynic. "Each time," he tells us, "it did not take me long to come to believe that my current attitude was not only best for me, because it put me on some kind of terms with my heart, but best in itself, absolutely."

When Todd loses his sense of the absolute, he is thrown into despair: one night—the date is either June 22 or 23, 1937—he suddenly realizes that "nothing has intrinsic value." Values are assigned to things from the outside, by people, so that all action and all things are "ultimately arbitrary," including the value of living; thus there is "no reason for living." Life is simply a floating opera, as old as Adam and Eve, made up of actors who play assigned roles to make people laugh. Such a boat appears in Todd's Chesapeake-oyster-and-crab town, piloted appropriately by Captain Adam. When pressed by little Jeannine Mack, Todd can give no final answer to the meaning of the floating opera—that is, the meaning of life:

> "[People] like to laugh because laughing makes them happy. They like being happy, just like you."
> "Why?" . . .
> "Why do they like being happy? That's the end of the line."

"Why do the actors?"

"Why do the actors act funny? They do that so the people will pay to come and see them. They want to earn money."

"Why?"

"So they can eat to stay alive. They like staying alive."

"Why?"

"That's the end of the line again," I said.

There are no final answers to "why," especially when it comes to "why live?" Life has no final meaning, no rational justification, but is absurd in the existential sense of the word. Once Todd comes to this realization he has no reason to live—or die. Like Hamlet, he must decide whether to be or not to be, knowing that whatever he decides has no real meaning. To live makes as much sense as to die, and vice versa; life is *de trop*, simply given. As a result, Todd has no reason to commit or not to commit suicide. When the novel ends, he finally decides to live, now convinced that the absurd must be turned into a way of life—aware that posturing gives life a kind of interest, less confident in his own use of masks, and more tolerant of the role-playing of others.

When Barth submitted the manuscript of *The Floating Opera* to Appleton-Century-Crofts, it was accepted with the provision that he change the ending. In the original manuscript Todd Andrews lighted three kerosene lanterns, a gas burner, broiler, an oven, and then turned on the acetylene gas valve which fed into the footlights. His plan was to kill not only himself but all on board the *Natchez*. We are never told why the explosion did not occur (probably a deckhand found and closed the open valve); but the ship does not blow up. After the show, Todd says goodbye to the Harrisons, whom he will hardly see again, and returns to his hotel with Captain Osborn where they discover that Mr. Haecker has attempted suicide by swallowing a bottle of sleeping pills. This version of the novel, published by Doubleday in

1967, is considerably different than the 1956 version in which Todd considers taking only his own life, leaving others to decide for themselves whether to live or die. From one point of view, the editor was probably right in wanting the change, since the 1967 version makes Todd into a hard-hearted killer, which is hardly consistent with his earlier character. From another point of view, the editor missed the point that Todd's concern is not with whether *his* life has meaning but whether *all* life has meaning. His concern is that of Kirillov who kills himself in the name of all men as testimony to the fact that there is no absolute justification for living. But Todd Andrews learns that such a philosophical truth makes all action gratuitous—the act of suicide as well as the act of living. So Todd will work on, trying to explain the inexplicable: why his father committed suicide and why he did not.

*End of the Road* pursues both the plot and the philosophical themes of *The Floating Opera*. On his doctor's advice, Jacob Horner takes a job teaching prescriptive grammar at the Wicomico State Teachers College in Maryland. There he meets Joe and Rennie Morgan who continually invite him to dinner followed by long philosophical discussions. Because Joe is trying to finish his Columbia doctoral dissertation, Rennie and Jacob spend much time together, finally making love one night when Joe is out of town. Filled with remorse, Rennie confesses to Joe, who makes her give herself again to Jacob in a kind of Nietzschean act of defiance to prove that they are beyond the mere conventions that regulate marital sex. When Rennie becomes pregnant, possibly with Horner's child, the Morgans are not quite sure that they are so completely beyond fixed concepts of good and evil. Rennie threatens suicide unless the child can be aborted. Jacob manages to get his own doctor, an obvious quack, to perform the abortion, and Rennie dies on the operating table.

*End of the Road* makes conscious use of French existentialism. Jacob first meets his doctor on the morning of March 17, 1951 when he is suffering from paralysis of the will. Unable to continue with his graduate study at Johns Hopkins, unable also to buy a train ticket to an arbitrary destination, Jacob falls into a trance and sits for twelve powerless hours on a bench in the Baltimore Penn Station. The doctor takes Jacob to his clinic where he tries to put him in motion, telling him, "Choosing is existence: to the extent that you don't choose, you don't exist. Now, everything we do must be oriented toward choice and action. It doesn't matter whether this action is more or less reasonable than inaction; the point is that it is its opposite." Action, an end in itself, prevents paralysis of the will and allows motion—undirected motion which is life.

Whereas Henry Adams felt despair at the idea of undirected motion, life as centrifugal rather than centripetal force, Barth turns such concern into a way of life and brings us face to face with Camus's Sisyphus—the man who finds purpose in what is purposeless. As the doctor tells Horner: "Energy is what makes the difference between American pragmatism and French existentialism—where the hell else but in America could you have a cheerful nihilism, for God's sake?" The doctor once again makes clear the novel's existential frame of reference when he explicitly advises Horner to "read Sartre and become an existentialist. It will keep you moving until we find something more suitable for you." Eventually Horner is to move on to "mythotherapy" or role-playing, the assigning of roles to oneself and others for the purpose of protecting the ego and insuring action. So long as we can see ourselves as characters in a play called life, we will not take ourselves seriously. As a result, we will have the comic perspective to avoid anguish and a final despair. Once again, Barth puts this idea in existential terms when the doctor tells Horner

"Mythotherapy is based on two assumptions: that human existence precedes human essence, if either of the two terms really signifies anything; and that a man is free not only to choose his own essence but to change it at will. Those are good existentialist premises, and whether they're true or false is of no concern to us—they're *useful* in your case."

As a novel, *End of the Road* gets its substance from examining such role-playing. Such posturing depends upon believing that it is important. When Rennie dies, however, Horner is too shaken with remorse to play any role at all. As a result, he is once again immobile, unable to act. "I couldn't decide," he tells us, "whether marrying Peggy would be merciful or cruel; whether setting police on the doctor would be right or wrong. I could not even decide what I should *feel*: all I found in me was anguish, abstract and without focus." Without a role to play, Horner is thrown back upon an emptied self and made one with the void with a resulting sense of anguish, the residual existential emotion. Staring at a bust of Laocoön caught in the grip of the serpent, Horner realizes that he is immobilized by the serpent of the naked self. In the face of naked reality all pretense to order has given way to chaos. When Joe Morgan calls to ask him about his plans, Horner cannot answer. When Morgan hangs up, Horner is left standing physically naked, holding the phone, "a dead instrument in the dark." The novel ends with Horner leaving the bust of Laocoön in his room as he moves to the bus station in search of the doctor. Mythotherapy fails Jacob Horner; reality is too much for fiction, and he is forced to abandon his role-playing in the face of Rennie's death. Perhaps the doctor can help him find another role; perhaps this is the end of the road. "Terminal," the last word of the novel, spoken to a taxi driver, leaves Horner's fate open-ended.

Despite the many differences between *End of the Road* and *The Sot-Weed Factor*, Barth's next novel, we do find in each the theme of man and his fiction. *The Sot-Weed Factor* is a wild, picaresque novel, set in the late seventeenth century, a twentieth-century version of

*Tom Jones*, which treats the life of Ebenezer Cooke who writes poems to celebrate his virginity and who preserves his virginity in order to have a subject for his poetry. As virgin-poet, Eben has a role in life, a role that is extended when the third Lord Baltimore appoints him poet laureate of Maryland, where he goes to write an epic poem, *The Marylandiad*, which turns into a satire and is later read as a poem of commemoration, so mercurial is the relationship between art and reality. Ebenezer's journey to America exposes him to pirates, savage Indians, swindlers, impostors, conspirators, and false priests. His companion of sorts is Henry Burlingame III, a protean character who changes roles as he journeys into the past in search of information about his ancestors. Ebenezer learns that his relationship with Henry, indeed with almost all of the characters in this novel, is unfixed, that the terms of it change as they assume different roles. As Burlingame tells him, "I wished only to establish that all assertions of *thee* and *me*, e'en to oneself, are acts of faith," and by faith he means "fiction." Ebenezer also learns that history is a fiction, "that we all invent our pasts, more or less, as we go along." This is proved by his inability to know if Baltimore or Coode is telling the truth; indeed at one point the evidence suggested that Coode, Lord Baltimore, Burlingame, and Andrew Cooke himself were involved in opium and prostitute traffic. That history is fiction is once again proved when they find two journals—one by the elder Henry Burlingame, the other by John Smith—giving two entirely different, albeit uproarious, accounts of the Pocahontas story. Most importantly, Ebenezer learns a truth that could save Jacob Horner: that man invents himself, creates the fictions that keep him moving, uses the imagination to open up the roads of endless possibility. Once again, Burlingame is the voice of wisdom: "The world can alter a man entirely, Eben, or he can alter himself; down to his very essence. Did you not by your own testimony resolve, not that you *were*, but that you'd *be* a virgin and poet from that moment hence? Nay, a man *must* alter willy-nilly in's flight to the grave; he is a river running seaward that is never the same from hour to hour."

Barth makes the idea of man and his fiction the subject of *Lost in the Funhouse*, a series of related stories. Particularly in "Life Story," where the writer tells us that he suspects "that his own life might be a fiction," and in "Lost in the Funhouse," Barth self-consciously discusses the creative processes, defining such terms as beginning, middle, end, and then treating their conventional meaning before he intentionally deviates from that meaning in practice. At one point he addresses the reader as a "print-oriented bastard," and asks him why he goes on reading instead of playing tennis or going to a movie. Barth is obviously concerned about the fate of the novel when Marshall McLuhan has told us that the printed word is becoming obsolete. In his concern to find narrative forms that are independent of print, Barth experimented with taping several stories in *Lost in the Funhouse*. Yet his self-conscious discussion of fiction takes us in circular fashion beyond the concern that the novel is dead or dying, a topic that he treats in the essay "The Literature of Exhaustion," and brings us back to the idea of the novel as form. In calling attention to the human origins of fiction, Barth, like Sartre before him, makes us aware that the God-like novelist is as dead as God. He opens up the novel and lets the characters out by showing that their existence depends upon his own imagination. In this context it is significant that the young boy in "Lost in the Funhouse" decides that he can build a better funhouse, "a truly astonishing funhouse, incredibly complex yet utterly controlled from a great central switchboard like the console of a pipe organ." He concludes, "Nobody had enough imagination."

The imagination gives the journey meaning. But we are not talking about the romantic imagination which was in tune with a transcendent realm of truth. Barth's imagination is a human faculty which works in a more diminished although equally complex way. In "Night-Sea Journey," Barth humorously tells his story from the point of view of a sperm cell swimming for its "life." The cell rejects the idea of a companion cell that their "Maker" made thousands of separate seas during his sexual lifetime, each populated with thousands of other sperm cells, and that in almost every instance both sea and swimmers came to naught. He rejects also the idea that both the Maker and the sperm "each generate the other," the life of one dependent upon the life of the other, the process dependent upon a cyclical rhythm. The process can even be more complicated because the Maker may also be the agent of a higher power who is using him in an equally symbiotic way. The rebel sperm is for ending the whole process, or at least his cycle within it, by committing suicide, thus becoming the sperm equivalent of Kirillov. At first incredulous, the narrator finds that this mad dream, particularly the desire to communicate it, sustains him. He drives across "this dreadful sea" with the single hope of convincing the ovum he fertilizes to "terminate this aimless, brutal business," to make fate the conscious product of choice rather than a chemical spasm called love. "Hate love," he concludes, proving that he is his own sperm, rejecting love as Nietzsche rejected God, and showing us that there are existentialists in both the womb and the tomb.

Jorge Luis Borges, the Argentine short-story writer, has had the greatest influence on Barth's recent work, an influence Barth recognizes in his essay "The Literature of Exhaustion." Borges, influenced by Lewis Carroll and H. G. Wells among others, has a unique way of looking at the past and the future. In the story "Pierre Menard, Author of the *Quixote*," Borges describes a turn-of-the-century French symbolist who, through an extraordinary effort of the imagination, is able to reproduce—not copy or approximate—several chapters from Cervantes's classic novel. While the words are the same, what has been added is three hundred years of history, so that the words can never be interpreted the same. As the historical perspective changes, so does the meaning of man's actions and the words through which those actions are ex-

pressed. Literature thus becomes action, an idea that
Sartre himself has expressed. Man must not only create
new fictions but reinterpret the old. As Barth has put it,
"Beethoven's Sixth Symphony or the Chartes Cathedral
if executed today would be merely embarrassing." Barth
has rewritten stories of Pocahontas and Scheherazade
from a twentieth-century—that is, ironic—perspective.

In several other stories in *Ficciones*, Borges treats time-
future or time nonexistent. In the famous "Tlön, Uqbar,
Orbis Tertius," Borges describes a purely imaginary
world, created by a secret society of scholars who au-
thenticate their creation by describing it in every possible
detail—its language, philosophy, history, science, mythol-
ogy—in an encyclopedia article. The imaginative reality
is so compelling that it competes with and then sup-
plants present reality, until "a fictitious past occupies in
our memories the place of another, a past of which we
know nothing with certainty—not even that it is false."
The scholars' creation proves that the imagination has
the power to change "the face of the world." Nietzsche's
superman has become the artist.

Yet Borges's fictional world can create its own tyran-
nies. In "The Garden of Forking Paths," he describes a
novel by one Ts'ui Pên in which all of the events that
can possibly befall the hero are portrayed. In this story
Borges presupposes that the individual has more than
one life to live and that in the course of time he will
exhaust all of his possibilities of choice. In "The Library
of Babel," Borges describes an infinite library with books
that register all the possible combinations of the alpha-
bet, thus expressing all that is given to express, everything, including "the minutely detailed history of the
future." Given this condition, the narrator of "The Library of Babel" is justified in fearing that the human
species is about to be extinguished, but the Library will
endure." In these stories man has become the victim of
fiction, which has gone ahead of him as fate, waiting for
him to catch up with it. To exalt fictional possibility at
the expense of human possibility is to substitute the

tyranny of fiction for the tyranny of God, to make man dependent upon a range of possibilities that lie outside his will.

Only the self-conscious artist can save man from Borges's labyrinth. At the end of Vladimir Nabokov's *Bend Sinister*, just before the fatal bullet hits Krug, Nabokov himself stands up, stretches himself, and goes to investigate the twang of something—a moth as it turned out—striking the screen window. Beckett's Moran begins his narrative: "Then I went back into the house and wrote, It is midnight. The rain is beating on the windows. It was not midnight. It was not raining." Nabokov and Beckett open up the novel, allow their characters to escape from a fictional God, force the reader to participate in the self-conscious process of creation, and reveal that fiction intrudes into life: that man makes himself through his fiction and that he must be self-conscious about what he is creating.

Life is a fiction: some fictions kill and some save. Ask Heller's Yossarian who is entrapped in the fiction of Catch-22; ask Pynchon's Benny Profane whose exhausted sense of fiction leads to yo-yoing; ask Barth's Jacob Horner who needs a fiction to get out of the corner. So long as modern man can recognize that his actions, personal and national, cannot be divorced from his fictions—from the modern myths about military invincibility or myths of the Red threat—he can try to save himself by changing his fictions, by altering the myth. "I whipped it all except the mind, the *mind*," says Ellison's Invisible Man, indicating why he is left immobolized for the moment on a coal pile. He is devoid of purpose because he is devoid of mind; he has exhausted his sense of history, which is to say that he has exhausted his sense of fiction.

If modern man has been left denuded by history, he has the capacity of mind to re-create himself. Our chronicle has shown man in search of the freedom to create himself, has shown him seeking to move beyond the restrictions of God, Church, rational philosophy and systems (including Freudianism and Marxism), theories of deterministic history, totalitarianism, and the prejudices of race. Nietzsche, Byron, Dostoyevsky, Sartre, Camus, Faulkner, Hemingway, Mailer, and Wright have all addressed themselves to one or more of the above forms of bondage. So also did Bellow and Percy, who emphasized at the same time man's responsibility to his human bond, who insisted upon human limits which distinguish civilized actions from the barbaric. Ellison, Pynchon, and Heller depicted what can happen when man loses a sense of his humanity, when a redeeming fiction fails him in a world gone power-mad. In their novels, man seems to be at the dead end of history. Heller holds out hope for a redeeming fiction, and so also does Barth, who turns history into fiction and fiction into history.

In making his fiction man makes himself. Man in motion is man with a dream. This idea, which can be found on the pages of the philosophical and literary existentialists, is no older than American literature. Mark Twain's Philip Traum told the children, "Dream other dreams, and better." He could easily have added, "Before it is too late."

# Notes

## 1 — Man the Redeemer

1. My discussion of Stavrogin is in debt to Richard Peace's *Dostoyevsky: An Examination of the Major Novels* (Cambridge: Cambridge University Press, 1971), pp. 150–56, 180–81.

## 2 — French Literary Existentialism

1. See Adele King, "Structure and Meaning in *La Chute*," *PMLA* 72 (1962), 660–67; and Roger Quillot, "Un monde ambiguë," *Prevues*, No. 110 (1960), pp. 28–38.

2. See Francis Jeanson, "Albert Camus ou l'âme révoltée," *Les Temps Modernes* 7 (1952), 2070–90; Francis Jeanson, "Pour tout vous dire. . . ," *Les Temps Modernes* 8 (1952), 354–83; Jean-Paul Sartre, "Réponse à Albert Camus," *Les Temps Modernes* 8 (1952), 334–54. The feud between Sartre and Camus became the subject matter for Simone de Beauvoir's novel, *Les Mandarins*. The controversy is discussed by N. Chiaromonte, "Sartre Versus Camus: A Political Quarrel," *Partisan Review* 19 (1952), 680–86, and by John Cruickshank, *Albert Camus and the Literature of Revolt* (Oxford: Oxford University Press, 1959), 120–27.

3. See Dominique Aury, "A Talk with Albert Camus," *New York Times Book Review*, February 17, 1957, p. 33.

## 4 — The Outer Limits

1. See Richard Lehan, "Existentialism in Recent American Fiction: The Demonic Quest," *Texas Studies in Literature and Language* 1 (1959), 181–202.

2. Allan J. Wagenheim, "Square's Progress, *An American Dream*," *Critique* 10 (1968), 45–68.

## 5—Into the Ruins

1. Walker Percy, "Symbol as Hermeneutic in Existentialism," *Philosophy and Phenomenological Research* 16 (1956), 528.

2. See George H. Mead, *Mind, Self and Society* (Chicago: Chicago University Press, 1934).

3. Walker Percy, "Symbol, Consciousness and Intersubjectivity," *Journal of Philosophy* 55 (1958), 632.

## 6—Man and his Fictions

1. Don Hausdorff, "Thomas Pynchon's Multiple Absurdities," *Wisconsin Studies in Contemporary Literature* 7 (1966), 258–69. Tony Tanner also pursues Pynchon's use of Henry Adams in his excellent *City of Words* (New York: Harper & Row, 1971), a book I came upon when my manuscript was in finished draft.

*Bibliographical Essay*


## 1. Nietzsche, Byron, Dostoyevsky, Melville, Conrad

The complete works of Nietzsche, edited by Oscar Levy, have been published by Macmillan Company (New York, 1924). *Thus Spake Zarathustra* was translated by Thomas Common and published by the Modern Library (New York, 1954). For commentaries on Nietzsche see William Mackintire Salter's *Nietzsche the Thinker* (New York: F. Ungar, 1968) and Walter Kaufmann's *Nietzsche: Philosopher, Psychologist, Antichrist* (Princeton: Princeton University Press, 1968).

*Manfred* and *Cain* are both available in a Everyman's Library edition (New York: Dutton, 1963). For an excellent discussion of Byron's rebel hero see Peter L. Thorslev's *The Byronic Hero: Types and Prototypes* (Minneapolis: University of Minnesota Press, 1962).

Dostoyevsky's *Notes from Underground* was translated by Constance Garnett and published by the Macmillan Company (New York, 1920). *The Possessed* was translated by Constance Garnett and published by the Modern Library (New York, 1930). *The Brothers Karamazov* was translated by Constance Garnett and also published by the Modern Library (New York, 1936).

The authoritative text of *Moby Dick* has been edited by Harrison Hayford and Hershel Parker and published by W. W. Norton (New York, 1967).

The complete works of Conrad are available in the Concord edition published by Doubleday (Garden City, N.Y., 1923).

For commentaries of a general nature on literary and

philosophical existentialism see William Hubben, *Four Prophets of Our Destiny: Kierkegaard, Dostoyevsky, Nietzsche, Kafka* (New York: Macmillan, 1952); William Barrett, *Irrational Man: A Study in Existential Philosophy* (New York: Doubleday, 1958), which treats Kierkegaard, Nietzsche, Heidegger, and Sartre; Thomas Hanna, *The Lyrical Existentialists* (New York: Atheneum, 1962), which treats Kierkegaard, Nietzsche, and Camus; Maurice Friedman, *Problematic Rebel: An Image of Modern Man* (New York: Random House, 1963), which treats Melville, Dostoyevsky, Kafka, and Camus; Ralph Harper, *The Seventh Solitude: Man's Isolation in Kierkegaard, Dostoyevsky, and Nietzsche* (Baltimore: Johns Hopkins Press, 1965); and Nathan A. Scott, *The Unquiet Vision: Mirrors of Man in Existentialism* (New York and Cleveland: World Publishing Co., 1969), which treats Kierkegaard, Nietzsche, Camus, Sartre, and Martin Buber.

## 2. Sartre and Camus

Sartre has written four novels and a collection of short stories all published in Paris by Gallimard: *La Nausée* (*Nausea*) (1938), translated by Lloyd Alexander (Norfolk, Conn.: New Directions, 1949); *Les Chemins de la liberté* (*The Roads to Freedom*) is the name of Sartre's trilogy, composed of *L'Âge de raison* (*The Age of Reason*) (1945), translated by Eric Sutton (New York: Knopf, 1947); *Le Sursis* (*The Reprieve*) (1945), translated by Eric Sutton (New York: Knopf, 1947); *La Mort dans l'âme* (*The Troubled Sleep*) (1949), translated by Gerald Hopkins (New York: Knopf, 1951); *Le Mur* (*The Wall and Other Stories*) (1939), translated by Lloyd Alexander (New York: New Directions, 1948). Sartre's theory of literature is best set forth in *Qu'ést-ce que la littérature? Situations II* (*What is Literature?*) (Paris: Gallimard, 1948), translated by Bernard Frechtman (New York: Philosophical Library, 1949). Sartre's literary essays appeared in *Situations I* and *III* (Paris: Gallimard, 1947 and 1949) translated by Annette Michelson as *Literary and Philosophical Essays* (London: Rider, 1955), which contains essays on Dos Passos, Camus, Faulkner, and American cities. Additional essays by Sartre were reprinted as *Situations IV* and translated by Benita Eisler

(New York: Braziller, 1965); it contains Sartre's reply to Camus. Sartre has also written full-length critical studies: *Baudelaire* (Paris: Gallimard, 1947), translated by Martin Turnell (New York: New Directions, 1950); and *Saint Genet, comédian et martyr* (*Saint Genet, Actor and Martyr*) (Paris: Gallimard, 1952), translated by Bernard Frechtman (New York: Braziller, 1963). Sartre's play *Huis clos* (*No Exit*) was published by Gallimard (Paris, 1945) and translated by Stuart Gilbert (New York: Knopf, 1947); it can also be found in a Vintage paperback edition translated by Gilbert and Abel. For an oversimplified account of Sartre's philosophical ideas see his *L'Existentialism est un humanisme* (*Existentialism and Humanism*) (Paris: Nagel, 1946), translated by Philip Mairet (London: Metheun, 1960). Sartre's most detailed epistemological study is *L'Être et le néant: essai d'ontologie phénoménologique* (*Being and Nothingness: An Essay in Phenomenological Ontology*) (Paris: Gallimard, 1943), translated by Hazel E. Barnes (New York: Philosophical Library, 1956). Sartre discussed his drift toward Marxism in an interview published in *The New York Review of Books*, 14 (March 26, 1970), 22–31. Wilfred Desan's *The Marxism of Jean-Paul Sartre* (Garden City: Doubleday, 1965) is the best book-length commentary on this matter. The best discussion of the political differences between Sartre and Camus is Michel-Antoine Burnier's *Les Existentialists et la politique* (*Choice of Action: The French Existentialists on the Political Front Line*) (Paris: Gallimard, 1966), translated by Bernard Murchland (New York: Random House, 1968). A useful bibliography of Sartre's work and the English and American criticism of it is Allen Belkind's *Jean-Paul Sartre: A Bibliographical Guide* (Kent State University Press, 1970).

Albert Camus wrote three novels and a collection of short stories published by Gallimard in Paris and Knopf in New York: *L'Étranger* (*The Stranger*) (1942), translated by Stuart Gilbert (1946); *Le Peste* (*The Plague*) (1947), translated by Stuart Gilbert (1948); *La Chute* (*The Fall*) (1956), translated by Justin O'Brien (1960); *L'Exil et le royaume* (*Exile and the Kingdom*) (1957), translated by Justin O'Brien (1958). Camus wrote two studies of a philosophical and literary nature, again published by Gallimard in Paris and Knopf in New York: *Le Mythe de Sisyphe* (*The Myth of Sisyphus*) (1942), translated by Justin O'Brien (1955) is a lyrical rejection of suicide; Camus treats the American novel in this study, particularly Hemingway. *L'Homme révolté* (*The Rebel*), translated by Anthony Bower (1956) is a study of metaphysical and historical rebellion; Camus draws upon Nietzsche and Dostoyevsky for many of his ideas. Camus's *Lyrical and Critical Essays* were edited by Philip Thody and translated by Ellen Conroy Kennedy (New York: Knopf, 1969): reprinted here are Camus's essays on Melville and Faulkner, including his foreword to *Requiem for a Nun* which he adapted for the Paris stage. The dramatic version has been published by Gallimard (Paris, 1956). Two of Camus's notebooks, originally published in Paris by Gallimard under the title *Carnets*, have been translated and published in New York by Knopf: the years 1935–1942 were translated by Philip Thody (1969), and the years 1942–1951 by Justin O'Brien (1966). For a thorough listing of primary and secondary material see Robert F. Roeming's *Camus: A Bibliography* (Madison: University of Wisconsin Press, 1968).

## 3. John Dos Passos, Ernest Hemingway, William Faulkner

Dos Passos's trilogy *U.S.A.* is made up of *The 42nd Parallel* (New York: Harper & Brothers, 1930), *1919* (New York: Harcourt, Brace, 1932), and *The Big Money* (New York: Harcourt, Brace, 1936); it has been republished in one volume by the Modern Library (New York, 1937). For an article related to Sartre and Dos Passos see Ben Stoltzfus, "John Dos Passos and the French," *Comparative Literature* 14 (1963), 146–63.

Hemingway's major novels have been published in New York by Scribner's: *The Sun Also Rises* (1926), *A Farewell to Arms* (1929), *To Have and Have Not* (1937), *For Whom the Bell Tolls* (1940), *Across the River and Into the Trees* (1950), *The Old Man and the Sea* (1952), and *Islands in the Stream* (1970). For an existential reading of Hemingway's fiction see John Killinger, *Hemingway and the Dead Gods* (Lexington: University of Kentucky Press, 1960). Also John Clendenning, "Hemingway's Gods, Dead and Alive," *Texas Studies in Literature and Language* 3 (1962), 459–63.

A related study is Roger Asselineau's "French Reaction to Hemingway's Work Between the Two World Wars," in his edition *The Literary Reputation of Hemingway in Europe* (New York: New York University Press, 1965). Audre Hanneman's *Ernest Hemingway* (Princeton: Princeton University Press, 1967) is a comprehensive bibliography of books by and about Hemingway.

William Faulkner published eighteen novels during his career. After 1935 Random House in New York published all his fiction: *Soldier's Pay* (New York: Boni & Liveright, 1926); *Mosquitoes* (New York: Boni & Liveright, 1927); *Sartoris* (New York: Harcourt, Brace, 1929); *The Sound and the Fury* (New York: Jonathan Cape and Harrison Smith, 1929); *As I Lay Dying* (New York: Cape and Smith, 1930); *Sanctuary* (New York: Cape and Smith, 1931); *Light in August* (New York: Harrison Smith and Robert Hass, 1932); *Pylon* (Smith and Haas, 1935); *Absalom, Absalom!* (1936); *The Wild Palms* (1939); *The Hamlet* (1940); *Go Down, Moses* (1942); *Intruder in the Dust* (1948); *Requiem for a Nun* (1951); *A Fable* (1954); *The Town* (1957); *The Mansion* (1959); *The Rievers* (1962). For related studies on Faulkner and existentialism see Ralph A. Cianci, "Faulkner's Existential Affinities," in *Studies in Faulkner*, ed. Neal Woodruff, Jr. (Pittsburgh: Carnegie Institute of Technology, 1961); John K. Simon, "Faulkner and Sartre: Metamorphosis and the Obscene," *Comparative Literature* 15 (1963), 216–25; Robert M. Slabey, "*As I Lay Dying* as an Existential Novel," *Bucknell Review* 11 (1963), 12–23; Jean V. Alter, "Faulkner, Sartre, and the 'noveau roman,'" *Symposium* 20 (1966), 101–12. William J. Sowder has published four articles on Faulkner's existentialism: "Colonel Thomas Sutpen as Existential Hero," *American Literature* 33 (1962), 485–99; "Faulkner and Existentialism: A Note on the Generalissimo," *Wisconsin Studies in Contemporary Literature* 4 (1963), 163–71; "Lucas Beauchamp as Existential Hero," *College English* 25 1963), 115–27; "Christmas as Existentialist Hero," *University Review* 30 (1964), 279–84.

## 4. Norman Mailer and Richard Wright

While Mailer has written many books, he has published only five novels: *The Naked and the Dead* (New York: Holt,

1948); *Barbary Shore* (New York: Rinehart, 1951); *The Deer Park* (New York: Putnam, 1955); *An American Dream* (New York: Dial, 1965); *Why Are We In Vietnam?* (New York: Putnam, 1967). Mailer links himself with the existential movement in *Advertisements for Myself* (New York: Putnam, 1959), and he discusses a "cosmic" existentialism in *Of a Fire on the Moon* (Boston: Little Brown, 1970). Donald L. Kaufmann discusses existential elements in Mailer's fiction in *Norman Mailer: The Countdown* (Carbondale: Southern Illinois University Press, 1969).

Richard Wright published four novels: *Native Son* (New York: Harper & Brothers, 1940); *The Outsider* (New York: Harper & Brothers, 1953); *Savage Holiday* (New York: Avon Publications, 1954); *The Long Dream* (New York: Harper & Brothers, 1958). Wright discusses his early years in *Black Boy* (New York: Harper & Brothers, 1945). Constance Webb's *Richard Wright: A Biography* (New York: Putnam, 1968) is a detailed account of Wright's life with some mention of Wright's relationship to Sartre. For a study of Wright and existentialism see Kingsley Widmer, "The Existential Darkness: Richard Wright's *The Outsider*," *Wisconsin Studies in Contemporary Literature* 1 (1960), 13–21. In this same issue is Jackson Bryer's useful checklist of literary criticism.

## 5. Saul Bellow and Walker Percy

With one exception, Bellow's seven novels have been published in New York by the Viking Press: *Dangling Man* (Cleveland: World Publishing Co., 1944), *The Victim* (1947), *The Adventures of Augie March* (1953), *Seize the Day* (1956), *Henderson the Rain King* (1959), *Herzog* (1964), and *Mr. Sammler's Planet* (1970). For a very important essay by Bellow in which he links recent fiction to Nietzsche and Dostoyevsky see "Some Notes on Recent American Fiction," delivered as a Library of Congress lecture and republished in *Encounter* 21 (1963), 22–29. Bellow was also interviewed by John Enck for *Wisconsin Studies in Contemporary Literature*, 6 (1965), 156–60.

Percy has published three novels to date: *The Moviegoer* (New York: Knopf, 1961), *The Last Gentleman* (New York: Farrar, Straus, and Giroux, 1966), and *Love in the*

*Ruins* (New York: Farrar, Straus, Giroux, 1971). In Ashley Brown's "An Interview with Walker Percy," *Shenandoah* 3 (1967), 3–10, Percy tells us that he has been influenced by existentialism, particularly Dostoyevsky, Kierkegaard, Heidegger, Gabriel Marcel, Sartre, and Camus; mentions that he modeled Will Barrett of *The Last Gentleman* on Dostoyevsky's Prince Myshkin; and insists that Sartre's *La Nausée* "is a revolution in its technique for rendering a concrete situation, and it has certainly influenced me." Percy again discusses some of these matters in another interview with Carlton Cremeens in *The Southern Review* 4 (1968), 271–90. For articles treating Percy and existentialism see Robert Maxwell's "Walker Percy's Fancy," *Minnesota Review* 7 (1967), 231–37, which treats Percy's existential vocabulary, and Lewis A. Lawson's "Walker Percy's Indirect Communication," *Texas Studies in Literature and Language* 11 (1969), 867–900, which treats Percy and Kierkegaard.

## 6. Ralph Ellison, Thomas Pynchon, Joseph Heller, John Barth

Ralph Ellison's *Invisible Man* was published by Random House (New York, 1952).

Thomas Pynchon's *V.* was published by J. P. Lippincott Co. (New York, 1963).

Joseph Heller's *Catch-22* was published by Simon and Schuster (New York, 1961).

John Barth's *The Floating Opera* was originally published by Appleton-Century-Crofts (New York, 1956) and then republished in a revised edition in 1967 by Doubleday which has published Barth's other novels: *End of the Road* (1958), *The Sot-Weed Factor* (1960), *Giles Goat-boy* (1966), and *Lost in the Funhouse* (1968). Along with some other important essays, Barth's essay "The Literature of Exhaustion," originally published in *Atlantic* (August, 1967), has been republished in *The American Novel Since World War Two*, ed. Marcus Klein (New York: Fawcett, 1969), 267–79. Richard Hauck discusses the inseparability of the real and the fictional in his chapter on Barth in *A Cheerful Nihilism* (Bloomington: Indiana University Press, 1971).

Some important books on recent fiction are Ahab Hassan's *Radical Innocence* (Princeton: Princeton University Press,

1961); Marcus Klein's *After Alienation* (New York: World Publishing Co., 1962); Robert Scholes's *The Fabulators* (New York: Oxford University Press, 1967); and Tony Tanner's *City of Words* (New York: Harper & Row, 1971).

# Index

Adams, Henry: and Norman Mailer, 85; *The Education of*, 146–47; on entropy, 149–50; and Ralph Ellison, 150, 155, 156; and Thomas Pynchon, 158–59, 161; and John Barth, 176

Anderson, Sherwood, 53

*Arbalète, L'*, 36

Ayme, Denise V., 46

Baldwin, James, 142

Barth, John: and Albert Camus, 173; on self-conscious fiction, 179; and Jorge Luis Borges, 180–82; and Vladimir Nabokov, 182; and Samuel Beckett, 182

—*End of the Road*, 175–77

—*The Floating Opera*: as existential novel, 172–75; and Camus's *Le Mythe de Sisyphe*, 173; revisions of, 174–75

—*Lost in the Funhouse*, 179–80

—*The Sot-Weed Factor*, 177–79

Beckett, Samuel, 182

Bellow, Saul: and existentialism, xix; fiction contrasted with Mailer's and Wright's, 107; his typical character, 107–9; use of Nietzsche, 128; rejects Heidegger, 128

—*Adventures of Augie March, The*: explicated, 115–18

—*Dangling Man*: compared to Sartre's *La Nausée*, 109; compared to Camus's *L'Étranger*, 109; explicated, 109–11

—*Henderson the Rain King*: explicated, 121–25; and Camus's *Le Mythe de Sisyphe*, 123

—*Herzog*: explicated, 125–30

—*Mr. Sammler's Planet*, 130–33

—*Sieze the Day*: explicated, 118–21

—*Victim, The*: explicated, 111–15

Bodin, Pierre, 35

Borges, Jorge Luis, 180–82

Bowles, Paul, 80

Brando, Marlon, 142

Byron, Lord George Gordon: anticipates modern existentialism, xvi; advocated a radical individualism, xvi, 3; his *Childe Harold*, 3–4; his *Manfred*, 4; his *Cain*, 4–5; influence on Nietzsche, 4–5

*Cahiers des Langues Modernes*, 36

Cain, James M.: his *The Postman Always Rings Twice* and Camus's *L'Étranger*, 62–66

Camus, Albert: and existentialism, xv; use of the American novel, xv–xvi, xviii; on fiction and philosophy, 13–

# Pirandello's Theater
## *The Recovery of the Modern Stage for Dramatic Art*

Anne Paolucci

WITH A PREFACE BY
Harry T. Moore

SOUTHERN ILLINOIS UNIVERSITY PRESS
Carbondale and Edwardsville

FEFFER & SIMONS, INC.
London and Amsterdam

To Eric Bentley
who, in search of theater,
led us to Pirandello

Library of Congress Cataloging in Publication Data

Paolucci, Anne.
  Pirandello's theater.

  (Crosscurrents/modern critiques)
  Bibliography: p.
  1. Pirandello, Luigi, 1867–1936—Criticism and interpretation.
I. Title.
PQ4835.I7Z723          852′.9′12          73–20324
ISBN 0–8093–0594–1

# Contents

## Preface

In 1972 we celebrated the appearance of the hundredth volume in the Crosscurrents/Modern Critiques series by publishing Anne Paolucci's From Tension to Tonic: The Plays of Edward Albee, a remarkably vital book. Now, as our 121st volume, we have Professor Paolucci's equally fine and thorough study of Pirandello, a demonstration of the continuing excellence of books which have been submitted to this series.

We are delighted to have another book by Dr. Paolucci, who knows the works of Luigi Pirandello so thoroughly, in their original Italian, not merely from reading them but also from directly participating in stage productions of them. And it is good, at this time, to have this examination of Pirandello, for he is becoming better known as his plays are being oftener produced than before, particularly by college drama groups, and because more people are reading his work. Pirandello, who wrote so trenchantly of modern man's problems, has become not only a man for this season, but one for future seasons as well.

Like Strindberg and O'Neill, Pirandello in his plays deals with the nervous tension characteristic of the twentieth century. Indeed, Strindberg (who influenced O'Neill) was working along such lines in his plays and novels of the preceding century, and he kept up this activity until his death in 1912. In this kind of writing, he had one predecessor among novelists: Dostoevsky. In the early years of our own epoch, modernists who were shattering older forms and attitudes flourished, in painting and music as well as in literature; and in

Pirandello's Italy there were the futurists, superficial in comparison to Pirandello who, after many years of writing fiction, turned to the stage in the year in which Strindberg died. And, like Strindberg, Pirandello drew upon fantasy as well as upon his unique brand of humor.

He took a doctor's degree at Bonn, in—of all things—philology. A brilliant teacher had interested him in the subject when he was studying at the University of Rome; the professor had made Pirandello aware of the fascinating folklore of his native Sicily and its quaint dialogues; he used the latter extensively in his early work. Before he became a playwright, he had been writing grimly of his world in novels and stories; impoverished by his family's financial collapse, he had to take a teaching position in Rome that paid meagerly. His wife went insane and, against advice, Pirandello kept her at home for many years until he finally realized that he had to put her into an asylum.

He was never fully successful as a dramatist until after the First World War, when he turned out his greatest plays, among them Six Characters in Search of an Author, in 1921, and Enrico IV, in 1922 (we should keep the Italian title for that one, if only as a convenience for people looking through indexes, since there are two other Henry IV plays about an English king, and a French monarch also wore that name).

Toward the end of his life, Pirandello was indirectly though publicly denounced in a speech by Mussolini, then (1933) beginning to learn tricks from Hitler, who had earlier learned from him. Mussolini didn't mention Pirandello's name in a speech that certainly referred to him: Mussolini attacked il teatro grottesco. Yet Mussolini imposed no objections to Pirandello's receiving the Nobel Prize in 1934, two years before he died.

The foregoing material is merely an effort to provide something of the background of the man whose plays Anne Paolucci so valuably writes about in this book. At the start of each chapter, she wisely provides synopses of the principal plays to be considered in that chapter. In literary criticism, some writers are opposed to synopsis; it seems to me that this is a limiting view, since synopsis is a form of criticism in that the points selected are a key to the critic's essential attitude. Some of the greatest commentators on literature use synopses; Edmund Wilson, perhaps the finest critic in this century, almost invariably worked with synopsis. And Anne Paolucci's idea of putting her summaries first is a most helpful one, for her analyses then can be straightforward, with no stops, in the chapter itself, to explain matters, although here and there she sensibly gives the material even more scope by developing some point or other which is implied in the synopsis.

As for Pirandello the writer, there is nothing further that I want to say here because Professor Paolucci deals with the entire subject so expertly, at the technical, philosophical, and critical levels, showing us exactly why so many interpreters of Pirandello find him to be "the playwright's playwright par excellence of the contemporary theater"—though he is also the audience's playwright, as we are learning with the passage of time. The reasons for this are implicit in every line of Dr. Paolucci's book, written as it is from a vantage point of so much enlightening experience, seasoned judgment, and critical skill.

HARRY T. MOORE

Southern Illinois University
November 16, 1973

## Introduction

Much has been written on Luigi Pirandello's theatrical art, but much still remains to be said. I have tried in this book to provide a set of guidelines for tracing the unity of his plays, placing in proper perspective his experimental quality and extending its application beyond the "theater" works. I wished, also, to dispel some commonplaces which suggest a sterile skepticism and a purely existential negativism. Pirandello's signature is a bold affirmation of life and theater; and I have attempted to trace it from the Sicilian naturalism of the early plays, to a commitment to "total theater," and finally to an exalted dramatization of art transcending itself, in the so-called myths.

To aid the reader who may not be familiar with all the plays discussed, I have—at the beginning of each chapter—summarized the content of the works dealt with. I have adopted, for convenience, the English titles of the plays, which appear in Glauco Cambon's chronological summary at the end of his excellent anthology of critical essays on Pirandello. For the sake of consistency, I have given my own English translations of all passages from Pirandello. Quotations from foreign critics—unless otherwise indicated in footnotes—have also been translated by me.

My grateful thanks to family, friends, and colleagues, at St. John's University and elsewhere, who expressed an interest in this book and sustained me with their constant encouragement. I am particularly grateful to Father Joseph T. Cahill, President of St. John's University, for having provided the academic environment which enabled me to make time for this work, in the midst of other pressing tasks. It is with admiration and thanks, finally, that I acknowledge the help of Henry Paolucci, whose invaluable insights into the Hegelian notions of the political, religious, and philosophic, as well as artistic, meaning of theater—particularly as applicable in the discussion on "Art for Life's Sake"—proved a constant spur and inspiration.

I wish to acknowledge with special thanks permissions granted by various copyright holders and publishers to quote from the following works:

"Theater of Illusion," by Anne Paolucci, in *Comparative Literature Studies* 9, no. 1, March 1972. Reprinted by permission.

"Luigi Pirandello," by Anne Paolucci, in *Forum Italicum* 7, no. 4, December 1973. Reprinted by permission.

A. P.

New York
June 1973

# Pirandello's Theater

*O what a thing is man! how far from power,*
*From settled peace and rest!*
*He is some twenty several men at least*
*Each several hour.*

                                    George Herbert

# 1

## The Invaded Stage

How does modern tragedy—from Shakespeare to our own contemporaries—differ from ancient Greek tragedy?

Pirandello raises the question in a paragraph of his most famous novel, *The Late Mattia Pascal*. And his imaginative, even comic, answer there is perhaps the best indication of what his own dramatic art is really all about.

> The tragedy of Orestes in a puppet theater! . . . Now listen to this crazy notion that just came to me! Let's suppose that at the very climax, when the puppet who represents Orestes is about to take his revenge on Aegisthus and his mother for his father's death, a great hole were suddenly torn in the paper sky of the theater, what would happen? . . . Orestes would still be bent on revenge, he would still be impatient to bring it about, but his eyes in that instant would be directed up there, to that ripped sky, where all kinds of evil influences would now filter down into the scene, and he would feel his arms grow limp. Orestes, in other words, would become Hamlet. The whole difference, Signor Meis, between ancient and modern tragedy is just that, believe me: a hole in the paper sky.[1]

Pirandello wrote those lines in 1903. Twenty years later, Georges Pitoëff, with genial intuition as to how Pirandello's *Six Characters in Search of an Author* ought to be presented to Parisian theatergoers, will literally rip open the ceiling of his set so as to lower Pirandello's six authorless characters

1

on to it in an old open stage-elevator that had once been used to bring on scenery. "In that surpassing moment," William Herman wrote many years later, "Pitoëff said everything in a single rendering: at once it was clear what the title meant. The central aesthetics of the playwright were demonstrated: the same elevator which dropped his ideas down on stage brought also a prophecy of how Pirandello was to be occupied for years to come." [2]

Was Pitoëff's ingenious opening a theatrical stunt? No doubt it was—just like the hole torn in the sky of Mattia Pascal's puppet theater that makes a strutting Orestes start to fret like Hamlet. When he first learned what Pitoëff planned to do with the opening scene, Pirandello was annoyed and tried to stop him. There was no sky-rending stunt in his text. But at the dress rehearsal, when he saw how the Director's eyes, and the eyes of everyone else in the theater, were drawn absurdly to those "influences" coming down upon what had been for decades the parlor-stage of the realistic theater, he must have sensed at once the power of that stunt to disarm more than just a puppet-Orestes. He had meant, as a dramatist, to tear a hole in the traditional theatrical stage; why not let his intention be registered, at least for the blasé audiences of a Paris opening, in this spectacular way?

When they opened at the Comédie des Champs-Elysée with Pirandello's Six Characters in 1923, George and Ludmilla Pitoëff and their troupe had been struggling along as one of the more than sixty foreign theatrical companies that had "invaded" France after World War I. Their success with the play raised them at once to a place of first rank, even as it established overnight an international reputation for their Sicilian playwright.

Pirandello was to dominate the Parisian international theater for the whole period between the two world wars. The Second World War, which ranged France against Italy, had a dampening effect; but after 1945, Pirandello enjoyed an enormous revival, there and elsewhere in Europe, and beyond. By then, Pitoëff's stunts (as well as the hypnotic spectral stage effects that Max Reinhardt introduced in the original German productions) had been set aside and the permanent features of Pirandello's dramatic art came to the fore.

In the late fifties, when Jean Paul Sartre was asked to name the one dramatist who, in his opinion, was the most timely and modern, he answered at once: "It is most certainly Pirandello." [3] To that same question, Georges Neveux replied:

> Without Pirandello and without the Pitoëffs (because one can no longer separate them, the genius of the Pitoëffs having given its form to Pirandello's) we would have had neither Salacrou, nor Anouilh, nor today Ionesco, nor . . . [sic] but I shall stop, this enumeration would be endless. The entire theatre of an era came out of the womb of that play, *Six Characters*. [4]

What Pirandello's first reception in America was like can best be judged from the record of Arthur Livingston's efforts to get the early plays translated and produced in the twenties. Professor Livingston was at that time (as Samuel Putnam identifies him) the "leading Italianist of the English-speaking world." [5] Livingston invited Pirandello to visit the United States, put him up as a houseguest, introduced him to the New York City intelligentsia, and undertook with producer-director Brock Pemberton to get his plays performed on a regular basis on Broadway—but with far less success, in the long run, than the Pitoëffs had in Paris.

In his "Prefatory Note" to a volume, published in 1922, of three plays by Pirandello (*Six Characters* and *Henry IV*, translated by Edward Storer, and *Right You Are [If You Think So!]*, translated by himself and now known as *It Is So [If You Think So]*), Livingston observed that *Six Characters* is by no means merely a theatrical "trick" exploiting in an unusually ingenious manner the old theme of the play within a play; on the contrary, he wrote, it is nothing less than "a dramatization of the artistic process itself," exploring with truly profound dramatic insight the mysteries of the creative imagination. "I suppose the human soul presents no mysteries to those who have been thoroughly grounded in the science of Freud," he concluded. "But in spite of psycho-analysis a few Hamlets still survive. Pirandello is one of them." [6]

After Livingston's time (which was also the time of an appreciative Stark Young), Pirandello suffered a virtually total eclipse in America—until the appearance of Eric Bentley's *The Playwright as Thinker* in 1946. In those days, the American critic who knew the Pirandello plays firsthand was rare; those inclined to reject him, fashionably, for his "tiresome ideas" were only too numerous. Against that tendency, Bentley wrote:

> Ostensibly Pirandello's plays and novels are about the relativity of truth, multiple personality, and the dif-ferent levels of reality. But it is neither these subjects nor—precisely—his treatment of them that constitutes Pirandello's individuality. The themes grow tiresome after a time, and those who find nothing else in Pirandello give him up as a bad job. The novelist Franz Kafka was long neglected because his work also gave the impression of philosophic obsession and willful eccentricity. Then another and deeper Kafka was discovered. Another and deeper Pirandello awaits discovery. [7]

Bentley has, in effect, repeated the labors of discovery that Arthur Livingston pursued in the twenties, but with far greater success. Following Bentley's lead, Francis Fergusson included a reevaluation of Pirandello in his book entitled *The Idea of a Theater: The Art of Drama in Changing Perspective*, which first appeared in 1949. Fergusson was much taken with Pirandello's notion of the stage as the life of the creative imagination literally "invaded" by the dramatis personae who become its reality. His assessment reminds us of the plight of Orestes under a rent puppet sky.

> The most fertile property of Pirandello's dramaturgy is his use of the stage itself. By so boldly accepting it for what it is, he freed it from the demand which modern realism had made of it, that it be a literal copy of scenes

off-stage; and also from the exorbitant Wagnerian de-
mand, that it be an absolutely obedient instrument of
hypnosis in the power of the artist. Thus he brought to
light once more the wonderful property which the stage
does have: of defining the primitive and subtle medium
of the dramatic art. "After Pirandello"—to take him
symbolically rather than chronologically—the way was
open for Yeats and Lorca, Cocteau and Eliot. The search
could start once more for a modern poetry of the theater,
and even perhaps for an idea of the theater comparable
to that of the Greeks yet tenable in the modern world.[8]

Since the reevaluations of Bentley and Fergusson, Pirandello has gradually come into his own in America, at least
in our university theaters if not on Broadway—although with
the production of *Henry IV* at Lincoln Center in 1973, the
ground was apparently broken for a change there too. Robert
Brustein has indicated in "Pirandello's Drama of Revolt"
what must now be regarded as permanent acquisitions for
contemporary Pirandellian criticism. Supporting the judgments of Livingston, Bentley, and Fergusson, he recognizes
as Pirandello's "most original achievement in his experimental plays . . . the dramatization of the very act of creation." Pirandello's dramatis personae, he says, are living
signatures of his artistry, "being both his product and his
process." Brustein asserts flatly that "Pirandello's influence
on the drama of the twentieth century is immeasurable."
Some who have felt his influence were perhaps better
artists, greater practitioners of the art "dramatized" in his
plays, but there is no doubt in Brustein's mind that even
a "partial list of influences marks Pirandello as the most
seminal dramatist of our time." Summing up his judgment,
the author of *The Theatre of Revolt* takes us to the very
threshold of what motivates us to add still another book to
the rapidly expanding Pirandello bibliography of our day.

In his agony over the nature of existence, he anticipates
Sartre and Camus; in his insights into the disintegration
of personality and the isolation of man, he anticipates
Samuel Beckett; in his unremitting war on language,

theory, concepts, and the collective mind, he anticipates
Eugene Ionesco; in his approach to the conflict of truth
and illusion, he anticipates Eugene O'Neill (and later,
Harold Pinter and Edward Albee); in his experiments
with the theatre, he anticipates a host of experimental
dramatists, including Thornton Wilder and Jack Gelber;
in his use of the interplay between actors and characters,
he anticipates Jean Anouilh; in his view of the tension
between public mask and private face, he anticipates
Jean Giraudoux; and in his concept of man as a role-
playing animal, he anticipates Jean Genet.

Beyond his vast seminal importance, Pirandello has of
course also left us a body of extraordinary plays which, as
Brustein readily admits, "continue to live with the same
urgency as when they were first written." [9]

In the chapters which follow, we shall examine this body
of extraordinary plays with a view toward increasing our
understanding and appreciation of them. Through an analysis of their dramatic action, seizing where possible the
characteristic acts that define the dramatis personae and
interpreting the rich network of interrelated themes as they
unfold in a bold and innovative language, we hope to
identify the dramatic excellence of these plays. I have
chosen for this purpose certain representative plays, which
I feel lend themselves best to the kind of examination here
outlined; but as a kind of general introduction I shall start
with a discussion of Pirandello's theater as a whole, exploring briefly the artistic impulse that gave it life and that
makes it an organically conceived dramatic world.

## 2

# Art for Life's Sake

Pirandello came to the theater late in life, when he was close
to fifty, and long established as a poet, short-story writer,
and novelist of considerable fame. He was born on June
28, 1867 in Girgenti, Sicily (since renamed Agrigento to
recall its original Greek name). The chronology of his pre-
dramatic writings begins with a collection of poems, *Mal
giocondo* (*Joyful Pain*), which appeared when he was
twenty-two. A second collection, *Pasqua di Gea* (*The Easter
of Gea Tellus*), followed in 1891. Then came his first volume
of short stories, *Amori senza amore* (*Loves without Love*),
in 1894; his *Rhine Elegies* (1895) and verse translations of
Goethe's *Roman Elegies* (1896); his earliest novels, *L'esclusa*
(*The Outcast*), 1901, and *Il turno* (*The Turn*), 1902; new
volumes of short stories spread out over a dozen years; the
novel that gave him an international reputation, *Il fu Mattia
Pascal* (*The Late Mattia Pascal*), 1904; and his much-
discussed literary essay, *L'umorismo* (*On Humor*), 1908.
These works in their very titles suggest the themes of the
major plays to come: the confounding of opposites, complexities of family relationships, adultery, unrequited love,
death, the multiplicity of personality, the irony of self-
consciousness — to name only a few.
Pirandello's first efforts at playwriting were, in fact, not
so much plays in the strict sense, as short stories and novels
adapted for stage representation. He used to insist, right
down to the completion of *Six Characters in Search of an
Author* in 1921, that he really had no interest in playwriting

7

as such, that he looked down upon stage representation as a mere technique for communicating the substance of stories that are much better told, for intelligent readers, in narrative form. Later, he most emphatically acknowledged that his first notion of dramatic art was all wrong. While that notion lasted, however, he used to shudder at the thought of submitting his imaginative creations to the "whims" of directors and actors. He much preferred, he said, the direct communication of lyric poetry and the fully controlled narrative techniques of the novel and short story.

But then, apparently, he experienced the kind of reversal that T. S. Eliot tells us about in "The Three Voices of Poetry," where he acknowledges that he did not learn what drama was really all about until *after* he had written *Murder in the Cathedral*. Like Pirandello, Eliot had written lyric poems and had narrated (in verse) a variety of tales. When he first tried to write plays, with his pageant-play *The Rock* and then *Murder in the Cathedral*, he thought his task was merely to *stage* his poems and narratives. "The third, or dramatic voice, did not make itself audible to me," he confesses, "until I first attacked the problem of presenting two (or more) characters in some sort of conflict, misunderstanding, or attempt to understand each other, characters with each of whom I had to try to identify myself while writing words for him or her to speak." Eliot then introduces an illustration as genial as Pirandello's account of the hole torn in a puppet theater which transforms Orestes into Hamlet.

> You may remember that Mrs. Cluppins, in the trial of the case of Bardell *v.* Pickwick, testified that "the voices was very loud, sir, and forced themselves upon my ear." "Well, Mrs. Cluppins," said Sergeant Buzfuz, "you were not listening, but you heard the voices." It was in 1938, then, that the third voice began to force itself upon my ear.[1]

It was in 1916, when he was forty-nine, that the "third voice" began to force itself on Pirandello's ear. By 1921, it had possessed him completely. In Pitoëff's words, from that moment "theater is in Pirandello; Pirandello is theater." [2] And Ionesco confirms the judgment, saying: "[Luigi Pirandello] is the manifestation of the inalterable archetype of the idea of the theater which we have in us." [3]

What poetry's third voice (and it was always *poetry* that talked to Pirandello) forces on the imagination is recognition that all the world's a stage and that all the men and women who appear on it generation after generation are caught up in its perpetually renewed drama of genuinely free personality. That vision of the world gave birth to tragedy and comedy among the ancient Greeks. Without seeking it, Pirandello relived the experience of that birth in himself.

In our everyday existence, we sense personality—human willful self-centeredness—all around us and in ourselves. But it is so mixed, so confused, that we cannot focus our attention on it easily. Our naïve self-concern in the pursuit of immediate goals and needs easily distracts our attention. Art no less than religion is a response to that all-pervading sense of personality in and around us: that mighty presence, as Wordsworth called it, in its first manifestation to him, when it haunted him like a passion—long before he learned to hear in it

> *The still, sad music of humanity,*
> *Nor harsh, nor grating, though of ample power*
> *To chasten and subdue.*[4]

From the lyric voice of poetry, Wordsworth had passed to that of lyrical narration; but he never heard the third—the dramatic voice of multiple personality, which is sad music still, but with power to purge us of our self-assertive and exclusive concern for ourselves.

Pirandello had his lyrical and narrative times. Viewing the confusion of wills around us, his first response was an anguished lyrical cry of sympathy, like Shelley's

> *Me, who am as a nerve o'er which do creep*
> *The else-unfelt oppressions of this earth.*[5]

Later, coming out of himself in his short stories and novels, Pirandello tried to represent sympathetically the confusion of wills in others (a confusion that impinges on our consciousness daily), seeking to give it a meaningful and communicable form. His narratives succeed; but as he develops his narrative skills, it soon becomes clear that it is the depths of willful personality that most interest him—which is to say that, though not quite consciously yet, he is all the while in search of theater.

When Pirandello finally hears that third voice—characters speaking for themselves to one another—his poet's eye leaps at once to the frenzied heart of the matter, and he bodies forth his dramatis personae as *maschere nude* (naked masks), which is the perfect Italian equivalent for the personae of drama in the ancient sense of the term. Personality in its nakedness is a phrase and a thought that takes us to the vital center of dramatic art. Pirandello places himself at that center; and from there, everything he sees, everything he remembers, everything that his friends—especially old Sicilian friends—tell him about life becomes dramatically provocative.

It has been observed that in any old Italian villa, or *palazzo*, or humble cottage, or city apartment, or rooming house, one can meet the very people Pirandello gives us in his plays—people as odd, as complex, as involuted. If we don't see them there, if we don't see them in our own homes, in ourselves wherever we are, it is because we just don't want to see them, because we resist the experience. Pirandello, as he makes clear in his short stories, saw with a lyric poet's eye the alienated types who feel themselves rejected in their families, in their village society, at work and at play. He saw also the opposite types who impose their will on everybody around them, forcing acceptance of what they insist is the truth of a situation when to most others—and to the alienated most of all—the situation is nothing of the sort. In Sicily such willfulness is, of course, at the heart of the life-style of the *mafiosi*, in whom a notorious sense of honor drives out every ordinary sense of truth when truth is likely to offend honor.

Alienation and aggressive self-assertion for honor's sake were most intense in the Sicily of Pirandello's youth. Yet, the tension between them was drawn to such extremes as to embrace within its range the infinite variety of personal conflicts that make up the social experience of men, women, and children everywhere.

Pirandello held up his dramatic mirror for all the world to see itself in it. He fashioned that mirror, first of all, with the materials of his native Sicily. His first significant play— the one which, in Eric Bentley's judgment, Americans ought to start with—has all the power and charm of the Sicilian world that fascinated Goethe when he wrote "Kennst du das Land?" It celebrates the ordinary, everyday life of rural, Arabic Sicily, whose exultant moods are splendidly voiced in the natural poetic genius of Liolà. Written originally in Girgenti dialect and first performed in 1916, *Liolà* springs full-blown into dramatic being, without laborious preparation, out of Pirandello's storehouse of narrated tales. It is deceptively light and comically realistic; but—as we shall see in the next chapter—the surface realism is under great tension, and the comic spirit cuts through the fibers of that surface until we sense the pressure of a world of tortured self-consciousness about to burst through from below.

After *Liolà*, Pirandello plunges headlong into that tortured underlying world. He starts, as a rule, with a seemingly solid, everyday situation which he then proceeds to tear apart. He does this in a parallel series of plays, one of which explores dramatically why theater came into being in the first place and why so many people still feel that its representations of human conflict can give meaning to man's earthly existence more adequately than most other forms of experience; while the other, plunging deeper, explores the lowest depths of human motivation, where we experience most directly the need for a theatrical catharsis to shape a personal self for ourselves out of the fragmented chaos of passions and emotions which is our everyday existence.

The first series consists of Pirandello's so-called theater

plays, with which he invaded the modern stage to recover it for dramatic art. In them he attempts to do for a thoroughly self-conscious age what Aeschylus, Sophocles, Euripides, and Aristophanes did for a Greek society which was anything but self-conscious. It was not until Greece had had its great tragedies that Socrates, a contemporary of Aristophanes, first took to heart the oracular utterance: Know Thyself. Even in Shakespeare's time, when Hamlet takes the place of Orestes, self-consciousness is not all-pervading, as it has become in our post-Kantian age.

What can the theater be for a self-critical, thoroughly self-conscious age like our own? Surely not the setting for a communal, religious, political ceremony such as it had been for the Greeks. What then? To answer that question, Pirandello takes our modern theater apart for us. He shows us its inner operation, how it works to shape personality *for* us on the stage, and *in* us through the dramatic catharsis we experience. The three plays that Pirandello himself grouped together as his "theater" plays (*Six Characters in Search of an Author, Each in His Own Way, Tonight We Improvise*) will be considered in detail from this point of view in the third chapter.

But what are we before dramatic art—which is our universal legacy in the Western world—succeeds in purging us, vicariously, to give us inner form? Pirandello shows us that too. In a series of plays, starting with *The Life I Gave You* and *It Is So (If You Think So)*, and running through *As Well As Before, Better than Before,* and *At the Exit,* to *Henry IV,* Pirandello forces us to experience for ourselves what happened to poor Orestes when a hole was torn through the marionette sky of his "classical" tragedy.

In this second series of plays on the complex depths of character, not less than in his theater plays, Pirandello anticipates the experimental efforts of our contemporary existential drama, our theaters of the absurd, of revolt, of protest, our "happenings." In one fell swoop, he—more than any other single playwright of this century—has shown the dramatic potential of certain philosophical questions *as theater,* translating difficult ideas into ingenious and immediate realities for the stage, redefining traditional "character" and "action" for the purpose, and transforming conventional language into a series of exchanges which defy standard "communication." He paved the way for the fragmentation of language which we find in Ionesco; he turned dramatic statement into a provocative reassessment of perception and experience, of the kind we find in Giraudoux and Genet; he explored the age-old questions of death and life in modern myths which invite comparison with Camus, Sartre, and Beckett. One must stress, however, that in all his ingenious reversals of traditional values and dramatic concepts, he never sacrificed the notion of "organic" theater.

It is worth noting here that the personae, or masks, of the ancient Greek theater were meant to *conceal* the confused complexity that makes us, before character is defined, some twenty several men at least each several hour. Those Greek masks were worn by actors who did not have to make their own faces and bodies into masks. They simply "put on" their dramatic personalities, and the playwright's words were intelligible to the audience on their own merit, regardless of whether the actors took emotional possession of them. The lines were recited; acting counted for next to nothing. In the modern theater, starting with the age of Shakespeare, *wearing* personality and *reciting* the playwright's words in an external fashion no longer sufficed—for the same reason that it was no longer acceptable dramatically to hold characters responsible for deeds they have not intentionally committed, as in the Oedipus cycle of Sophocles.

Pirandello grasped fully the difference between the ancient and the modern sense of personality. The modern consciousness of right and wrong, the Judaic-Christian "conscience" and notion of guilt, the subjective attitude of self-conscious individuality as distinguished from the objective fact of accomplished deeds, have dictated a new mold for modern drama. The heroes of modern drama since Shakespeare's time have made their tragic decisions in the complex depths of personality, where the sanctions of moral law or social responsibility have no compelling force. Whether morally justified or wrong and criminal in their deeds, they invariably act as they do, not out of interest in the "ethical vindication" of the external absolutes they subscribe to but for the simple reason that they are the kind of men they are.

This new dramatic imperative of the modern world was given its first memorable expression in Shakespeare; but Pirandello is the first dramatist to express dramatically a *total* absorption in it. Shakespeare had already revealed that, when we look deeply into the motives of our actions, even when caught on the horns of a tragic dilemma, we are always faced with an absurdity that borders on the comic. Greek society, with its objectively confirmed absolutes of family and political values, concealed from itself the sense of "comic relief" that inevitably gnaws its way into our consciousness in moments of high, even tragic, drama.

That sense of comic relief, in tragedy, already strong in Shakespeare, becomes all-pervasive in Pirandello. His one major literary essay, *On Humor*, was devoted to an analysis of its significance for the full development of personality. It is ultimately a humorous experience to know oneself self-consciously. Each of us is an individual claiming "personal" rights objectively before the law; but each of us is also a moral subject claiming rights (and wrongs) of conscience, a family member claiming the love of parents, brothers and sisters, children, a "burgher" in the rat race of civil society, manifesting needs and struggling to secure the co-operation of others for the satisfaction of those needs, and, finally, a "citizen" with the rights and responsibilities of integration in a political fraternity. In those several roles, we manage to maintain a sense of personal unity on the strength of habit. But that unity is threatened again and again by the strain we feel internally as we pass out of one role into another, even in the course of a single ordinary day. In such moments, we are apt to see ourselves suddenly as we imagine "others" see us. We hold up a mirror to ourselves and, whether consciously or not, share at least for a moment in the essential process of creative art.

That is Pirandello's tour de force. We see ourselves

mirrored, but we're aware that we are somehow not what
we seemed, and the mirrored image embarrasses us, often
to the point of laughter. We may instinctively reject the
image. But not for long. Sooner or later, we admit to ourselves that we are what we were embarrassed to see mirrored back to us. And then our "humor" becomes a painful
awareness of the grotesque posturing our lives must seem
to be to others.

Humor, says Pirandello, is the uneasy acknowledgment
of the trial of personality as it is forced to recognize its
many masks. This is what links humor, or comedy, with
tragedy in the historic origin of drama among the Greeks.
In an essay on the history of the Italian theater—completed
late in his life—Pirandello tells us that the Greeks conceived
their plays as trials, offering the public what is, in fact, the
very essence of theater:

> a public trial of human actions as they truly are, in that
> pure and everlasting reality which the imagination of
> poets creates as an example and warning for our common-
> place and confused natural life—a trial both free and
> human, which spurs the consciences of the judges them-
> selves to an ever loftier and more rigorous moral life.
> This, in my judgment, is the value of the Theater.[6]

A public trial, both free and human—to catch our con-
sciences. Again and again, in the Greek theater, the question
is raised: What does it mean to be free? And in the answers
provided by Aeschylus, Sophocles, and Euripides, the Greek
audience—through emotional vicarious involvement in the
dramatized action—experienced the arrogance of freedom,
which makes us claim responsibility for all that we do or
suffer to be done to us, despite the fact that, by objective
analysis, by scrutinizing ourselves and our situations in detail, it is easy to "see" that a hundred, a thousand, a
hundred thousand "forces"—internal as well as external—
act on us to make us do what we do.

Pirandello displays the full complexity of that kind of
"trial." We are one, externally, in our many social and
legal masks; but under analysis, our oneness disintegrates,

breaks up into fragments. We are one—or, rather, we are a hundred thousand different "ones," as many as there are others around us mirroring our reflection differently each moment.

The dialectical struggle of the will to hold that complexity together is what Pirandello puts on display as a public trial. It is the common denominator of all his plays, and that is why we must dwell on it here. The Greeks, whose sense of family memberships and social commitment was much stronger, depicted that public trial or struggle in relatively simple terms. Shakespeare's trial of personality coming to know itself is much more complex. But Pirandello's burden—which is the moral burden of our age—is to deal with a world in which, the minute we stop seeing ourselves as one, we immediately see ourselves as no one, or as a hundred thousand ones. It is the same dramatic purpose at work, however: to put on public trial the complexities of human nature and conduct. When we look around us in everyday life, all we get is an image of ourselves in a shattered mirror. The playwright's burden is to give us something else: the reality of our fragmented wills, indeed, but so nakedly exposed, so focused, that it makes us whole at least in the shock of self-knowledge that makes us free.

Pirandello's is "difficult" theater, to say the least. But not more difficult than the reality which is the subject matter. The encrustations of habit are not easily cracked. How exactly do we go about "seeing ourselves" in the depths of our consciousness? Pirandello pictures it for us, usually, by having one of his characters look at his reflection in a mirror. That way we can get to see ourselves as others see us. And, as we usually try to get into the real consciousness of other people by looking steadfastly into their eyes, so we imagine we can do the same with our mirrored image; and with better results, since we are, after all, looking out of the same eyes we are looking into. That's our instinctive expectation. Yet, when we try it, what we actually see is an utterly distracting look with which we are not in the least able to identify ourselves. We realize at once that we can do better by closing our eyes, by not looking out at all, so that the mind's eyes may turn inward upon themselves.

Consciousness turned inward is self-consciousness. Even before a mirror, consciousness is very different from self-consciousness. Consciousness, at best, must have a naïve confidence in its sensory experience. Facing the world of things it can see, hear, smell, taste, and touch, things that are *here* and *now*, consciousness says simply: *così è—it is so.* But that initial sense of certainty is easily destroyed. The *here* and *now* which is the basis of our certainty of things disappears the moment we turn our attention away. *It is so* only if that's how you see it: *se vi pare.*

So we turn away from things that only appear to be and focus our consciousness inward upon itself (as Socrates advised). There, needless to say, we get a totally different impression of things. Our first impulse, then, is to empty our consciousness of all its sensory impressions, so as to see it in its nakedness. The immediate effect is like an empty mirror reflected into an empty mirror ad infinitum. There is great depth, but no content. We have, indeed, our *self* mirroring itself; but, without specific content, it could be *any* self, in any body; and that, we quickly recognize, is the antithesis of what is ordinarily meant by personality.

We were *somebody*, however confused, in simple consciousness. Now, in our first attempt at self-consciousness, we are suddenly *nobody*. Pirandello forces the sensation of this experience on us repeatedly in his plays. It is by no means a theatrical stunt. But neither is it a psychological or phenomenological tour de force that were better left to philosophers. The ancient Greek drama, in fact, discovered its tragic and comic masks—its dramatis personae—in the very depths of this dialectic of self-consciousness. The nothingness, the nobody or anybody we initially find there is the naked will whose task it is to shape us a proper persona, or mask, which will hold together, according to its strength, the confusion of our everyday conscious experience which makes us twenty several men at least each several hour.

But there is a dilemma in the experience of the naked will mirroring itself in empty self-consciousness. Which is the original, real will and which the mirrored image? Which was the original consciousness that emptied itself of its empirical experience of the world to study itself and which —in the act of self-reflection—is the reflected consciousness?

The question is worth exploring even apart from its strictly theatrical importance (which is critical for any serious study of the idea of drama) if for no other reason than that it has literally revolutionized our contemporary society, on and offstage. Students of Karl Marx know how fascinated he was by Hegel's discussion of the dilemma of self-consciousness in the *Phenomenology*.[7] Whether he actually read Hegel or not, Pirandello certainly knew the experience and has dramatized it with great daring, and convincingly, in many plays. It is a dilemma each of us can experience for himself. In what is perhaps his most brilliantly conceived novel, *Uno, nessuno, e centomila* (*One, No One, and a Hundred Thousand*), Pirandello explores the progression from full consciousness, as somebody, to empty self-consciousness, as nobody in particular, to the third level of awareness that combines the fullness of the first with the infinite self-reflection of the second, in a dizzying experience of mirrored fullness where the confusion is a thousand times, a hundred thousand times what it originally was, and we are no closer than before to discovering which is the original self-conscious will and which the reflected image.

In his *Phenomenology*, Hegel reminds us that entire ages, entire civilizations—as, for instance, the ancient Hindu— have been wrapped up in it, to the point of abandoning any commonsense awareness of our so-called objective world. Each of us, even here in the West, where empirical science reigns, must plunge into it at least momentarily if we are ever to know what "knowing" really is. Hegel characterizes the experience as that of the "unhappy consciousness." It is difficult to come out of it without an act of "hybris," as the ancient critics of drama defined the term—without an arrogant assertion of willful self-mastery, such as the protagonists of the Greek tragedies displayed onstage for the moral edification of the Greek citizenry.

It takes a creative, dramatic arrogance to make "one" out of the division of mirrored consciousness mirroring its mirrored consciousness. In that experience, our original naïve consciousness is literally beside itself, as if it were another self; and when it seeks to overcome that division, it literally *crowds* itself in infinite self-reflection, like that fiend in William Blake's cloud who *crowds*, in his fierce madness, after night.

In the end, one side of mirrored self-consciousness must overwhelm the other—or surrender itself to the other (which is really the same thing)—if we are to be made whole. Hegel calls it a conflict between lord and bondsman, or master and servant, in which the roles end up being reversed before they are confounded. Karl Marx, as we know, saw his Communist revolution of the proletariat as accomplishing in civil society precisely the reversal of roles which Hegel indicates as the inevitable outcome of the master-servant struggle in the divided self-consciousness. Following Hegel's specific indications, the author of the *Communist Manifesto* argued that, by arming its servants with industrial skills and the weapons of war, the bourgeois ruling class of modern industrial society was giving its very being, with all its strength, to its enemy and thus virtually committing suicide. Marx's "final solution" to the bourgeoisie-proletariat struggle (in which the proletariat triumphs absolutely with its dictatorship) is the antithesis of Hegel's view of the ultimate outcome. Hegel emphasizes that the I-Thou opposition in self-consciousness is truly resolved not when one side insists that the other side is nothing, a *not-I*, but when the opposed sides of consciousness recognize their higher unity as "we" in creative reason.

Pirandello's dramatization of the experience follows the course of the Hegelian analysis. Out of the dramatized conflict in play after play written late in his career, he brings us to a new sense of "we," of a unity of personality in self-consciousness; and in that unity or synthesis, the Greek tragic catharsis finds its modern equivalent.

Just as he explored in one series of plays what the stage is and has been for civilized society, and in another the depths of personality that provide the substance of dramatic art, so Pirandello gives us a third series of plays that dramatize, onstage, the experience of dramatic catharsis itself. His last great plays—the so-called myths of *The New Colony*, *Lazarus*, and *The Mountain Giants*, taken together with *Diana and Tuda* and *When Someone Is Somebody*, are an integral and culminating part of Pirandello's dramatic world. They can stand alone, of course, on their own merits as distinct works of art; but, like Shakespeare's *Tempest* and, even more, like his *Henry VIII*, they reveal their full dramatic significance only to those who are thoroughly at home in the dramatic world of which they are the culminating achievement.

In ancient Greek drama, the tragic catharsis was by no means complete in the first or second work of a grand trilogy. Aeschylus's *Prometheus Bound* needs not only a Prometheus unbound to complete its dramatic effect, but also a play establishing Prometheus in Attica as a benignant deity. In the *Agamemnon-Cheophori-Eumenides* trilogy, the cycle is not complete until Orestes is tried in a rational court and acquitted by a vote of Athene which puts the family curse to rest. Sophocles's trilogy of *Oedipus Tyrannos*, *Antigone*, and *Oedipus at Colonus* gives us, in fact, three distinctly different masterpieces, in which the third takes on a transcendent importance it could not otherwise have had as a work of art, when it is read as the culmination of that particular trilogy.

In his last plays, Pirandello is in effect drawing the chief meridians of his theatrical world upward to converge at a single pole. This whole business of life can be for us all no more than a tale told by an idiot unless we get deep enough below the surface of conventional values to the substantive core. What blind Oedipus "saw" at Colonus, what Orestes experienced in Athene's court of ultimate appeal, what Shakespeare reveals to us in the magic art of Prospero and in Cranmer's prophecy at the christening of the child destined to become Queen Elizabeth—such is the substance of Pirandello's myth plays. In them he gathers up all that he had already dramatized, into a new synthesis, to show us its social, religious, and artistic reality, in its rightness, its holiness, and its beauty.

Pirandello's theatrical world is planted deep in the common soil of human experience, with a sturdy weathered and twisted trunk of theatrical expertise that enables him to review for us dramatically the meaning of theater, and with marvelous branches of evergreen leaves that come and go imperceptibly, laden with seasonal fruit. Just before he died, Pirandello had a vision of such a tree—the great Saracen olive of Sicily. He explained to his son, on the morning of the day before his death, that with that tree planted in the center of the stage, for the curtain to come down in the unwritten final act of *The Mountain Giants*, he would solve everything he meant to show. That great tree, whose roots he had revealed in his masterful *Liolà*, was meant to symbolize the completion of his theater.

How that tree was nourished through its Sicilian roots— how the characteristically Sicilian origins of Pirandello's theater nourished the growth of a truly universal dramatic art—is not the least of the themes we mean to pursue in the chapters that follow.

# 3

# The Arabic-Sicilian Microcosm of *Liolà*

*Liolà.* The women of the village, hired by Zio Simone for the day, are shelling almonds, singing and gossiping as they work. Like a wizened Greek chorus, they complain (not altogether without sympathy) about the old man's crankiness and miserliness, especially since his young wife, Mita, it appears, will not produce the heir expected of her. When Mita joins the group, her husband berates her publicly for her "inadequacy"; but behind his display of righteous grievance, everyone has recognized the truth: Mita is simply the victim of the old man's impotence. Liolà, to whom the young women of the vallage are irresistibly drawn, appears. At their bidding, he sings, teasing the girls with lyrics about his free and easy ways and playing on his notorious reputation as a Don Juan. Tuzza—sullen and moody—is the only one who does not respond. It soon comes out that she is pregnant with his child; but Tuzza vows she will never have Liolà as her husband because she will not share him with other women (he has already fathered three illegitimate children, whom he cares for with his old mother, Ninfa). Tuzza plots with her mother Zia Croce to offer the yet unborn child to Zio Simone, as his "heir," in return for security and a special place in his household. Simone agrees. But Liolà, infuriated by Tuzza's deception, works out his own counterplot and makes Mita conceive. When Zio Simone learns that his wife is pregnant, he is overjoyed. He refuses to believe that it is not his child, and Tuzza is thus deprived of all that she had hoped to gain by "giving" Simone her own illegitimate offspring. Having thus accomplished—with Liolà's help—what was expected of her, Mita is restored to her rightful place in her husband's home (1916).

"In reconsidering Pirandello today," writes Eric Bentley, "the first play to read is *Liolà*." Although it is the most lyrical of Pirandello's plays, and thus must lose much of its poetry in translation, "enough of the original comes through," Bentley insists, "to remove the anti-Pirandellian prejudice. It is a play that lives by an evident loveliness. . . . Amid the spurious apocalyptics of the few and the genuine hysteria of the many—so far the only spiritual manifestations of the atomic age—anything that recalls us to sanity is welcome. Pirandello's tidings of great joy are the best 'message' any theatrical manager of today could find."

Bentley, sharing what he calls its holiday mood, would have us relish the "breath of a happy paganism" in the play, and he calls it, in that spirit, the "last Sicilian pastoral." [1] And yet, when the curtain goes up and we hear a chorus of peasant women singing the "Passion" of Jesus while they shell nuts, we are at once made aware that, for all its promise of a breath of happy paganism, *Liolà* belongs to that postpagan world of "aching pleasure" that turns "to poison while the bee's mouth sips." [2] In Pirandello's Sicilian pastoral, as in Boccaccio's *Ninfale fiesolano*, it is too late for the joys of pristine pagan innocence. What joys there are— meant to suggest that pagan innocence—are really infected to the core, or spiced, if one prefers, with a Christian popular sense of sin. Boccaccio, in his most pagan mood, had longed for the times when lovely nymphs were pursued and often caught by wanton satyrs in the Fiesolean hills above Florence. But he realized that there is really no turning back; Christianity had enveloped that pagan world, now grown old, like a gloomy cloud, or rather in the form of a spiritual plague more noxious than the physical plague from which the storytellers of his *Decameron* had fled. When the curtain goes up on Pirandello's *Liolà*, the women of Arabic-Christian Sicily sing:

> *When Jesus was being scourged,*
> *Mary was at the gate.*
> *"Don't strike so hard," she cried,*
> *"His flesh is delicate."*

The verses of this "passion" are punctuated with gossip that anticipates the play's action, and as a distraction from the monotony of shelling almonds their words are highly suggestive, symbolic even, of the true spirit of the play. In the original dialect version of the last two lines—

> *Nun cci dati accussi forti,*
> *su' carnuzzi delicati!*

—the diminutive "carnuzzi" suggests even more powerfully the premature ripening into maturity which is the underlying theme of the play.

In *The Late Mattia Pascal*, Pirandello tells how fruit vendors force the ripening of what has been picked from the tree prematurely, using the illustration to suggest what life has done to Mattia Pascal. Old science manuals explain, under the heading "What causes ripeness?" (Mattia Pascal notes), that ripening takes place naturally when the heat of the sun acts on the native cold temperature of the pulpy fruit. But fruit vendors have discovered, by experimentation, he says, that fruit can be made to ripen by "bruising" it. This practice enables them to bring to market a preseason sampling of fruit and sell it at a high price. That, he explains, is how my soul was made ripe, while it was still green and bitter.

In his brilliant and unpretentious study of Pirandello's Sicily (*Pirandello e la Sicilia*), Leonardo Sciascia cites this passage from *The Late Mattia Pascal* as a key to Pirandello's dramatic art. In Sicily especially (though it is a universal experience), young men and women often get "bruised" to maturity while their flesh is still as delicate as that of our Lord, in the "passion" sung at the opening of *Liolà*.

What bruises most, and earliest, in Sicily is, of course, the traditional sense of family honor. From his first moments of awareness, the Sicilian child is made conscious of what things he must value more than life if he is not to risk staining the family honor. Family property is to be valued in that way. Property is accumulated not to be consumed or enjoyed personally but to be passed on as a family legacy. The chastity of women is to be valued similarly, with honor to be saved at all costs.

But when is honor really safe? Only with a "successful" death of the kind that Socrates, Plato, and Aristotle talk about when they say that to have lived a truly happy life means to die happy. For most people, the pursuit of happiness rarely goes beyond the pursuit of pleasure; but in some lands like modern Sicily the pursuit of happiness is bound up almost wholly in the pursuit of honor. In this kind of situation, those who long for other forms of happiness are forced sooner or later to deny their instincts and are "bruised" in the process of trying to avoid being rejected by their society. A few become total outcasts.

Liolà, "the poet," lives at least superficially in open defiance of all the norms of traditional Arabic-Sicilian society. Love in all its varied and joyous expressions—carnal, filial, charitable—is the sum and substance of his existence. He comes and goes with the winds, always ready to improvise a song. "Sing for us!" the country girls cry out when he first comes on the scene, as they shell almonds. And he gladly obliges, entertaining them with a provocative improvisation.

> Where you have a brain in your head,
> I've got a windmill instead.
> The wind turns the mill and the world as well,
> Round and round like a carousel.
>
> Today I burn with love for you, dear,
> From the top of my head to my toes,
> But tomorrow, don't look for me, I won't be here—
> I'll be gone with the first breeze that blows!
>
> So, keep the brain in your head,
> And I'll keep my windmill instead.
> The wind turns the wheel and the world as well,
> The whole world's my carousel.

But his characteristic "song of love" is plaintively tender, even though he sings it as if to mock an old "man of honor," Uncle Simone, for his shameless jealousy, greed, and constant apprehension. "Don't be afraid of me," says Liolà, "you don't have anything I could possibly want."

> Last night I slept in an open field,
> With a few feet of earth for a bed,
> Under a blanket of stars I slept,
> With a thistle tucked under my head.
> Worry and hunger, debts to pay?
> Not for me! I just sing them away.
> I sing and my heart is filled with the joy of my song,
> I sing and the hills echo back every rhyme of my song!
> I have health, the bright sun above,
> These blond kids of mine and the girls that I love,
> And a tiny old woman, of course—like my mother! [3]

He kisses his mother, and the girls—ecstatic—clap hands around him.

*Liolà* is the most self-contained and complete of the Pirandellian plays. The tensions of human relations, of self-scrutiny, which in the later plays take us to the brink of madness, darkness, and death are barely noticeable here. Roberto Rebora correctly cites it as the only play in the Pirandello repertory in which the protagonist stands out fully defined and whole in a natural setting, the values of which are fully affirmed and accepted, despite the tendency of the social environment to "bruise" the natural instincts and emotions to premature ripeness. Indeed, not until we reach Pirandello's grand "myths," in which social, religious, and artistic values are again asserted as unambiguous truth, do we find anything resembling the self-contained world of *Liolà*. [4]

This early play is no doubt Pirandello's dramatic statement of his naturalistic or veristic heritage. But, as we have already suggested, the naturalism of the action and characterizations is anything but naïve or simply descriptive. We are led very early in the play, with marvelous simplicity, to recognize that its "realism" is, if not deceptive, at least misleading. We are already in the "theater of illusion," even though the romantic nostalgic mood, which later erupts into emotional paroxysms and destructive evocations of the past, here remains only a melancholy feeling, barely discernible in the self-righteous argument which, as we shall see, is advanced in the play to justify an unusual inversion of traditional moral codes. In *Liolà*, innocence survives the "dissolution of character." And that alone would suffice to make it unique in the corpus of Pirandellian plays.

It is also unique in other ways, however. *Liolà* moves forward at an even pace, uninterrupted by dramatic novelties; its characters never betray themselves in the tortured intensity of self-analysis. There is no effort to probe motivations beyond the given situation, no probing of the dark corners of the soul, no deliberate heightening of dramatic illusion through the unexpected and the absurd. Facts and events are what they are, and they are confronted squarely. The telescoping of past and present, the psychological stratification of such plays as *It is So (If You Think So)*, *As Well As Before, Better than Before, Naked, Henry IV* are not to be found here. From the standpoint of construction, it is perhaps the most formal and traditional of Pirandello's plays. It is to the later repertory what *Julius Caesar* is to Shakespeare's later tragedies: a relatively undisturbed action, beautifully integrated into an artistic whole, yet restlessly suggestive of what is to become for the playwright a new dramatic experience.

The hero of *Liolà* is, according to the author himself, a kind of sun-inebriated deity, a combination Pan and Dionysius in a Christian setting—the god of song and love seen against a compelling backdrop of religion and morality. The very names of the characters suggest a strange contrapuntal play of biblical and mythological elements: Ninfa, Mita, Gesa, Croce, Simone. One might even argue with a certain amount of success that the play is a subtle parody of Christian values; the climax—the scene between Mita and Liolà, the night of Zio Simone's acknowledgment that Tuzza's child is his—contains, in fact, a number of significant references to the Virgin birth. Mita herself has been cast out, as it were, and has been forced to take refuge in her aunt's poor hut. That a symbolic pattern exists would be hard to deny, but it remains an unobtrusive commentary, felt rather than grasped consciously. One can see or read the play any number of times without really becoming aware of that pattern. Nevertheless it is there; and once recognized, it becomes significantly obvious.

We have already noted how the symbolic suggestions are felt in a troubled pastoral atmosphere not unlike that of Boccaccio's *Ninfale fiesolano*. It is far more important for our purpose to stress that the underlying irony in the romantic setting of Pirandello's play recalls another great masterpiece, Machiavelli's *Mandragola. Liolà* too, in a sense, is an attempt to integrate pagan innocence—or indifference—and Christian morality.

Comparison with *Mandragola* is especially interesting and deserves our attention here since it helps to illustrate what has been said thus far about Pirandello's preoccupation with translating conventional reality into internal conviction. It is no mere coincidence that in his first major work as a dramatist, Italy's greatest modern playwright should have attempted what is virtually a revision—or, rather, a dramatic turning-inside-out—of what deserves still to be regarded as the first masterpiece of the Italian theater. The two plots deal with the same kind of deception: an old wealthy man marries, beneath his status, a virtuous young woman who finally produces the heir he longs for by allowing herself to be seduced by a young lover.

In *Mandragola*, the old wealthy Florentine Nicia actually helps in the plotting which culminates in the seduction of his young and beautiful wife, Lucrezia. He does so unknowingly—that is, unaware of the true motive behind the planning of Callimaco, the young "playboy" who comes all the way from France with a burning desire to see for himself the beautiful woman about whom everyone, far and wide, raves. Having seen her, naturally, he falls in love; and to get what he wants, he works out an elaborate plan which the old man not only agrees to but also helps to bring to pass. Nicia wants an heir so badly that he falls in im-

mediately with the arguments put forward by the priest, Fra
Timoteo, Callimaco, and the others, ready to do the most
dreadful things (including accessory to murder) in order to
have his son. Lucrezia is suspicious at first and will have no
part of the mad plot; but having realized that her own
confessor is ready to go along and is prepared to give her
arguments in favor of the seduction, she agrees. Finally,
having experienced the difference (as she says) between an
old husband and a young lover, she emerges at the end of
the play ready to accept her new life, confident in her
ability to handle the situation, and her husband, from that
moment on. The role of the priest is central to the play, and
—of course—reminds us of the larger Machiavellian canvas,
where political fragmentation results inexorably in the
fragmentation of all moral and personal values.

In *Liolà*, the old man, Zio Simone, is not a fool and
there are no arguments of the kind we find in Machiavelli's
cynical assessment of the situation. Mita, Simone's young
wife, is a virtuous woman to the end; Liolà is not a
scoundrel seeking to satisfy his lust; there is no one in
Pirandello's play like the hypocritical monk or the disreputable but loyal servant of Callimaco. Mita's mother,
unlike Lucrezia's, is unsuspecting and good; one feels she
could never be party to the kind of plot Lucrezia's mother
allows herself to be drawn into, in Machiavelli's play, and Zia
Gesa is never put to the test. Liolà, it is true, talks Mita into
sleeping with him; but his argument is sincere and selfless:
he will give her the child her husband craves only because
Tuzza has already tricked him into making her pregnant
and is offering the illegitimate child she now carries to
Simone as the heir he longs for in exchange for economic
security for her own family. She actually confesses to Zio
Simone that Liolà is the father of the child and leads him
to a private understanding whereby Simone—who wants
nothing more than to "pass on" his property to an heir—
will claim the child publicly as his own. Tuzza's illegitimate
child will give her an advantage over Mita, who has been
unable (so Simone claims) to bear him a son. Liolà, infuriated, decides to unmask the deception practiced upon

him by Tuzza; but he does so indirectly, by giving Mita the baby which Simone obviously cannot give her. And Zio Simone, for the reasons suggested (which dramatically remain beautifully ambiguous and which do not betray him as a fool) acknowledges Mita's child as his own and repudiates Tuzza.

It is the old story of the rape of Lucrece, stripped of its rigorous stoicism, in *Mandragola*, and revised as a romantic paradox in Pirandello's *Liolà*. Pirandello knew Machiavelli's play very well and ranks it, in his "Introduzione al teatro italiano," [5] as a masterpiece of world theater. Like Machiavelli, Pirandello wants to salvage the human situation. For Machiavelli, the rigorous sense of virtue is turned into a ruthless and cynical exposure of human nature, a desperate attempt to destroy all romantic illusions. For Pirandello, deception becomes an act of faith; the protagonists themselves accept it sincerely in their will and in their hearts. For Machiavelli, the outcome is accepted merely as convenience; the unspoken bond of necessity and a willingness to mask the illusion thus created provide a cynical justification for deception. For Pirandello, the situation is translated into convincing reality. The reasons for the deception are taken seriously; convenience becomes a romantic truth or, rather, a romantic lie. For, considering the matter with some of the later plays in mind, we cannot shake off the feeling that in translating convenience into self-deception the characters of *Liolà* have set up psychological tensions much more dangerous than anything suggested in *Mandragola*. A closer look at the two plays will show the profound gulf that separates them in spite of extraordinary similarities. The contrasts which emerge will help to define the Pirandellian world in its most essential features.

Machiavelli's uncompromising cynicism is embodied in the figure of Fra Timoteo, who not only turns logic into casuistry—in a brilliant argument which includes references to the Old Testament—but also disguises himself to join the others in effecting the hero's disreputable purpose. In his monk's garb he argues for a demonic inversion of Christian values.

When confronted with a good that is certain and an evil that is uncertain, one must never renounce that good for fear of that evil. Here we have a good that is certain: you will become pregnant, you will win a soul for our Good Lord; the uncertain evil is that the one who, after the potion, lies with you will die—but it also happens that some do not die. Still, since the thing is doubtful, it is well for Messer Nicia not to run that risk. As for the act itself, to call it a sin is empty talk; for it is the will that sins, not the body. What makes it sinful is to displease the husband, and you please him; to take pleasure in it, and you find only displeasure. Besides, it is the end that must be considered in all things; the end for you is to fill a throne in Heaven, to make your husband happy. The Bible says that the daughters of Lot, believing themselves to be the sole surviving women in the world, mated with their father, and because their intention was good, they did not sin.[6]

In his disguise, Fra Timoteo recalls the very values he has subverted; but without pangs of conscience. On the contrary, he has already sized up the situation and turned it to his advantage.

There's truth in the old saying that bad company leads men to the gallows; and often a person gets into trouble as much for being too easygoing and good-natured as for being too vicious. God knows I had no intention of harming anybody: I kept to my cell, I recited my office, I tended my flock; then this devil of a Ligurio crossed my path, who got me to stick a finger in a mess, into which I've sunk my whole arm, and my whole body, and I still don't know where I'll end up. But my one consolation is that when there are many people involved in a thing, many have to look after it.[7]

These passages are typical of Machiavelli's insistence on distinguishing the two levels of appearances and reality. Fra Timoteo, like all the other characters of *Mandragola*, must justify his actions in some way—but never by betraying basic values. For him, life is a matter of shrewd compromises; piety is simply maintaining certain appearances. He is perhaps the most farfetched embodiment of the Machiavellian dichotomy; hypocrisy is transparent in him. But he in no way differs in this respect from any of the other people in the play.

Pirandello's cynicism has a very different effect. Liolà, who like Fra Timoteo has the task of convincing the woman whose virtue must be sacrificed that the projected seduction is not wrong, seems to have justified his arguments to himself: they ring true. He too falls back on religious illustrations, but in his case they are perfectly believable. There is nothing rhetorical about them. They spring from the situation and are psychologically powerful and convincing. The only deception here is Tuzza's. When Mita says that she has resigned herself to the will of God and is ready to suffer in silence the wrong that is being done to her by Tuzza, Liolà lashes out:

> God, that's right.—He should take care of things.—He did, once.—But no matter how good you are, how modest and true to the holy commandments, you don't really believe you're the Virgin Mary, do you?

The argument is hammered home, with angry sarcasm. Mita can't seriously expect the Holy Ghost to descend upon her and make her conceive! God won't perform that kind of miracle! And she's a fool if she thinks even for a moment that everything will be resolved automatically. God can't extricate her from her predicament. "And you say I'm blaspheming!" he scolds. It is Mita who is blaspheming, thinking that God will take a hand in the matter.

Liolà's argument rises out of the situation; it has nothing of the perverted logic of Fra Timoteo's. Although he enjoys the reputation of a Don Juan, Liolà is not out to seduce Mita. His concern for her is genuine; he wants to help her. Mita has been cast out of her own house and an impostor has been welcomed in her place; Liolà will not allow Tuzza to prevail. His argument contains many references to God and the Virgin Mary, but these do not constitute a subversion of faith. On the contrary. Liolà must convince Mita that the divine precepts they hold dear have been undermined by their enemy and that heaven itself is on their side.

Tuzza's seemingly righteous plot must be counterbalanced with Liolà's seemingly unrighteous plan. In carrying out his plan, Liolà is, in effect, doing God's will. This equation is not spelled out in detail; it is only suggested in the careful allusions to religious motifs called forth by Mita's innocent appraisal of the predicament in conventional terms. The whole question of whether or not the seduction constitutes a sin is carefully avoided. The implications are further softened by suggestions on the part of others that Mita deserves a "miracle" such as the one Liolà has proposed for her. Aunt Gesa sets the mood for the romantic transvaluation of values:

> Rest assured, Zia Croce, not even a saint from heaven would tolerate the ill-treatment of that old wretch, the insults he throws at her in front of everybody. Even the Virgin Mary would cry out against such treatment. "You want a son, do you? Well, here's one for you!"

The religious motifs are woven into the texture of the play subtly and unobtrusively, setting the psychological mood for the "miracle" which finally occurs and taking the accomplished fact somewhere beyond hypocrisy. The Machiavellian universe has been turned upside down with the fine hand of poetic justification. As Piero Gobetti has commented: "In Pirandello dialectic itself becomes poetry." [8]

Mita's seduction in Pirandello's play arises from the natural sequence of events and involves no plotting of the usual kind. It appears, in fact, almost divinely inspired, a moment created by a strange unexpected juxtaposition of events, which no one could have foreseen. Liolà simply catches the moment: ripeness is all. His action is not selfish indulgence but the righting of a wrong. We see Mita onstage going back to her aunt's hut, after Zio Simone, in a fit of anger inspired by his declaration that Tuzza will now be part of the household and annoyed at his wife's reaction, drives her out. Mita's aunt has gone on an overnight trip to a neighboring town to see a lawyer about protecting Mita's interests. Liolà, who lives directly across from Mita's old home, sees Zio Simone come after his wife, to take her back with him, and hears Mita's vehement refusal. It is at this point that Liolà presents his case—or, rather, *her* case— to Mita. The argument is motivated by justice and real concern for Mita's welfare. Others, he tells her, have shown you what must be done, but you refuse to learn by their example. You're encouraging Tuzza in her despicable plot. For your sake, I have denied fathering her child . . . and I will continue to deny it so that our counterscheme can work. It's for your good—he tells her—because there is no other way out now.

> You think you're the only one who's suffering? God only knows what I've had to swallow! When I went there, to do my duty as a man of honor, and saw with my own eyes that beast of a mother invite your husband where Tuzza was waiting—ah! I saw the whole plot in a flash; I saw you, Mita, what would happen to you, and I swore to myself that they wouldn't get away with it! I closed my lips. And I waited for this moment! No, you musn't let them get away with it, Mita! It's up to you to pay them back in kind. God himself dictates it to you! She musn't be allowed to take advantage of me, that wretch, to destroy you!

The logic is convincing; what ordinarily would be reprehensible in the acceptable morality of Mita's world becomes a divine command rooted in another kind of justice. The hard realism of Machiavelli's demonic arguments here becomes a romantic illusion rooted in a rigorous sense of right. Tuzza is making use of Liolà to ruin Mita, his childhood sweetheart, married against her will—for family reasons and economics— to an old man with money. Tuzza's monstruous plot is an "infamia" which God himself must want to see punished. Liolà argues convincingly that he is simply protecting her honor and her rightful place from the machinations of Tuzza and Zia Croce.

There is no one in *Mandragola* who, subjected to humiliation in this way, maintains his integrity to the end. Everyone is included in Machiavelli's intrigue; Nicia himself plots with the others, unwittingly, for his own dishonor, but he is not an innocent victim. He is, in fact, the grossest materialist of them all, indifferent to the fate of the young man who must drain the mandrake potion and worried only as to how he can get away with it. In *Liolà*, Zio Simone retains his dignity and the deception practiced on him is transformed into an act of faith. Mita's triumph at the end of the play is not at his expense; her arrogance is directed against their common enemy, Tuzza: "That's right. The deception is exactly where you least expect it: in my husband's property, which you were ready to claim at the expense of your own dishonor!"

Like Tuzza and Zia Croce, Lucrezia almost gives her deception away at the end of the play, but only in her brazen arrogance toward a husband for whom she can no longer have any respect. Nicia, with his usual caution and his jealous concern for his public image, warns his wife to walk in fear of God. Lucrezia underscores the irony of his comment with open contempt. Nothing he can say or do can ever again affect her. The trap laid for her had become, for Machiavelli's Lucrezia, a means for self-indulgence. The deception which set the action into motion is fully acknowledged and strengthened by the end of the play. It is the one thing that all the protagonists have in common; it holds together the fragmented purposes and particular ends of the various characters in the play.

Pirandello, instead, distinguishes sharply between the deception practiced as such and the deception which is the reaction to it. Tuzza has tried to draw Zio Simone into a carefully prepared trap but has instead been caught in her own unscrupulous designs. Mita's deception is merely self-protection. It is the righteous reaction to the threat posed by Tuzza's scheme. Zia Croce is right when she says that the deception is in Mita—"in whom it doesn't show!"—but Mita's answer reaffirms the values that Tuzza would have destroyed and exonerates her. Zia Croce agreed to a plot against Mita at the expense of her daughter's honor; Mita is forced into a counterplot to save her own honor. And in the justification and acceptance of Liolà's plan, Mita's deception is thus transformed into righteous indignation and appearance and reality are made one in the conscience.

The profound significance of Pirandello's theme is made clear in Liolà's explanation to Mita that nothing he or anyone else could possibly say would ever convince Zio Simone that his wife's child is not his very own. Even if Liolà himself were to "confess"—who would believe him? Maybe the others, but not Simone: "He'll never believe it, simply because he doesn't want to believe it! Try convincing him, if you can! He'll never believe the child isn't his, even if you skin him alive!" Tuzza herself realizes the truth in this when she confronts Mita at the end. And Zio Simone proves the point himself: "It's mine! mine! mine!—and don't anyone dare speak a word against my wife!"

Mita's assertion that her way is "dritta e giusta" (straight and righteous) and Tuzza's way is "torta e falsa" (wrong and crooked) is the perfect summing up of the theme of illusion made real. The lie has taken root in the will and appears to have the strength of truth. And yet, in this seemingly successful transformation of illusion into reality other forces are unleashed which must ultimately shock the will out of its self-deception and destroy the presumption. We see this inevitable conclusion in many of Pirandello's later plays. In Liolà, the illusion is taken seriously. But one cannot help feeling that eventually Mita will have to pay for the deception she has practiced on herself. The plays that follow in the Pirandellian repertory take up the burden of reassessing such self-deception and spell out its consequences.

Liolà deceives the spectator, even as its hero deceives Mita into accepting his logic. The Mandragola, on the other hand, never confounds morality with expediency; the outlines of sin and virtue are never blurred. Agrigento is far removed from Florence—morally as well as geographically. In both plays, the end seems to justify the means; but in Liolà these means are transformed before our very eyes to accord with the end. The scene in which Liolà convinces Mita that she must allow him to give her the child her husband yearns for is a psychological as well as a dramatic tour de force. The immorality of the action itself and of the deception which follows it is softened by a romantic argument. One is reminded, in that scene, of the romantic justification of Francesca's sin in the fifth canto of Dante's *Inferno*; the sin itself is momentarily forgotten in Francesca's beautiful account of the irresistible promptings of love. Mita yields to her lover in much the same spirit as Francesca abandons herself to the memory of the *dolci sospiri*. The will gives its consent and makes the *libido licito*, the "libidinous" "licit."

There is no trace in *Mandragola* of the self-deception which is the heart of Pirandello's play. Machiavelli's characters define their intentions explicitly and call them by their true names: Callimaco succeeds in satisfying his lust; Lucrezia enjoys a young lover and produces a son for her old, impotent husband; Nicia finds happiness in the birth of an heir; the monk gets his material reward and—even more important—enjoys the satisfaction of knowing that he has helped to neutralize an explosive situation in the most efficient and delicate manner. In brief, scandal is averted and everyone gets what he wants. The different vectors which motivated the characters remain distinct to the end, but, through skillful mediation by the monk and clever planning by Callimaco, they are made to resolve ultimately into a single fact.

In Pirandello's play, the hero combines in himself the roles of mediator and doer—planning, arguing, blessing, and carrying out the seduction. And when the "miracle" has been effected, he moves graciously out of the picture with an uncorrupted disposition that is more than human and escapes moral censure. Uncorrupted and uncorrupting—for he retains his carefree joy to the end, leaving no hate, no tragedy, no destruction in his wake. Even Tuzza is forced to admire Liolà's beautiful handling of the matter. Her attempt to stab him, at the end of the play, is simply frustration at having failed where he succeeded. Tuzza, in fact, is the villain of the piece, but here too Pirandello has softened the implications by making her, at the same time, her own victim. It is not

Liolà who initiates the intrigue; he merely brings it to its conclusion. Even in the matter of her own relationship with Liolà, Tuzza makes clear that it was she who took the initiative, planning her own seduction, as it were, in order to spite Mita and achieve her own ends. Liolà holds our affection throughout because of his serene detachment in the midst of petty actions and his profound sense of justice. When he acts, it is to right the wrong done to Mita, not to satisfy his own lust. His instinctive goodness goes so deep that he can even consider giving up his freedom to save Tuzza from disgrace. He bestows his grace upon one and all, indifferent to the merits of the recipient or to the profit he himself might expect.

In Liolà's magnetic generosity, in Mita's final victory through loving trust, in Tuzza's unhappy attempt to rise above her despair by deception, and in Zio Simone's unruffled faith, we have all the makings of Pirandello's "theater of illusion." Mita succeeds where Tuzza failed, because she has accepted the promptings of her heart and consented to them in her will. In rejecting Liolà, Tuzza has rejected herself as well. All her plotting, all her protestations at the end, serve merely to expose her abortive illusion. The cold facts she insists on appear as gossip pure and simple; they are inspired by envy, and the more she insists on them, the more she reveals herself a fraud. Zio Simone himself emerges not as the naïve, gullible Nicia of *Mandragola* but as an early version of the hero of *Henry IV*: nothing and no one can destroy the illusion to which he has subscribed. Tuzza herself has all the force and willfulness of Pirandello's later heroines, but nothing of their self-awareness.

Liolà alone seems to defy comparison. In the impressive gallery of Pirandellian heroes, he stands alone. His godlike freedom and his contagious joy give the world the appearance of innocence and bring to the human heart that sense of the miraculous which is the gift of faith. If anything, Liolà is like Signora Ponza, the illusion made flesh, but fully realized as the consummate and marvelous embodiment of an inspired will.

# 4

## From Person to Person to Nonperson: The "Theater" Plays
*Six Characters in Search of an Author; Each in His Own Way; Tonight We Improvise*

*Six Characters in Search of an Author.* A rehearsal of one of Pirandello's earlier plays is interrupted by the sudden appearance of six people, obviously a family, who tell the theater director that they are looking for an author to induce him to dramatize their story. They say that they are characters conceived by another author who has now left them on their own. At first the Director is impatient. But curiosity gets the better of him. He lets them "act out" parts of their story, instructs his actors to study their performances closely, and he himself tries to write down some of their dialogue. Stage props are moved this way and that, the actors try to take over, there are interruptions, quarrels, new beginnings. The strangers insist that the drama is in *them* and cannot be "acted." By their obsessive strength of will, they manage to piece together their story bit by bit, taking full possession of the stage. We learn that the Father had encouraged a liaison between his rather simple-minded wife and one of his employees. When his only Son was still young, he had forced his wife to go a long way off, with her lover. Years passed. Three children were born to the Mother in her new union. But then her lover died. Poverty forced her to return to the City; and poverty also led her eldest daughter to be seduced secretly into prostitution. One day, the Father, succumbing to a carnal desire that he had not felt for years, went to a brothel run by Madam Pace in the rear of a shop to make love, by arrangement, with a young girl. While he is there, Mother arrives. She is horrified to learn that her daughter is a prostitute and that the man embracing her is her husband. The Father is overwhelmed with shame. Condemning himself for the lust that had brought him to Madam Pace, he is determined to salvage all that he can by bringing everyone back home—Mother, grown daughter, and two younger children—to live with him and his Son. But it doesn't work. The daily confrontations of Father, Stepdaughter, Mother, and Son are a perpetual agony. In the final scene, the young children accidentally die, meaninglessly; and the adult characters, obsessed by the knowledge of what had brought them together, abandon themselves to unutterable despair. Yet it is impossible to tell, in the end, whether they are playing their parts or living them, and, if living them, whether they are to "enact" their agony again and again, as in a play, or only once, and finally, as in everyday existence (1921).

*Each in His Own Way.* The play starts in the theater lobby, where a handbill has been distributed explaining that the play about to be performed is based on the recent scandal involving the actress A. Moreno, who had run off with Baron Nuti, driving her fiancé—the sculptor La Vela—to suicide. In the theater, the curtain goes up on a palatial drawing room where guests are discussing the awful news of the suicide of the painter Giorgio Salvi. Two young men, Doro and Francesco, have argued vehemently over who was to blame, Doro placing the responsibility on Delia Morello, Francesco exculpating her. Doro reports all this to his friends, among whom is Diego. Under Diego's analytical probing, Doro completely reverses his stand. It is clear that he, like so many others, is fascinated by the woman. When Francesco comes around to apologize for having quarreled with his friend, Diego forces him into the opposite camp. The double reversal sets up a new confrontation. Quarreling again, Doro insults Francesco, and the two agree to a duel. Delia suddenly appears, causing great consternation among the people in the house. She has come to thank but also to apologize to Doro for having taken her part when, in fact, she deserved to be condemned. She explains that she had run off with Michele Rocca to spite her fiancé's family, who had always regarded her with contempt. The first act ends here, but the curtain goes up almost immediately again, showing a replica of the side corridor of the theater, extending from the lobby back to the stage itself. Groups of people come together to talk about the play (including critics, who expound on the good and bad features of Pirandello's play). The "intermission" is almost over when a woman rushes down from her box protesting that her life should not be exposed on stage in this way. It is clearly La Moreno. Her friends try to quiet her and lead her back to her place. In the second act, Michele Rocca comes to discourage the duel. Delia returns. Rocca urges her to leave with him, but Delia refuses. Their violent and passionate exchanges bring to light the fact that they are bound by something more compelling than either love or hate: their shared guilt. Before the stupefied onlookers, the two embrace and go off together. The second act ends here; but the curtain is again raised quickly, showing the same portion of the theater as in the first interlude. A few spectators begin to emerge when, suddenly, La Moreno, again "invading" the scene, rushes through to the door leading to the side of the stage. There is a great commotion and then a dramatic scene—very like the one just enacted onstage—is "performed" by the "real" people involved. The stage is invaded, and the actors, fed up with the "real-life" interference, walk out, refusing to finish the performance. An announcement is made that the third act of the play must be called off (1924).

*Tonight We Improvise.* The lights in the theater go out, but the curtain fails to go up when expected. It is obvious, after a while, that a quarrel is taking place onstage. There are shouts of protest from the impatient audience. Eventually, the Director of the play (for which no author is listed in the playbill) comes forward to explain that what the audience is witnessing is the delayed beginning of a "happening" and that everything is proceeding exactly as he has prescribed. He gives a brief summary of the plot to be improvised. The curtain goes up, finally, but the actors (not yet in their "parts") register their displeasure with the direction. The Director keeps insisting that this is all part of his plan. What follows is a series of scenes in rapid succession, punctuated by exchanges between the actors and the Director, and comments from the audience. The story being "improvised" reveals itself in bits and pieces. Mommina, with her three sisters and her mother, are shown with a variety of admirers, who escort them to all sorts of places. Their father, fascinated by a local singer, spends most of his time in a Cabaret, where he is the butt of jokes inspired by the behavior of his women. One day he gets into a brawl over his favorite, La Chanteuse, and is stabbed. He comes home, mortally wounded. After his death, his family breaks up. Mommina marries one of the suitors who, mindful of the girl's past, keeps her locked up in the house, forbidding her to use cosmetics or even to look into a mirror. Mommina languishes and grows old before her time. Her two little girls are her only happiness —but even this is poisoned for her by the fact that they too are virtual prisoners in the house. We learn in bits and snatches that one of Mommina's sisters has become a professional singer in the province and is in town for an operatic performance. Mommina's husband, still mad with jealousy about her past, abuses her and leaves the house. In a climactic scene, in which she dramatizes for her children the very opera her sister is singing that night, Mommina dies. Her husband, meanwhile, has been persuaded by her family to change his ways. He returns with them to the house, only to discover that it is too late. At this point, the actors step out of their roles for a final brief exchange in which they vow never to improvise again. It is too risky (1928).

In *Liolà*, Pirandello touches, as we have seen, on what is to become his driving dramatic obsession: the destruction of personality through self-deception. But he does not focus on it. The play belongs not to its one genuinely tortured character, but to those who somehow "get away" with the deception, consenting to it in the will. Mita and Liolà are "saved" in spite of the terrible lie to which they have subscribed with full consent. Yet, there are here, quite unmistakably, all the traces of the inversions, paradoxes, contradictions, and reconstituted "morality" which are to be found full-blown in the later plays. Deception itself has many faces: Tuzza's in using Liolà for her scheme and hiding the attraction she feels for him first in the guise of indifference, then in hate; Zio Simone's in allowing the deception to be used to his advantage; Mita's and Liolà's, in countering Tuzza's with a deception of their own; the willingness of other characters to accept the situation without any serious probing. The thematic lines—like the obsessive characters of *Six Characters in Search of an Author*—seem to follow an inexorable course of their own toward what must be described in this case as an enigmatic and suggestive conclusion. Who is really good? With the later plays in mind, one is forced to conclude that Mita—despite her inherent virtue and her righteous indignation—is a potential embodiment of the Pirandellian paradox. She deceives Simone no less than Tuzza does. Her new mask does not trouble her. The irresistible existential probing which will haunt us in the later plays is here resolved neatly and expeditiously.

The paradox embodied in Tuzza's forced betrayal of self and in Mita's relaxation in self-deception cloaked in righteousness contains implicitly the agonizing process of the dissolution of character. In the obsessive action of the later plays, there can be no semblance of rest till the whole substance of the paradox—everyone and everything involved in it—has been brought out into the open. Mommina, Delia Morello, the Stepdaughter, in the plays we are about to consider, are each extensions of the double image with which *Liolà* closes. That double image is itself the key to the master theme; it is tortured in the later plays into a spectrum of possibilities, a mosaic of opposites, a sequence of reversals not unlike the self-evoked levels of consciousness associated with psychoanalysis.

Pirandello develops his master theme, as we have noted, in

two distinct series of plays that parallel one another. As the playwright himself indicated by grouping them together at the beginning of his collected plays, the best way to begin a discussion of that master theme is with the so-called "theater" plays, where Pirandello dramatizes with greatest immediacy the tortured dissolution of character that results from obsessive concern with the question of identity and reality. As Francis Fergusson observes, in his theater plays Pirandello has shattered the illusion of the stage as the mirror of everyday life and forces us to look upon it as a reality itself. Stage drama becomes the extension of life.[1] And in insisting on this dramatic principle, Pirandello makes himself, as Georges Neveux points out,

> the great prestidigitator of the Twentieth Century, the Houdini of interior life. In his most important play, *Six Characters*, he took the very center of the real world and turned it inside out right in front of us, as the fisherman turns inside out the skin of an octopus to lay bare its viscera.
>
> But what Pirandello laid bare before us is not only the work of the actors, nor that of the author, not only the other side of the scenery, but something much more universal: *the other side of ourselves*.
>
> It is our inner life which is suddenly found projected on the stage and decomposed there as if by a prism.[2]

The theater plays shatter stage conventions in order to force us to look into the magic mirror of art. They are our initiation into the dialectic of self-consciousness through a familiar medium. In plays of a second series, which we may call "personality plays," or "masks" in the technical sense, the medium is the eye that projects our vision of the stage rather than the stage itself. We get a sensation of being "looked at" in such plays as *At the Exit*, with its heightened sense of death-in-life; *As You Desire Me*, with its struggle to articulate the inner identity which is recognized intuitively through self-evoked crises; and *Henry IV*, which with its alternating currents of lucidity and madness that illuminate the tragic assertion of self, is unquestionably the masterpiece of this second kind of Pirandellian drama. The theater plays offer us its reverse, objective side, but only to shatter it. The stage is objectively before us, ready for the presentation of a typically "well-made play." Instead we see it literally stripped of its familiarity by a series of invasions or "happenings."

Who are the six characters who suddenly appear in the midst of a rehearsal, disrupting the proceedings and insisting on their own private "play"? It is easier, perhaps, to begin by saying what they are *not*. They are not "unfinished" characters, even though they may at times suggest that. They have sprung full-blown on the stage; and although they insist that they seek an author and make feeble efforts to help produce a script, they follow their own inexorable inner law, from beginning to end.

As Pirandello himself tells us in his genial preface to the play, his six characters carry in themselves their own law of being and must be heard. "I have not been defined dramatically, as a character," says the Son, but the phrase simply proves what we already know: he does not choose his role, it has chosen him. His very recalcitrance is the keynote of his dramatic life. He is driven to take part in the preconceived "script" since it is the only life that exists for him. Like the others in his family, he is compelled to express the characteristic act which defines and sustains him. He keeps apart, a stranger in the midst of these proceedings, to register his protest and to escape his guilt. His silence is part of the obsessive drive toward expression; but it is the Mother who defines the momentary characteristic act which each of them must forever embody: "It takes place now, forever! . . . I live here and now, always, in every moment of my suffering, which renews itself constantly, always here and now." In their characteristic posture, each of them recollects the spontaneous overflow of emotion associated with the eternal moment which is their entire being. They are fully determined in themselves; and together they produce a dramatic harmony which the Director cannot hope to imitate. This is underscored by the Director's empty insistence that the Stepdaughter control her passionate outbursts. Like

Hamlet directing the players who come to Elsinore, the Director insists on the "well-made play." But the six characters know they must not adhere to such rules. They have no choice: "we are exactly what you see; we have no other reality beyond this illusion!" says the Father. "The play is in us; it is us; and we are impatient to put it on, exactly as our passions dictate!"

Like the great heroes of classical tragedy, they are doomed to an inexorable moral compulsion to assert themselves in the one single thrust which is the fulness of their being; but their commitment lacks the awesome confidence of insight into necessity. They cannot explain; they can only narrate and act out the key moment that has shaped them. They come onstage masked; but this too is a paradox, for they are the most alive and, in spite of their straining for precise and unambiguous terms, the most articulate characters on the stage. In them the entire spectrum of emotional life and the painful dialectic which it demands for expression is put forth as the key to meaning. And yet, Pirandello will not let us forget, they embody a dramatic paradox too—for, although we may be tempted to look upon them as "real" in the same way that so many of us regard Shakespeare's Hamlet as a "real" person, they, no less than Hamlet, are characters playing a part in a provocative and exciting play. Onstage, real actors must play the roles and convince us that they are nevertheless roles beyond the capabilities of "mere" actors!

In the beginning—so the book of theatrical genesis must begin—was the Mask.[3] "Each of us," says the Father, who is himself a naked mask, "thinks himself 'one,' but it's not true. He is 'many,' my friends, as 'many' as there are possibilities in us. 'One' with this fellow, 'one' with that other. . . . And always under the illusion that we are 'one and the same' for all, and always that same 'one' we *think* we are, in all we do."

Those characters who invade the stage are not an interruption, obviously, but the heart of the matter. The paradox they contain in themselves is extended, through Pirandello's ingenious use of stage conventions, into the larger paradox of the artistic "illusion" attempted by the actors and, beyond that, to the ultimate confrontation with the audience.

"What is for you people an illusion waiting to be shaped, for us is our only reality. Not for us alone, mind you. Think about it. Can you tell me who you are?" The Father thus unexpectedly strips the illusory, everyday mask from us all. As long as the dichotomy "illusion-reality" persists, neither the Director nor the audience can hope to understand. The characters have shown the way: "If *we* have no other reality beyond this illusion, you'd better look again at what you think is *your* reality, the one that you breathe and touch to-day, because—like yesterday's—it will turn out to be an il-lusion, tomorrow." The simplistic notion of a relativist phi-losophy, which has so often been called upon to explain this and other plays of Pirandello, is death in such a context. The six who embody the "immutable reality" of a multifaceted, ever-shifting and ever-whole persona remind us of this. They are the elusive moment of life, the assertion—not the nega-tion—of it. In their struggle for self-assertion they show us the way we too must go.

The difficulties in that struggle are dramatized, within the duality he has created on stage, with every effort made by the Director and his company to interrupt the proceedings and get on with their playacting. And here it is necessary to point out that the company players are not bad actors, but extremely good ones; the very stage directions point up the fact. In their rendition of certain "scenes" they are manifestly the polished and talented professionals which every director would like to have in his company. What is lacking is not artistic skill. Their very interruptions tell us how closely they are listening and watching and absorbing. They pick up lines easily and quickly (and though the smallest departure from the original lines brings on eloquent criticism of the "performance" on the part of the Father and Stepdaughter, this is no serious reflection on their talent) and resent asper-sions cast on their art. They are distracted again and again from their professional task by the others who manage to carry on, as though some internal mechanism were driving them to play out the scenes as they have "lived" them, and continue to live them. The characters never lose their place; they follow their own internal script, picking up their "lines" without cues, carrying the sequence to its inevitable con-

clusion. One is scarcely aware of this; only in retrospect do
we realize how subtly Pirandello has managed to keep them
on their track. Their drama eludes the possibility of a
script, even though they try their best to cooperate with the
Director, who would like to record the dialogue as they speak
it.

An uncontrollable necessity seems to spur them on, the
necessity for self-definition. In this the theme transcends
theater and characterization and becomes universal. The dissolution of character is thus suggested in the most immediate
and visual terms, within the accepted stage conventions, in
the confrontation of actors and characters. The actors are
convinced they can take on anything; the characters insist
on their unique dramatic posture. They are dramatic embodiments of will; and in their single-minded purpose, the
dramatist has recognized the multiplicity of intentions and
actions which make up personality. The Italian critic Bon-
tempelli has aptly defined one side of this important equation.

> The Pirandellian theater is the most tragic and exalted
> document (and monument) of a fatalism which seemed,
> at the start of a new age, to threaten civilized man and all
> his achievements of twenty-five centuries, making him into
> a squirrel whose entire life is spent spinning his little cage
> around. The life of the Pirandellian figures is terrible and
> grotesque. They are no longer, as in Sophocles, the vic-
> tims of a cruel Olympus, hurling bolts from the clouds;
> no longer, as in Shakespeare, victims of their own uncon-
> trollable passions; no longer, as in Ibsen, victims of a
> moral law which is nothing more than social convention.
> They are the victims of a clear and restless consciousness
> of the nothingness which surrounds man—the center and
> the outermost limit of a universe of infinite radius—vic-
> tims of an attitude which has replaced the vital need for
> rules with "it is so (if you think it is)." [4]

In the passionate intensity of their struggle toward self-
assertion and light, the Pirandellian characters may indeed be
described as "tragic." But they rise above the existential void

just as the characters of Sophocles and Aeschylus rise above their destiny to awe-inspiring resignation in self-knowledge. In their final recognition of their own limitations, the Pirandellian figures go beyond tragedy, to the very limits of art. And if, at the end, they seem to hover on the edge of a chaotic madness, their utter faith in themselves saves them from it. In the reconstituted soul thus coming to unflinching self-consciousness, Georges Duhamel sees, in fact, the paradoxical meaning of the Pirandellian "persona."

> Where are we? Beyond darkness? Beyond the world? Beyond life, perhaps. Precisely that: all these characters are familiar to us; we recognize the profile, the gestures, the sound of the voice—they are all we know! And yet, we know nothing about them. We soon discover that they are "beyond," on the "other" side. And a kind of terror fills us. Just think: instead of two faces, they may turn out to have a hundred, a thousand.[5]

The tragic feeling is in those who recognize the multiplicity of the Pirandellian persona. The clever gimmicks and the paradoxes that dazzle us—illusion-reality, being-nonbeing, self-nonself—all tend to reduce the experiences to commonplaces. But Pirandello himself warns us against this when he describes his theater as the tragedy of the modern soul. "O what a piece of work is a man!" Hamlet intuits the paradox which Gaston Baty had characterized in Pirandello's work as "the eternal man, one and whole in the changing accidents of his appearances." [6]

Finally, the Pirandellian characters are not in themselves destructive forces. They are independent creations seeking expression within an inadequate world; only a supreme creator, God, can give unity to their reality. Like the characters of Flaubert's *Madame Bovary*, they call for providential direction of their lives, the kind we see in Manzoni's *The Betrothed*. They set up reverberations in our will and move toward recognition like a magnet which draws everything else toward it which is essential, leaving unimportant things behind. The "fact" of incest in *Six Characters* is meant to be terrible and shock us; but even more terrible is the Oedipus-like unfolding of that fact. What is most terrible, ultimately, is the repudiation of self, which like a vengeful ghost seeks out the betrayer and forces him to acknowledge the lie buried in him.

To those who cannot identify with them, Pirandello's characters seem indeed unfinished dramatically and inadequate to their task. The tragic feeling they evoke may appear exaggerated; the existential premise on which they build their drama can be misinterpreted as an interruption which is arbitrary and unwelcome. And yet, they have in fact been called forth out of their eternal limbo by the unanswered questions in all of us. And, most significantly, it is only in the theater that Pirandello shows us this kind of "morality" play, for the theater is the very act of creation which, for a moment, makes us gods. It is no accident that the lesson should come about on the stage, where actors are striving to strip away the confusion of life for the "eternal moment" each of us harbors in himself. What the Pirandellian characters are *not* is precisely the confusion we need to strip away to define them. Only then can we take part in the Pirandellian transformation ourselves; we are all *maschere nude* in the dramatic catharsis of Pirandello's theater, where the protagonists have double identities, where plays do not "end," where the action is telescoped in reverse in at least three planes (as the dramatist himself tells us in *Each in His Own Way*), where the theater invades life itself. Auréliu Weiss sums up this argument as Pirandello's commitment to abolish "real" characters as distinguishable from the "masks" of drama.

> *He has banished from his plays all characters*, the foundation and pillars of traditional drama.
>
> His entire dramatic work is nothing more, in effect, than a categorical negation of the existence and reality of stage characters.[7]

In their all-consuming purpose to strip away everything but the single moment of recognition, the intruders in *Six Characters* dramatize in the most memorable way the dissolution of what in everyday life we take to be "personality." In their spirallike movement toward insight, they assume postures, or personae, which define them in their essential relationships. The struggle toward light may seem confused and inarticulate; but it is, in fact, the dialectic of conversion, in which the paradoxical assumptions which seduce us are laid aside. Although the author keeps reminding us that the creator's will is not operating in them, the truth is that they are fully defined in the only possible way, as a true mirror of distorted images.

The three levels of insight—characters, actors, audience—first attempted in *Six Characters* are structured even more boldly in *Each in His Own Way*. In the second of his theater plays, Pirandello brings the audience right into the play (the theater was empty in *Six Characters*) and makes it an integral part of the action. In the three-year interval between these two plays, he wrote several other pieces—including *Henry IV*—a fact which may help explain the beautifully organic structure of this tour de force. The drama on the stage is the professional execution by actors of a play which is alluded to and repeated in snatches offstage in the interludes between the acts. The sharp dichotomy of *Six Characters* here is resolved as a perfect mirror image; the stage business is reflected in the "real" business in the lobby of the theater at the beginning (where handbills are being distributed and the first of several commotions takes place), then in the replica of the side corridor of the theater, *onstage*. The "stage" drama is repudiated in the "real-life" drama—but the two are themselves a new whole mirroring the real audience.

The internal play—unlike the abortive rehearsal in *Six Characters*—is fully realized and is meant to be perfectly transparent. It is not disrupted by the "real" drama until the very end, when the actors are thrown into confusion by the unrestrained invasion of their stage by La Moreno, whose notorious goings-on have been the substance of the stage drama. But the interludes mirror much more than the reality depicted on stage; they contain a whole series of mirror images of another kind and draw us into the play directly, through critical appraisals and arguments about the value of

Pirandello's entire dramatic conception, as well as the play being performed.

In the stage action of *Each in His Own Way*, Diego is the catalyst who forces hidden secrets to the surface. We meet his instinctive drive for truth again and again in Pirandello—Laudisi in *It Is So* (*If You Think So*) is possessed by it, and so are Cotrone in *The Mountain Giants*, the Father and Stepdaughter in *Six Characters*, and La Spera in *The New Colony*. Here it is Diego who spoils the outward complacency and self-assurance of his friends, forcing them to reveal the contradictions they harbor. But it is Delia Morello—the actress who has driven lovers to suicide and who exerts a deadly fascination on men—who provides the unerring direction toward self-awareness. Her emotional commitment never wavers: she is always and perfectly true to herself. Thus we see her hate become love, in her own terms; and we watch her undergoing an agonizing reappraisal of motives before the world. She is the embodiment of the paradoxes of the six characters in the earlier play, the very center of the concentric circles which are drawn so clearly here, from the inner play to the outermost action; everything is defined by her struggle to articulate her predicament. When she finally acknowledges her hate and love (they are one thing in her, ultimately) as a necessity to share the guilt of her lover who had put her to the "test" and thus forced her fiancé to kill himself, the play is in fact over. But Pirandello creates a disturbance, which is really the epilogue to all this, and ends the play with this "interruption." It is clear that the dramatic structure here is beautifully integrated into the organic development of the theme.

In the interludes which follow the two acts, Pirandello offers us, through a variety of voices, a discussion of the angry debate which is the focus of action onstage. Critics and spectators come together in these intermissions and give us contradictory and revealing assessments of the meaning of the play and the value of the performance. "Do you think it's right," asks one dissatisfied critic, "to destroy the personality of characters like this? to let the action go every which way, without beginning or end? to pick up the thread arbitrarily, from an argument?" Pirandello has stolen the thunder from his severest critics, who, long after his time, can still be heard asking: Can the play be simply a mass of arguments, a cerebral indulgence? In *Each in His Own Way*, a second critic answers: "But the argument you speak of is the very play. It *is* the play!" Another chimes in: "Which comes to life, after all, in the woman!" These exchanges are not self-indulgence on Pirandello's part (although he must have enjoyed the chance to get even with some of his more persistent critics); he is battering down, by means of an unanswerable dialectic, the misleading notions put forth by some and suggesting in the clearest terms where the meaning of the play lies. "But I would simply like to see a play performed, that's all!" says the first critic, unabashed. And another replies: "But the play lives in the woman!" And once again we are reminded of what must eventually be recognized as the Pirandellian trademark—the mirror gone crazy: "If you want to know what I think . . . it's like flashes in a mirror gone mad." The acknowledgement is the beginning of the Pirandellian dialectic. The mirror gone crazy takes us to the very threshold of recognition—but so long as the distinction between image and "real," subject and object persists, nothing can come of that moment of insight.

This internal polemic in itself has many levels of meaning. It defines the limits of critical perception and, in so doing, suggests the difficulty of interpreting the play; it records faithfully the full spectrum of impressions which must always be the basis for intelligent appraisal; it sets up opposing camps (as indeed there were) and gives them ideal and eloquent expression; it uses the critical barbs to advantage as a mirror of the conventional rules which must be broken through to get at the meaning of the play; it sets all of this up as a kind of prelude to a final convergence of the action of the stage play and the real-life drama which erupts during the interludes. It is Pirandello's self-analysis as a critic, his appraisal of himself as a "third" person in his own many voices.

What is the lesson of such self-analysis? It is that the

image of the conventional stage must be destroyed to arrive at the true significance of playacting. Conventional plot and action—no less than conventional "character"—must be sacrificed, by exquisite surgery, to restore vitality and health. The well-made plot cannot serve any longer, nor can the pleasant living rooms which mirror our familiar surroundings on the stage. The setting for the action onstage in *Each in His Own Way* is only vaguely familiar—although described in detail; it gives the impression of a surrealistic painting. The room is, in fact, full of religious paintings and objects and suggests a large chapel. And the stage itself disappears in conventional terms in the interludes, where the illusion of a theater within a theater is itself an infinite reflection not unlike—much later—Albee's use of the replica of the mansion in *Tiny Alice*.

Here also, as in *Six Characters*, conventional character is replaced by something which is the multiplicity of internal drives. Delia comes into the action fully aware of her confusion and seeks desperately the meaning and resolution of that confusion in the many mirrors of opinion around her. Diego has grasped the contradictions in himself and in his friends and—although he never goes beyond the moment of dialectic in himself—he leads others to the brink of insight. This splintered reality is reinforced by the violent reaction of La Moreno and Baron Nuti—the real-life celebrities who are in the theater (unknown to one another) witnessing their own painful drama. Like the six characters in the earlier play, they are in a state of passionate awareness of self; and, as in the other play, their drama is concluded when their relationship is properly recognized and acknowledged. In the course of the stage action, however, they remain separate— each unaware of the other's presence in the theater—and, in that isolation, their suffering is hardly bearable. The stage action ends with their compulsive acceptance of an almost indescribable relationship which fluctuates from hatred to love to something not unlike the necessity which holds Paolo and Francesca forever together in Dante's fifth canto of the *Inferno*. And, although the real-life celebrities have objected all along to the manner in which their tragic destiny is portrayed in the stage version, they reaffirm the truth of their relationship through the stage drama, echoing it and bringing the play to its organic end with the confession and acceptance of their bond.

*Each in His Own Way*, like *Six Characters*, makes much of the theater, using the familiar setting as an organic part of what is, in effect, an unfamiliar dramatic structure. The novelty of this is the most striking thing about these plays. The very limitations of the stage are put to advantage. The extension of the stage business into the replica of the very aisles of the theater is a telescoping technique which creates a misleading impression of realism to lure us into an ingenious transparency. The technique forces us to adjust our sight quickly to inner and outer meaning, expands the image of distant things in a flash, superimposes what seems at first irrelevant on what appears basic. It forces us to set up an equation which extends from microcosm to macrocosm in a series of instantaneous flashes of insight; we *see* the very dialectic which is the language of the play.

Pirandello's insistence on introducing a "play of critical opinions" in the interludes is not just a whim. There is much here that is autobiographical, as we have suggested, but it is not mere self-indulgence. He is reminding us that the comments about the play are indeed part and parcel of it—the search for meaning. The critics are not, after all, so far removed from the rest of the action. They too must be purged. The dramatic thrust is outward as well as inward; we move from the larger stage back behind the footlights, each time, with a new advantage. Meaning is possible only through this continuous spiraling dialectic.

It is—as the author tells us elsewhere—"difficult" theater. The strain of communication is at times almost unbearable. Early in the play, one of the young women remarks: "So long as there is a doubt inside us, we should keep our lips sealed. We go on talking; and we ourselves don't know what we're saying." "Bastard thoughts" surprise us, rising to the surface like unwelcome ghosts. But these are the beginnings of self-knowledge. They spur us to define, record, probe our initial impulses, express the inexpressible. Diego's account of how he surprised himself in the mirror one day, as he bent over his dying mother, is like Jerry's account of the Cerberus-like dog in Albee's *The Zoo Story*: it fixes in a flash the symbolic meaning of an experience through an irresistibly suggestive image. The reflection of almost cheerful expectancy, Diego confesses, distressed him to the point of guilt: he couldn't wait for his mother to die. He had rationalized that it would be better for her to end her long agony; was not his expression in the mirror a kind of relief at the prospect of her release from pain? He comes to the very edge of truth in this stumbling toward expression. And in this context, the account he gives of how, as his mother lay dying, he was distracted by the efforts of a fly to get out of a glass of water into which it had fallen, is a related image. He missed the moment his mother died, for he was too busy watching the fly drown. This is not "perfect" communication, but it is perfectly transparent. The mirrored reflection and the reflected image of death in the water—the dead woman herself—are epiphanies of a truth struggling to the surface.

Delia Morello strikes the same note when she says,

> I take out my mirror; and you can't imagine my reaction . . . the cold horror that comes over me, when I see my painted mouth in the circle of the mirror, this face which I have made into a mask.

The mirror image is the stripping away of her assumed role. Just as the author sees himself reflected in the prism of the critical opinions he records, so too the chief characters begin their painful self-assessment with the recognition of their image in a mirror. In this flash of illumination, words become inadequate—or so it seems. "Words, precisely that. Words shown in their inconsistency!" says one of the critics in the interlude. And Diego recalls, in this vein, the negativism of trying to grasp meaning through the obvious, of attaching significance to ready-made concepts, when he notes,

> —We know about each other and each of us knows about himself some scrap of certainty today, which is not the

same as yesterday's, which will not be the same as tomorrow's—

Words, concepts, and truths accepted at face value can only destroy intuition. The assortment of comments during the interlude points up the confusion which comes with such acceptance.

"I've had it, with this spasmodic nihilism!"
"—And this desire for annihilation!"
"—Denial is not constructive!"

The mirror gone crazy is the beginning of the constructive process. Diego makes this clear when he tells his friend Francesco not to take too literally what Doro had said to him in anger, earlier. When he called you a clown, Diego observes, Doro was accusing himself, lashing out at his own shortsightedness. "You haven't understood. He was striking out at the little clown which he did not recognize in himself but which he saw in you—in what you mirrored back to him!" At the very end, in the second interlude, the intelligent critic sums up the unexpected resolution of the stage drama and the real-life drama with the words: "They saw themselves as in a mirror and rebelled against it, especially against that last scene!" So long as the inadequacy, in any form, persists, identification is impossible. Words, conventions, facts, the duality of mirrored image and true "reality" must disappear before meaning can emerge. La Moreno and the Baron meet, at the end, and in that last painful confrontation, which is the mirror image completed, they recognize themselves reciprocally and their relationship is acknowledged. The stage play and the real-life drama become one in a painful identity. Their play has nothing more to tell us.

What we witness in all this is the buildup of self-knowledge through intuitions translated into an act of will. "Each of us must build for himself the ground under his feet," says one of the speakers in the stage play, "every turn, every step of the way, demolishing everything that isn't yours, that wasn't laid down by you, the ground you made use of like a parasite, a parasite." The road we travel must be engineered and constructed step by step. The task can take us to the very edge of madness—as Agnes tells us in Albee's *A Delicate Balance* (perhaps the most Pirandellian play in the American repertory). It is one of Pirandello's driving themes. The ready-made conscience which seeks to justify our actions to ourselves is, as Diego reminds us, "a rubberband. Once it grows slack, pfff! the madness burrowing inside each of us comes rushing out." The danger is always lurking in us, and the most innocent word or gesture can let it loose. The trick is to let go and force oneself to build from scratch.

*Each in His Own Way*, we may conclude, is the best example of the shattered mirror that Pirandello holds up for us to guide us from level to level in our spiraling journey to the center of personality. The stage play is itself many plays: the indifferent, the curious, the complacent, the conventional all walk on uncertain ground; the leading characters let go and find their dreadful way alone. The struggle to understand hidden intentions and motivations is best articulated by Diego, who although not fully aware of the final outcome of his probing nevertheless understands the necessity of it; the goal of identity is achieved by Delia Morello and Michele Rocco in the stage play and by La Moreno and Baron Nuti in the real-life drama. The interludes contain also the shattered, isolated judgments which are the critical mirror of the play. As in *Six Characters*, the multiplicity of masks is reconstituted for us in *Each in His Own Way* through a striking series of reflected images, each perfect in itself and perfectly integrated into the meaning of the whole. In the splintered consciousness itself, which is the dissolution of identity, Pirandello seeks to show us a way toward personal reintegration.

The theater-as-mirror is employed for the third and last time on a grand scale in *Tonight We Improvise*. In place of the sophisticated upper-class milieu of the earlier play, we have here a Sicilian town where the rigorous local mores and conventions offer a stark and highly dramatic contrast to the "advanced" sensibilities of the main characters. Here, as in the other theater plays, Pirandello builds layers of meaning through a stratification of situations, each an infinite reflection in itself. We have a Director (Hinkfuss) who tells a live audience that the evening's performance is a kind of improvisation which follows, however, his plan and general direction. We have actors cast in dual roles—that is, they are part of the company and part of an idea which is to be dramatized on stage; we have the same penetration of the stage action into the audience, the same disregard for the conventional intermissions—the play continues even during the formal intermissions—the same gradual identification of the actors with the roles they play, the same rejection of stage conventions for "real" portrayal; we have the same preoccupation with critical judgments, but here in the context of the relationship of actor-director, improvisation-script, performers-audience.

The "transformation" which is the explicit keynote of Pirandello's theater plays is introduced at the outset with Hinkfuss's comment to the audience that the work of art continues to live only by virtue of the life given to it by each one of us. "If a work of art survives, the reason is that we can redeem it from the inflexibility of its form, we can dissolve that form inside us." In the constant renewal of drama, the "actors" must in a sense destroy themselves as actors and assume their roles as their very substance and being. They must, in short, do precisely what the actors who play the six characters succeed in doing, while protesting that it cannot be done. The leading actor is the spokesman for this idea; his frequent objections to any sort of direction are indicative of the transformation which must take place. "Once life emerges, no one can tell it what to do!" he insists. And, at a certain moment late in the play, the entire cast rebels and drives Hinkfuss from the theater. Having assumed the very substance of the roles they portray, the actors—like the six characters—become self-directed, moving from within, with the confidence of self-sufficiency.

The problem of communication persists, however. It is, as we have already seen, an inevitable corollary to the main theme. But here, Pirandello articulates something new, something which was implicit in the other two plays and which now is brought out into the open. Although they have recognized the fact that they no longer need Hinkfuss's direction, the actors insist on a script. Improvisation cannot work. In his penetrating essay on the Italian theater—which, as we have already indicated, is a mine of insights and deserves to be studied closely in connection with Pirandello's theater—Pirandello states very clearly his conviction that no serious theater can rely on improvisations, on "happenings" which are really impromptu. The harmony of the whole will not allow it. Speaking of the *commedia dell'arte*, he points out that this genial creation of the Italian theater was not "an accidental discovery of mere actors. Anyone having even the slightest acquaintance with the way an actor works on the stage, with the precise directions he requires if he is to take a step to the right instead of to the left, will readily see that the idea of improvising their performances could never have occurred to actors." [8]

The paradox he puts before us is perfectly transparent in this case: we see actors struggling to reach their ideal roles and dismissing all direction at a certain point—but the whole thing (as Hinkfuss keeps insisting) is part of a carefully devised sequence and a rigorous direction. The contradiction in the play is only apparent; it spells out for us the different stages in the slow movement toward perfect theater and provides valuable insights into the demands of the stage.

The abortive effort to produce a script for the life drama of the six characters here becomes a driving necessity for actors compelled by their own inner exigencies to assume the mask of the characters they embody as their own. This is not the illusion to re-create characters professionally (and yet it is that too!), but the very *becoming* of personality as an independent reality. The paradox need not be labored; the whole sequence is part of an ingenious script, as Pirandello reminds us. In the essay just cited, he urges that old plays be modernized, redone in the mirror of current habits and usage—and this too must be borne in mind. The script is not a dead book if we translate it into the language of our own emotions and insight: "in the Theater a work of art is no longer the work of the writer (which, after all, can always be preserved in some other way), but an act of life, realized on the stage from one moment to the next, with the cooperation of an audience that must find satisfaction in it." [9] The actors in *Tonight We Improvise* reject both the author and the director—but they insist on the script they have "created": "Not the author! The script, yes—so that we can for a moment at least give it life again."

On the most immediate level, therefore, the play recalls the confrontation between staging the illusion of life and the life drama itself. But one must not stop here. Pirandello is not setting up an easy opposition to amuse us; here more than anywhere else he warns us against the apparent relativism of such a contradiction. The resolution is spelled out for us in many ways in the course of the play.

The interruptions which figure so dramatically in the other two plays are here more frequent and better integrated on the whole—serving to jolt us again and again into the heart of the problem. They are indeed part of the "improvised" production—which, we should stress, is not a rehearsal (as in *Six Characters*), but a finished product presented to a live audience in the guise of a "happening." Within this format, the stratification of themes is beautifully crystallized. Utter confusion marks the opening of the play; the Director explains that it is all really part of the show, but then his actors confront him publicly and insist it is not. Again and again they complain about his direction. Scenery is changed while the curtain is open; the actors mingle in the aisles of the theater with the spectators and carry on their roles. The life of the play is constantly being extended into the theater.

When in the second half of the play Mommina—now a virtual prisoner in her jealous husband's house—beats her head against the four walls, repeating each time "This is a wall," she is expressing the death throes of the soul buried alive. Later, her sisters and mother come back with her husband to free her from her prison; they talk to her from the other side of the prop which serves as a wall, and one of the group remarks: "This is a wall! This is a wall! You're not supposed to be heard in there!" The parallel, with all its poetic reverberations, reminds us of the invisible wall between the stage and the audience. We are there with Mommina—but not really. Communication, we are told, is indeed impossible; and yet, paradoxically, it is taking place in that recognition of its limitations. Mommina cannot possibly know—in her role—that they are there, standing outside; and yet that knowledge is what makes the suggestive parallel work. On a higher plane of action, communication is effected in the suggestion of a nemesis at work—in the same way that Macbeth's pregnant repetition of the witches' "Foul is fair and fair is foul" links him up at once with a demonic plan. Like Shakespeare, Pirandello moves easily in a multifaceted kind of symbolism which, in its rich suggestions, is almost Dantesque. The audience (and the reader) is at every moment at the heart of things.

For Pirandello, communication is ultimately not in words but in the mirroring of intuitions—through phrases that echo one another, through parallel situations, through the very image of the mirror. When the women of the company are preparing Mommina for her final scene, they hold up a mirror for her to see the effect of the makeup which has transformed her into an old woman before her time. But the actress—who is now deep in the role—pushes it aside impatiently: "No! He took all the mirrors away, there are no mirrors in the house. Do you know how I get to see my reflection? In the window panes, like a shadow, or in the distorted image in the moving water of the cistern—and it takes my breath away!" Her true reflection, of course, is in her role. The transformation which the mirror reveals is artificial and false. The stage mask has disappeared, as our own conventional mask must give way before such an infinitely suggestive series of intuitions.

The theater plays were written within a span of seven years: *Six Characters* in 1921, *Each in His Own Way* in 1924, *Tonight We Improvise* in 1928. In between, Pirandello wrote much else—including the masterpiece in which the multiplicity of roles and the continuum of dramatic insights reach dramatic perfection of a new kind. Comparisons here are apt to mislead us into facile judgments, and—as Benedetto Croce reminds us—are apt to deaden the critical perception. The theater plays are, after all, unique and perfect in themselves, a disarming, immediate expression of the dissolution of character as it is mirrored in the life of actors, directors, and author—all of whom are the vehicle for its explication. The stage itself becomes, in these three plays, a distorted, shattered mirror of life, full of imperfections and impurities. In that mirror, which is first and foremost the mirror of his own creative personality, Pirandello has embodied the notion that "life's a stage" and has taught us how to see the drama of our own lives. In the plays that are to be discussed hereafter, the stage disappears from the scene; but its influence is never lost. The theater plays must be recognized as a seminal inspiration for all of Pirandello's other works.

# Through a Shattered Mirror: The Infinite Reflections of Self

*At the Exit; It Is So (If You Think So); As Well As Before, Better than Before; The Life I Gave You*

**At the Exit.** The setting is the back entrance (or exit) of a country cemetery, where the ghost of a Fat Man sits on a worn bench. He is joined there by the ghost of a Philosopher. They still have their earthly forms which will last, we learn, until the last desire attaching them to earthly existence has been fulfilled and the will surrenders itself to death. What holds the Fat Man to life is his desire to confront his unfaithful wife again. He predicts that she will be killed by her lover, and he will see her weep. At once the Murdered Woman enters, but she is laughing irresistibly over the irony of having been forced back to her husband by her lover. A child then appears, clutching a pomegranate, his last unfulfilled wish. The Murdered Woman helps him peel the fruit and eat it; and the boy, satisfied, soon vanishes. The Murdered Woman weeps at the loss, for her one desire was to have a child. Her weeping gratifies the Fat Man, who vanishes while leaning on his cane, which then falls noisily to the ground. At the sound, the Murdered Woman looks around fearfully, suddenly realizing her isolation in death. A cart comes into view, pulled by a donkey. The Philosopher, still clinging to his earthly curiosity, hides behind a tree to watch, motioning to the Murdered Woman to join him there. The donkey stops to nibble on the pomegranate rinds left behind by the vanished child; but the little girl who sits on top of the cart, behind her parents, covers her eyes as though sensing something strange. When they finally move on, the Murdered Woman rushes desperately behind the cart, her arms outstretched toward the child. Only the Philosopher is left to continue his eternal argumentation (1916).

*It Is So (If You Think So).*   The Agazzi women have been slighted by their new neighbor, the mother-in-law of Agazzi's assistant, Signor Ponza. The woman has refused to invite them into her house, when her neighbors had called—even though, in deference to Agazzi's superior social station, she should have called on *them.* Prodded by the friendly sarcasm of Laudisi, Signora Agazzi's brother, the women (including friends who have dropped in out of curiosity) confess that they have been gossiping about Ponza's strange family arrangements: he has put up his mother-in-law in an expensive flat next to that of the Agazzis, while his own wife lives on the edge of town, in an inexpensive walk-up. Moreover, he keeps Signora Frola from her daughter, allowing the two to greet one another only at a distance. In the Sophoclean unraveling which follows, we learn that Signora Frola visits her daughter twice a day, looking up at her window from the courtyard. They exchange notes by means of a basket which is lowered and raised again for the purpose. Signora Frola now calls, explaining that she could not receive the ladies earlier because her son-in-law would be upset. He has suffered a serious breakdown—she informs them; when her daughter Lina (Signora Ponza) was taken ill and had to be surreptitiously left in a nursing home, Ponza almost went mad. When Lina was restored to him, he refused to believe that it was his wife. In his mind, Signora Frola says, he was convinced she had died. A second marriage had to be "performed" in order to restore Lina to her husband. In short, Signora Frola tells them, Ponza is mad. But she quickly assures them that her son-in-law is not at all dangerous. On the contrary: he is most considerate and tender. Soon after she leaves, Ponza enters. His version of the facts is very different. He convinces the group that his mother-in-law is mad, not he; that he keeps the mother and daughter apart because Signora Frola believes her daughter to be still alive, when in fact she has died. The woman who is now his wife is another, not Lina. The Agazzis and their friends accept this story. But under Laudisi's destructive and inexorable questioning, the others conclude that the only way to get at the truth is to confront the two. When this happens, Signora Frola defers to her son-in-law, who excitedly orders her back to her flat. After she has gone, he suddenly grows calm and explains that his anger was feigned to humor the old woman. The Agazzis want the facts now more than ever. "Evidence" finally arrives from the little town where the newcomers had lived—but it is very ambiguous evidence and, because of an earthquake, what little is known cannot be checked out. At this point, the Chief of Police steps in at Agazzi's request and orders Ponza to bring his wife to them. When the woman arrives, she is heavily veiled. Under questioning she says simply: I am Signor Ponza's second wife and Signora Frola's daughter. Laudisi's skeptical and brilliant probing of "reality" thus shapes an unanswered question (1917).

**As Well As Before, Better than Before.**   Fulvia Gelli, who abandoned her husband and infant baby girl to pursue a life that brought her down to the depths of moral degradation, is saved from a miserable death by the husband she abandoned. She returns to him, but in order to spare her daughter—who treasures the false memories of her mother which have been fed her—Fulvia comes back into her own home as Doctor Gelli's second wife. A lover follows her there, but she dismisses him. Soon she becomes pregnant again. Her daughter, Livia, however, grows even more cold with this news. Full of hate for her "step-mother," the girl makes inquiries and learns that her father has never really married this "other woman" who obviously has a sordid past. With this knowledge, she angrily confronts Fulvia, and the mother reveals her true identity. Meanwhile, after a year, her still-fervent lover—Marco Mauri—returns, ready to go with her anywhere. In

the realization that her husband has not really changed
at all and that Livia cannot tolerate her now any more
than she could before, Fulvia decides to leave with Mauri
—who has given up position, family, and security for her
sake. But this time, she does not leave her baby behind.
The newborn infant will accompany her into her life with
Mauri (1920).

*The Life I Gave You.*    Donn'Anna Luna's only son has just
died. The women of the neighborhood are reciting a
litany for the dead. They leave when, from the room
where the corpse lies, the parish priest emerges with a
neighbor. These two are soon joined by an old servant,
who had cared for the son as a child. In hushed whispers
they reveal their consternation at Donn'Anna's insistence
that her son has "gone away" and will eventually "return." For Donn'Anna, her son's death is a fiction; she
will keep him alive willfully, in the same way that she
gave him life at birth. His life is now in her hands; she
will not let go. Unexpectedly a young woman, Lucia, arrives and asks to see Donn'Anna's son. Unaware that he
is dead, she reveals that, until his recent return to his
mother, the son had been her lover, that she is pregnant
by him, and that she has now abandoned her family and
children to be with him. Donn'Anna, turning it all to her
purpose, tells the young woman that her son has gone
away on a trip but will return—convinced that Lucia will
eventually understand. Together they will keep the
young man "alive." But when Lucia's mother also arrives
and learns that the young man is dead, she insists that
Lucia be told the truth. The girl is ready to remain with
Donn'Anna, but the older woman agrees, finally, that she
must be made to return to her family. The play ends
with Lucia protesting that she will stay on, and
Donn'Anna letting go of her fiction in the reality of
events crowding around her (1923).

The theater plays dramatize Pirandello's commitment to
naked masks (*maschere nude*) in the most striking and

provocative way, as we have seen. It is no wonder that
*Six Characters*—the least "defined" in terms of a particular
human situation, and therefore the most translatable of the
theater plays—should have proved to be Pirandello's most
popular play in the United States. In it the business of
theater is described most directly, reduced to its essentials.
Life invades the world of art and shatters the dichotomy of
"reality-illusion," taking over that world and resisting all
attempts to adjust to anything else. It is the most "contemporary" of the theater plays, also, in its existential insistence on the incommunicability of corrosive passions—
this, too, translated directly into terms that are immediately
appealing to a theater-conscious public. But to see in this
transparent work about the stage simply a "clever" play is
analogous to reducing the greatness of *Hamlet* to what
Shakespeare had to say about actors and acting in his play-
within-a-play. Ultimately, the play's the thing—but the
conscience which is the heartbeat of the Pirandellian experience does not reside in the gimmicks which show to advantage the stagecraft of dramatic art. The full implications
of *Six Characters*, and of the theater plays generally, remain
to be discovered in a very different direction.

Not communication of feelings and thoughts, but the
externalization, expulsion, expression of these, regardless
of the possibility of "communication," is the main business
of the theater plays. In *Six Characters*, communication is
declared to be impossible, though necessary, throughout the
action; in *Each in His Own Way*, the confrontation is more
effective but the main characters resist the effort to be
absorbed in the trial of communicating and escape instead
into their own dark despair. In *Tonight We Improvise*, that
dark world is invaded by others, but at the last moment,
Mommina succumbs to her tragic necessity to close herself
up in herself, and dies. The effort at communication is the
soul of Pirandello's plays; that effort contains everything
else. The theater plays dramatize the *difficulty* of that effort;
in the plays we are about to discuss, it is the *psychological*
process itself which is dissected, magnified, studied in all its
possibilities.

The difficulty of externalizing the inward passionate experiences of life has been beautifully summarized by Coleridge, in his answer to Wordsworth's great ode.

> *A grief without a pang, void, dark, and drear.*
> *A stifled, drowsy, unimpassioned giref,*
> *Which finds no natural outlet, no relief,*
> *In word, or sigh, or tear—*[1]

But Pirandello reminds us that the Wordsworthian insight into the matter is just as valid as that of Coleridge. The "spontaneous overflow of emotion"—which becomes truly communicable emotion only in the process of being "recollected in tranquillity"[2]—is dramatized in his plays as the very movement from inward agony to expression in all its variety of possibilities. There is a great deal of posturing, groaning, moaning, and weeping; there are thoughtless accusations; there are fearful efforts to make contact; there are characters who, again and again, insist on adequate verbalization of their inner torment, and fail. The Father in *Six Characters* is an eloquent reminder that the "actors" watching and listening to him must be moved out of their tranquil passivity by being forced to "recollect" somehow a "spontaneous overflow of emotion" which was never theirs, before they can begin to understand his "performance." The real-life drama is the recollection of emotion in its spontaneity. And, if we forget that it is, in fact, an actor who is playing the role of the Father, we may indeed get the impression that we are actually witnessing a nonartistic recollection of spontaneously overflowing emotion. In all great plays, the protagonists—Oedipus, Hamlet, Othello—recall their agonies for us in this way; but Pirandello's Father does it before fellow actors in a second dimension of theatricality, setting up the equation in visual dramatic terms.

How does one externalize, express, expel, emotional experience? Laughter is one way. Weeping, sobbing, sighing, violence are others. But all of these fall short of language; they become dramatic only when the attempt to verbalize them begins. Laughter then becomes a kind of grotesque humor which catches us in its trap: we laugh at the expense of someone else, but it immediately turns against us and becomes an outlet for our own pain. Through the verbalizing of emotion, the everyday masks are slowly stripped. In the process, contradictions are exaggerated, humor interrupts and forces us momentarily to step back, arguments are reversed, commonplaces are turned inside out. Communication in Pirandello rarely succeeds; but the dramatic articulation of it gives rise to the Pirandellian dialectic, which is expression of the inexpressible.

With the effort to verbalize intense emotions, Pirandello moves into what must be recognized as his true dramatic stride. The ineffable must somehow be voiced, even though in most cases (and *Liolà* is a marvelous exception) speech proves inadequate for the experience. In trying to find words for the inner life of spirit, Pirandello's characters must project a high "sincerity level," and in so doing they inevitably set up a contradiction. They say such and such; but do the words really reflect what they feel and think? The characters themselves feel the inadequacy. In translating their emotions into words, are they not really negating the inward experience? What can be externalized, what is finally externalized, becomes in the doing, the very opposite of what it purports to be: the reality of the inner experience in its *inwardness*. More often than not, Pirandello's characters convince us not by what they actually say but by the conviction that animates their facial expressions, gestures, and general physical restlessness. Explanations contradict other explanations; the past contradicts the present; facts contradict conviction. Again and again Pirandello reminds us that we cannot attach ourselves to any of these isolated moments of the verbalization of experience: language forces us back into ourselves. But, by the same token, that necessary *distance* makes possible a new awareness of things. In the effort to verbalize one's deepest feelings, one creates for himself the adequate objective correlative of his emotional life.

Pirandello exacerbates the difficulty of this dilemma in many of his plays. His characters keep harping on the limitations of words. But the total effect is obviously the very opposite.

In the series of plays we are about to consider, Pirandello approaches the dilemma in much more complex terms and with subtler insights, demanding of his audience much greater concentration. In *Henry IV*, this obsession with the problem of dramatic communicability takes us—as in Shakespeare's *Hamlet*—to the very brink of the inexpressible.

The difficulty of communication in Pirandello is pursued, of course, far beyond the difficulties of merely verbal expression. The trials of verbalizing emotions and states of mind are only an immediate reflection of the difficulty of holding together the many "masks" of character. The protagonists of *Six Characters* are six personae, each complete and whole in the characteristic act he represents—although the process of depicting that whole appears at a certain moment a splintered reality, a disintegration of personality. It is the will that holds together the multiplicity of masks, drawing the seeming fragments together in the nervous movement which is the disorder and revitalization of life.

To suggest that, in his preoccupation with the paradoxes of communication and the multiplicity of personality, Pirandello was toying with philosophical ideas at the expense of dramatic effect is wholly misleading. The problem of identity, the transformation of a pragmatic and social "reality" into a provocative question, the undermining of facts and events as commonly understood, the insistence on the creative role of the will in perception and apprehension, are always, in his plays, human and immediate dramatic situations triggered, almost always, by a deception forcing its way to the surface. Far from being cerebral exercises, his plays are intensely personal. Moral questions are explored in precisely the open-ended ambiguous forms in which they overtake us in our lives. Pirandello is firm in his insistence that "morality" be preserved; but for him, morality is the unwavering commitment to oneself, in the honest appraisal of intentions. His protagonists are, as a rule, "lost" men and women consumed by passion; and if conventional rules are upheld in the end, it is only because those men and women have accepted them in the depths of their souls, while acting contrary to them. By the same token, the hypocrisy of those who accept an external set of rules with complacent self-assurance is attacked at every turn. The undermining of conventional morality, in other words, is never an end in itself in Pirandello, but simply the means to force a confrontation with self.

The plays discussed in the pages that follow are representative of Pirandello's treatment of moral questions. In *As Well As Before, Better than Before*, the "unconventional" seems to win out; in *The Life I Gave You* the unconventional is softened by a kind of retributive justice which exonerates the offenders; in *It Is So (If You Think So)* social conventions and "position" are undermined in the short-sightedness of those who insist on external assurances. In all of them, external conventions are shattered, to be reconstituted or replaced wholly by a Hamlet-like assertion of personal *will*.

Donn'Anna, in *The Life I Gave You*, knows perfectly well, from the very beginning, that her son in the next room is dead. Sooner or later she will have to bury him. But she delays the preparations, determined to keep him alive by sheer strength of will. What does this mean? Her relatives and friends interpret her decision as the result of the shock she has suffered. But she is calm and lucid in her determination, and manifests tender concern for those around her. As often happens in Pirandello's plays, we are thrust from the outset into an unusual situation, deceptively familiar but pregnant with unforeseeable complications.

For Donn'Anna, the conviction that her strength of will can keep her son alive is, paradoxically, an assertion of death: the entire play is built on this contradiction, explored in many subtle ways. For her, the boy's physical death is nothing recent, we soon discover. He had died long before when, in defiance of her will, he had left home. This paradox is further complicated by her explanation that the life she is now eager to preserve is the life she had recognized as the very being of her son before he left home. The worn yet living man who returned after so many years was already dead for her, a stranger she could not recognize as her son.

One point, at least, deserves mention here as characteristic of Pirandello's superb handling of dramatic structure. The son, for whom so much emotional energy is expended, is never seen—alive or dead. And the fluctuations between life and death, which are the substance of the play, are compressed, like the melodic phrase that introduces a series of variations, in the unseen event with which the play begins: the event of the boy's death. Throughout, it is this point of no dimension between life and death which we keep coming back to. The boy has just died, but his mother is determined to keep him alive as something more than a memory; the boy lives again but in another dimension, as the child the mother loved, who mirrored her joy and her affection; that child has died in the silent stranger who returned to her home, but it is to live again in the new child who will be born to Lucia. The dizzying effect of these paradoxes makes the obvious parallel between her own dead son and the lively children of her sister Donna Fiorina, recently returned from the city, all the more effective: they too have suffered change, and Donn'Anna recognizes in their fascination with their new life away from home the beginning of the separation she has already gone through. The play suggests "distances" all through: the distance of physical separation, the distance of new habits and a new life, the distance between life and death, the distance of time, which can separate and bring together again in the memory past and future in the single reality of the present.

Lucia, the woman who bears the child of the dead man, is the only person in the play who comes close to understanding Donn'Anna's determination. Until she learns of her lover's death, Lucia responds to Donn'Anna with full sympathy, creating in the older woman the illusion that she has succeeded in shaping the reality of her will. But the distance between them becomes clear when Lucia, learning the truth, decides to remain with Donn'Anna to comfort her. Yet the sacrifice has no meaning. In accepting the "fact" of her lover's death, Lucia has destroyed Donn'Anna's trust in her. For the young woman, death has won out.

A simple fact, after all! Life and death are distinguishable. There can be no mistake, surely. But again and again, Donn'Anna shakes our sensibilities with her dogmatic in-

tuition of things, questioning the most obvious "facts."
What is life? Her sister, Donna Fiorina, weeps at the change
in Donn'Anna's life, with the death of her son; but Donn'-
Anna sees in her sister's countenance a much greater change.
The lovely memory of the past they shared makes the
present seem like a vague dream.

> It's all like that. Exactly. A dream. And if your body can
> change right under your hands like this, change like
> this . . . the things you remember—this thing or that
> one—what are they? Memories of dreams. That's how it
> is. This . . . that. . . . Everything.

Life's but a dream whose shapes return. And the memory
gives them substance: "Well then, I say that so long as my
memory lasts my dream is alive. There! My son as I see
him . . . alive! alive! Not what's lying in there. Try to
understand me!" Communication is painfully frustrating.
Inner certainty cannot be rendered in words. The problem is
as acute here as it is later in Ionesco and Albee.

And yet, the words are everything for Pirandello. He
twists them and pulls them apart, pumps them dry for suggestions, repositions them in different contexts, uses the
ready-made molds to solid advantage, producing an easy
naturalness rooted in the realities of speech, at once vivid and
suggestive, precise and symbolical.

Lucia's description of her lover's aspect just before he left
her to return to his mother's house echoes an earlier, similar
description by Donn'Anna: "Dying, he was dying for years.
His eyes had already lost their light. He was dead already
when he left! I saw how pale he was, how pale . . . how
miserable he looked, and I knew he would die!" For a
moment, Lucia and Donn'Anna recognize a reciprocal intuition. And in that infinite reflection of two mirrors giving
back the same insight, impression and expression coincide,
and Donn'Anna leaps to a final, terrible conclusion.

> I . . . I embalmed you when you were still alive! You
> were alive and I embalmed you . . . as you no longer
> were, as you could no longer be . . . with your full head

of hair and with those eyes which could no longer laugh!
And because they could not laugh, I didn't recognize
them!—How, then? How could I make you live outside
of your life? that life that had worn you down. . . . Poor,
poor flesh of my flesh that I will never never . . . see
again? Where are you? . . . Where are you?

The tender simplicity of these passages is charged with
electrifying paradoxes. Donn'Anna is here acknowledging the
futility of trying to preserve life in a memory that was a
truncated experience, or—in a different perspective—embalming the image of a happy past when it was still, in spite
of the frightening change that had taken place, very much
alive. In thinking she could preserve her son's "ideal"
image, Donn'Anna has deceived herself no less than her
son had in thinking he could cut himself off from his roots.
For a moment, Donn'Anna allows herself to be deceived
again: Lucia will remain with her and keep her son alive
for her. "Don't take him away! Don't leave me! Don't
leave me!" But, as in most of Pirandello's plays, darkness
closes in almost immediately, and the action rushes to its
appointed end. Lucia's resolve to remain with Donn'Anna
is meaningless in the light of her account of her lover's willful retreat from life. Donn'Anna's decision to make him live
through her own powerful will proved shortsighted. He had
chosen death; and against that choice, she has no weapon.
This final, clear intuition is a kind of Leopardian resignation in the face of despair. "What shall I do with myself,
now?" Lucia asks, when Donn'Anna insists she must go back
with her mother. "And what about me, here?" Donn'Anna
replies.

That's what death is all about, my child. . . . Things to
be done, whether you want to or not . . . and things to
be said. . . . First, a timetable to check out, then the car
to the station . . . a trip. . . . That's what we are, busy
ghosts. . . . To torture oneself, resign oneself, find rest.
. . . That's what death is.

In one of his most unusual and "contemporary" plays—
*At the Exit* (although in anticipation of Sartre's *No Exit,*

it might more properly be called, simply, *Exit*)—Pirandello probes with the most delicate nuances of his art the notion of death as an act of will, the resignation of the spirit once the last overwhelming desire of the soul has been satisfied. This remarkable one-act play, which owes something, as E. L. Master's *Spoon River Anthology* does, to the *Greek Anthology*,[3] may have been the inspiration for Thornton Wilder's *Our Town*—only, it is much more profound, more dramatic, less sentimental. The protagonists are, at first, the "ghosts" of a Fat Man and a Philosopher: ghosts by virtue of definition, since they are dead; but clearly still in their human, earthly forms (invisible to others) since they have not as yet given up their attachment to life. The Fat Man leans on his cane, on a bench, waiting—in death—for the coming of his unfaithful wife who, he insists, will soon be killed by her lover. Soon the Murdered Woman's ghost appears as anticipated, and then, after they have reviewed with the Philosopher the circumstances of the Fat Man's death and the Woman's murder, the ghost of a child appears. A pomegranate satisfies the last earthly desire of the child, so he vanishes. The Murdered Woman weeps to see him go, and, since to see her weep was the Fat Man's last wish, he too is satisfied and vanishes. Next, the Woman disappears; but she goes out screaming, in effect, since it is total despair, not fulfilled desire that finally detaches her from earthly life. Only the Philosopher remains, yearning for the world's highest good, beauty, truth, etc., without hope of realizing it, yet yearning still. He alone keeps the ghostly limbo vigil. We are reminded of Dante's Virgil in the fourth canto of *Inferno*, who sums up the lot of the "virtuous pagans" condemned to Hell only for want of the saving grace of faith in Christ with the words: "without hope we live in desire." It is the least common denominator of Hell.

*At the Exit*, for all its brevity, is a masterpiece of its kind. In its one act, Pirandello manages to explore the perverse relations of betrayed husband, faithless wife, and bestially passionate lover; the natural longing of a woman for a child and of a child for sensory pleasure; and of a philosopher for a kind of perpetual intellectual masturbation. Relationships are always the substance of ethical structure in Pirandello; and here they are reduced to their essential core. The play contains the theme of *No Exit*, but goes beyond it to a Dantesque intuition of the nature of Hell: the eternal separation from light and love and the pain of knowledge, now revealed in its true form. In the moment of their articulation, the twisted relationships of these four people are established no less permanently in their consciousness than are those of Sartre's characters in *No Exit*; but Pirandello goes beyond, into the implications of their everlasting isolation. There is no judgment here based on "good" or "bad"; the adulteress is by far the most sensitive of the four. Her fate is the most dreadful, not because she has "sinned against man" but because she feels cursed in her profoundest being as a woman, where desire itself dies finally, face to face with her despair of having a child.

Pirandello's superb skill as a narrator is particularly evident in the compressed and therefore heightened structure of this one-act play. We come to know, or, rather, we are made to see vividly, the events which lead to the Fat Man's death and the murder of the Woman by her lover. And through the Philosopher's probing, the Fat Man is induced to say,

> I confess that my pleasure at being alive depended in large measure on my indifference to things and my having no great illusions. Don't think for a moment that my wife's betrayal was a shattering blow. Oh, I brooded about it, all right; and I would say to myself that I brooded because I had been hurt. But inside me I knew that I was really relieved. But it was not wholly relief, because—you see—even her lover failed to satisfy her, nothing satisfied her, no one.

The Woman herself corrects with devastating openness many of his impressions, betraying the same kind of indifference and compulsive drive for truth reflected in the account she gives of her last moments on earth, with her tormented lover. The play has the outer form and external appearance of Thornton's *Our Town,* but in its sense of incommunicable emotions and in the abstract isolation of the Philosopher it is perhaps much closer to Albee's *Quotations from Chairman Mao.* Each of the busy ghosts, in this Sicilian Spoon River play, is enclosed in his own cocoon, his own self-imposed limits, his all-consuming wish. Each represents a different theme, an independent form of life. As in *The Life I Gave You,* death is here translated as the assertion of self through an act of will; and life is the memory which survives, the last hope, the extension of an illusion in the moment of death.

In exploring these provocative themes, Pirandello never sacrifices the drama of personality for the abstraction of pure thought, the immediacy of content for clever gimmicks of form. His difficult themes are embedded in the realities of personal crises, difficult relationships, poignant emotions. What could easily become melodramatic situations in less capable hands—long self-analyses, personal tragedy, sin and suffering, moral reevaluations—mesmerize us in Pirandello's handling. He draws us to the very center of the soul. Even such relatively early plays as *At the Exit, Six Characters, It Is So (If You Think So)* reflect the playwright's instinctive preference for the *personal* situation that slowly evolves into a kind of phantasmagoria which gives rise to philosophical suggestions. The dramatic situation which emerges is thus, from the beginning, an organic whole. It is worth remembering in this context that plays like *At the Exit* (1916) and *It Is So (If You Think So)* (1917) were written around the time that *Liolà* appeared (1916), perhaps the most realistic and "even" of Pirandello's plays. Art is life, for Pirandello; but life becomes very early in his career as a dramatist the unraveling of difficult and profound questions about individual motives and human relationships generally.

The potential traumas of *Liolà* and the compressed but profound insights of *At The Exit* are given full scope in *As Well As Before, Better than Before* through grotesque and bitter humor. In this play, the chief characters are mercilessly exposed in all their weaknesses; and in the course of that devastating probing—which is the Pirandellian equivalent of a psychoanalytical therapy—a kind of laughter spills out. To call this "comic relief" would be an absurdity; on the contrary: though humorous there is little relief in it. Fulvia's sarcasm and frustration, directed as much against herself as against others around her, find an outlet in almost hysterical irony at those moments when on one else around her sees the dilemma of her situation. She must pose as a "stepmother" for the sake of her daughter's sensibilities; she must be grateful to her husband, who has taken her back and tries to be understanding; she must greet her own aunt as a stranger; she must go along with "mourning" and the Mass said for her—the "first" wife—on the occasion of the anniversary of her "death" (an anniversary whose date was fixed arbitrarily years before, for Livia's sake). Fulvia's laughter and humor are the private expression of an insupportable deception into which she has fallen out of sheer necessity. The more she tries to "save" the memory of the "dead" wife and mother—the unsoiled memory of her former self—the more difficult her isolation becomes. Her husband encourages the deception although he senses her pain; her daughter has not adjusted to the "new" mother, even after a year's time; she is a trapped stranger in her own house. The psychological tensions are immediate and profound. There is nothing here of the distinctly Freudian commonplaces found in O'Neill, or the purely conventional realism with which Ibsen defines such situations. Pirandello is closest to Strinberg in his insights, and much more devastating in his manner of stripping bare the illusions of "right" and "wrong."

Fulvia (who comes back as Flora and Francesca) deserted her husband Silvio and her infant daughter Livia because of her disgust with Silvio's hypocritical posture. Her life has been a complete abandonment on her part of all conventional behavior, an almost savage necessity to destroy her former image, created by her husband. At a certain moment she agrees to return to Silvio, leaving behind a lover who has abandoned everything for her. Marco Mauri follows her, nevertheless, and urges her to return to him: they belong together. But Fulvia is anxious to resume her role as mother and wife. She soon discovers that Silvio has not changed at all, but she adjusts to that fact because of her desire to be with Livia, who is now sixteen.

It is a painful dilemma. Livia worships the memory of her dead mother and resents the intrusion of the "donnaccia" who has presumed to occupy her place. She maintains a cold distance; nothing Fulvia does to woo her back seems to have any effect. To make matters worse, by straining to uphold the image of her former self in the eyes of the world, Fulvia isolates herself more and more by contrast. She is two distinct people; and because she really embodies a contradiction, she cannot destroy one without destroying the other. Her past is real; she is as much the old Fulvia as she is the new one. It is the Lord and Bondsman confrontation.

By the time Mauri returns, after a lapse of a year—during which time Fulvia has given birth to a second daughter— Fulvia is almost ready to call the bluff. Matters come to a head through Livia's determined efforts to find out about the intruder's past. She discovers that there is no marriage record, and that the woman living in her house has a sordid background. But in her triumphant unmasking of "Francesca" Livia is crushed by the discovery of the woman's true identity. Fulvia realizes that she can no longer live in that house. Livia will never forgive her; and Silvio means nothing to her. He has understood little of her shattering experience and even enjoys the idea, secretly, of having for his own pleasure, a woman who has been the sexual object of so many other men. When Mauri appears, Fulvia is ready to leave with him. But this time, she will not make the same mistake: the new baby goes with her. Her love for the child will see them both through the difficulties that lie ahead. And Mauri is faithful and considerate, in a way that Silvio never was. Her child will learn to love her without judging her harshly. And, most important, there will be no deception to perpetuate.

The death-in-life theme is present here from the beginning. "I was as good as dead," Fulvia says to her husband, early in the play. "It was a miracle, for you too!—If you only knew how much I believe in miracles now!" But the initial ela-

tion which follows her return, the hopes she nourishes, are
gradually destroyed as she realizes that she has come out
of one deception into another. The agony of her separation
from her family and the degradation of her former condition must be reassessed in the light of the lie hidden beneath
the respectable surface of her family life. By insisting on the
ridiculous mask of a "second" woman, Silvio has forced her
into another kind of degradation. The whole conventional
structure is thus reversed: her lover was honest with her, at
least, and she was never forced to live out a parody of this
kind. She realizes, in the course of this reversal, that her
husband's hypocrisy had been the cause of her dissatisfaction
and eventual flight, years before—as it will be, again, now.

Fulvia comes to understand that her new identity cannot
be a way of life. What she has suffered and what she has
been in the past must be part of the present, if she is to
remain truly alive. In her daughter's memory of her dead
mother, she feels her own present death. But in the image
which comes back to her, she does not recognize herself.

> I've felt it! I'm dead. Really dead! I'm right there, in front
> of her, and I'm dead! It's not me, not this one, who is
> alive—her mother is someone else . . . dead, out there!
> I'd like to take her by the arms, shake her, look straight
> at her and say: No! no! Listen to *me*, dear girl: because
> *she's* dead. . . . The dead can't hurt us any more, and
> so, in time, we think only good things about them. My
> dear girl, even death can be a rotten lie!

If she is to take up again the thread of her life, Fulvia must
kill the lie of her own death: "It must be destroyed, this
lie, destroyed, because I am alive, alive, alive!"

The respectability of Silvio and Livia is pitted against the
immorality of Fulvia and found wanting. But not quite in
those terms. As in most of his plays in which immorality
and sexual deviations are the central themes, Pirandello
phrases the confrontation in another way. In this case, it
is—more properly—a confrontation between the hypocrisy
of appearances and the search for identity. Fulvia (and she
is typical of this Pirandellian category of "heroines") is not

*seen* as an immoral "lost" woman at any moment in the play. We know what she has been because she tells us, and her words ring true. We also learn, indirectly, that her so-called immorality, though not condoned, appears much less pernicious than the "immorality" of those who have forced her to live a lie. Pirandello, like Dante, can condemn the sin and exalt the sinner at the same time.

In trying to restore the organic unity of her life and the continuity of her actions, Fulvia comes face to face with an opposition which must prove tragic. She cannot remain Livia's stepmother; but she cannot resume her legitimate role as mother, either. She must come to terms with the old Fulvia trying to fit into her new identity as though a miracle had really taken place. But miracles in Pirandello do not happen by chance or fate; they are the Promethean effort of the will. And, more often than not, they fail: Donn'Anna cannot preserve her son's life by a sheer act of will; Mita has accepted a "miracle" from Liolà but its consequences are never spelled out; Ilse expects a sudden transformation to take place in the rough peasants who witness her play but is killed in the effort; Diego Spina is skeptical of miracles but is raised from the dead by the miracle of modern drugs; La Spera hopes to convert her friends to a new life but fails; Fulvia hopes that her daughter will "raise" her from the dead but discovers that she has never really been alive for Livia. Yet, miracles can happen; and in some plays, like *The Grafting*, Pirandello reminds us that love can cancel all difficulties.

But a miracle—if one were possible in Fulvia's case—must destroy one of her two "relationships," her vital role as Livia's mother. For, to reveal her true identity means to shatter Livia's whole life—built on a lie—and to degrade herself in her daughter's eyes. Yet not to reveal it is even more terrible, since her whole identity rests ultimately on her relationship with her daughter. Like Oedipus, who contains in himself both the good king and the patricide, and who in destroying the latter must also destroy the former, so Fulvia cannot expect to extricate herself from the dilemma of self-contradictory roles. The dilemma is reflected in other similar difficulties: Livia has actually never known her mother, except in death—only a miracle could bring her back as a living, breathing, human being; Silvio has never understood her and never will; the towns-people and relatives see only the conventional pattern of things and cannot respond to her profound inward con-viction of what is "right." Love might indeed work the miracle, but Fulvia's love has a tragic flaw in it which renders it ineffective. As in the tragic dilemmas of the Greek heroes, Fulvia is finally forced into a revelation and realizes her inherent limitations.

Her final decision is for the lesser of two evils: she escapes the complex life for the simple one. Livia cannot accept her "sinful" mother, and Fulvia is forced to dis-appear again into her "sinful" world with her lover. Silvio too, it is clear, lives a lie. His real attachment is to the dead woman, the one who lives in his memory, not the one who is alive with him now. He wants her, he uses her; but he resents her.

Here as elsewhere, Pirandello explores this complex human drama with truly Augustinian insight into psy-chological realities. He does not condemn; he simply records the consequences which haunt the doer in his deed. There is nothing false or exaggerated in the picture he draws; instinct is never pitted against reason. The real issue lies elsewhere. His "lost" women, his passionate lovers, his sinful and tortured people are remarkably disciplined in their quest for reality and truth, single-minded in their purpose. In their relentless search for identity, they expose the limitations in others, as well as their own. In the Pirandellian world, fallible human forces are given free reign to remind us that "sin" and "morality" are meaning-less in conventional terms when insight into necessity is at stake. Freedom is a heavy burden, and that message is driven home with ruthless clarity.

The struggle toward freedom is translated into phe-nomenological terms in *It Is So (If You Think So)*. The play is a brilliant dramatic statement of the destructive process of dialectical inversion, where our deceptive image of the world is slowly eroded through irony and skepticism.

Laudisi, like Diego in *Each in His Own Way* and Fulvia in *As Well As Before, Better than Before,* is the catalyst who forces us to redefine "facts" and restructure the world as a conviction of the will. "What do we really know about others?" he asks. He presents himself as the devil's advocate in the "case" which evolves. He is the passion of reason, incapable of giving unity to the world but very effective in destroying the ready-made notions about it.

A set of disturbing facts are presented to us regarding a husband, his wife, and his mother-in-law; evidence is marshalled to test the validity of those facts. The son is possessive and cruel, it seems—to the point of keeping his mother-in-law from seeing her own daughter at close range. The wife is not seen until the very end of the play. The contest of wills is between Signor Ponza and Signora Frola. The mother-in-law is depicted as indulging her son-in-law in his deranged claim that his first wife has died and that the woman he lives with is really a second wife. Signora Frola goes along with the "masquerade" for, as she explains, when they returned her daughter to Ponza after a long absence necessitated by Lina's physical breakdown, he refused to recognize her as the same woman who had been taken from him. He was convinced his wife had died, and a second "marriage" had to be concluded before Ponza could resign himself to his "new" wife. For him, Signora Frola explains, Lina is a *second* wife; and she goes along with that deception to keep him calm.

But the very same facts are convincingly restructured by Ponza to prove that the old woman is mad and that he must humor her in thinking that *he* is mad. In this dramatic and psychological tour de force, Pirandello encourages the characters on the sidelines (and, by extension, of course, the audience and readers of the play) to examine the "facts" in two contradictory contexts, undermining our easy convictions about things and forcing reality as we know it to a rigorous test. We hear Ponza's account of things, and it rings true and convincing; we hear Signora Frola's, and she creates a whole new set of possibilities. When "evidence" is finally searched out to get at the "true" facts, it proves meager and ambiguous. Finally, Ponza is ordered by his superiors to present his wife to them. Surely she will be able to settle the matter! But when the young woman appears, heavily veiled, she can only agree that she is indeed Ponza's second wife and, also, Signora Frola's daughter. The play ends with this provocative paradox.

Laudisi has prepared us for this "revelation" all along. What are facts? What can anyone tell us that will be proof of anything? What kind of evidence can disprove Ponza's conviction or demolish Signora Frola's quiet assurance? The veiled figure who appears at the end is the embodiment of the dialectical process: I am what you believe I am, she tells the assembled company. But this is not an affirmation of the relativity of things, of skepticism and doubt. She is not an illusion but the abortive truth which they have created for themselves. For Ponza she is indeed what he claims; and for Signora Frola, she is truly the daughter who was taken away and then restored to her husband. Signora Ponza remains outside the possibility of true knowledge for those who counted on her words to decide the doubt. The conviction of my husband and mother has shaped me for them clearly, she is saying; but to you others I must remain veiled. She is the mirror of their misunderstanding. Conventional rules have determined their conclusions about her. They are on the threshold of the truth, but will never know it. She is the symbol of their abortive labor to reveal her identity. It *is* so, if you will it. And they have not.

Confusion here as elsewhere in Pirandello is only apparent. If the substance of reality escapes us, it is because we have refused to undertake the full journey of discovery. So long as we subscribe to the premise that reality is outside us, an external "fact" to be catalogued and filed away, it will elude us. Truth is the mirror image of the soul.

Mirror images, in fact, abound in this play and in very obvious ways. Laudisi, in spite of his skeptical daring, is still in a limbo of "reality-illusion." He questions to provoke the repudiation of external facts, yet he does not affirm anything but the doubt in himself. Like Diego in *Each in His*

*Own Way*, Laudisi retains his composure in the devastating Socratic experience he inspires. His will is not whole. In the final resolution, he must be counted with his sister and her family and friends: a double image, still out of focus. He remains outside looking in. His very skepticism is a sign of his inability to recognize truth. He sees the difficulty and forces others to see it, but that is the whole of his commitment.

Laudisi takes us to the very brink of discovery. At the end of scene 2 in the second act, one of the women, annoyed at his questions and his air of skeptical superiority, refuses his outstretched hand and takes a brusque leave of him. "Then, Madam, I take leave of myself for you!" he says, and shakes his own hand. A few lines later, at the opening of the next scene, he is alone, gazing into a mirror.

> Ah, there you are! My dear man!—Which of us is mad, eh? Yes, I know: I say *you* are, and you point at *me*.— Come now, between us, we know each other well, we two!—The trouble is that others don't see you the way I do! And so, my dear fellow, what does that make you? For my part, here in front of you, I see myself, touch myself—you, as others see you, what are you? A ghost, my dear fellow, a ghost!—And yet, look at these madmen here! They ignore the ghost they carry with them, in themselves, and go running, bursting with curiosity, after the ghosts in others! And they really believe that it's different!

In setting himself up as the critic of the others, Laudisi, with his self-conscious criticism of the others, creates in us the illusion that he is himself a sort of living embodiment of the answer to the play's problem. But he is not. The true image and the reflected image are not resolved, by his insight, into an organic whole. Laudisi cannot, therefore, have the last word in the play's dilemma, and the dialogue again and again makes that clear. The three people who have caused so much turmoil represent the last true phase of consciousness, where the duality of internal and external reality is resolved into inner certainty.

The mirror is a favorite device with Pirandello; but the eyes of the characters are also reflections of doubt, division, uncertainty, and deception. In the eyes of his relatives and friends, Laudisi sees their difficulty and describes it for them in many different ways. They think they "see" but they do not. They think they know, but in the very act of asserting what they think they know, they are undermined. The clear "facts" are true barometers, they think; but the facts themselves work against them.

In all of this, Pirandello obviously chooses the most extreme set of circumstances to dramatize his point. Nothing speaks for itself—not even the documents which finally arrive. The earthquake in the village from which Ponza has come has destroyed almost all "evidence." What they manage to get hold of is ambiguous. The very woman who has given rise to all the speculation is herself an ambiguous "fact." Pirandello exhausts the argument, hammers it home with an obsessive intention spiced with humor. The plot is an "ideal" characteristic situation—that is, the exaggerated circumstances are pushed to the limits of credibility so as to present a foolproof "case." Within that structure he unfolds the perfect trial.

We have in *It Is So (If You Think So)* an immediate emotional experience; but we have also, as in most of Pirandello's plays, a highly complex dramatic structure, infinitely suggestive. In the "myth" plays, Pirandello introduces a new dimension. Emotional and psychological immediacy and dramatic complexity are there woven into a transparent allegory reminiscent of Spenser's world in its details and of Dante's in its artistic yearning for completeness. Those remarkable allegories will occupy our attention in the penultimate chapter. But first, we must consider that play of Pirandello's which sums up in the most memorable dramatic way the themes and ideas discussed so far: *Henry IV*. In it, the identity crisis and the dissolution of personality are brought by their internal dialectic to the very edge of non-theater. Its infinite psychological reflections suggest, also, literary reflections: Hamlet, Dr. Jekyll and Mr. Hyde, Dorian Gray, Dostoyevsky's Idiot all come to mind. And in its pervasive sense of the inexpressible, it reminds us of the Terror in Albee's *A Delicate Balance*. With *Henry IV* we come to the center of the Pirandellian universe, where the Dantesque journey into the depths of personality finds its darkest and most sublime expression.

# 6

# The Creative Madness of *Henry IV*

*Henry IV*.  The curtain rises on the "throne room" of a villa reconstructed to look like an eleventh century German imperial castle. From the talk of the servants, we learn that the master of the house is insane, that he thinks he is the "tragic" German Emperor Henry IV, enemy of Pope Gregory VII, that his entire staff has been hired to sustain the fiction, and that all visitors are obliged to pretend that they are historical personalities of the eleventh century. The main action begins with the arrival of Carlo Di Nolli, the madman's nephew, who has lately assumed full responsibility, as a sort of legal guardian, for his uncle's welfare. He comes accompanied by his fiancée Frida, her mother the Marchesa Matilde Spina, the mother's lover Belcredi, and a Doctor Genoni, all of whom (except Di Nolli) are visiting the place for the first time. The idea, advanced by the doctor, is to apply shock treatment by "turning back the clock" for Di Nolli's uncle. Twenty years before, during a Mardi Gras masquerade, the Marchesa Matilde had dressed as Matilde of Canossa, friend of Pope Gregory VII, and the play's protagonist (then an overzealous, almost feared suitor) had dressed as Henry IV, so that he could "go to Canossa" as a penitent. Having rehearsed for a month to play the role well, he was deeply absorbed in it, when, during the actual masquerade, he happened to fall from his horse and was knocked unconscious. The result was a mental derangement that left him embedded, so to

speak, in the role he had assumed. Suspecting that a cure
is now possible, Di Nolli and the doctor set their elaborate
counterfiction in motion. After a preliminary meeting, to
enable the doctor to observe Henry's reactions to a variety
of "eleventh-century" visitors, the plan is to confront the
mad emperor with two versions of his beloved Matilde of
the Mardi Gras masquerade, dressed as Matilde of Canossa
(or rather, of Tuscany, to be historically precise). One
will be the actual Matilde, manifestly advanced in age,
and the other will be Frida, her daughter, dressed in the
very costume that she had worn twenty years before. The
expectation is that the contrast will force the mind's clock
back to where it had stopped and shock it into moving
forward again. But Henry IV has already informed his
retainers that he is really no longer insane, that his full
recovery took place eight years before, and that he had
then decided to continue in his role as Henry IV only
because he felt it would be too painful, for others as well
as for himself, to try to cope with a world that had moved
on without him for twelve years. Now he will tell his
visitors the truth. Yet, when he comes to them for that
purpose, there are the contrasted Matildes, with Frida (unknown to Henry) looking just like her mother looked
twenty years before. The fiction sustained in his insanity
has come to life. The shock treatment at once backfires.
Perhaps he is not cured, or perhaps these people before
him now are more insane than he ever was! But his old
love for Matilde rekindles to a feverish passion at the sight
of young Frida in Matilde's dress. He wants her; he claims
her. In a heated confrontation, he reveals that he had not
fallen off his horse accidentally twenty years before. The
Marchesa's lover Belcredi, even then his rival, may have
made the horse rear. The clock has really been turned
back. In a final angry scuffle, Henry stabs Belcredi. The
blocked deed has been done. Belcredi cries: "He is *not*
insane! He is not insane!" But the play ends with the
feigned emperor's realization that, with his revengeful
blow, he has now further embedded himself, perhaps forever, in his "role" (1922).

"We are born, and we die! Did you perhaps choose to be born, Sir?" says Henry IV to one of his guests. "Not I.— And between one event and the other, many things happen that we would rather not have happen, and we sadly resign ourselves to them."

Resigning ourselves means, we more or less willingly play the parts forced on us by chance, fate, providence—call it what you will. And so, all the world's a stage; and what fools these mortals be who fret and strut their hours upon it and then are seen no more!

The first actors to appear on stage in Pirandello's *Henry IV* are "stagehands" in a sort of theatrical company that has been putting on a "history play," day in and day out, for twenty years. The lead in the play has remained the same for those twenty years, because it is *his* play. But the stagehands and bit-part players come and go. And in the opening scene a new bit-part player is being broken in. Unhappily, he has made a mistake and can't immediately pick up his lines again. He knew when he applied for the part that it was an historical play built around the character of Henry IV— but he had mistakenly assumed it was Henry IV of France and so had boned up on the fifteenth-century French milieu, when in fact—as he discovers upon his arrival—the central character is Emperor Henry IV of Germany, the great pseudo penitent who, as everyone knows, had to "go to Canossa," to kneel before Pope Gregory VII and beg forgiveness for having defied the papal will.

In the first exchange of the play, the oldtimers are explaining the business to the new man, and we have the typical prologue of a Renaissance comedy.

LANDOLFO [*to the new man, Bertoldo, by way of explanation*].    And this is the throne room.
ARIALDO    At Goslar.
ORDULFO    Or at Worms.
LANDOLFO    According to the event we're representing, it hops around with us, here this time, there the next.
ORDULFO    In Saxony.

ARIALDO  In Lombardy.
LANDULFO  On the Rhine.

At this point, Bertoldo realizes he has made a mistake. "This room . . . these costumes," he says. "Which Henry IV is it? I'm a bit confused. Is he Henry IV of France or not?" "Henry IV of Germany, my boy: the Salian dynasty." "The great and tragic Emperor!" "The one at Canossa. Every day we carry on here the terrible war between Church and State, by Jove." "The Emperor against the Papacy!"

Bertoldo grows more and more upset. How will he be able to play *this* part? They might have been clearer in telling him what it was all about, before he arrived. And so, he enters the "play" not knowing what his part is to be. Nor do his new companions. The only one in the play who knows what it's all about, as a play, is its "protagonist," the madman who has been in the leading role for twenty years, since the time when he first played the part in a carnival masquerade.

From its very beginning, Pirandello's *Henry IV* is a mirror of madness, that form of divine madness which excites a playwright to write plays, producers and directors to put them on, and audiences to sit and watch and listen until they are transported wherever the playwright's fancy leads. And the best characters in the best plays are almost always divinely mad poets in their own right, in whom the creative genius of their authors is most adequately embodied. King Lear and Hamlet, in their madness are their own playwrights, even as Cervantes's Don Quixote in his madness is his own novelist.

All of us have at least a touch of such creative madness in us, or we could not be taken in by the literary artist's creative will. And many of us who are not artists have much more than just a touch of it. Pirandello, as we know, saw his wife grow mad; but before he was forced to put her away, he was able to observe her madness—often a mad jealousy—at close range. It was a madness that insisted things were so which—except in the strength of her will—were not so. And after he had her put away, Pirandello went to Canossa as a "madman" himself (by writing this play) to do penance and to explain to himself and to the rest of us what madness is all about.

People have been dressing up stages, and themselves, for millennia—to play Oedipus, Hamlet, Lear. We must say of the best of them who assume such roles:

> *Is it not monstrous that this player here,*
> *But in a fiction, in a dream of passion,*
> *Could force his soul so to his own conceit*
> *That from her working all his visage wanned,*
> *Tears in his eyes, distraction in his aspect,*
> *A broken voice, and his whole function suiting*
> *With forms to his conceit? And all for nothing!*
> *For Hecuba!*

[Hamlet, 2.2.561–68]

But we know that it is to the actor playing Hamlet, or Oedipus, or Othello that the words best apply. So it is with the madness, the feigned madness—and most of all, with the feigned feigned-madness—of Pirandello's mad Henry IV in his permanent masquerade.

"Do you know what it means," says the mad Henry, "to find yourself face to face with a madman—face to face with one who tears down the foundations of all you have built up in you, and around you, your logic, the logic of everything you have pieced together! Well—what do you expect? Happily for them, they don't fashion things by logic. . . . They don't have to rely [for what is real to them] on the witness of a hundred thousand other people who are supposed not to be mad!" What makes one mad, he concludes, is to imagine that we can look into the eyes of another and really find our way into his inner sense of reality: "You stand there, at best, like a beggar before a door he can never enter: for he who enters is never you, with the world you have in you, as you see it and touch it—but someone unknown to you, like what you appear to be to the eyes and touch of that other in his own impenetrable world." And the set grows dark as Henry finishes this speech and pauses.

In *Henry IV*, Pirandello shares with us the highest excitements of creative madness. Although it was written about the same time as the first of the theater plays and comes relatively early in Pirandello's already late development as a playwright, it is by far the most sophisticated expression of his "third voice of poetry." The action never flags, nothing is repeated or wasted in the dramatic conception, the most difficult themes are brought together in a beautifully organic whole which is both characteristic and new. The entire construction is a piling up of roles—conscious and deliberate—and a spanning of time, all of which are handled with masterful ease and transparent suggestivity. The play is, in fact, the epitome of the theater plays: a series of masks put on and taken off sometimes in the twinkling of an eye or a change of tone, as it were, and a play within a play in a series of stratifications.

The opening, as we said, prepares us for this network of roles and masks. The emperor's retainers consider their dual roles as servants and as "secret counselors"; visitors to the "imperial palace" must assume historical roles in accordance with the milieu created by their host; the portraits in the throne room are themselves a double dimension—"modern" with respect to the rest of the furnishings in the room, but "set" in time through the costumes which the figures represented are wearing. The visitors, led by several men and women who had participated in the original carnival masquerade of twenty years before, are Donna Matilde (whom the protagonist had wooed), her daughter Frida (whom he has never seen), Belcredi (who had been his rival and is now the Marchesa's lover), the Marchesa's confidant, Di Nolli, and a psychoanalyst-doctor (who has been brought along to examine and perhaps cure the madman). The visitors are five in all, and with Bertoldo—the new retainer— they add up to six characters, who literally invade the stage that has been set for the twenty-year run of the protagonist's stellar performance. Unlike the Father and his pathetic family searching for an author in the play written only a few weeks before *Henry IV*, these six characters have no trouble, initially, fitting themselves into the continuing action al-

ready on stage. Frida, the Marchesa's daughter, is induced
at a certain moment to impersonate her mother, playing the
part of Matilde of Tuscany, as portrayed in one of the two
paintings flanking the throne; mad Henry's nephew Di Nolli
assumes the figure of the tragic emperor himself as represented, youthfully, in the other painting; the Marchesa
assumes the role of Adelaide, mother of Berta and mother-
in-law of the historic Henry; the Doctor plays the part of
Ugo of Cluny; Belcredi, the Marchesa's lover, puts on the
robe of a monk of Cluny, attending Ugo.

The idea, plainly, is to shock the protagonist out of his
madness. Time, in the process, becomes a kaleidoscopic,
ever-shifting reality. We feel it shift, first of all, in the tele-
scopic suggestion of the portraits painted twenty years earlier
and depicting a period eight hundred years before that. But it
shifts also in the dramatically doubled image of the
Marchesa, who sees her daughter in the portrait that is
actually the representation of her own youth, as also in the
error of the new retainer who boned up on the period of
1500 in France, when he ought to have boned up on Germany in 1000. Time intrudes again and again to disrupt the
period piece, the superimposition of generations is suggested
in various ways a number of times, the present becomes a
single moment eight hundred years before. There is no
mistaking the link, in this dramatic format, with the theater
plays. Landolfo, one of the retainers, in fact tells his colleagues: "We've got everything here; our wardrobe contains
whatever is needed to come up with a beautiful historical
production, the kind that's so popular in the theater today." His conclusion that the form is there waiting for its
content is perfectly correct; and the visitors who come on
the scene unannounced "come to provide the content." The
real drama begins in the recognition scene.

Masks, mirrors, and portraits, are the transparent symbols
of this play which is authentically "Pirandellian" in every
turn of phrase, from start to finish. The portraits are
described early in the first act as "reflections" in a mirror;
but the Marchesa, seeing her portrait, recalls the Pirandellian suggestion of the infinite reflections of a double mirror.

"That's not me," she says about the figure in the portrait, "it's you!" What she sees in that youthful representation is her daughter Frida; and the opinions expressed by the others mirror the confusion of the false identity. The mirror image echoes the masked images of the carnival party: "I'll never forget that scene, all of us wild and loud, our faces masked, in front of him—that terrible mask that was not a mask anymore, but Madness!" And those past masks are suddenly mirrored back in the present where Henry says reprovingly to the Marchesa:

> I tell you that, although you're perfectly serious, you too are masked, Madam; and I'm not referring to the great crown you're wearing—which I pay homage to— or to the royal cape you have on.

Henry is reproving the Marchesa for having dyed her hair, as if to embalm the ideal image of youth in her. But he too has dyed his hair. So, in censuring her, he is also censuring himself.

There are masks beneath masks; images superimposed on images. "I am here, today, masked as a penitent," Henry says. But the penitent is part of the historical mask. The case of the Marchesa is even more complex. She puts on her historical robe, dyes her hair to seem to be what she no longer is, asks for a mirror to see her masked self, sees her daughter Frida in the portrait of her youthful self, puts on the identical historical dress of Matilde of Tuscany as a "double" image to shock Henry, yet fails to recognize her true reflection in the eyes of her old suitor who urges her to take up her true role ("look into my eyes!" he insists). True communication begins when the isolated self has come to recognize itself in the reflections given back to it by others.

The opening scene of the second act, where the intruders discuss the possibility that Henry may have recognized Matilde as his former friend, proves the difficulty of communication where the evidence advanced is of the kind already seen in *It Is So* (*If You Think So*). Facts are inadequate; and the analysis of words is death, "The weight of the dead!" Henry's "madness" is a carefully constructed universe; and the so-called real people who assume the fiction are themselves the walking dead. They don't belong there. "You're chewing the life of the dead!" their host tells them.

In the second act, Henry drops his mask of madness to show them what they ought to have seen long before.

> Tell me, can you really stand by quietly, knowing someone is knocking himself out trying to convince others that you are really what he sees, that they should accept his judgment of you?—"Mad!" "mad"!—I don't mean now, I'm joking now! But before, back there, before I hit my head in that fall.

Like Laudisi, he destroys their complacency. "Can you look into your eyes?" Their confusion and embarrassment is obvious. "What do you see there?—Am I or am I not?—Go on, say it, I'm mad!" The best mirror is the eyes. Matilde has already experienced a terrifying moment, when her former suitor looked into her eyes and recognized her. The others have assured her it is impossible, but her instincts tell her she is right. The eyes are the windows of the soul; through them communication is established when nothing else succeeds. And when one sees the reflection of one's own terror in the eyes of another, the outer image, the public image, the other self, will suddenly appear as an embalmed puppet, fretting and strutting, moving and talking, like the famous fatally wounded warrior of a Renaissance mock epic who, not having felt the blow, went on fighting even though he was dead! "We've grown comfortable," says Henry, "in the fine estimates we have of ourselves." And our comfort undermines our sense of reality.

Henry's madness, like that of Hamlet, is the inner conscience reaching out into the world of the dead. It is the madness of illumination, and we identify with it *outside* the framework of the play as a revelation of intimate personal experience. But Pirandello's Henry, like Shakespeare's Hamlet, is a variety of contradictory postures; and all of them, taken together, are the true role. In this sense, with its complex multifaceted, vibrantly taut characterization, *Henry IV* is the epitome of *personality* as well as of the theater plays.

The visitors to the villa are the means whereby Henry comes to know himself fully. In them, he sees his own self-deception; and in their insistent probing, he is forced to reconsider the entire "production" he has staged. "There he goes, picking up his cues again!" Belcredi snaps late in the play. And Henry replies: "I suppose, for him it's a masquerade out of season, eh?" The irony is directed against Belcredi, but it also suggests a new insight for Henry himself. It *is* a masquerade out of season. But not his.

> I'm well, my friends: because I know perfectly well that I'm posing as a madman here; and I do it quietly!—The trouble is with all you people, who live your madness with so much fuss, not realizing it, not seeing it.

What is especially remarkable about this play is the fact that it contains perhaps more echoes of Pirandello's other works than any other single play of his—and yet the total impression is that of something wholly new and unexpected. Though elaborately staged, it is nevertheless a fast-moving, eccentric, absorbing production in which everything rises out of the dramatic frame of the story and is explicated in the framework of the action. Roles and costumes are put on and discarded; images come alive and step down from their picture-frames; the eyes become the perfect mirror; phenomenological questions abound; but all within the powerful illusion of the play which has been literally created for us by the protagonist.

The theme of madness is explored here in all its paradoxical implications: the visitors collapse before the devastating single-mindedness of their host; the retainers, on a lower level, are forced to come to terms with their own lightly assumed roles; Henry himself moves in and out of insanity with the expertise of a fencing master; the terms of the equation keep changing from one moment to the next. Madness serves an immediate allegorical purpose, the key to which lies in the cluster of mirror images. Like the child-blood-milk images in *Macbeth*, which suggest at once the theme of life cut short, potential crushed, goodness perverted, the mirror images in *Henry IV* are the genial expression of the mad search for identity through layers of "roles." And in the final resolution of those "roles," Pirandello's Henry inevitably invites comparison with Shakespeare's Hamlet.

Henry professes, like Hamlet, to be in love with the woman from whom he has been wrenched; but in Pirandello's play, that woman is many different women—the Marchesa as she was, the Marchesa as she is depicted in the painting, the Marchesa as she sees herself in her daughter Frida, the Frida-Berta image created by the new "masquerade," the Marchesa before she dyed her hair, the Marchesa grown old but recognized by her former suitor. Like Hamlet, Henry writes his own account of things and keeps a record— he literally rewrites history in his own image. Like Hamlet, he has assumed the mask of madness in order to be left to his own devices—although for the rest of the world, he appears mad all through; like Hamlet, he stabs his enemy, who hides behind the "role" assigned him; like Hamlet, he defines and redefines his decisions to make them appear right.

The reversals of personality in *Henry IV*, the gradual dissolution of character as it moves from certainty to uncertainty to new certainty, are the most complex and suggestive in the entire Pirandellian repertory. The outsiders in *It Is So (If You Think So)* remain unchanged and unshaken at the end of the play; the actors and director in *Six Characters* are only briefly drawn into the drama of the intruders; no one in *Each in His Own Way* undergoes a shattering catharsis that we can identify with; but the intruders and retainers of *Henry IV*, no less than Henry himself, are made to see themselves at close range, as false masks, puppets who think themselves free, actors playing an assigned part—many parts. The villa itself, like the strange mansion in Albee's *Tiny Alice*, seems to expand and contract as the past rushes in and the future closes down on the scene.

Henry's past contains the same suggestion of a "premature ripening" noted in connection with Liolà. He was "bruised" literally, when Belcredi made his horse rear in the Mardi

Gras masquerade; and at once the green, even sour, role he had chosen to play opposite Matilde of Canossa, ally of his archenemy Pope Gregory VII, ripened prematurely. Henry himself uses the word *ammaccato* ("bruised") in telling what happened to his head when it got "knocked" on the ground. The aging process was hurried, generation was superimposed on generation, and he leaped from youth to middle age, from a life yet to be lived to one long since solidly registered in the annals of history.

Henry IV does to us from the stage exactly what he says the insane do to us when we dare to look into their eyes. The madman, he says, destroys the very foundation of our logic with his madly penetrating gaze. At the end of the play, when Henry is provoked to violence by the taunts of his old rival Belcredi, we see an obvious reversal of roles. It all happens so quickly that one is apt to miss the dramatic essence of the moment. Belcredi, listening to the protagonist's reasonings, concludes cynically that if things were as the other represents them, Henry would be the sane one and they would be insane. Henry replies: "But if you weren't crazy, you and she together, would you have come to me?" "But I came, you know, thinking that the madman was you." "And what about her?" Belcredi hesitates to defend the Marchesa's sanity. He can't be sure about her, he says, because she seems charmed out of herself by what Henry has been saying. The Marchesa must take up her own defense.

But the final turn comes when Henry, still staring their logic down with his madman's frenzied eye, suddenly claims that Frida—dressed to look like the portrait of Matilde of Tuscany, who is the Marchesa in her youth—is his by right. He embraces her, shouting to his retainers to keep the others away. Belcredi shouts back: "Let go of her! You're not insane!" And Henry lashes back: "Not insane? How's this!" and digs his sword into Belcredi.

It is Belcredi who is led off, protesting "You are not insane! He's not insane!" And the madman remains standing there, the majestic embodiment of "imperial authority." The logic of his visitors has crumbled. His own has not.

The critic Ferdinando Pasini, in his widely read book *Luigi Pirandello (As I See Him)*, tells of the effect of the play on him, as often as he saw it, in words that reflect the experience of many of us. While admitting that the plot's logic appears to break down under close scrutiny, he nevertheless avows:

> I have seen the play two nights in a row, superbly acted by Ruggero Ruggeri, I've read it and re-read it many times, and I have always felt that, even while I noted the logical breaks, the mental effort I made to grasp and formulate my logical objections was unmistakably overwhelmed by the artistic emotion communicated to me.[1]

Everything in the imperial house of madness has a reason for being there, or for happening, but it is a reason mirrored back at us out of a shattered logic. The whole play, indeed, consists of compulsive attempts to piece together broken continuities of time, reason, love, relationships, historical fact, and present fiction. And what is it, finally, that has been pieced together? As in *Hamlet*, nothing, everything. Nothing, if we apply the usual rules—Henry, like Hamlet, has swept all pretense aside with the impulsive show of retributive justice at the end; everything, if we consider the psychological distance we have come. We all share, aesthetically, in his extraordinary madness. "No," we say. "You're not insane. He's not insane." And the tragic catharsis is complete.

In this paradox lies the greatness of the play. In the telescoping of time, distance, and roles; in the juxtaposition of the living dead and the mad who claim life for themselves; in the disintegration of experience into large human questions and intimate personal drama, each of us invades the stage and assumes a role which is the equivalent of a full cast.

# 7

## Art Transcending Itself
*Diana and Tuda; The New Colony; Lazarus; When Someone Is Somebody; The Mountain Giants*

*Diana and Tuda.* Sirio Dossi, a young sculptor is obsessed with the notion of making a huge statue of Diana. His model is the breathtakingly lovely Tuda, whom he finally marries, as a working arrangement, to keep her from posing for others. Nono Giuncano, an old friend who is also a sculptor, visits Sirio often in his studio and tries to discourage him in his mania. The old sculptor had, in fact, destroyed his entire collection of statues because, he explains, compared to the vitality of a Tuda, sculpture is death. But Sirio cannot be swayed from his purpose and drives Tuda to distraction. She breaks their agreement, in her loneliness, and resumes posing for a painter who had sometime before started a canvas representing Tuda as Diana. Sirio, enraged, wounds the man and slashes his painting. Tuda then disappears, but Sirio searches and finds her. He gets her to come back temporarily. There is a violent confrontation in the studio. Tuda seems about to smash the statue of Diana. Sirio rushes to stop her, threatening to kill her, if need be. The old sculptor struggles with him, and in the scuffle, Sirio falls, hits his head, and dies. Tuda then realizes that in Sirio's death, she also has died. The statue has destroyed them all (1926).

*The New Colony.* A group of ex-convicts, smugglers, and thieves decide to leave their miserable surroundings, near the docks, and at the suggestion of La Spera (a prostitute) find haven and a new life on an island, formerly used as a penal colony. Their desire to escape the past and set up their own utopian community is too tempting to dissuade the poor wretches from going to the island which, rumor has it, is fast sinking into the sea. La Spera with her child, Currao (the child's father), and the others manage at first very well, but a certain Crocco is jealous of Currao, the leader of the group, who lives with La Spera as her husband. Crocco instigates the others against La Spera and, after a quarrel with Currao, leaves the island. But he soon returns with Padron Nocio—whose young son Dorò had accompanied the group to protect La Spera. Crocco has convinced Nocio that the island is a fertile paradise and that it should be exploited. He has also convinced women to accompany them, to start a new profitable center on the island. With the newcomers, however, all the old habits and vices return. Currao's leadership is contested, and Nocio is put in command by Crocco and his gang, who plan to kill Dorò and put the blame on Currao. Crocco gets La Spera to denounce Currao, who is planning to marry Nocio's daughter Mita and take La Spera's child from her. In the confrontation, Crocco's duplicity is discovered. At this point, however, the island starts to sink. In the end, La Spera and her child, having fled to a makeshift hut at the top of the mountain, are the sole survivors (1928).

*Lazarus.* In a frenzy of pious self-righteousness, Diego Spina has decided to turn over his huge estate to the poor of his district. Those in his household object to what they consider to be an inconsiderate gesture which will deprive many people of a livelihood and his two children of their inheritance. The matter is aggravated by the fact that Lia, the girl, is a cripple and Lucio, the son, is still studying in the seminary, to become a priest. His wife Sara, who had left him when Diego had taken it upon himself to separate the children from their mother and send them away to school, has been living on a distant part of the estate with Arcadipane, Diego's overseer. They have two children who, unlike Lia and Lucio, are healthy and happy. Sara is not concerned about Diego's move to give up his estate. She and her family can always find a good living elsewhere. When she suddenly appears at her husband's house, it is to tell him that Lucio has left the seminary and gone to her. Diego rushes out to talk to his son and on the way is run over and killed. He is brought back to life with an injection of Adrenalin, but no one dares tell him that because he is suspicious of medical miracles. He learns the truth, however, when he finally confronts his son. The knowledge shatters him, for it proves in his eyes that there is no God and life after death: he remembers nothing of the interim between the moment of his dying and his return to life. In this new frame of mind, his pent-up jealousy gets the better of him and he tries to kill his rival Arcadipane. Lucio, seeing his father's despair, decides to return to the seminary so as to lead Diego back to a new faith in God as something more than a cold, pious abstraction. Sara had been right. The play ends with Lia returned to her mother. In the new-found strength inspired by Sara's belief in God as the source of natural religious faith, Lia rises from her wheelchair and walks again (1929).

*When Someone Is Somebody.*   The celebrated writer ★★★ has gone to rest at the house of his American nephew, who has come from the United States to publish the poems of a new young poet, Délago. With them is Natascia, Pietro's wife, and her sister Veroccia, with whom ★★★ is infatuated. In their youthful company, ★★★ is rejuvenated. But the world soon forces its way back into his life: his wife Giovanna and his two children, together with his publisher and Giaffredi, an influential friend, come to take him away. ★★★ realizes he must return with them; it is no longer possible for him to start again. He takes leave of his young friends and his nephew Pietro and returns to the deathlike legend he has helped to create around him. The new poet, Délago, we learn, had been his own creation, a new style of poetry, which could have given *** a whole new inspiration. But his family, learning the truth, will not permit publication of the poems, arguing that their appearance could undermine the established fame of ***. Back among his family and admirers, *** agrees to a public announcement admitting the authorship of the poems as a huge joke. Public honors are conferred upon him, in the midst of which his nephew and the two young women arrive in a desperate attempt to force him to reconsider. But *** is no longer accessible; he is deaf to all their pleas. The curtain comes down on *** seated in a thronelike chair, immobile, a kind of statue of himself, his own public image rendered lifeless (1933).

*The Mountain Giants.* The Countess Ilse, together with her husband and several others of her theatrical company, comes to "Villa Cotrone," a fantastic place where dwarfs, old women, apparitions, and a strange assortment of types have found a haven. Cotrone, master of the villa, is a kind of Prospero who indulges the poetic fantasy of all who attend him in his isolated home. He urges the newcomers to stay, and they seem at first content to do so. But they soon weary of the "magic" of the place, particularly the apparitions that inhabit it and come alive at the bidding of the imagination. Ilse is determined to perform her play—the one play of their repertory, written by a young admirer of hers who committed suicide for her. She wants to move audiences to take the work to heart. Cotrone finally agrees to arrange for her to perform for the Giants of the Mountain close-by, and he promises to go himself to persuade the Giants to allow Ilse's company to put on the play. (The actual text ends here, since Pirandello died in the middle of this work. What follows is Pirandello's own summary of the final act as reconstructed by his son Stefano Pirandello.) Ilse's players go to the mountain, but the rough people there are unreceptive to her play. They prefer rowdy comedy and marionette theater entertainment to high art. Cotrone had warned Ilse, but she was determined to present the play. The crowd jeers at her. Ilse grows angry and insults them. In the orgiastic abandonment which is let loose, Ilse is killed and others are literally torn to pieces. The survivors return to the villa, where Cotrone explains that although Ilse has died, the poetry she embodied still lives. It will be recognized in time. The Giants, who never appear, send emissaries with apologies for what has happened (1936).

The dilemma of freedom, out of which Greek tragedy originated and in which it perfected itself as an awe-inspiring social catharsis, absorbed the last eight years of Pirandello's artistic life. The dilemma was by no means a philosophical abstraction for him. The plays in which he explores its depths to the final tragic catharsis acquire in the end, as he himself acknowledges, a "mythical" aura that tends to carry them beyond the traditional limits of art. In them, art offers to serve higher values than itself, yet with full awareness that, in so doing, it attains its own perfection.

The culminating achievement of those years is a series of three plays grouped together by Pirandello as "myths." They were for him quite clearly a new art form: embodiments of what might be called a Platonic vision of the ideal form of creative life or, preferably, an Hegelian drama of the absolute moments of spirit. The earliest of the three, *The New Colony*, depicts a society based on love and mutual cooperation, precariously fashioned, in virtual despair, by the criminal dregs of our actual society. The second, *Lazarus*, erects a new faith based on a kind of Augustinian or Pascalian pessimism about man's knowledge of God and the afterlife. Finally, in *The Mountain Giants*, left incomplete by his death, Pirandello gives us a phoenixlike vision of the death of art. In all three, pessimism about the existential human condition looms large: truth and nontruth are confounded, as are beauty and ugliness, religion and irreligion, good and evil, freedom and necessity. But in this confounding of opposites, beyond being, beyond thought—as Plato explains at the very heart of the mystery of the Socratic dialectic—is the transcendental oneness of all that is and is not: *to agathón*, source of all being, all beauty, all goodness, all truth, and the opposites that define them, without which they could not be. It is the culminating expression of Pirandello's "sentimento del contrario" (his feeling that he ought always to support the contrary) and his most accurate reflection of the revolutionary state of mind that gripped the European-American scientific community in the opening decades of the twentieth century.

Physical science itself, in the genius of an Einstein or a Max Planck, could already show us, beneath the hard surfaces of our everyday world, a reality of such energetic stuff as dreams are made on. In Pirandello's genius too, with matter's destruction, form and idea are rehabilitated. The result is a dramatic rehabilitation of law, religion, and art. His myths are thus an affirmation of the divine nature of the human will in its tragic, often self-destructive struggle for universal freedom.

*Liolà* represents that struggle in its most naïve and beautiful expression. With Liolà, "the poet," we are on the threshold of insight. Conventions and morality are destroyed as *matter* and restored as *form*; the dichotomy of right and wrong is resolved in the conviction of the will which recognizes the shortcomings of the one and accepts the truth of the other. In *Liolà*, "right" is the irresistible force which determines the outcome; but it is the "right" of the protagonist's natural, instinctive conviction about things. He accepts without reservation the Socratic voice which dictates to him what must be done. In later plays, of which *Six Characters* and *Henry IV* are typical, Pirandello struggles with the dichotomy of inner and outer "imperatives," the discovery of self and the rejection of the "image" others have of us. In a variety of situations—all of which are triggered by crises verging on paranoia, sexual aberrations, morbid desires, death, and psychological obsessions of one kind or another—he explores the difficult moment of self-consciousness when the soul comes to know itself and rejects the conventional notions about itself. In the "myths" this psychological probing is extended into a kind of allegorical statement about the larger content of the search for freedom through insight into necessity. In each, the individual resurrection into light is shown as part of a social context which itself is shaken to its roots. In them, for the first time, the tragic outcome of "discovery" is redeemed by a kind of universal hope. The very "particulars" of a situation are transformed before our eyes into allegorical utopian terms: a kind of Kafkian mountain with a Matilda-like figure on its Dantesque peak (*The New Colony*); a fertile countryside which like the Franciscan settings of Giotto's paintings is stamped with the breath of a divine influx (*Lazarus*); an old villa which is transformed as if by magic into an open vista without end, and a rugged mountain where the Olympian gods hide (*The Mountain Giants*). Like the figures of Dante's *Divine Comedy*, the Pirandellian characters in these three extraordinary plays retain all their particulars, all their quirks and individual traits, while taking on the transparency of universal meaning. All great works of art do this, of course; and Pirandello does it in all his plays. In the "myths," however, one is aware of the deliberate purpose and sees the slow transformation as part of an acknowledged artistic plan, a new vision.

These three myths come to us with an entourage of supporting plays, narratives, and literary essays that greatly illuminate their significance as works of art. The most important of these supportive works for our purpose here are the plays *Diana and Tuda* and *When Someone Is Somebody*, and the critical essay "Introduction to the Italian Theater," published in 1936, the year of Pirandello's death, as the preface to Silvio D'Amico's *Storia del teatro italiano* (*History of the Italian Theater*). Because they bear most directly on the theme of *The Mountain Giants*—the tragedy of art's self-consummation, or liberation from self, for life's sake— consideration of them will be integrated with our discussion of that play.

*The New Colony* reveals the new Pirandellian vision in a variety of ways. The outcasts who are to form the new society are shown in their wretched state, hounded by the law, at first, doomed to their life of crime without hope of reprieve. Almost all of them have served time on a penal colony situated on an island off the mainland—an island which threatens to sink into the sea. It is there that the prostitute La Spera suggests they all go, not as criminals but of their own accord. They get permission from the authorities (the island is now abandoned because of the danger of further volcanic eruptions) and move there together, to set up their ideal community. La Spera's new-found hope is contagious; and at first everything seems possible. La Spera suddenly gets a flow of milk, after five months, and can breast-feed her baby by Currao, the leader of the group. Initially, at least, the island seems to all a virtual paradise. "Il paradiso degli uomini cattivi" ("the paradise of evil men") takes on new meaning. La Spera with her selfless example provides the inspiration for the group. Currao is drawn into the new life immediately and recognizes the need for a new kind of social structure. "Now that the other law is gone, you've got to make your own." Tobba, the "prophet" of the group, old in years and experience, predicts that the island will not go down so long as they remain true to their purpose and do not sin against one another.

The notion of a social contract—for what we might call a "participatory democracy"—is explored in all its dramatic implications. The ultimate question, of course, is this: Is it possible for human beings to live under enforceable laws, without being tyrannized by those who are charged with administering those laws? Can there be ordered freedom, or must one escape legal order completely to be free? It is the problem most aptly defined for the modern world by Rousseau in his *Social Contract*. It has agitated the hearts of American intellectuals at least since the days when Emerson's friends put it on trial at Fruitlands. Yet it was already old for the ancient Epicureans and Plato, and older still when revived by Marsilius of Padua, Hobbes, Locke, and Hume—to name only a few. Pirandello does not take on the burden of a philosophical answer; he is first and foremost a dramatist. The attraction of this idea was for him the ultimate expression of his dramatic commitment to probe the mystery of freedom. And yet, the conclusions he suggests are consistent and convincing, even on philosophical grounds.

So long as La Spera—a kind of Mary Magdalen figure who will appear in just that guise, as a secondary character in

*The Mountain Giants*—continues to provide the inspired conviction which first moved the group to take on the new life, everything goes well. There is a hitch, however. One of their number, jealous of Currao (who is not only the "leader" but also enjoys La Spera in a monogamous relationship) begins to brood. Crocco, as he is called, tries to force his attentions on La Spera, but the woman protests and explains that they must not think of her according to the old dispensation any longer. But the man is already corrupted by his own undisciplined appetites. He deserts his friends, but soon returns with a large group of "new" colonists, including the rich Padron Nocio, whose young son has gone with the outcasts secretly to "protect" La Spera. Currao recognizes the danger and predicts the outcome:

> He'll spoil everything! He'll make good things come easy. There. Do you hear? They're already restless, singing, playing, dancing over there. . . . You've brought idleness, self-indulgence; and envy will come out of it, and jealousy; ambition and intrigue will take over. You've brought back all the vices of the city, and women, and money. The city, the city we ran away from, like from the plague.

The description recalls St. Augustine and Camus. The plague of the city has entered the new community; the island itself must suffer. In Augustinian terms, the City of Man—with its built-in disposition to seek its own, its greed and lusts and self-interest and self-righteousness—has invaded the community of rehabilitated free men and condemns them to resume their old habits. La Spera sees it happening and tries her best to reverse the forces at work; Currao sees it too, but he ultimately falls prey to it himself and singles out Mita, Nocio's daughter, as his new bride. For a brief moment in the play, Currao shares the tragic insight of La Spera. In coming to this place, he tells the new arrivals, you have placed yourselves outside your own law and have destroyed ours. Nocio has come to establish a commercial enterprise on the lovely island, convinced by Crocco that all is well and that they can make a fortune there. Crocco has also managed to convince the others that there is much gain in the venture—and the license to do anything they please. But the truth is that La Spera is holding things together, that her faith and loving supervision of all things keeps the outcasts together in harmony. With Crocco's self-deception in asserting that the well-being of the inhabitants is not a matter of faith and selfless cooperation, the whole illusion disintegrates.

Crocco brings the outside world back into the picture, and for the outcasts this is the beginning of the end. La Spera is denigrated and insulted. The others, following Crocco's example, turn against her in the same way. Currao himself abandons her for Mita and the promise of wealth and power. At a certain moment in the third act, someone says about the "feast" that is being prepared for the crowd: "It will be a lovely masquerade out of season!" The phrase (echoing Henry's ironic retort to Belcredi in *Henry IV*—"For him, it's now only a masquerade out of season, eh?") reminds us, by suggestion, that the inner world of will and faith can only be sustained by taking it seriously.

The Pirandellian theme of the world as will and faith is here interwoven with the notion of the limits of individual freedom. The community of outcasts has created its new world by a Promethean effort and an almost superhuman sacrifice. But that new community has its own laws, and to prosper it must insist on them. Freedom, Pirandello seems to be saying, is not license; and the fact that the restrictions which oppressed the group while they lived on the mainland have been lifted does not mean that the new colony can continue without any laws or regulations. Restrictive laws must be replaced by constructive laws; the "don'ts" must be replaced with a spontaneous "do," the law of love which obeys instinctively its own commands. La Spera leads the way; but when Crocco refuses to join the community of love, he destroys, in effect, everything and everyone.

Only La Spera is saved at the end. The island, which had sustained itself above the sea all through the early part of the experiment, is suddenly torn apart by volcanic explosions and the sea rises to engulf it. All are lost, except La Spera who—in seeking refuge from Currao's wrath—had run to her dismal hut at the very top. From that vantage point, she watches the island swallowed up by the sea. Only the ridge on which she stands, clutching her infant boy, remains above sea level. She will survive alone, in her deserted Eden, with her boy.

*Lazarus*, written the year after *The New Colony*, traces a different meridian to the same pole. In it the dialectic of faith, the opposition between accepted conventions and inspired truth, is explored in a daring dramatic content in which a man dies and is resurrected. We are reminded of O'Neill's *Lazarus Laughed*—although the latter play was written earlier (1922) and lacks the spontaneity of dialogue and the difficult probing of Pirandello's theme. O'Neill assumes, through an abstract kind of allegory in historical terms, the catechismal notions of death and the afterlife. Pirandello is much more original in his appraisal of the doubts that beset inquiry into first causes; he is not satisfied with commonplaces. The "miracles" in O'Neill's play are the abstract rhetoric of the traditional accounts; in Pirandello, the miracle is translated into terms which are more than logical and yet admissible as events in which the human will has played a part.

The religious affirmation of *Lazarus* is similar to the new faith in loving community described in *The New Colony*. The trilogy of myths is grounded in the miracle of belief—which, as St. Augustine pointed out almost fifteen hundred years ago, is the greatest of all miracles. In *Lazarus* this theme is traced in its religious context, shown as the new life in a new concept of God. Diego is the religious formalist, bordering on the fanatic—the man who, trapped in his own sense of sacrifice and suffering, insists on making it true for others as well. His son Lucio is forced into the seminary at an early age, although everything in him rejects the notion of retreat from the world. His younger child, Lia, is sent to a boarding school run by nuns, where she contracts an illness which paralyzes her legs. All three represent, together with the priest who nurtures these false illusions, the rigorous straitjacket of formal piety which survives only by keeping the world at a distance. There is here a reminder of Boccaccio's tirade against the "plague" which destroys the world outside, in the *Decameron*—the plague of restraint, of formalism, of rhetorical absolutes, and more especially, of the Church of his day, which combined in its teachings all these things, according to Boccaccio. Pirandello, however, is not bitter or skeptical. In *Lazarus*, a Franciscan peace covers the world, an acceptance of God in all His manifestations, an indelible conviction that God does exist and that faith is possible; there is no undermining of the Church in the way that there is in Boccaccio. Pirandello's play traces the conversion from darkness to light—but it is a true religious conversion.

One of the most impressive features of the play is the manner in which Lucio, Diego's son, describes his sensitive appreciation of the sensory world. Even as a young seminarian, religion was for him the mystery of the senses—the sounds, smells, and sights of the religious services and the impressive darkness of the church.

> My faith, when I was still very young, in the seminary, was . . . was smell, taste . . . the smell of incense, of wax . . . the taste of the host . . . and a kind of awe at the sound of steps echoing in the empty church. . . .

Lucio's recognition of the true motives that led him back, suddenly, to his mother's house after many years is the beginning of his conversion to a new faith. But he must explain that new faith to others.

His mother instinctively understands. Lucio at once recognizes in her the law of love, the discipline of nature, God mirrored in the instinctive goodness of her life and happiness. For the first time, the woman can talk openly to her son, as an equal. Lucio grasps her tragic frustration at having had her daughter taken from her, against her will, and brought back a cripple in a wheelchair. Diego's formalism and rigor, cloaked in a religious posture, was too much for her. She has watched at a distance as her children wasted away, forced to live in isolation. By contrast, her children by her lover Arcadipane are healthy and happy. The new family is the symbol of love and insight into nature. Lucio's conversion thus is related—in time—to that of his mother. In grasping the reasons behind her actions he is asserting his own new understanding of divine providence. His conversion becomes now the catalyst for Diego's own agonized search for truth.

Diego is brought face to face with his true self when he rushes to Sara's house to talk to his son, after having recovered from the "accident" which—everyone else admits—was the occasion for a miracle. He is not told that he had been declared dead. Earlier in the play, Lia's pet rabbit had died, and the doctor had brought it back to life with an injection of Adrenalin. Diego had refused, at the time, to believe that the rabbit had really stopped breathing. A miracle comes from God, not medicine. When he himself is brought back from the dead in the same way, the doctor warns his family and friends not to tell him, because in his weakened condition, he might go into shock and die. At Sara's house, he learns the truth. His old faith is shattered. If he was dead, why can't he remember something of the afterlife, why hadn't he seen God? It simply proves, he concludes, that there is no God, no afterlife, nothing. In his new skepticism, he lashes out against those around him, particularly at Arcadipane, whom he now admits to be his rival. His previous indifference was only a posture like everything else. He still loves Sara, but he knows that it is too late to win her back.

Sensing his father's terrible despair, Lucio decides to return to the seminary for Diego's sake. Not for appearances, not to calm him in the knowledge that his son is doing what is expected of him—but because he understands that he alone now can help Diego find a new content for his faith. A pattern emerges from all that has happened. Nothing is accidental; nothing happens in vain. Providence is redeemed in the knowledge that Lucio's conversion has brought on the painful but ultimately rewarding reevaluation of things: Sara has been exonerated; Diego has been cut loose from his unsteady moorings and is on the way to a new and deeper sense of life; Lia is restored to her mother, who is able to transmit to her the will and faith that will make her whole again. In Lucio's "sacrifice" there is nothing that suggests self-denial. He is doing precisely what his love dictates. He is happy in the decision. As he explains to his father, God wanted you to wake from the dead without a memory of that experience. It is His way of granting you a new grace, a new chance to discover what it's all about. Nothing has been lost.

The moving personal drama is laced with philosophical comments which rise out of the circumstances and give the play its sinews. What is immortality? The only possible way we can formulate thoughts about it is by recognizing signs of it in this life. It's not something "else"; it is the present moment, in which the past and future merge. Every flash of insight is a flash of immortality. God surely is something else, on that other side; but here and now, he is the joy and love and faith that we experience in the life He gave us. It is not reward and punishment in abstract terms. God does not contradict life; and if *we* do—as Diego does through most of the play—that in itself is punishment enough already.

> To believe in this kind of Immortality, not strictly ours, not for ourselves, not the hope of reward or fear of punishment; to believe in this eternal present moment of life, which is God—that's quite enough.

The psychology of conversion is spelled out in human terms that are rooted in logic. Diego's own argument is used against him by Lucio: if you truly believe that you were not dead when we found you (as you insisted you could not have been), then your doubt about the afterlife is meaningless. You were never there. You have nothing to report back. And if you believe you were dead after all—might not God have wanted you to come back precisely as you did? Isn't it conceivable that he was testing you for some reason, or granting you a special experience to put you back on the right track? But ultimately, Lucio points out, the difficulty is in your insisting on a "here" and "there."

> If our soul is God in us, then what can science and the miracles of science possibly mean, except that they occur

by His leave? And what can you possibly know about
death, if there is no death in God, and God is now inside
you again, as in all of us, here and now, eternal, in this
moment of ours which becomes eternal only in Him?

And, in more personal terms, the argument goes like this:

Don't you see? You had closed your eyes to life, thinking
that by doing so you would see that other one, beyond.
This was your punishment. God blinded you to that one,
and now opens your eyes again to this one, which is His,
for you to live it and let others live it, working and suffering and finding joy like all the rest of us.

In Pirandello's vocabulary, the "miracles" of the play are
underscored by warnings against accepting them in their
formal definitions. The resurrection of the rabbit, the new
dimension granted Lucio, Sara's insight into life—repeated
and explicated in key moments of the action—the resurrection of Diego and the coming to terms at the end of the play,
all suggest a sort of turning inside out of old religious mysteries that serves to renew their essential meaning. In the
natural setting which Pirandello creates, these moments of
conversion are intensely personal, yet fully consistent with
formal definitions. For each protagonist, the experience is
drawn against the range of his own convictions. The shattered mirror of faith reflects many such experiences.

When it was first performed, *Lazarus* precipitated heated
controversy in Italian religious (and antireligious) circles.
Although it was clearly antidogmatic in its treatment of religious and particularly of Catholic themes, some leading
Catholic spokesmen defended its manifest sincerity in dealing with the fundamental doubts and fears that are the inevitable concomitants of any religion of hope—for hope is
inseparably linked to and saturated with doubt. What happens, dramatically, in *Lazarus*, is an almost Lutheran mystery
—or, rather, Augustinian or Pauline—which is the assertion
that if there is no God, nothing is true and man is a beast
among beasts. When Diego loses his faith in God and His
eternal laws, he becomes a violent beast, ready to kill. And

before the spectacle of the abject fall from grace to primal instinctive life, in the chaos of the soul, the Christ-like figure of Lucio takes on the burden of faith and reconstituted nature. Compared with God and His laws, man is nothing—but sooner or later, that absolute moment of darkness must give way, either to demonic self-sufficiency or sublime dependence on faith. The Leopardian sinking into oblivion is rare. For Pirandello it is only the beginning of self-conscious life. If we know only ourselves, we rise almost instinctively to a dizzying existential sense of certainty and glory; Sartre and Camus sustain that moment of nothingness, but Pirandello resists with all his spiritual might the instinctive urge to glorify oneself in the recognition of one's nothingness.

Knowing oneself obviously is not enough—an empty mirror facing an empty mirror. Knowledge of one's own limitations is the existential abyss; beyond that is knowledge of the divinity in us, which is not *us*. In the fearful, faithful, hopeful, but always doubt-ridden recognition of God in self, the empty mirror becomes an infinite full reflection. Pirandello's plays—and the myths are the most powerful elucidation of this—are a warning against the existential certainty that the sense of nothingness elevates man to a kind of divine being. The Lutheran transfiguration that turns despair into presumption is abandoned in Pirandello for the Augustinian paradox. Humility—the nothingness of man confronted by the divine—exists side by side with the exalted experience of spiritual strength. The Pirandellian posture is the ambiguous posture of Hamlet.

The difference lies, ultimately, in Pirandello's insistence that natural grace is not enough. Nature is good in itself; but man's nature has been corrupted. Grace doesn't deny, doesn't destroy nature; on the contrary, it perfects it. *Grazia non tollit natura, sed perficit.* Diego has risen from the first death, the death of the body, but is in grave danger of sinking into the second death, that of the soul, which comes upon us when we accept our nothingness as puppets and deny the divinity which is already present in the knowledge we have of our limitations. In *Lazarus*, God is restored in these terms. Lucio overcomes the emptying out of faith, and his momentary posture as a freethinker is destroyed before the certainty of the divine task set for him. Diego, on the edge of absolute despair after his dogmatic certainty has been shattered, is saved by contact with the state of natural grace embodied by Sara, infused with the love of God.

The impossible utopian myth of *The New Colony* and the hard religious myth of *Lazarus* are extended in *The Mountain Giants*, where Pirandello confronts the difficult articulation of a third inspired "myth": that of art.

Shortly before his death, Pirandello explained to his son that he had resumed work on the last of his mythtrilogy plays, after a long interruption, and that everything had finally fallen into place. He had had, he said, a sort of vision of a Saracen olive tree during a restless night, and with that insight he felt he could soon put on paper the final act resolving dramatically the whole question of the meaning of dramatic art, a matter to which he had literally dedicated his life after having heard the "third voice of poetry." In the Pirandellian chronology, *The Mountain Giants* becomes, therefore, significant as the dramatist's last statement about art in general, and particularly about the art of drama.

Before taking up the significance of *The Mountain Giants*, however, it will be worth our while to prepare for it by reviewing his earlier dramatizations of the artistic experience in *Diana and Tuda* and *When Someone Is Somebody*.

*Diana and Tuda* is Pirandello's Pygmalion. Diana is the ideal statue, Tuda the model whose vitality a young sculptor, Sirio Dossi, wants to "seize," to externalize, in clay and eventually in stone. Tuda loves to pose for painters and sculptors. She is gay and bohemian. Mindlessly, the young sculptor—who is also independently wealthy—attracts to himself her almost selfless love. He, on the contrary, treasures the beauty of her body with an artistic jealousy that finally prompts him to marry her, to keep her from posing for others.

But art should be generous. The true sculptor, painter, composer, poet, is supposed to share his joy, spread it—to borrow Wordsworth's phrase—in widest commonality. Here, on the contrary, Sirio is using Tuda destructively. To give artistic life to a stone Diana, he literally abuses the life out of his living model.

Yet the play is by no means an allegorical abstraction. It is dedicated to the young actress Marta Abba, for whom it was written. The first act, which ends with Sirio's marriage-for-art's-sake proposal (Tuda's wedded life is to be literally a model marriage) is worthy in spirit of the finest pages of Henry Murger's *Scénes de la vie de Bohême*. We learn that Sirio's friend, the old sculptor Giuncano, gray and past seventy, has in a fit of temper and rage destroyed all his own statues because of the deathlike calm of their classical beauty. His life, he says, is sinking out of him; he has wasted its precious years making statues only to be left with a wretched old body, soon to become a lifeless corpse. He prefers Tuda's youthful beauty to all the statues that ever were or can be made, though he knows that her beauty will fade, and she too will become a wretched rotting thing, like the old models who do servants' work in the artists' quarters. Sirio torments his model-wife by letting another woman come and go as she pleases in their house, until Tuda in desperation decides to leave, with old Giuncano, if he will have her, or with another artist, or simply to be gone from her torment. Sirio, desperate because he cannot finish his statue without her, tracks her down and forces her to come back for a final confrontation. In the shaping of his Diana, he had wrought a constant transformation, keeping up with Tuda's feelings, and he appears to have tormented her deliberately so as to work such a transformation to perfection in his statue.

In the end, it appears that Sirio has indeed worked Pygmalion's magic. He has poured Tuda's life into the statue, draining it out of her body which is now prematurely wasted. In the last scene of the play, Tuda rushes angrily at the statue, crying that she wants to pour the rest of her burning life into it. "Don't touch it!" cries Sirio, seizing her, "or I'll kill you!." Old Giuncano leaps after him with a threat of his own. He clutches the young man by the throat; both fall off the scaffold supporting the statue, and Sirio is killed by the fall. Giuncano, who loved him like a son and had grown to hate him because of Tuda, sees now that he has been blinded spiritually by the approach of death in his aging body. Sirio has paid with his life to make his statue live. And Tuda, wasted, blames herself: "Yes, me, me . . . because I didn't know how to be what he wanted of me . . . To be her! Her! . . . And now, look at me. . . . Nothing, I'm nothing."

There is no moral here of the usual kind. What we have is the dilemma of the life-death of art. On one side, it is Keats's "Grecian Urn" with its young lover fixed by art in the moment of budding love, to whom the poet says,

> never, never canst thou kiss,
> Though winning near the goal—yet, do not grieve;
>   She cannot fade, though thou hast not thy bliss,
>   For ever wilt thou love, and she be fair! [1]

—and and on the other, it is Yeats's "Sailing to Byzantium," with its aged man who is

> but a paltry thing,
> A tattered coat upon a stick, unless
> Soul clap its hands and sing, and louder sing
> For every tatter in its mortal dress. . . .
> Once out of nature I shall never take
> My bodily form from any natural thing,
> But such a form as Grecian goldsmiths make
> Of hammered gold. [2]

Tuda is a taste of art's purgatory, written with a tragic impetus for a young actress. The warmth of life cannot be poured into the clay or bronze of statues which must always offer us blank eyes. But it can be poured into the dramatis personae of theatrical art—who are virtually statues of flesh and blood, less subject to time's destructive power than those of stone. But what of the literary artist, the dramatist who fashions dramatic characters for the stage? What hold has he on his "living words"? It is one thing if he becomes thoroughly confounded with his works—like Homer, or Shakespeare, or, in some measure, Dante too. Homer, Shakespeare, Dante, are what they wrote, nothing more, nothing less. But most literary artists don't have that good fortune. Most have concrete, very definite "biographical" existences apart from their works, existences of fixed shape, unalterably defined in the public mind. That is the theme of Pirandello's *When Someone Is Somebody*, performed and published in 1933.

The play is a "comic" counterpart of *Diana and Tuda*, evidently written by Pirandello to purge his own vanity as a celebrated writer by reversing the Pygmalion myth. It is not a statue that is to be made to breathe with life, but a living man to be hardened into a statue by the deadly power of his living fame.

The protagonist, an old and famous Italian writer, namelessly identified as \*\*\*, feels suddenly rejuvenated by the visit of an American nephew, Pietro, who is accompanied by his Russian-American wife Natascia and her sister Veroccia. These three, but especially Veroccia, induce him to strip away the reality of his years and start a new career as a fresh young poet, concealed behind a bookseller's publicity photo of himself as he actually looked in youth—an appearance which all who have honored him in his maturity have long since forgotten. Veroccia, enthralled by the prank, charms the old man with the sort of appeal that America makes to the old world in Emily Dickinson's verses

> *I'm nobody! Who are you?*
> *Are you nobody, too?*
> *Then there's a pair of us—don't tell!*
> *They'd banish us, you know.*
>
> *How dreary to be somebody!*
> *How public, like a frog*
> *To tell your name the livelong day*
> *To an admiring bog!* [3]

Old \*\*\* comes to hope, indeed, that the young nobody he pretends to be will succeed, in time, in eclipsing the fame of the old Somebody he has been. A book of his love lyrics

under the pseudonym Délago is to be published and widely
publicized as rivaling in excellence the works of \*\*\*. The
picture of "Délago" begins to appear everywhere, beside that
of his old rival. His ruse is unmasked, however, when \*\*\*'s
relatives and friends rise to defend his fame; \*\*\* is forced
to give up his feigned youth as "nobody," and reconciles
himself sadly to the inescapable living death of being Somebody. His American nephew and nieces who had urged him,
impishly, to run off with them to America, lose patience—
especially Veroccia—and he is left, in the last scene mentioned, on the stage, alone in his study. There, he addresses
himself tenderly to the absent Veroccia, explaining her error
in taking the reflection of her vitality in him as a genuine
rebirth of youth; and as he speaks he assumes the appearance
of a statue, at his desk: "Really, when you're Somebody, you
have to take care that, at the right moment your death be
officially decreed, and that you be locked in—like this—to
stand guard on yourself."

When Someone Is Somebody was performed in 1933. The
following year, it was indeed as Somebody that Pirandello
was awarded the Nobel Prize, in competition with Paul
Valéry and G. K. Chesterton. Asked by photographers in
Stockholm to pose for them at a desk and typewriter, he
inserted a piece of paper in the machine and typed on it the
word "pagliacciata"—a "comic" scene fit for puppets of straw
—over and over again until the "pagliacciata" was over. It
was his way of standing guard over himself as Somebody in
self-decreed death.

Marta Abba, for whom Pirandello wrote Diana and Tuda
(his description of the model in the stage directions is a
description of the actress), tells us in the introduction to her
own English translation of The Mountain Giants that Pirandello was in the midst of writing the first two acts of that
great myth when the idea for When Someone Is Somebody
came to him late in 1929, after he had already separated
from it a subplot, which later became one of his most popular plays, As You Desire Me. Four years were to pass before
Pirandello returned, with renewed fervor, to his final dramatic statement on the meaning of art in its highest form.

It is only fair to point out here that critical opinion about this last, incomplete play has polarized to extremes—not unlike the critical polarization to which Shakespeare's last play, *Henry VIII*, has given rise. Whatever the final judgment on its artistic merit, it must stand, at any rate, as Pirandello's maturest statement about the value of art.

The play tackles head on all the paradoxes of the earlier theater plays, the full drama of *maschere nude* let loose in a frenzy of creation. Cotrone, the central figure of the play, is Pirandello's Prospero—the poet-magician whose creative imagination holds all things together. In the villa where he lives with his people (it is known as *La Scalogna* and its inhabitants as the *scalognati*), dream fantasies come to life, poetry and drama unfold spontaneously, each inhabitant can take on different and varied roles. Dwarfs, old and young people, an array of life-size marionettes inhabit the villa. Into this sanctuary of self-absorbed imaginative life comes the Countess Ilse, leading the weary remnants of her theatrical company and accompanied by her faithful and loyal husband, who has wasted his fortune to please her in her dramatic pursuits. The action of the play, in true Pirandellian fashion, begins with the intrusion of this handful of actors into Cotrone's world. Ilse and her people are thus the spokesmen of the repudiated ideal, artists scorned and reduced to poverty, but who still hold fiercely to their inspired vision of art. Cotrone and his people are the ideal embodied in all its fantastic shapes and forms: art not so much for its own sake, but in complete freedom to assume whatever form it must. What we have is a poetic Garden of Adonis, where instead of souls, artistic fancies come into being, as formed in the mind of the creator. Ilse does not, however, understand the full meaning of this; and though Cotrone explains that she will find there a haven and the peace she seeks in her pursuit of art, the woman is obsessed with her desire to perform. For her, drama as art lives in its production, in its projection into an audience which will be shaped and changed by it. Ilse is the ideal of artistic communication. Sensing this, Cotrone promises to speak to the Giants who live on the nearby mountain. Whether there can be a performance is up to them. They must be handled carefully, he warns. Ilse must not do anything unless the Giants have given their permission and agreed to the performance.

That is where the two acts of the play completed by Pirandello and published in his lifetime end. According to the outline for a concluding act, transcribed by Pirandello's son, Cotrone gets a kind of "foundation" authorization from the Giants—who are really great captains of industry—for Ilse's company to perform for the recreation and edification of the working classes of the mountain society. The Giants apologize for not having time to attend the performance themselves, for they are too busy with other things—projects which add to the general material well-being of mankind by making the fullest possible use of nature's resources.

Here, it should be noted that there is in the industrious spirit of the mountain people a distinctly *American* element. Pirandello's earlier plays, when first produced on American stages, had paradoxically pleased Henry Ford, who offered quite seriously to back their mass-dissemination. In the industrialist's view, Pirandello was a "man of the people," whose plays could be presented to popular audiences everywhere. Ford's proposition, advanced as a money-maker, was never taken up seriously. And it seems to be somewhat brutally satirized in the projected conclusion of *The Mountain Giants*. But there is also a distinct dramatic appreciation of the American productive spirit, living for the future, in several Pirandellian writings and late interviews. That too is reflected in the outline for the concluding act of his last great myth.[4]

Cotrone himself leads Ilse and her band of actors, who now perform only one play, into an open space before one of the dwellings of the Giants. Leveling off an open space is, after all, etymologically, the original root meaning of the word "Theatrum." It is as if we were to witness a new birth of "theater" in strange surroundings, a new world. But it is really the actors and the play that their leader insists on performing, no matter what, that are strange. The audience of workers, eager to be entertained, have no idea that the Countess Ilse is irresistibly driven to perform *The Tale of the*

*Changeling* whenever and wherever she can, in quest of spiritual redemption for having driven the play's young author to suicide by refusing his love.

The atmosphere that greets the performance is that of a circus. The workers had hoped for clowns or marionettes to entertain them, and they make that clear with their impatient responses. Ilse's sensitive soul cannot endure it. She breaks down and proceeds to insult the crude taste and boorish ways of her audience. The crowd grows angry. There is a violent confrontation in which Ilse is killed and others in the company are literally torn apart. The satyrs have destroyed the divinely inspired artists.

Cotrone, the all-knowing wizard of art, explains what has happened. It is not poetry that has been rejected. The fanaticism unleashed against the actors was provoked by them. Ilse had wanted to convert the ordinary people to her own vision, when the conditions were not propitious. The rough audience in the mountains felt the emptiness for them of such "missionary" art and rejected it for life. Ironically, Ilse's actors had felt exactly the same, in their own fanatical way, about the talking puppets in Cotrone's villa. Puppets should amuse, and that's all there is to it. The Count, mourning over his wife's body, cries out that mankind has destroyed poetry in the world. But Ilse is not all there is to poetry. She was possessed by the power of art, but it was by no means true that in her death art also died.

Cotrone's somber assessment of the meaning of Ilse's "sacrifice" for art's sake accords with Pirandello's own final critical statement on the significance of drama in his "Introduction to the Italian Theater" published in the last year of his life. The theater, he says there, cannot put on a work of universal and eternal value without accepting the world of ordinary existence. The audience must be moved, but not by the theater's turning its back on the pressures of the world. Those realities must be respected; and the writer's work must find its ideal communication within those limitations.

*The Mountain Giants* upholds this view of art, without undermining the *scalognati* and their existential solution, private and limited. The actors, on the other hand, emerge as ambiguous spokesmen for their artistic ideal. They want the work of art to live among the people—but for the work's sake, not the audience's. The actors thus represent a sterile aestheticism which they fail to recognize as sterile, even though they know that Ilse's commitment to perform the same play endlessly is part of her own love-sick longing for death. What the rough public rejected was something that was not addressed to them in their ordinary life, with its ordinary demands. In Cotrone's villa, drama can survive the demands of communication; but when it moves out to seek a public, an audience, it must become what it was for the ancient Greeks: a social ritual of initiation into the mysteries of personal freedom. Poetry in its highest reaches must universalize itself dramatically, as a shared experience. To sum up the aesthetic doctrine of *The Mountain Giants*, A. Leone de Castris has written aptly:

> Pirandello realizes that, at the very limits of its mystic flight and in its secret self-satisfaction, poetry might indeed have saved itself, but the humanity of poetry would have been destroyed. What he attempted in fact was the breaking down of the barriers between the barbarized and regimented humanity of his time [*i servi fanatici della vita*] and the elusive and aristocratic isolation of art, abstractly protesting its advantage [*i servi fanatici dell'Arte*].[5]

De Castris explains that Pirandello had interrupted the writing of *The Mountain Giants* and had considered taking up a "new beginning" in the story of Adam and Eve, admitting the impossibility and futility even of that brand of poetics that betrays its purpose of mirroring reality with honest criticism; for he was after a form of "art which, however depressing the vision of the world that nurtured it, had never forgotten the daily striving of man in his search for a better world." [6]

In the context of our earlier discussions, the identity crisis in *The Mountain Giants* must be recognized as that of the self-consciousness of the artist seeing himself in a glass darkly.

Ilse does not recognize her own limitations in the response of the rough mountain people; her awareness has not gone beyond the dichotomy generated by the inevitable confrontation. She sees herself as the very opposite of her audience; she is pure and inspired, they are rough and deaf to art. She thus precipitates by her one-sided self-assertion her own martyrdom, her own negation as an artist in a dialectical moment of nothingness raised to an absolute. She does not live to see beyond that moment. But Cotrone assures us of it; poetry cannot die in Ilse, for it is not at stake in her artistic fanaticism. His respect for the Giants is an allegorical statement that the gods who bestow such gifts know best how to distribute them. Ilse insisted on her absolute commitment in spite of Cotrone's warning. She thus destroyed the possibility of communication. The crowd remains what it was, and Ilse is killed by her zealous belief in her own adequacy.

Ilse's suicidal impulse does not differ in final analysis from that of Diego despairing in his dark knowledge of God's ways, or that of Henry IV reshaping his dead past for the sake of his erstwhile friends, or that of the six characters who force their way into the consciousness of the actors. In retrospect, *Six Characters* clarifies the central theme of *The Mountain Giants*; the six living "fantasms" must find a way to reach the actors and, by implication, the audience. Pirandello does not explicate the failure; but the many diverse ways in which the intruders hold the attention of their "audience" to the point of total absorption is the beginning of the lesson. Cotrone has understood it; but Ilse, in her impetuous desire to know herself in the fulness of art, fails. She is properly described as "un'esaltata," swept up into her own grand vision. The work which she treasures, which she would force on the listeners on the mountain, is as we have already indicated the drama of her dead poet friend, to whom she had denied herself in life and for whom she now sacrifices herself. She holds on to this. It is her one great act of faith. But, as Doccia reminds us: "the world becomes yours only when you have no where else to go. You go on and on, then you come to rest in the grass under the silence of the sky; and you are everything and nothing . . . you are nothing and everything." And Cotrone adds:

> One does not choose his mask. . . . None of us is in that body that others see; but the soul that talks, who knows where; no one knows; an apparition among apparitions, with this comic name of Cotrone. . . . The body is death: darkness and stone. God help those who see themselves in their body and in their name. We're fantasms. All those that go through our heads.

Cotrone claims that the work of the poet lives in itself for itself, but Ilse objects that it lives in her. And Cotrone concludes: "Just as the poet did not enjoy your love, so too the work of art will not enjoy glory from mankind."

*The Mountain Giants* is, in effect, a long defense of theater in which the critic-dramatist puts forth his notions about the subject and makes them walk on the stage. The stage has its own demands; the play has its own life; the audience comes with the full potential of being absorbed into the experience; the actors must allow their roles to claim them. And the dramatist—if he is honest and inspired—will let the fancy take over and the creations of his imagination take shape of their own accord, as the six characters (Pirandello tells us) took shape before his eyes, even as he tried to dismiss them when they first "appeared" (as the Director, in the play, tried to dismiss them when they first came on stage). What is especially curious and interesting about Pirandello's handling of this large theme about the translation of art in communicable form is his insistence that the abstract ideals— both Ilse's and Cotrone's—are destructive; and that the life of theater justifies its vast expenditure of energy finally only with the resolution of the dialectic of consciousness, in the act of dramatic representation itself which is a shared creative experience of the audience as well as the actors, director, set designers, stagehands, managers, producers, and author.

Whatever Pirandello might have had in mind for the very end of *The Mountain Giants*, there can be little doubt that the work would have resolved the two extremes—the esoteric self-indulgence of the artist and the impetuous and inflexible insistence of the actor in search of an audience—in a dramatically visual way. The Saracen olive tree, ever green and fruitful for centuries, long surviving in Sicily the dominance of the Mohammedans who planted it, might indeed have solved everything, as Pirandello claimed for it in the dramatic excitement of his last days on his deathbed. The roots of the giant tree sink deep into the soil; its gnarled and tortured trunk, riddled with holes, has manifestly weathered the worst tides of outrageous fortune; and its branches, that twist out with pitiful generosity to bear fruit for generation after generation, welcome the birds of the air to nest and sing in their seasons. It is a tree that seems to have wounded itself in a rage against life only to learn in the pain of it that beyond pain, deeper than pain, is joy.

With *The Mountain Giants* we return to the theatrical vision of Pirandello as it was in the beginning, in the bitter-sweet pastoral comedy of the natural poet, *Liolà*. But we have come a long way. What was barely implicit in *Liolà*—the affirmation of traditional social, religious, and even artistic values through their apparent rejection—is made explicit as we trace those themes through the main body of plays of which *Six Characters, It Is So(If You Think So)*, and *Henry IV* are representative, into the great myths where they begin to reconverge like meridians far removed at the equator and drawn up to meet once more at the pole. La Spera in *The New Colony*, Diego in *Lazarus*, and most of all Cotrone in *The Mountain Giants* bring to tragic resolution —tragic in the sense that *Oedipus at Colonus* is tragic—the dilemmas of self-consciousness with its mirrored halves that seek to overcome one another, and of the social outcasts who are judged mad whether they seek to hide their alienation or force its acceptance on their neighbors. Liolà lived comfortably with those dilemmas. But neither we who look on, nor the playwright of *Liolà*, are able to be comfortable with him. We are in Dante's condition on the edge of Hell, where Virgil first comes to him. We see the light on the distant hilltop which is our desired goal. Liolà the "poet" enables us to see it. But our guide tells us that the direct road to it is blocked and we must go a long way around—*a te convien tener un altro viaggio*—through a hell first, and then a purgatory.

Liolà, with the three waifs he has fathered in encounters with three different women, is surely typical of Pirandello's outcasts. But with his carefree spirit, which makes him a latter-day Pan, able to make women pregnant with a mere touch, he doesn't let himself be an outcast. With the children he loves, and supported by his mother and most of the young girls of the neighborhood, he is able to fashion for himself a social order that lives freely by its own laws, anticipating what La Spera and Currao will try to make for themselves and their outcast band in *The New Colony*.

Diego Spina's "resurrection" in *Lazarus* is also a return, by way of Hell and Purgatory, to the divine naturality of *Liolà*. Just as the old dispensation of social order is rooted out forever in the new insights provided by the picture of the "new colony," so that of the prevailing conventional religion is uprooted by the new insights of husband, wife, and son in the Pirandellian myth of religious renewal. Diego's wife Sara, like Liolà, longs for the land, sun, rain, and plants which are the gifts of God. Like Liolà, she is responsible for miracles, even though she is hardly disposed to call them that. Liolà scoffs at Mita's reluctance to do what he suggests; she clings to conventional views. Her kind of "miracle" is impossible, but Liolà does in fact provide it—just as Sara produces a kind of miracle in inspiring Lucio to return to her and later to "resurrect" his father from his second, spiritual death, a miracle that has the power to raise the crippled Lia out of her wheelchair. In both plays, the natural child is exalted as the greatest of miracles. In both the mother-child relationship is depicted as the greatest source of strength, the most powerful, most civilizing statement of divine grace in the world.

The misfits of *Liolà* and *Lazarus* are exalted in their self-sustaining strength. In the intervening plays, Liolà's world of natural grace cracks; we see the self-sustained "misfits" as distorted reflections in a shattered glass. But Pirandello remains on course. Having gone the long dialectical way around, he returns in *Lazarus*—with full awareness of where he has been and of having been cleansed spiritually by the experience—to his starting point, to the dominant theme:

instinctive nature is good but does not of itself suffice. From the almost pagan natural goodness of the early play, we come, in the end, to a goodness rehabilitated, perfected, by Christian grace in which nature is infused not with the kind of joy that Boccaccio pursues in his *Ninfale fiesolano*, but with a joy whose natural growth is bathed in the light and love of God. Liolà gives Mita a child, out of bountiful natural grace; Lucio, restored to his mother, restores his father to spiritual life out of divine bounty.

*The New Colony* and *Lazarus* are plays deeply rooted—like the Saracen olive tree (and *Liolà*)—in the soil of Sicily. But it is the last of the myth plays, *The Mountain Giants*, that reaches down most deeply for the richest cultural sustenance of that soil, even though it is set impressionistically beyond ordinary place and time. The link between *Liolà*'s world and that of *The Mountain Giants* is brilliantly traced for us in Roberto Rebora's brief but excellent study, "*I giganti della montagna* e la crisi di *Liolà*." Rebora notes that the judgments of Cotrone, particularly those that interpret for us Ilse's suicidal longing to communicate art's mysteries for art's sake, are a sophisticated restatement of Liolà's judgment that the inspired life of song cannot be overwhelmed by the world but is rather itself the world's saving grace. Liolà asserts this judgment instinctively. It is an expression of his unity of character, his personal integrity, an integrity which all of us who see the play have long since lost, for it is impossible to sustain it in its naïve naturalness. "Liolà," writes Rebora,

> is self-contained within the limits of the natural and possible. If he passes in the least beyond the natural appearances of things it is only in his characteristic southern melancholy which becomes song, life, love, and never a scrutiny of things, never an analysis of song or life or love. Pirandello could not do otherwise than leave his Liolà as he first conceived him, defined to perfection as a self-contained dramatic personality.

Thus left to himself, Liolà becomes the symbol of the Pirandellian crisis which will point the way to his masterpieces, and natural reality ceases at once to coincide with truth. Liolà, willfully set aside by Pirandello as a character complete in himself, becomes—in a manner more or less obvious, though sometimes deliberately veiled—the type of protagonist who constantly batters himself against the prison-house walls of incommunicability if not of non-being itself.[7]

It is a Liolà prematurely bruised to ripeness by the trials of life that returns to us in the protagonist Cotrone of *The Mountain Giants*. Cotrone is Liolà now king of the fairies, poet-legislator, creator of worlds. (The play forces comparison with *A Midsummer Night's Dream* in many ways: the intrusion of one world upon another, the magic "play" seen only by those who have been initiated into the magic world, the attempt at reaching an audience [more successful in Shakespeare's play], and a God-figure [Theseus-Cotrone] who gives organic meaning to the parts.) In one sense, at least, *Liolà* succeeds where *The Mountain Giants* does not: the poet-singer of the early play creates his magic world and proves that it can be communicated to others. No one is sacrificed in *Liolà*. The poetic imagination conquers all.

The whole of Pirandello—Rebora correctly observes—may be summarized in the identity of Liolà-Cotrone. The poet Liolà springs up out of the Sicilian ground to sing as unacknowledged legislator of the world. It's a very real world, with all the vices of real people. Liolà knows them, shares them, and rises above them, naturally; but there is, as we noted, a certain sourness in all this that disturbs and makes us unnaturally self-conscious. Pirandello's subsequent work is the examination of the agony of that self-consciousness, first felt as a bittersweetness in *Liolà*. The final artistic catharsis comes late, and when it is done, Pirandello sums up its significance as an ultimate defense of theater, in *The Mountain Giants*. There all sourness is gone, all the agony is reduced to proper perspective in the larger canvas—where allegorical distance provides the key to all paradox.

In the last of the myth plays, Liolà does indeed reappear

as Cotrone; but the naïve poet-singer, untroubled by the tortured dialectic of self-knowledge, no longer exists. Cotrone must face that tortured dialectic in Ilse, as well as in his own memories. His task as the supreme poet is to reconcile the absolute alienation of art, in and for itself, and to find ways to offer the poet's gift to the world at large. It is hardly a task for Liolà.

It is no surprise that one of the characters in *The Mountain Giants*, hearing the terrible thunder of the Giants of modern industrialism, who are threatening to descend on their poetic sanctuary in Cotrone's villa, cries out: "I am afraid!" Those words, repeated twice, give rise to provocative speculation when we realize that they were the very last Pirandello wrote for that play. The great poet-singer who does not fear—as Dante feared as he set out in his "piccioletta barca" for the great unknown which poets before him had not dared to explore—the vision of his Master, is presumptuous and foolhardy. The Giants, like the gods of Olympus, can consume the onlooker. They never appear, of course; but Pirandello never was closer to them than in this clear statement about their power and their gracious bestowal of poetic grace. The Giants never speak; but their message as interpreted by Cotrone reassures us that communication is possible and warns us that the poet's task in seeking to enchant his audience is not more difficult than that of the Giants who must make known to the poet what he is to do to have meaning for life.

# 8

# Empty Stage

Pirandello has told us that it was an urge to give the characters of his fiction greater independence that led him to write plays so late in his successful literary career. But even after he had written several significant works for the stage, he expressed a very low estimate of the art of acting and of theatrical performances generally. He coupled the stage with booksellers' stalls as mere marketing places for literary works which are complete in themselves long before actors or printers get their hands on them. Acting out a play, he thought at first, was like illustrating a story with pictures, or translating it into another language. Only very gradually did he come to feel that the characters that pressed him in his imagination to liberate them from the descriptive narratives of his fictions were pressing also to compel producers, directors, and actors to give them a stage where their external environment not less than their very selves could have independent existence.

It is a stage already in the business of presenting plays to a paying public that is "invaded" by Pirandello's six characters. And yet, from another point of view, those characters thrust us back to the remotest origins of the theater, when it was first leveled out by human art as a temple for the performance of religious rites. Priests and the public gathered on that level ground and, by the rites of worship, they called upon the divine presences vaguely sensed in nature to show themselves more distinctly, in more meaningful forms. In the progression of the arts among the ancient Greeks, it was architecture that first leveled a ground for sensory manifestations of divinity; sculpture then fashioned its adequate sensory shapes; then painting emerged to mirror the divine perception of that environment, followed by music to measure externally the vital pulse of its inner life. But for the Greeks it was poetry that completed the progression of the arts: first with its epic voice that could construct for the mind's eye a whole world of beauty; then with its lyric voice that fills that world with rhythmical, melodious, rational sounds; and finally with the dramatic voice that compels the training of actors, the construction of stage sets, and the assembly of audiences once again for the performance of what remains essentially (in Pirandello's maturest judgment, at any rate) religious rites.

Dramatic art in its perfection requires a stage, actors, and audiences no less than it requires its creative playwright. All the world's a stage, to begin with. The playwright's passion, or gift, is to re-create it—this everyday world—so that it manifests in its least detail an essential intelligence. Thus the empty stage of the dark theater is already a work of art, an expression of human intelligence in its every detail, potentially full of all that can be dramatized upon it. Pirandello's irresistible sense of the dramatic potency of the stage itself is what underlies all of his plays after *Six Characters* and *Henry IV*.

Insofar as a play is a literary work complete in itself as the author conceived it, the place for its "preservation" is the printed book that can be stored on the shelves of a library. In his "Introduction to the Italian Theater" Pirandello summed up his maturest sense of the difference between the play complete in itself and its theatrical performance.

> The Theater is not archaelogy. Unwillingness to take up old works, to modernize and streamline them for fresh productions, betrays indifference, not praiseworthy caution. The Theater *welcomes* such modernization and has profited by it throughout those ages when it was most alive.

The original text can be read leisurely at home; what the theater offers is the *current* translation of the text into fresh, updated language, adapted to contemporary taste and habits, revitalized so as to make possible communication with a living audience reflecting a living and immediate reality.

Why is this legitimate?

Because in the Theater, a work of art is no longer the work of the writer (which, after all, can always be preserved in some other way), but an act of life, realized on the stage from one moment to the next, with the cooperation of an audience that must find satisfaction in it.[1]

Earlier in that same essay, Pirandello notes that drama was in its very origin among the Greeks "an act of life realized upon a stage." In the days of its perfection in Athens, of its continuance in Rome, its revival in the Italian Renaissance, and its new birth out of medieval church rituals, civilized human societies, Pirandello observes, "celebrated the Theater as a religious or quasi-religious rite; that is, as a genuinely 'vital act' that united all the spectators in a reality expressly created by the poet to exalt their feelings." An instinctive need to see ourselves in a "living mirror" brought the dramatic art into existence; but it is by no means fully satisfied where the theater is nothing more than relaxation for an audience after a hard day's work. Hardly less satisfactory is the communication of rhetorical brilliance that merely entertains. The stage can be "used" for such purposes, says Pirandello, but that is not its reason for being. It fulfills its true purpose, it becomes truly alive only where the spectators—no matter how few and scattered —are lifted out of their ordinary lives temporarily "by virtue of that magic power which poetry acquires when its characters take on flesh and come to life on the stage."[2]

In that experience, Pirandello continues, the audience becomes the eyes and ears and soul of a people, and the living stage becomes its voice. The confusion of ordinary everyday existence is sifted and explained on the stage in what may be called, as we noted earlier, "a public trial of human actions as they truly are, in that pure and everlasting reality which the imagination of the poets creates as an example and a warning for our commonplace and confused life." For the mature Pirandello, who had long resisted the idea, the playwright and spectator must meet on the stage to consummate together the "vital act" of drama. The spectator who holds back, who refuses to make the spiritual effort required to share in the experience, and the author who shrinks from the effort to communicate in terms suitable for his audience are both betraying—each in his own way—the high purpose for which the theater exists in civilized society, a purpose to which they have at least implicitly given their consent.

Perhaps in this respect the theater has been betrayed beyond remedy. What it had been and could conceivably again become it certainly was not in Pirandello's day. Writing in the last weeks of his life, when virtually all his own plays had been performed, and his fame had become international, Pirandello observed with candor: "It is difficult for us to realize the importance of the Theater in the civic life of a people, after having sat through the kind of play that is usually offered the public these days—and not only in Italy." [3] That was in 1936. In 1949, Francis Fergusson, exploring the same grounds in *The Idea of a Theater*, drew the same conclusion. Where the theater has really flourished, whether in Elizabeth's England or in the Athens of Pericles, its end—as Hamlet puts it—"both at first and now, was and is, to hold, as 'twere, the mirror up to nature; to show virtue her own feature, scorn her own image, and the very age and body of the time his form and pressure." Fergusson acknowledges with Pirandello that such a mirror is rarely formed at any time, and that the experience of looking into one to see ourselves there in Hamlet's sense is hardly the promise of any established theater of our day. "We doubt," Fergusson writes,

> that our time has an age, a body, a form, or a pressure; we are more apt to think of it as a wilderness which is without form. Human nature seems to us a hopelessly elusive and uncandid entity, and our playwrights (like hunters with camera and flash-bulbs in the depths of the Belgian Congo) are lucky if they can fix it, at rare inter-

vals, in one of its momentary postures, and in a single bright, exclusive angle of vision. Thus the very *idea* of a theater, as Hamlet assumed it, gets lost; and the art of drama, having no place of its own in contemporary life, is confused with lyric poetry or pure music on one side, or with editorializing and gossip on the other.[4]

Fergusson is at pains to emphasize that our twentieth century has produced some superb playwrights—and we may add that, since 1949, it has produced several more. His point is that the art of drama simply has "no place of its own in contemporary life." When we try to take our best playwrights together, "we cannot tell what to make of them," for we have no conception, valid for our time, of the dramatic art in general.

It is from such a perspective that Pirandello's labor to give us an "empty stage"—a stage for genuinely dramatic art, no longer confused with lyric poetry or editorializing, pure music or gossip—reveals its most impressive aspect. In Fergusson's apt expression, Pirandello's dramatic art has literally invaded a stage long possessed by craftsmen of marvelous skills who have at best a mistaken "idea of the theater." For Pirandello, between 1916 and 1921, when the "third voice" of poetry was forcing itself irresistibly on his mind's ear, the stage of his time seemed no place at all for living characters. Almost cynically, he concocted the idea of invading that stage with his *Six Characters in Search of an Author* to cast the rascals out. Can real characters find on the contemporary stage successful playwrights worthy of them? For that is the real point of Pirandello's tour de force. Here is a family of characters to mirror our contemporary state of mind and heart back to us. They have come out of the creative imagination of a man who writes novels and short stories to be marketed in booksellers' stalls. But they are searching for an author who can give their drama a fitting stage, a proper "place of its own in contemporary life." Those who grossly buy and sell mere entertainment in drama's temple, says Pirandello, are to be cast out, and so his six characters move in to overturn "the tables of the moneychangers and the seats of them that sold doves" and all the other props of those who make the temple of dramatic art a den of commercial swindlers.

What Pirandello achieved by his disdainful invasion of the theater as he found it was, in Fergusson's words, "the restoration of the ancient magic of 'two boards and a passion,' frankly placed in the glare of the stage light and the eye of the audience." [5] It is the "empty stage" of purest theatrical potency. Pirandello did not, for he could not by himself, put on that stage a completely satisfying theater for our time, mirroring to its own age and body their true form and pressure. But for all who "search for a theater," the author of *Six Characters*, of *Henry IV*, and of *The Mountain Giants* has shown where the search must begin and to what end. He is, in other words, precisely what our Livingstons, Pitöeffs, Sartres, Bentleys, and Brusteins—to name but a few—have acknowledged him to be: the playwrights' playwright par excellence of the contemporary theater.

Pirandello argued that we have the playwrights for genuine theater always, either actually or potentially, and there is always, in civilized societies, a potentially fitting audience. It is the place where the two must meet that is usually unavailable for the purpose. When a true playwright finds a proper stage, the thing can be done as it should be done; his audience, however sparse, can be made to share, through the dramatic catharsis, in the highest spiritual experience of which the theater is capable. And when the audience is few, it can be said of those few (as of Henry V's soldiers at Agincourt) "so much the worse [the words are Pirandello's] for whoever stayed away; he missed the chance to participate in an experience of spiritual life actually and wholly realized within the circle of the community of which he is a part, and there can be nothing to boast of in his having turned his back on it." [6]

Georges Piroué ends his richly suggestive book on Pirandello with what appears on first reading to be a devasting critique of the "emptiness" of Pirandello's theater, with respect to dramatic content. Pirandello, he says, is in no

sense the "national" playwright of his people, whether we
take him as an Italian or a Sicilian. Liolà is the only
memorable Sicilian represented for us on Pirandello's stage;
after him, the only fully formed character is Henry IV, a
madman whose life is a madman's tale, full of sound and
fury. Pirandello, PirQué argues, gets on his empty stage and
stamps his feet at us. He mocks everything we are or would
be: our words, our pride, our family, our social class, our
religious conventions. And yet, there is no mistaking the
fact that he himself has nothing better to offer us on those
levels; he is one of us, addressing himself no less than us
with his disquieting judgments.

In just such terms, page after page, Piroué presses his
final critique of Pirandello's dramatic art, until just when he
appears to have said the worst he suddenly makes what can
only be called a dramatic Pirandellian reversal. What Pirandello does on the stage, he concludes, is—after all—typical
of the southern European and particularly the Sicilian critical spirit. It always seeks, as a point of honor, to vindicate
itself publicly after it has riotously disturbed the established
conventional order of things. Pirandello, writes Piroué,
"abandons himself to public vindication, to sarcasm, all for
the purpose of obtaining from us, like his Henry IV, the
forgiveness and reinvestiture of Canossa." [7] The playwright
demands that we share with him the experience of emptying
himself out of all respectful remembrances of things past and
hopeful anticipations of things to come. Condemning as
false the hopes and dreams, the masks and modes of our
everyday existence, which he refuses to dramatize for us, he
proceeds with the talent of a Prospero to "invent *ex nihilo*,"
writes Piroué, "another society more supple and transparent
than ours, even though it too has a prodigious coherence,
where Pirandello and we together can savor fully all that
life had denied him: the world of the theater, the universe
of the theater, at once new and re-established in its primitive
ingenuity where author, actor, and public, stage and audience, find themselves intimately associated in a comple-
mentary and convergent unity of being." [8] For Piroué, finally,
it is the Promised Land of theater at its best, for the recovery

of which Pirandello was amply justified in stamping his feet.

Pirandello, as we know, eventually went onstage himself to direct his own plays. In the printed versions of his works, directions for sets, for the "masking" and costuming of actors, and for the "blocking" of action are copious. He was most concerned to have his invented world adequately visualized while his characters spoke with the authentic "third voice" of poetry by means of which they gained for themselves the prerogatives of dramatic independence. Orlando di Collalta, in his "Introduction to a Scenographic Interpretation of Pirandello's Theater," notes that, for every act of a play that he wrote, Pirandello supplied, on the average, 108 words of stage directions—not including incidental directions for actors.[9] For the one-act play, *Our Lord of the Ship*, where the dialogue-text adds up to 2703 words, the author supplied an additional 2972 of set and character descriptions. But the words and deeds of the characters contribute even more to the final effect of a fully conceived world, not in the least less real—however more vibrant it can be made to appear on an empty stage—than the life that is to be daily observed, as Collalto notes, in the villas, *palazzi*, *pensioni*, humble dwellings, and bourgeois living rooms across the length and breadth of Sicily and Italy. Pirandello's men, women, and children in *Liolà*, his Agazzi family in *It Is So (If You Think So)*, his Marchesas, even his Cotrones, have about them the very essence of the real Sicilian character, in which sensuous obsession is one with religious exaltation, and attachment to property, instead of being the materialistic obsession it seems, becomes an apprehension and acceptance of death. Death's musty smell is ever-present in the straining for security, in the accumulation of family heirlooms, old chests and bedposts, and of sons who will give their parents a proper burial. Pirandello's plays reject the external aspect of that Sicilian show of values, but not the spirit throbbing beneath it, of which those values are a mere local encrustation.

Though his art is rooted in the life of Sicily, Pirandello is not, however, in the final analysis, a Verga or a Capuana, or Lampadusa. For him, the Sicilian spirit rooted realistically in the soil is an affirmation to be erased first, so that it may, in self-negation, universalize itself. That is what he means when he says: "There's a compulsion in my art to create, as it were, the ground under one's feet, step by step, as my characters move; and between one step and the next there is an abyss."

Before he turned to writing plays at the age of forty-eight, Pirandello had completed over two hundred and fifty short stories and seven novels. But then, like Molière and Goldoni, he became wholly a "man of the theater," with the advantage of long years of experience with the literary art of narration. As we learn from Corrado Pavolini, who worked closely with Pirandello onstage, the novelist-turned-playwright used his narrative expertise to grip the sensibilities of the actors he directed in what must certainly have been a breakthrough to new ground for the director's art. In his essay, "Pirandello at Rehearsals," Pavolini tells us what it was like for members of the company, when the Sicilian playwright was in the midst of giving imaginative birth to a new play and bursting with an urge to try it out, to share and test it on the strength of their objective response. He would begin by narrating the action of the projected play in the third person, telling, describing, interpreting. And then, without any marked transition, the "third voice of poetry" would gradually take possession of him, and he would begin to dramatize rather than narrate, "taking on the voice and manner of first one character then another then another still, until, instead of the little man himself, we saw a whole crowd of people on stage," literally invading it, "with as many voices and passions and reasons for being as the figures pullulating in him."

In this picture of Pirandello literally "creating" his characters we have something resembling Plato's grand Demiurge shaping all this world of sight and sound out of a vast bin of formless space, with his eye fixed on the eternal prototypes beyond space and time. It is the very picture that Shakespeare's Theseus alludes to when he speaks of the poet's shaping art that "gives to airy nothing a local habitation and a name." Pavolini, who thrilled to see it, says that Pirandello would use his hands as he verbalized his half-conceived works, literally shaping his figures with his sculptor's thumb. From all this there would emerge a whole world, fully elaborated in all its details, as a backdrop for those figures of his imagination; and it was almost

> as if footlights and overhead lights had suddenly been turned on. That's how we, in fact, listened day after day to the birth even of his very last creation: we saw "performed" in this fashion the whole of those *Mountain Giants*, who, on paper, have remained voiceless and motionless after the second act; nor is it possible, with death having struck just then, that they will ever wake and live again.

Once he had found his "empty stage," his Demiurge's bin of airy nothing—which is potentially all that imagination can fashion for it—Pirandello came to view it as a grave responsibility to follow day by day the work of the theater. Again we have Pavolini's eyewitness account for it that Pirandello let himself be absorbed in the life of the theater till he came to grasp its most hidden secrets, to know its workings in and out, its cunning twists and turns, its daggered jealousies, feverish rivalries, its loves and hates, its daily routine of taxing work. Except for Goldoni, Pavolini notes, Italy had not had before Pirandello, a playwright imbued with a sense of theater so real and immediate. Like Shakespeare and Molière, he made the players' life his own, traveling with his "theater" and abandoning himself to its fascinations and miseries. His company soon became for him a microcosm of all civilized social life with particulars highlighted and intensified in every detail. With its well-defined personalities on and offstage, and full as it is (again in Pavolini's words) of "rhetorical flourishes, extravagant impulses, generous aims, malicious plots, financial failures, bureaucratic hierarchies, it is exactly like a busy city on the move." And Pirandello ignored no part of it. He was at home with the tasks of stagehands, set-builders, electricians, carpenters, and wardrobe mistresses; the worries of the box-office people and administrators; the excitements and boredom of apprentices and the posturings of prima donnas. He moved among them for many years, "following their fortunes with the humility of a craftsman, and, when the need arose, with the liberality of a Maecenas."

He loved the theater, but he was also a hard taskmaster. At rehearsals he was tireless in noting the inflection of a line, the pitch of an actor's voice, and in correcting what needed correction. He would get his actors "under" the parts by his own masterful example as a natural actor of the very kind he conceived in his *Six Characters.* In other words, in rehearsals, he made his actors see and hear the characters they were supposed to become, and he taught them precisely how to wear such "naked masks" conjured into being by his theatrical art. He would himself often go through a whole "concert" of parts, indicating the speed and pulse of the speeches with, as Pavolini notes, " a truly astounding bravura in the shifting of tone, expression, gesture, posture even, from one line to the next, producing among his awe-struck admiring company, a sense that they were witnessing a full orchestration of voices, characters, and emotions."

Pitöeff had been the first to say it: Pirandello *was* theater. For it, Pavolini reminds us, he abandoned his home, "the peace of his study and his books, and went abroad in the world with his actors," putting up in small hotel rooms where, "still dazzled by the heat and brilliance of the footlights, he would sit at his typewriter to peck out the words of so many of his plays." [10] In the solitude of those moments, the empty stage would come alive again in his imagination, and a whole crowd of figures would fill the room like the puppets come to life in Cotrone's villa.

Liolà, Cotrone, Pirandello: a full circle. In the morning of the last full day of his life, Pirandello told his son Stefano (as we already mentioned) that he had lain awake all night, trying to resolve the last turns of action for the concluding act of *The Mountain Giants*—otherwise fully conceived in his mind and outlined for his son to transcribe. Fitfully indicating the solution he had found, he said: "There's a Saracen olive tree, very large, in the middle of the stage; and with that I've solved everything."

With that image his vision of art's profoundest mysteries —which is the substance of his last play, as of his entire life as a dramatist—comes to an end. "The curtain is drawn on it," were his last words of explanation to his son, and he was content with them.

How are we to take that olive tree thus planted on an empty stage? Is it a symbol of the dramatist's tragic inspiration? Many of his best interpreters—Sciascia in his *Pirandello and Sicily*, Guido Salvini (who staged many of the plays) in his provocative essay "On Act Three of *The Mountain Giants*" [11]—have thought so. As Pirandello pictures it for us, that Saracen olive stands, finally, on level ground cut into the side of a mountain where the giants of our modern industrial society have authorized and subsidized the performance of plays. We are not yet on the topmost heights of the mountain, where the constructive giants (without whose labors there can be no civilized life) themselves live. But even to that leveled ground, the climb has been for art a painful purgatorial ascent. Ilse has died in attaining it, and her company of fanatically committed actors has been overwhelmed by the difficulties. Still, this is no deterrent. Like the Saracen olive tree, the art of theater has deep roots in rich soil, and its branches reach fruitfully high into the air. And Pirandello has nurtured it well.

Sometime before his death, Pirandello left instructions that his body be cremated and the ashes scattered—or, if the giants would not allow such "pollution of the air," that those ashes be placed in a rock in his native Sicily near a place known locally as "Chaos." The law, indeed, ordered his return to "chaos." Nearby is a giant olive tree. And in that place, with its solitary tree, Pirandello clears for us his empty stage, to be flooded with light and crowded with living figures as often as we look inward, imaginatively, and surprise the stranger in our midst. "I'm nobody," he is saying. "Are you nobody too?" And in a split second, one, a hundred, a hundred thousand figures come rushing into our consciousness, like characters who have found their author and their play.

# Notes

## 1 — The Invaded Stage

1. Sciascia, pp. 17–18. (Unless otherwise indicated, all passages from foreign works—including Pirandello's original texts—have been translated by me.)
2. William Herman, "Pirandello and Possibility," in Cambon, p. 154.
3. Thomas Bishop, "Pirandello's Influence on French Drama," in Cambon, p. 51.
4. Ibid., p. 64.
5. Putnam, p. 7.
6. Livingston and Storer, pp. v–vi.
7. Bentley, *The Playwright as Thinker*, p. 148.
8. Fergusson, *The Idea of a Theater*, p. 193.
9. Robert Brustein, "Pirandello's Drama of Revolt," in Cambon, p. 133.

## 2 — Art for Life's Sake

1. T. S. Eliot, "The Three Voices of Poetry," *On Poetry and Poets* (New York: Farrar, Straus & Cudahy, 1957), p. 99.
2. Cited by Sciascia, p. 78.
3. Thomas Bishop, "Pirandello's Influence on French Drama," in Cambon, p. 60.
4. William Wordsworth, "Lines Composed a Few Miles above Tintern Abbey," *Complete Poetical Works*, ed. John Morley (London: Macmillan & Co., 1928), p. 94.
5. Cf. James Thomson, "Sympathy," *Essays and Phantasies* (London: Reeves & Turner, 1881), p. 237.
6. Paolucci, "Introduction to the Italian Theater," p. 14.

7. See the discussion on "the conflict of self-consciousness in self-opposition," Hegel, pp. 228–40.

### 3—The Arabic-Sicilian Microcosm of Liolà

1. Bentley, *Naked Masks*, pp. viii–x.
2. John Keats, "Ode to Melancholy," *Poems*, ed. C. W. Thomas (New York: Ray Long & Richard R. Smith, 1932), p. 107.
3. All passages from the plays are from Luigi Pirandello, *Maschere nude*.
4. Roberto Rebora, "*I giganti della montagna* e la crisi di Liolà," *Atti*, p. 471.
5. Paolucci, "Introduction to the Italian Theater," pp. 22–23.
6. Paolucci, *Mandragola*, p. 36.
7. Ibid., p. 47.
8. Piero Gobetti, cited in the preface to Pirandello's *Maschere nude*, 1:19.

### 4—From Person to Person to Nonperson

1. Francis Fergusson, "Action as Theatrical: *Six Characters in Search of an Author*," in Cambon, pp. 40–42.
2. Thomas Bishop, "Pirandello's Influence on French Drama," in Cambon, p. 61.
3. See Sciascia, p. 31.
4. Pirandello, 1:21.
5. Ibid., p. 22.
6. Ibid., p. 24.
7. Weiss, p. 48.
8. Paolucci, "Introduction to the Italian Theater," pp. 23–24.
9. Ibid., p. 28.

### 5—Through a Shattered Mirror

1. Samuel Coleridge, "Dejection: An Ode," *The Poetical Works* with a critical memoir by William Michael Rossetti (New York: Ward Locke & Co., n.d.), p. 128.
2. See William Wordsworth, "Preface to the Second Edition of the *Lyrical Ballads*," *Complete Poetical Works*, ed. John Morley, pp. 849–77.
3. See Sciascia, p. 34.

### 6—The Creative Madness of Henry IV

1. Pasini, p. 437.

7 – Art Transcending Itself

1. John Keats, "Ode to a Grecian Urn," *Poems*, ed. C. W. Thomas (New York: Ray Long & Richard R. Smith, 1932), pp. 105–7.

2. William Butler Yeats, "Sailing to Byzantium," *The Oxford Book of 20th-Century Verse*, chosen by Philip Larkin (New York: Oxford University Press, 1973), pp. 82–83.

3. Emily Dickinson, "I'm nobody! Who are you?" *Selected Poems and Letters*, ed. Robert N. Linscott (Garden City, N.Y.: Doubleday & Co., 1959), p. 75.

4. Giudice, p. 378.

5. De Castris, p. 219, n. 32.

6. Ibid.

7. Roberto Rebora, "*I giganti della montagna* e la crisi di *Liolà*," Atti, p. 471.

8 – Empty Stage

1. Paolucci, "Introduction to the Italian Theater," pp. 27–28.

2. Ibid., p. 13.

3. Ibid., p. 11.

4. Fergusson, *The Idea of a Theater*, pp. 1–2.

5. Ibid., p. 186.

6. Paolucci, "Introduction to the Italian Theater," p. 13.

7. Piroué, p. 221.

8. Ibid., p. 222.

9. Orlando di Collalto, "Introduzione ad una interpretazione scenografica nel teatro pirandelliano," Atti, pp. 363–64.

10. Corrado Pavolini, "Pirandello alle prove," Atti, pp. 922–24.

11. Guido Salvini, "Il terzo atto dei *Giganti della montagna*," Atti, pp. 925–28.

# Selected Bibliography

Abba, Marta, trans. *"The Mountain Giants" and Other Plays by Luigi Pirandello*. New York: Crown Publishers, 1958.

Abete, Giovanna. *Il vero volto di Luigi Pirandello*. Rome: A.B.E.T.E., 1961.

*Atti del congresso internazionale di studi pirandellani, Venezia, 2–5 ottobre 1961*. Florence: Le Monnier, 1967.

Bentley, Eric. *The Playwright as Thinker*. Cleveland and New York: World Publishing Co., 1955.

———, ed. *Naked Masks: Five Plays by Luigi Pirandello*. New York: E. P. Dutton & Co., 1952.

———, ed. *The Genius of the Italian Theater*. New York: New American Library, 1964.

Cambon, Glauco, ed. *Pirandello: A Collection of Critical Essays*. Englewood Cliffs, N.J.: Prentice-Hall, 1967.

Cantoro, Umberto. *Luigi Pirandello e il problema della personalita*. 2d ed. Bologna: N. U. Gallo, 1954.

De Castris, A. Leone. *Storia di Pirandello*. Bari: Laterza, 1966.

Di Pietro, Antonio. *Pirandello*. 2d ed., rev. Milan: Vita e Pensiero, 1950.

Fergusson, Francis. *The Idea of a Theater*. 1949. Reprint. Princeton University Press, 1968.

Giudice, Gaspare. *Pirandello*. Turin: UTET, 1963.

Guasco, Cesare. *Ragione e mito nell'arte di Luigi Pirandello*. Rome: Editoriale Arte e Storia, 1954.

Hegel, Georg W. F. *The Phenomenology of Mind*. Translated by J. B. Baillie. New York: Macmillan Co.; London: George Allen & Uwin, 1931.

Janner, Arminio. *Luigi Pirandello*. Florence: La Nuova Italia, 1948.

Livingston, Arthur, trans. *"Each in His Own Way" and Two Other Plays.* New York: E. P. Dutton & Co., 1923.

——, and Storer, Edward, trans. *Three Plays by Pirandello.* New York: E. P. Dutton & Co., 1923.

Murray, William, trans. *Pirandello's One-Act Plays.* New York: Minerva Books, 1970.

Nardelli, Federico Vittore. *Vita segreta di Luigi Pirandello.* Rome: V. Bianco, 1962.

Paolucci, Anne. "Theatre of Illusion: Pirandello's *Liolà* and Machiavelli's *Mandragola." Comparative Literature Studies* 9, no. 1 (March 1972): 44–57.

——. "Luigi Pirandello: Experience as the Expression of Will." *Forum Italicum* 7, no. 4 (December 1973).

——, trans. "Introduction to the Italian Theater by Luigi Pirandello," in *The Genius of the Italian Theatre.* Edited by Eric Bentley. New York: New American Library, Mentor Books, 1964.

—— and Paolucci, Henry, trans. *Mandragola.* Indianapolis and New York: Bobbs Merrill Co., 1957.

—— and Paolucci, Henry, eds. *Hegel on Tragedy.* Garden City, N.Y.: Doubleday & Co., 1962. (Reprinted by Harper & Row, New York, 1974).

Pasini, Ferdinando. *Luigi Pirandello (come mi pare).* Trieste: La Vedetta Italiana, 1927.

Pirandello, Lugi. *Maschere nude.* Preface by Silvio D'Amico. 2 vols. Milan: Arnoldo Mondadori, 1958.

Piroué, Georges. *Pirandello.* Paris: Donoël, 1967.

Puglisi, Filippo. *Pirandello e la sua lingua.* Bologna: Capelli, 1962.

Putnam, Samuel, trans. *"As You Desire Me," by Luigi Pirandello.* New York: E. P. Dutton & Co., 1931.

Renda, Umberto and Turri, Vittorio, eds. *Dizionario storico-critico della letteratura italiana.* Turin: G. B. Pravia & Co., 1941.

Sarazani, Fabrizio. "Luigi Pirandello." *Il Borghese.* April 4, 1971, pp. 881–85.

Sciascia, Leonardo. *Pirandello e la Sicilia.* Caltanissetta: S. Sciascia, 1961.

Vicentini, Claudio. *L'estetica di Pirandello.* Milan: U. Mursia, 1970.

Vittorini, Domenico. *The Drama of Luigi Pirandello.* London: Oxford University Press, 1935.

Weiss, Auréliu. *Le Théâtre de Luigi Pirandello dans le mouvement dramatique contemporain.* Paris: Librairie 73, 1964.

# Index

153